God in the Natural World

Edited by Ted Peters and Marie Turner

God in the Natural World

Theological Explorations in Appreciation of Denis Edwards

Editors
Ted Peters and Marie Turner

Adelaide
2020

Birds – front cover by Yvonne Ashby
The artwork 'Birds' depicts our natural world in its purest form. Balanced and in harmony the land is sustained by its life force, water. Stillness is broken by a flight of birds freely moving across the land. The bird is coloured in affectionate memory of Denis Edwards who expressed a strong liking for the red used in my palette. I hope I have captured the colour; it represents spirit, protecting the heart of our great Australian wonderland.

Cover design: Myf Cadwallader
Cover Art work: Yvonne Ashby
Layout, in Minion Pro 11, by Extel Solutions, India.

ISBN: 9781925612059   soft
           9781925612080   hard
           9781925612035   epub
           9781925612097   pdf

Published by:

An imprint of the ATF Press Publishing
Group owned by ATF (Australia) Ltd.
PO Box 234
Brompton, SA 5007
Australia
ABN 90 116 359 963
www.atfpress.com
Making a lasting impact

Table of Contents

Introduction

This book is a collection of essays written by scholars from various geographical locations and inclusive of different ecumenical perspectives. The contributors are colleagues or dialogue partners familiar with the work of Denis Edwards. They have written to honour the memory of a theologian whose later works on eco-theology contribute significantly to the scholarly discussion on deep incarnation. In preparation, contributors were invited to read, in particular, two works by Denis, namely, *The Natural World and God. Theological Explorations* (Hindmarsh, SA: ATF Theology, 2017) and *Deep Incarnation. God's Redemptive Suffering with Creatures* (Maryknoll, NY: Orbis Books, 2019).[1] The writers write from the perspective of their own research expertise but engage, to various extent, with these two works and other writings by Denis. All have a focus on eco-theology.

For Denis, his eco-theological body of work was not purely an intellectual engagement. His own geographical location contributed to his deep personal love of landscape, with its myriad life-forms, and from that love grew a practical and authentic commitment to ecological responsibility. He was born in the South Australian city of Port Pirie and although the city is an industrial environment, it stands on the very edge of the magnificent Flinders Ranges. At his funeral in February, 2019 at St Francis Xavier's Cathedral in Adelaide, where Denis had been ordained a priest fifty-three years earlier, the Eulogy was given by his niece, Michelle Thomas, and her words give us insights not only into the deeply loved and loving human being that Denis was, but also into the foundations of his theological vision.

---

1. Awarded first place in the 'Faith and Science' category of the 2020 Catholic Book Awards (USA).

As Michelle told us, he was influenced by the deep faith of his parents and felt the calling to become a priest, joining the seminary at twelve years of age. To continue in Michelle's words, 'he was also a great footballer and never one to shirk away from a contest, with his height as a ruckman being used to full advantage in the seminary team . . . He loved nature and walking on the beach, camping in the Flinders Ranges and sleeping in a tent and wearing his Tilley hat. He didn't like mobile phones and would often not carry one, or have it switched off. He cherished his holidays, spending time at Maslins (Beach), never wanting expensive trips away, just happy being near the ocean and connecting with what gave him the greatest joy. Having time to quietly reflect was a great gift for him'.

In this volume Denis' own personal story is included, where he gives an account of the hold that the Finders Ranges had over him, and how this ancient land inspired his concern for justice for the Aboriginal inhabitants. He returned often to that part of the country, both in person and in his writings. It nurtured in him a sensitivity to the many landscapes he would encounter in his journeys across the Earth. In his chapter, Ernst M Conradie refers to a walk he and Denis took at the Serafino Conference Centre in McLaren Vale where a 2014 conference on ecology was held amidst the vines. There they appreciated a 'mature red wine' and shared a theological commitment to what is material, bodily and earthly'. Christopher Southgate recalls a time he and Denis walked up a South African mountain, but when the weather turned it was Denis who, with 'wisdom and judiciousness', advised the group to curtail their walk to reach only as far as the waterfall. In Denis' life as in his writings, the bigger picture of mountains and cosmic skies and oceans sits side-by-side with a quiet observation of a river red gum tree or a rock-wallaby or a single flower. All of these spoke to him of the Creator and the Creator's commitment to the 'material, bodily and earthly'. But he was also acutely aware of the rawness and violence inherent in the evolutionary process. His theological consideration of the place of all creation in the mystery of the incarnation and its salvific role encouraged him to engage with the concept of deep incarnation, in which the saving work of Christ is seen as effective for all of creation, and not only for humankind.

Denis Edwards was a deeply intellectual thinker. His writings give evidence of a very fine systematic theologian who constantly refined his work to clarify and explicate his arguments. He was in constant engagement with the great thinkers of the Christian theological tradition, such as Rahner and the early Patristic writers, whose works on the place of creation gave him a solid foundation for his later ecological concerns. He was also in constant contact with some of the finest theological contemporary minds engaging with eco-theology and, in recent times, the concept of deep incarnation, and several of these scholars have generously contributed to this collection in his honour.

This volume offers a richness and variety of ecumenical eco-theological thought offered by scholars and colleagues of Denis who have been touched by his life and his work. Several of them were personal friends, for he was a participant in discussions on science and theology in many parts of the world. The contributors come from places across the globe such as the United States of America, Australia, South Africa, the United Kingdom and Malaysia. Lutheran, Roman Catholic, Anglican (Episcopalian), Uniting Church (Protestant) and Eastern Orthodox traditions are represented.

The expression 'deep incarnation' was first coined by Niels Henrik Gregersen in his article 'The Cross of Christ in an Evolutionary World', *Dialog: A Journal of Theology: A Journal of Theology* 40/3 (Fall 2001): 192–207. In Chapter One of his book, *Deep Incarnation*, Denis conducts a dialogue with Celia Deane-Drummond and Christopher Southgate, two of the contributors to this collection. In her chapter Celia asks the question, how can an articulation of the continuing work of God in the natural world understood in pneumatological categories still make sense? She explores Denis' pioneering work in articulating a theology of the Spirit in the natural world, and seeks possibilities of theological alternatives to his developed Rahnerian notion of self-transcendence. She argues that there is a need not only to develop an adequate theology of the Spirit in creation, but also to situate this alongside an awareness of current philosophical currents that are influencing popular science to speak either directly or indirectly in the language of the sacred in the natural world. As well as engaging with Denis' work she highlights two important contemporary philosophers of nature, Michael Serres and Erazim Kahák.

Christopher Southgate compares and contrasts the work of Denis Edwards, Niels Gregersen, Celia Deane-Drummond, Ted Peters, John Haught, Ernst Conradie, RJ Russell, Paul Fiddes and Neil Messer, several of whom are to be found as authors in this present collection. Referring to the unsustainability of the Western tradition that has seen a fall-event at the heart of a disordered creation, he argues for an eco-theology developed out of an evolutionary narrative that can find no place for such a sudden late-onset disordering of the cosmos and its Darwinian state. He speaks instead of three great phases of God's action in the world in line with evolutionary processes, and which can be integrated into the Christian narrative of creation and redemption.

Ernst M Conradie focuses on Denis' Christology and his endorsement of the deep incarnation theology, relating this to Denis' affirmation of an Athanasian notion of divinisation. He challenges this approach, asking whether it is deep enough to sustain an unwavering, eschatological commitment to God's creation in the sense of *creatura*, to that which is material, bodily and earthly.

Alexei V Nesteruk writes from the perspective of the eastern Orthodox tradition which, as he says, is not as attracted to the concept of deep incarnation as are Roman Catholics. Nevertheless, he argues that deep incarnation can contribute to Maximus the Confessor's idea of the *macro-anthropos*. In this idea, the world acquires the features of humanity constantly effecting its own incarnation, through knowledge of the universe and all organic and inorganic nature in the image of the Logos made flesh. It sees humanity as a mediating agency between divisions in creation and between creation and God. Thus, he argues, deep incarnation can be treated as a new expression of the moral mediation between creation and God already exercised by Christ through his Resurrection and Ascension.

Mark Worthing, for several years a dialogue partner together with Denis on the Australian Lutheran- Roman Catholic Dialogue team, gives an insight into Denis' strong commitment to Receptive Ecumenism when he narrates an incident during one dialogue meeting when Denis drew Mark's attention to his own Lutheran stance on the theology of the cross. Mark employs this theology of the cross when he argues that deep incarnation underscores the true power of the Christian message, at the centre of which is the crucified God. He draws upon the literary voice of Christos Tsiolkas to remind us of the God who suffers not only for, but also with, creation.

Our co-editor, Ted Peters, widens the discussion to include the work of astro-theologians in an expansive deep incarnation theology which encompasses the entire material history of all galaxies and all extra-terrestrial creatures into the eternal perichoresis of God as Trinity. Another contributor, the philosopher-theologian Stephen Downs, widens the discussion in the opposite direction, arguing for more focus on plant life in the redemptive theme proposed by deep incarnation. He urges readers to listen to indigenous voices and, as with Mark Worthing, to voices from literature.

Ted Peters reminds us of the historical context surrounding Joseph Lenow's entry. When we turn to addressing the ecological crisis, we remember how the World Council of Churches alerted us to the danger in the late 1960s, shortly before the first Earth Day environmental movement in 1970. With apocalyptic fervour, the futurist theologians of the day challenged the global public to wake up to the signs of impending doom and to the need for urgent repentance and renewal on a planetary scale. Jürgen Moltmann's *Hope and Planning* (translated by Margaret Clarkson, New York: Harper, 1971) was followed by two alarms by Ted Peters, *Future—Human and Divine* in 1978 (Louisville KY: Westminster John Knox Press), and *Fear, Faith, and the Future* in 1980 (Minneapolis: Augsburg). And in 1981, scientist Charles Birch along with theologian John Cobb published *The Liberation of Life* (Cambridge UK: Cambridge University) employing process metaphysics to structure a holistic treatment of life on Earth. Because both liberation theologians and feminist theologians took a strong stand against eco-theology, on the grounds that ecological theology shared a partnership with natural science, and natural science is both patriarchal and imperialistic, theologians along with the Christian churches lulled themselves to sleep while the planet continued to burn.

After the nuclear disaster at Chernobyl in 1986, both liberation and feminist theologians began to wake up and take notice. So did church leaders. In the wake of this late awakening, three extent models for treating the ecological crisis theologically have been developed, namely, ecojustice, stewardship, and ecological spirituality.

This is where Joseph Lenow picks up the story. In his chapter, 'Following the Deeply Incarnate Christ: Discipleship in the Midst of Environmental Crisis', Lenow builds on Denis Edwards' deep incarnation to propose a *Christic ecology* that recognizes the interconnection of natural and biological process; the localisation of analysis of Christ's presence in the natural world, in service of eco-liberation; and the development of new liturgical and devotional practices rooted in deep incarnation.

Joseph Bracken critiques the rigour of Denis' philosophical method in regard to the distinction between the primary causality of God and the secondary causality of creatures from moment to moment. He argues for a systems-oriented interpretation of the

Christian doctrine of the Incarnation and offers a way in which the term 'deep incarnation' can move beyond the realm of symbol and metaphor and into a systematically organized world view that is basically compatible with the Christian understanding of the Christian God-world relationship.

John F Haught explores ways in which Denis' reading of Teilhard de Chardin, done in the light of Karl Rahner, could have been developed more to fully participate in the radical metaphysical reconfiguration of Catholic thought that Teilhard envisaged. He identifies this as a loophole in Denis' efforts to hold together the philosophical ideas of early Christian thought, and the drastically different world view of contemporary scientific thought. He believes that Denis' efforts to summarise the thought of the early Christian writers is his most important contribution to Catholic thought.

Part of the attraction that Teilhard held for Denis as a committed and pastoral Roman Catholic priest, was his concept of creation as the Eucharistic table. Two of our writers who engage with the Eucharistic theme are Anthony J Kelly and Mary E McGann. Kelly acknowledges Denis with assisting his thinking on the ecological dimension of the Eucharist, while McGann focuses on the Eucharist in reference to the hunger of Earth's poorest, a theme prominent in Pope Francis' *Laudato si'*.

Ilia Delio explores a new God-world relationship, a relational holism, through Teilhard's ideas on mind, matter, evolution and God. She argues that by including consciousness as part of the material world, Teilhard opened up a place for religion within nature, transcending the abstraction of supernaturalism and reframing religion as the depth and breadth of evolution. She aims to retrieve the evolutionary epistemology and cosmology of Teilhard in order to overcome the Kantian split between matter and mind too often assumed in today's dialogue between theology and science.

Three of our contributors are early researchers, having either recently completed doctoral degrees are near completion. Julie Trinidad was one of Denis' final doctoral students. Her work on Kasper offers ways in which his pneumatology can be developed within the deep incarnation discussion, and shows that Kasper has been influential in Denis Edwards' work on ecology. Lawrence Ng Yew Kim explores how Denis' engagement with his friend and discussion partner, the late astronomer and theologian William R Stoeger (Bill), influenced Denis' concept of divine action within the concrete realities of the world. His chapter works with a Thomistic perspective and addresses the issue of miracles more robustly in a non-interventionist but genuinely theological way. From the perspective of her Lutheran background, Jamie L Fowler is interested in the physical presence of Christ in the Eucharist in an effort to make the doctrine scientifically and theologically accessible. She does this through a consideration of the deep incarnation of Christ into the multidimensional unity of life which establishes a relationship between the divine and material reality, thus shining a light on the self-giving nature of God in the Eucharist.

While Denis was first and foremost a systematic theologian, he was consistently conscious of the importance of the biblical tradition as a theological foundation. Two of the contributors to this volume are biblical scholars who were colleagues of Denis at the Adelaide College of Divinity which formed the School of Theology of Flinders University where Denis was based for many years. Michael Trainor was a long-standing friend and colleague of Denis, and Scripture, especially the New Testament, often featured in their professional as well as their cordial conversations. Michael has written the *In Memoriam* as well as a chapter on the Gospels. He has long been a member of the Earth Bible team under the leadership of Professor Norman Habel. His chapter offers an ecological reading of the Gospels of Mark and Luke and focuses on the transformation of Earth by the Jesus event. In reference to Denis' work he explores Earth-related insights in Rahner's work. A colleague of both Denis and Michael, Vicky Balabanski, an ordained minister of the Uniting Church also active in the Anglican/Episcopalian Church, has worked for many years in the Letter to the Colossians. In Vicky's chapter she offers a reading of Colossians 1:14 and the hymn of 1:15-20 engaging closely with Denis work in *Deep Incarnation*, and she concludes with reference to *Laudato si'*. Her chapter examines in particular the crucial concept to be found in the Colossians hymn of God's redemptive suffering with the whole of creation. With Michael Trainor and myself, Vicky is also a foundational member of the Earth Bible team under the leadership of Professor Norman Habel. While I have not contributed a separate chapter in this volume, my work in the biblical wisdom literature with its richness as a source for ecological readings of the bible was first inspired by Denis' insights on wisdom Christology, which I experienced first as a student and then as a privileged colleague.

Beside our writers there are many others who have helped in some way to bring this collection to fruition. Gerard Kelly, former head of the Catholic Institute of Sydney, a long-time friend of Denis and his colleague on the Lutheran- Roman Catholic Dialogue team, gave generously of his time in helping to collate a bibliography of Denis' works, as did Peter Malone. Cris Henriksson, formerly Administrative Officer at the Catholic Theological College in Adelaide and now at the Australian Catholic University campus in Adelaide, co-operated in helping with the bibliography. Denis would be the first to appreciate the way in which Cris is always on hand to help struggling theologians circumnavigate the more practical tasks of academic life! We are grateful to Robert J Russell (Bob) for allowing the use of Denis' article, 'A Story of a Theologian of the Natural World', which relates his pathway to his developed eco-theology. We thank Patricia Fox, dear friend and long-time colleague of Denis both in his academic and pastoral work for giving us an early indication of this work and other unpublished works of Denis.

Yvonne Ashby's delicate yet powerful artwork has been influenced by the classes she took at the Adelaide College of Divinity, often led by Denis. Denis took a great personal interest in art and music and was often to be found in art galleries and at orchestral concerts. He found in Yvonne's art much that delighted him. We are grateful to Yvonne for her generosity in contributing the cover design, which encapsulates so well the themes of Spirit and creation.

Finally, sincere thanks go to the publisher, Hilary Regan. In a time when theological publishing faces many difficulties, Hilary has been an untiring champion of quality publications. Through ATF Press he gives a voice not only to theological writers in his homeland of Australia, but far and wide throughout the globe. Several of Denis' books have been published through ATF.

This present publication honours a man and a priest of 'infallible courtesy, and quiet kindness', as Christopher Southgate puts it. Denis' gracious and faith-filled personality shines clearly through his own writings and those of the contributors who knew him well, and their insights give us a sense of what it means to live well and with deep integrity. We will miss the 'genial companionship' to which Anthony Kelly refers, but the richness of the thinkers represented here, including the newer writers who have begun their eco-theological journey, attests to his ongoing legacy.

Marie Turner
October 2020

Contributors

Vicky Balabanski is senior lecturer in New Testament at Flinders University Department of Theology and Director of Biblical Studies at the Uniting College for Leadership and Theology, in Adelaide, South Australia. She has lived and worked in various parts of Europe, the Middle East and Asia, including a year in Jerusalem as the Golda Meir post-doctoral fellow at the Hebrew University. She is a writer and editor of the international Earth Bible Project, which has produced a series of books that seek to read the Bible in the shadow of the ecological crisis facing the Earth community, including her Earth Bible Commentary on *Colossians: An Eco-Stoic Reading* (Bloomsbury T&T Clark, 2020). Vicky is actively involved in supporting the development of indigenous writers in the field of spirituality. She has long been revegetating land on the Southern Yorke Peninsula, in South Australia, a region now designated as a 'Great Southern Ark' to rewild and reinstate ecological processes.

Joseph A Bracken, SJ, is a Jesuit Priest, Professor Emeritus of Theology at Xavier University in Cincinnati, Ohio. He has specialised over the years in linking the metaphysical scheme of Alfred North Whitehead with classical Roman Catholic Church doctrine, above all, in dealing with the philosophical presuppositions of interreligious dialogue and the proper relation between religion and science. His latest book publications are *Does God Roll Dice? Divine Providence for a World in the Making* (Liturgical Press, 2012), *The World in the Trinity: Open-ended Systems in Science and Religion* (Fortress Press, 2014), and *The Church as Dynamic Life-System; Shared Ministries and Common Responsibilities* (Orbis, 2019). In preparation is a new book tentatively titled as *Universal Intersubjectivity in an Event-Filled World* to be published by Fortress/Lexington Academic later in 2020.

Ernst M Conradie is Senior Professor in the Department of Religion and Theology at the University of the Western Cape where he teaches systematic theology and ethics. His most recent monographs are *The Earth in God's Economy: Creation, Salvation and Consummation in Ecological Perspective* (LIT Verlag, 2015) and *Redeeming Sin? Social Diagnostics amid Ecological Destruction* (Lexington Books, 2017). With Sigurd Bergmann, Celia Deane-Drummond and Denis Edwards he is the co-editor of *Christian Faith and the Earth: Current Paths and Emerging Horizons in Ecotheology.* (T&T Clark, 2014), and with Hilda Koster he is the co-editor of *The T&T Clark Handbook on Christian Theology and Climate Change* (T&T Clark, 2019).

Celia Deane-Drummond is Senior Research Fellow in Theology at Campion Hall, Oxford University and Director of the *Laudato si'* Research Institute, Campion Hall, Oxford University. She is also Visiting Professor in Theology and Science at Durham University and Adjunct Professor in Theology at the University of Notre Dame, where she was based from 2011-2019. She was Chair of the *European Forum for the Study of Religion and Environment* from 2011-2018. She is co-editor of the journal *Philosophy, Theology and the Sciences*, published with Mohr Siebeck. Her more recent single author works include *Ecotheology* (London: DLT, 2008); *The Wisdom of the Liminal: Evolution and Other Animals in Human Becoming* (Grand Rapids: Eerdmans, 2014); *A Primer in Ecotheology: Theology for a Fragile Earth* (Eugene: Wipf and Stock, 2018); *Theological Ethics Through a Multispecies Lens: Evolution of Wisdom Volume One* (Oxford: Oxford University Press, 2019) and edited volumes, with Sigurd Bergmann and Markus Vogt, *Religion in the Anthropocene* (Eugene: Wipf and Stock, 2017); Agustín Fuentes, *The Evolution of Human Wisdom* (Lanhan: Lexington, 2017) and with Rebecca Artinian Kaiser, *Theology and Ecology Across the Disciplines: On Care for Our Common Home* (London: Bloomsbury, 2018).

Ilia Delio, OSF, holds the Josephine C Connelly Chair in Christian Theology at Villanova University. She is the author of over twenty books including *Making All Things New: Catholicity, Cosmology and Consciousness,* a finalist for the 2019 Michael Ramsey Prize and *The Unbearable Wholeness of Being: God, Evolution and the Power of Love,* for which she won the 2014 Silver Nautilus Book Award and a 2014

Catholic Press Association Book Award in Faith and Science. She is also founder of the Omega Center, an online educational resource for the work of Teilhard de Chardin and the integration of science and religion in the twenty-first century.

Stephen Downs' interest in what came to be known as ecological theology began when he first studied environmental ethics around 1980. Early in his academic career he was asked to teach Catholic seminarians about science and religion, Christian anthropology and the place of human beings in the world; and later, Catholic social teaching, which includes care for the environment. Since then he has mostly taught introductory and foundational units in theology. But he has continued reading ecological theology and discussing it with colleagues and students. He is currently National Head of School, Theology, at Australian Catholic University.

Jamie Fowler is trained in molecular biology and systematic theology. She is finishing her PhD studies in theology at the Graduate Theological Union in Berkeley, California, USA.

John F Haught (PhD Catholic University, 1970), is Distinguished Research Professor, Georgetown University, Washington DC. He was formerly Professor in the Department of Theology at Georgetown University (1970–2005) and Chair (1990–95). He is the author of 22 books: *God After Einstein* (New Haven: Yale University Press, forthcoming); *The New Cosmic Story: Inside Our Awakening Universe (New Haven: Yale Univ. Press, 2017); A John Haught Reader: Essential Writings on Science and Religion* (Eugene, Oregon: Wipf & Stock, 2018); *Resting On the Future: Catholic Theology for an Unfinished Universe* (New York: Bloomsbury Press, 2015); *Science and Faith: A New Introduction* (New York: Paulist Press, 2012), *Making Sense of Evolution: Darwin, God, and The Drama of Life* (Louisville: Westminster/John Knox Press, February 2010); *God and the New Atheism: A Critical Response to Dawkins, Harris, and Hitchens* (Louisville: Westminster/John Knox Press, 2008); *Christianity and Science: Toward a Theology of Nature* (Maryknoll NY: Orbis Press, 2007); *Is Nature Enough? Meaning and Truth in the Age of Science* (Cambridge: Cambridge University Press, 2006); *Purpose, Evolution and the Meaning of Life* (Ontario: Pandora Press, 2004); *Deeper*

Than Darwin: The Prospects for Religion in the Age of Evolution (Boulder, Colo: Westview Press, 2003); *God After Darwin: A Theology of Evolution* (Boulder, Colo: Westview Press, 2000); *Science and Religion: From Conflict to Conversation* (New York: Paulist Press, 1995); *The Promise of Nature: Ecology and Cosmic Purpose* (New York: Paulist Press, 1993); *Mystery and Promise: A Theology of Revelation* (Collegeville: Liturgical Press, 1993); *What Is Religion?* (New York: Paulist Press, 1990); *The Revelation of God in History* (Wilmington: Michael Glazier Press, 1988); *What Is God?* (New York: Paulist Press, 1986); *The Cosmic Adventure: Science, Religion and the Quest for Purpose* (New York: Paulist Press, 1984); *Nature and Purpose* (Lanham, Md: University Press of America, 1980); *Religion and Self-Acceptance* (New York: Paulist Press, 1976).

Anthony J Kelly CSsR, is a priest of the Redemptorist Order; his doctoral and post-doctoral studies were in Rome, Toronto and Paris. He was for many years involved in Yarra Theological Union in Melbourne and was President of YTU for ten years. Formerly, he was President of *Australian Catholic Theological Association* and Past Chair of the *Forum of Australian Catholic Institutes of Theology*. Anthony was Head of Sub-Faculty of Philosophy and Theology at the Australian Catholic University from 1999 to 2004. Anthony has been Professor of Theology and Philosophy at Australian Catholic University, Research fellow in the University's Institute of Critical Inquiry, and was a member of the International Theological Commission from 2004 to 2014. He has written numerous books and articles many are with ecological topics in relation to spirituality and theology with his interests being in the Thomist theological tradition, Trinity, Theology and Culture, Lonergan Studies, ecology and social justice. His publications include: *Deus Ineffabilis Trinitas: The Theologian in the Presence of the Revealed God* (Washington: The Thomist Press, 1970); *The Wings of the Morning. Theological Meditations.* (Melbourne: Spectrum Publications, 1977); *Wondering about God* (Liguori, MO: Liguori Publications, 1978); *Love Remains. A Meditation on Christian Love* (Melbourne: Spectrum Publications, 1979); *The Range of Faith. Critical Questions for a Living Theology* (Homebush: Paulist Press, 1986, and Collegeville: The Liturgical Press, 1989); *The Trinity of Love. A Christian Theology of God.*: Wilmington: Michael Glazier 1989);

Eschatology and Hope (Maryknoll, NY: Orbis, 2006); *The Resurrection Effect: Transforming Christian Life and Thought* (Maryknoll, NY: Orbis, 2008); *God is Love: The Heart of Christian Faith* (Collegeville, MN: Liturgical Press, 2012); *Upward: Faith, Church and Ascension of Christ* (Collegeville, MN: Liturgical Press, 2014); *Laudato si': Integral Ecology and the Catholic Vision* (Adelaide: ATF Press, 2016).

Joseph E Lenow is Resident Assistant Professor of Theology at Creighton University in Omaha, Nebraska, USA, and a priest in the Episcopal Church. His works have appeared in the *International Journal of Systematic Theology, Religious Studies, Studia Patristica,* and the *Anglican Theological Review.*

Mary E McGann, RSCJ, is a member of the core doctoral faculty of the Graduate Theological Union in Berkeley, and is Adjunct Associate Professor of Liturgical Studies at the Jesuit School of Theology. Her recent research and writing focus on the global water and food crises, the challenges these present to Christian worship and sacramental practice, and the need to pursue deep liturgical renewal that honors and acknowledges our planetary independence. McGann inaugurated the Ecology and Liturgy seminar at the North American Academy of Liturgy in 2009 and served as its convener for several years. Among her recent publications are her fourth book, *The Meal That Reconnects: Eucharistic Eating and the Global Food Crisis* (Collegeville: Liturgical Press, 2020); and 'Troubled Waters, Troubling Initiation Rites', in *Full of Your Glory: Liturgy, Cosmos, Creation,* Teresa Berger, editor (Liturgical Press, 2019). She teaches courses in 'Ecology and Liturgy', and 'Spirituality of the Earth', collaborates with the faculty-student Climate Justice Initiative at the Jesuit School, and engages with her community in permaculture gardening.

Alexei Nesteruk holds PhD in Physics and Mathematics, as well as DSc (Habilitation) in Philosophy. He is visiting research lecturer at the University of Portsmouth, UK, as well as a research fellow and lecturer at the Russian Christian Academy of Humanities in St Petersburg, Russia. He is author of *The Sense of the Universe: Philosophical Explication of Theological Commitment in Modern Cosmology* (Fortress Press, 2015).

Lawrence Ng Yew Kim is currently a graduate student at the Jesuit School of Theology of Santa Clara University. He is also a diocesan priest from Malaysia who was ordained in 2003. Like many people, he describes his life as a journey. It is a journey that begins with the question 'how' and 'why'? A catechism taught his class once that Jesus lives in the tabernacle inside the Church. He remembered thinking (in Malay), 'bagaimana? (how?)' and 'kenapa? (why?)'. The questions never stopped since for him, which led him to the priesthood and to his interest in the theology and science dialogue at the Graduate Theological Union.

Ted Peters, co-editor of this volume, serves as co-editor of the journal, *Theology and Science,* published by the Center for Theology and the Natural Sciences at the Graduate Theological Union in Berkeley, California, USA. He is author of *God—the World's Future* (Fortress, 3rd edition, 2015) and *God in Cosmic History: Where Science and History Meet Religion* (Anselm Academic, 2017). He is editor of *Artificial Intelligence and Intelligence Amplification: Utopia or Extinction* (ATF Press, 2019). He is author of a fiction thriller with a Transhumanist plot, *Cyrus Twelve,* with Aprocryphile Press [http://tedstimelytake.com/series/leona-foxx-thriller/]. See his website: tedstimelytake.com.

Christopher Southgate is a Professor of Christian Theodicy at the University of Exeter, UK. Trained originally as a biochemist, he has since worked as a house-husband, bookseller, lay chaplain, and a trainer of Christian ministers. He has taught the science-religion debate and its application to ecological issues since 1993. He is also a much-published poet. He is author of *The Good and the Groaning: Evolution, the Problem of Evil, and the Call of Humanity* (Westminster John Knox, 2008).

Michael Trainor is senior lecturer in biblical studies with the Australian Catholic University and Parish Priest of the Adelaide western suburb parish of Lockleys in the Archdiocese of Adelaide. He holds an MA in biblical literature and languages (Chicago), MEd (Boston) and DTheol (Melbourne). His area of specialisation is the study of the New Testament with particular focus on the gospels and their relevance for our contemporary world and pastoral life. Michael is co-chair of the Uniting Church-Roman Catholic Dialogue of South Australia, co-chair of the South Australian Council of Christians and Jews, immediate past president of the Australian Catholic Biblical Association, Chair of the Australian Council of Christians and Jews, Member of the Australian Catholic Bishops Council for Christian Unity, and Executive Board member of the International Council of Christians and Jews. In 2007 Michael received an Order of Australia (AM) for his services to theology, archaeology and inter-faith relations. His latest books include *About Earth's Children: An Ecological Listening to the Acts of the Apostles* (Bloomsbury/T&T Clark, 2020), *About Earth's Child: An Ecological Listening to the Gospel of Luke* (Sheffield Press, 2012), *The Body of Jesus and Sexual Abuse: How the Gospel Passion Narratives inform a Pastoral Response* (Wipf & Stock, 2015), and *Owning and Consuming: Neo-Liberalism and the Biblical Voice* (Routledge, 2018—co-authored with Prof Paul Babie of Adelaide University Law School). Michael is also a contributor to the forthcoming volume, *Enabling Dialogue about the Land: A Resource Book for Jews and Christians* to be published by Paulist Press/Stimulus Foundation, edited by P Cunningham *et al.* Michael and Denis Edwards lived in community for several years.

Julie Trinidad is a lecturer in Catholic Studies at the University of South Australia and a member of the Staff Spiritual and Religious Formation Team at Catholic Education South Australia. Julie holds Bachelors and Masters degrees in both Education (Adelaide and Flinders Universities) and Theology (Flinders University and the Catholic University of Leuven). Her PhD, awarded by the Australian Catholic University, was supervised by Denis Edwards. Julie has been Ministry Formation Program Coordinator and Coordinator of Youth Ministry for the Catholic Archdiocese of Adelaide. She is a member of the Australian Lutheran–Roman Catholic Dialogue and convenes the Gender Justice Working Group of the Australian Catholic Theological Association.

Mark Worthing is Pastor of Immanuel Lutheran Church, North Adelaide. He was formerly Senior Researcher at the Australian Lutheran Institute for Theology and Ethics (ALITE) (2013–2015) and Senior Research Fellow of the Graeme Clark Research Institute at Tabor College, Adelaide (2010–2012). Mark is a Fellow of the

Institute for the Study of Christianity in an Age of Science and Technology (ISCAST), and a founding member of the International Society of Science and Religion (ISSR). Mark's publications include *Unlikely Allies: Monotheism and the Rise of Science.* (Melbourne: ISCAST/Nexus books, 2019); *Iscariot* (Melbourne: Morning Star, 2018); *Martin Luther: A Wild Boar in the Lord's Vineyard* (Melbourne: Morning Star, 2017); *Graeme Clark. The Man Who Invented the Bionic Ear* (Sydney: Allen&Unwin, 2015); and *God and Science in Classroom and Pulpit*, with G Buxton and C Mulherin (Melbourne: Mosaic Press 2012). *God, Creation and Contemporary Physics* (Minneapolis (Fortress Press, 1996), won the international 1997 Templeton science and faith book of the year prize.

From God to Nature and Back Again

A Story of a Theologian of the Natural World[1]

Denis Edwards

When Robert 'Bob' John Russell invited me to contribute to this series of accounts of intellectual journeys in the field of science and theology, I initially resisted the idea. But Bob is persuasive. He is also a wonderfully generous man, someone from whom I have learnt a great deal and a person I much admire, so I ended up saying yes to his invitation.

One of the reasons for my initial reluctance was that I do not see myself as one of the major players in this field. This self-assessment does not spring from false modesty, but from my sense that in the dialogue between science and theology there are three broad groups at work: those who are specialists in science/theology, those who are principally scientists who are committed to the dialogue, and those who are principally theologians who see engagement with science as a fundamental part of their theological work. I see myself as belonging to this third group rather than among the specialists.

My theological base is the mainstream of Christian systematic theology, in Christology, the theology of the Trinity, and in the theologies of thinkers such as Irenaeus, Athanasius, Thomas, and Rahner. In a great deal of my writing, however, I have been engaged in some way with the sciences. Professor Manuel, SJ, surprised me in 2013, at the Seminar of the Sciences and Theology in Barcelona, by introducing me by offering a systematic analysis of my publications over the last twenty years. He showed that I have alternated in consecutive publications almost exactly between articles or books

---

1. This autobiographical essay by Denis Edwards was written at the invitation of Robert John Russell, co-editor of *Theology and Science*. It will subsequently be published in that journal as well as here in this memorial volume.

focused on ecological theology and those centred more directly on issues in science and theology. For many academics, of course, these are distinct areas of interest. Pondering the largely unconscious choices I have made to alternate publications between these two areas has led me to greater clarity that what unites them in my own work is the endeavour to contribute to a twenty-first century theology of the natural world.

So in this article, I look back from this conclusion and ask: What has led to this conviction that I am called to be part of a community of scholars seeking to build a theology of the natural world, one that can respond, on the one hand, to the insights of scientific cosmology and evolutionary biology, and, on the other, to the great issues we face in the global community of life Earth, such as climate change and the loss of biodiversity? I will begin with some short reflections on what I see as the early beginnings for this conviction. In the second section I will reflect on the 1970's, a time of commitment to social justice and theological education. In the third section, on the 1980's, I will trace the development of my ecological consciousness and engagement with the sciences. The fourth section, on the 1990's, will be focussed on international collaborations, and the role in my story of the Center for Theology and the Natural Sciences at Berkeley (CTNS) and the Vatican Observatory. Finally I will name some developments in my journey during the early twenty-first century.

Beginnings

Two early experiences of the natural world are important in my story. The first is of the Flinders Ranges, which run close to Port Pirie, an industrial town north of Adelaide where I was born. From my teenage years on, I have gone back from Adelaide to spend time in these ranges and there found that the pressures of everyday life begin to lift and are replaced by a sense of wholeness. Often in the early days I would camp in Brachina Gorge, a place that had its origins 800 million years ago, as a low-lying basin filled by the sea. Amazing, pre-Cambrian fossils have been found in this gorge, fossils of soft-bodied, highly developed creatures that lived 600 million years ago. These are the Ediacara fossils, after which a new period of life on Earth is now named. Brachina Gorge is a place of morning bird-song, of beautiful, yellow-footed rock wallabies, of emus leading their young along the creek bed, trees full of noisy cockatoos, and ever-changing reds in the cliffs above. For me this has been a place of wordless peace, a place of God's Spirit.

The second experience of the natural world occurred once a week during my years of seminary training. Our college was located where the Adelaide plain meets the hills of the Mount Lofty Ranges, and bordered a nature reserve that is now the Morialta and Black Hill Conservation Park. It is an area that had long been important to the indigenous Kaurna people, a place of waterfalls, great River Red Gums, some of them many hundreds of years old, of rare Yellow-Tailed Black Cockatoos, of brilliant blue green and orange Rainbow Lorikeets, and delightful tiny Fairy Wrens. Each week we walked in these hills. One of my friends loved birds and could name all the species of those we met. Another knew the botanical names of all the plants, including all the endemic species of delicate orchids growing in the Black Hill area. Looking back I think that there were times when I have learnt more about God in these hills than I did in my seminary classes.

From my present perspective, however, two aspects of my early studies have been particularly important in my journey into the theological dialogue with science. The first is the way we were taught to interpret the two Genesis accounts of creation. We were led to understand them in their contexts, and to see them as offering profound theological truths, such as that there is one God who creates everything and who finds the whole creation good. The cosmology of the ancient authors, and their structuring of the order of events, were not seen as having authority for Christians today. It is the salvific truths of the Scriptures that we were taught to hold as precious gifts of God. I remain deeply grateful for the clarity of the teaching I received. It has constituted a permanent freedom to embrace fully scientific cosmology and evolutionary biology, without in any way compromising my embrace of biblical faith.

A second aspect of this early story that comes to mind is that in my late teens and early twenties I began to read the works of the Jesuit palaeontologist, Teilhard de Chardin, particularly *The Human Phenomenon*,[2] *Le Milieu Divin*,[3] and *The Mass on the World*.[4] Later I would be deeply engaged by his *The Heart of Matter*.[5] Along with

2. Now re-translated by Sarah Appleton-Weber, as Teilhard de Chardin, *The Human Phenomenon* (Portland, Oregon: Sussex Academic Press, 1999).
3. Teilhard de Chardin, *Le Milieu Divin: An Essay on the Interior Life* (London: Collins, 1957).
4. In Teilhard de Chardin, *Hymn of the Universe* (London: Collins, 1957).
5. Teilhard de Chardin, *The Heart of Matter* (London: William Collins, 1978).

many others at the time, I found Teilhard's work exhilarating and transformative. It would be hard to overestimate its importance in my journey. Ever since my first reading I have embraced his idea that what science tells us about evolution can be held together in one vision with the theology of the crucified and risen Christ, particularly the cosmic Christ of Colossians and Ephesians. While I now bring a more critical approach to some aspects of Teilhard's work, I see his fundamental vision as an enduring foundation and inspiration for my later focus on ecology, and on science and theology, on what I am now calling a theology of the natural world.

The 1970s: From Social Justice to Theology

At the beginning of the seventies I was a young priest working in parishes in Adelaide, with much of my work focussed on young people through the Young Christian Workers and Young Christian Students movements. These movements were inspired by the Belgian priest, and later Cardinal, Joseph Cardijn. They brought young people together to reflect on their lives in the light of the gospel and to take action, using the methodology of see, judge, and act. In Latin America this same approach of action and reflection gave rise to the Basic Ecclesial Movements, to Liberation Theology and to the centrality of the option for the poor.

Looking back, I think it was a passion for social justice that largely shaped my early ministry, a passion supported by the commitment of the young people I worked with, and also by the theologians I was reading, particularly Gustavo Gutiérrez.[6] I was doing something I believed in deeply. It was disconcerting, then, when my archbishop asked me to take on a new project that involved working with a team of people forming catechists and developing adult education in the archdiocese. Eventually I decided that I could bring the same commitments to this new work.

Moving into adult education demanded further education on my own part and I was sent off to Fordham University to do a master's degree. I found myself in a wonderful cohort of students, with very good teachers, and began to learn what I did not know, about Scripture,

---

6. See particularly Gustavo Gutiérrez, *A Theology of Liberation: History, Politics and Salvation* (Maryknoll, NY: Orbis Books, 1973, 1978).

theology, and spirituality. I discovered the transforming power of good theology. In the process I came upon Karl Rahner's theology of faith, and the interconnection in this thought between the transcendental experience of God by grace in everyday life and the explicit faith of the Christian tradition. I came to Adelaide, determined to work with my colleagues to make good theology available to the people of the local church, and we began to offer serious courses in Bible, theology and in the prayer tradition of the church.

Later in the decade I was sent back to study, this time at The Catholic University of America, to do doctoral course work and then write my thesis, which I did under the direction of Avery Dulles, on the relationship between the experience of God and explicit faith, in the work of Karl Rahner and John of the Cross. It was a good time to be at Catholic University, with excellent and highly committed lecturers who led us into a deep appreciation of the great Christian tradition, in its biblical, Patristic, medieval, Reformation, and more recent expressions, but who also had an open and searching approach to contemporary issues. Karl Rahner's work was pivotal in my own theological development, not only for his content on an astonishing range of issues, but also because of his theological approach, which is always ready to engage issues of everyday life with the depth of the Christian tradition, and to see them in the light of God-with-us in the Word made flesh. In the next decade, when I became convinced of the theological importance of ecology, and felt the need to engage theologically with recent science, I would find rich resources in Rahner's works.[7]

The 1980s: From Social Justice and Theology to Ecology and to Science

When I came back to Adelaide from doctoral studies, one of my colleagues insisted that I offer a course on what I had learnt through

---

7. This engagement with Rahner on these issues has continued in, for example, 'Resurrection of the Body and Transformation of the Universe in the Theology of Karl Rahner', in *Philosophy & Theology* 18/2 (2006): 357–83; 'Resurrection and the Costs of Evolution: A Dialogue with Rahner on Noninterventionist Theology', *Theological Studies* 67/4 (December 2006): 816–33; 'Teilhard's Vision as Agenda for Rahner's Christology', in, *From Teilard to Omega*, edited by Ilia Delio (Maryknoll, NY: Orbis Books, 2014), 53–66.

doing the thesis. She overcame my reluctance by insisting that since I had been given the opportunity for this kind of study it was only fair that I should share the fruits of it with others. So I set about designing a course that I then taught each year for about five years. After teaching it several times I realised that I had the makings of a book, so I began to write as I taught. The result was my first book, *Human Experience of God*.[8] It many ways it was an attempt to interpret Rahner's thought, but while Rahner consistently refers to negative experiences of human suffering or emptiness when he gives examples of the experience of God, something he does often, many of my examples are positive, and unlike Rahner's, they are often experiences of God that occur in an through the encounter with the world of nature.

It began to become clear to me, along with many others, during the early eighties that commitment to social justice needed to be enlarged to include the natural world. The poor of the Earth are the ones most afflicted by ecological disasters. I was certainly influenced towards a more ecological consciousness by reading Charles Birch and John Cobb's *The Liberation of Life*,[9] Thomas Berry's early writings, and his *The Dream of the Earth*,[10] and particularly Sean McDonagh's *To Care for the Earth*.[11] It was greatly encouraging to find some systematic theologians beginning to do ecological theology, in books such as Paul Santmire's *The Travail of Nature*,[12] Jürgen Moltmann's *God in Creation*,[13] Sallie McFague's *Models of God*,[14] and Gabriel Daly's *Creation and Redemption*.[15]

An important influence for me as an Australian was the voice of the indigenous peoples of this land. Any talk of social justice in Australia had to address the extreme injustice experienced by many Aboriginal

---

8.   Denis Edwards, *Human Experience of God* (New York: Paulist Press, 1983).

9.   Charles Birch and John Cobb, *The Liberation of Life: From Cell to the Community* (Cambridge: Cambridge University Press, 1981).

10. Thomas Berry, *The Dream of the Earth* (San Francisco: Sierra Club Books, 1988).

11. Sean McDonagh, *To Care for the Earth: A Call to a New Theology* (Santa Fe, New Mexico: Bear & Company, 1986).

12. H Paul Santmire, *The Travail of Nature: The Ambiguous Ecological Promise of Christian Theology* (Philadelphia: Fortress Press, 1985).

13. Jürgen Moltmann, *God in Creation: An Ecological Doctrine of Creation* (London: SCM, 1985).

14. Sallie McFague, *Models of God: Theology for an Ecological Nuclear Age* (London: SCM, 1987).

15. Gabriel Daly, *Creation and Redemption* (Dublin: Gill and McMillan, 1988).

people. In thinking about this theologically, it seemed essential that we newcomers to this land adopt an entirely different stand before indigenous Australians—we need to stand before them as learners. We need to learn to respect their historical and ongoing role as custodians of this land, as people who know the spiritual significance of the land. So I attempted to write about this theologically, in terms of a God-given invitation to Christians to see themselves as apprentices in faith to Aboriginal people in their view of the land.[16] Listening to Aboriginal voices led me towards my own ecological conversion.

The growing conviction of the centrality of the ecological to theology in our time drew me more and more to reading in science, and not simply to scientific ecology, but also to evolutionary biology and to cosmology. In order to understand the community of life on Earth it seemed important to understand what science has to say about where we come from. So I was busy reading Steven Weinberg's *The First Three Minutes*,[17] Stephen Hawking's *A Brief History of Time*,[18] a whole series of books by Paul Davies, and writers like John Barrow John Gribbin and Martin Reese, and books on biological evolution from diverse biologists including Ernst Mayr, EO Wilson, Richard Dawkins and Stephen Jay Gould. The eighties for me were a time of committing myself to learning some science, and I have kept reading it since. Much of my interest has been in the large story that cosmology tells us and in the further story of the evolution of life on Earth. I became convinced that theology for the twenty-first century had to engage creatively with these two interconnected stories.

I began to try to do theological work on the dialogue between cosmology and biology on the one hand and the Christian story on the other. Probably because of my ongoing engagement with Rahner's thought, I was convinced that a Christian theology that engaged with nature could not draw simply on creation theology. If it was to be truly Christian, it would need to draw on the whole story of God's action with regard to creation, involving both creation and saving incarnation. I well understood the argument of Christians involved

16. Denis Edwards, 'A Local Church in Apprenticeship to the Aboriginal View of the Land', in *Called to Be Church in Australia* (Homebush, NSW: St Paul Publications, 1989).
17. Stephen Weinberg, *The First Three Minutes* (London: Basic Books, 1977, 1993).
18. Stephen Hawking, *A Brief History of Time: From the Big Bang to Black Holes* (London: Bantam Press, 1988).

with ecology who felt that the churches in recent centuries had spent far too much time worrying about individual human salvation. But it seemed to me that the appropriate response to this was not to retreat from the theology of the saving incarnation back to a simple creation theology or spirituality, but to push further into the theology of the salvific meaning of the Christ event, not just for human beings, but for the whole inter-related universe of creatures.

In this context I wrote *Jesus and the Cosmos*,[19] beginning the book with the scientific account of the emergence of the universe, of life on Earth, and of human consciousness, and also with the story of Jesus of Nazareth. I then attempted a theological correlation between these two stories, drawing on some of Rahner's major insights: that the divine self-bestowal involves both creation and salvation in Christ; that the radical self-giving of God to creation in the incarnation is not simply the response to human sin, but was always the divine intention; that the resurrection of the crucified Jesus was the beginning of the transformation of the whole interrelated universe. In this same period I began work on another little book that became very popular, perhaps because of its title, *Made From Stardust*,[20] which explored a theological anthropology in which human beings were understood as springing from the primordial big bang, made from stardust, part of the evolution of life on Earth, companions with other creatures in one Earth community, and as the universe come to self-awareness, able to respond personally to God's gracious self-giving love.

The 1990s: CTNS and the Vatican Observatory

It was easy to feel isolated doing theology on the natural world in the eighties in Adelaide. Very importantly, I had the active collaboration of Alastair Blake, professor of physics at Adelaide University, who was always ready to help me with my grasp of the sciences and equally interested in dialogue about the theological positions I was developing. But I felt the lack of wider dialogue with others working in the same area. I see the nineties as the time when this need was met, the time when I began a more active engagement with colleagues

---

19. Denis Edwards, *Jesus and the Cosmos* (New York: Paulist Press, 1991).
20. Denis Edwards, *Made from Stardust: Exploring the Place of Human Beings within Creation* (Melbourne: Collins Dove, 1992).

around the world working in science and theology, and the start of my involvement in various international collaborations that have greatly helped my thinking and writing.

It all began for me with one book. While wandering into a college library during a theology conference in Sydney in 1990, and looking at the new books section, I came across a large volume entitled *Physics, Philosophy and Theology*.[21] It was a *eureka* moment for me, a book that opened up to a whole world of scholars engaged in the issues that concerned me. The book springs from a research conference held at Castel Gandolfo outside Rome in September 1987. It is edited by Robert John Russell, director of CTNS at Berkeley, and two Jesuit of the Vatican Observatory, George Coyne, the Observatory director, and William Stoeger, a staff astrophysicist. Although I knew of the existence of both groups, I knew very little about them, and had had no contact with them.

I decided that this had to change. So I wrote to Bill Stoeger asking if it would be possible for me to come to Tucson to spend some time with him, and to Bob Russell asking to do a sabbatical at CTNS in the first half of 2003. Bill responded to me very graciously and invited me stay with the Jesuit community of the Vatican Observatory Research Group in Tucson. I asked Bill to give me things to read on the sciences each day, and in the evenings we spent time discussing them, usually on long walks around the streets of Tucson, and sometimes over a Mexican meal. Bill wisely told me not to try and learn the mathematics I would need to become fully at home in physics, and encouraged me rather to continue to see myself as a theologian informed by the sciences. He suggested ways I could keep up with the sciences, including subscribing to a scientific journal that has been a regular part of my reading ever since. From then on Bill read critically many of the things I wrote, and I visited him for further conversations on later journeys to the USA.

Bob Russell warmly welcomed me to Berkeley and to CTNS. I took regular seminars with him and with Ted Peters, and began to learn my way around the key issues in science and theology, and to read the key players more deeply, including Ian Barbour, Arthur Peacocke and

---

21. Robert John Russell, William R Stoeger, and George Coyne, editors, *Physics, Philosophy and Theology: A Common Quest for Understanding* (Vatican City: Vatican Observatory, 1988).

John Polkinghorne, all of whom I would later get to know during the nineties. I was intellectually challenged by Bob Russell's commitment to the sciences, particularly physics, and learnt from him to respect the integrity of the sciences. I was moved by his enduring passion for the active dialogue between science and theology, and his evident deep commitment to the Christian gospel. While I was at Berkeley I worked on *Jesus the Wisdom of God*,[22] an attempt at a Wisdom Christology that embraced the natural world, and which opened out into a trinitarian theology of creation, inspired by Bonaventure and his concept of the universe as the self-expression of the Trinity.

At Berkeley I became aware of a series of five research conferences on divine action that were being co-sponsored by CTNS and the Vatican Observatory during the nineties, with the organising theological theme of divine action. This theme was taken up in the light of five scientific areas: quantum cosmology, chaos and complexity, evolutionary and molecular biology, neuroscience, and quantum mechanics. The focus was on the Christian conviction of God's particular acts in the history of salvation and in human lives ('special divine action'). I was invited to participate in the conference on 'Chaos and Complexity' held at Berkeley in 1993 and the one on 'Evolutionary and Molecular Biology' held at Castel Gandolfo in 1996.

These conferences, the ones in which I participated actively, and the others that I engaged with through the volumes produced as a result of each of them, challenged and enlarged my thinking about science and theology and have a big influence on my thinking and research. My own approach differed from that of the substantial group of important scholars (including Bod Russell, Nancey Murphy, George Ellis, and Thomas Tracy) who explored the idea that God acts in the indeterminacy of quantum events to bring about particular outcomes in the macro world. I agreed with Bill Stoeger, who through the whole series of conferences, built upon and developed the Thomist tradition of a God who acts through secondary causes that have their own integrity. The vigorous engagement that these conferences represented pushed me to work hard to clarify my own thinking, resulting, a decade later, in the book *How God Acts*.[23] Much

---

22. *Jesus the Wisdom of God: An Ecological Theology* (Maryknoll, NY: Orbis Books, 1995)
23. Denis Edwards, *How God Acts: Creation, Redemption and Special Divine* Action (Minneapolis: Fortress Press, 2010).

more recently, since Bill Stoeger's untimely death, I have offered an interpretation of his contribution to the series of conferences, and of his legacy to the wider theological community.[24]

There were other conferences in the nineties that widened my horizons. I had been involved in teaching a seminar course for Flinders University on 'Theology, Cosmology and Evolutionary Biology', and so became eligible to attend Templeton-funded 'course-prize' conferences on Science and Religion that were held at Cambridge University and at CTNS in Berkeley, where we heard from many of the key figures in science and theology, and met scholars of like mind from all around the world. Other examples are a major conference on science and religion sponsored by the University of San Francisco, and a four day conference in Granada, Spain, in 2001, that gave rise to the International Society for Science and Religion.

I see the nineties, then, as the period where I became exposed to at world-wide community of scholars on science and religion, and had wonderful opportunities to learn from them, and then to become part of this group of colleagues. This has been a great gift that has shaped my research and my life, a gift given largely by CTNS, the Vatican Observatory, and the Templeton Foundation. Towards the end of the nineties I tried to give expression to a genuinely trinitarian theology of the natural world that fully embraced evolution, and published *The God of Evolution* in 1999.[25]

Beyond 2000: Towards a Theology of the Natural World

By the beginning of the third millennium, it had become increasingly evident to me that systematic theology, apart from notable exceptions like Jürgen Moltmann, and those like Ted Peters and Bob Russell deeply involved in the science-theology dialogue, was still not focussed on the natural world. It was still all about human beings and God, although in the light of Latin American Liberation theology and European political theology, the human was now understood much more socially and politically. The old threesome of God, the human,

---

24. Denis Edwards, 'Towards a Theology of Divine Action: William Stoeger, SJ, on the Laws of Nature', in *Theological Studies*, 76/3 (September 2015): 485–502.
25. Denis Edwards, *The God of Evolution: A Trinitarian Theology* (New York: Paulist Press, 1999).

and the wider creation, found in the Scriptures, Patristic writers and medieval theology, had been reduced to a twosome from the time of the Reformation and the Enlightenment and this reduction of theology had persisted into the later twentieth century. This was at a time when two distinct issues of the natural world confronted theology, the urgent crisis of life on the planet, and extraordinary developments in science that seemed to have left Christian faith and theology far behind.

It was clear to me, then, that the priority in my own theological research needed to be on contributing to the development of a theology that fully embraced the natural world. And it seemed necessary to me, at least, that this theology took engagement with the sciences, such as biological evolution, with utmost seriousness, and at the same time contributed to building an ecological consciousness by showing that animals, plants, ecosystems, rivers, seas and the atmosphere have value before God that human beings must respect. It needed to involve the field of science and theology on the one hand, and ecological theology on the other.

While it is obvious that great theologians of the past did not have to confront the kind of scientific and ecological issues that Christian theology faces today, it seemed to me that a theology of the natural world for today needs to be deeply grounded in the tradition, and build creatively on, for example, the insights of Bonaventure that I had discussed in *Jesus the Wisdom of God*. So, when early in the new millennium, I recognized that I needed to deepen my understanding of the Holy Spirit dynamically at work in the emergence of the universe and the evolution of life on Earth I began from the great theologian of the Spirit, Basil of Caesarea. With the completion of my book on the Creator Spirit, *Breath of Life*,[26] I felt that I was moving towards a richer, fully trinitarian, theology of God continuously at work in the creation through the Word and in the Spirit.

It seemed the time, then, to attempt a synthesis of ecological theology, which took seriously its pneumatological and christological dimensions. Above all, in this new work, *Ecology at the Heart of Faith*,[27] I was seeking to show how the ecological is not extrinsic to

---

26. Denis Edwards, *Breath of Life: A Theology of the Creator Spirit* (Maryknoll, NY: Orbis Books, 2004).
27. Denis Edwards, *Ecology at the Heart of Faith* (Maryknoll, NY: Orbis Books, 2006).

Christian faith, and not at its edge, but is to be located at the very heart of it, in its trinitarian depths. The book goes on to propose that ecological faith is central to the Eucharist and to Christian spirituality, and to explore its outcome in ecological practice. While I meant this to be an accessible book, and I think it is, I was delighted a few years later to be approached by a publisher to write a book aimed at helping teachers in Christian schools, senior students, and general readers, with ecological theology, in the form of a picture book. The result was *Jesus and the Natural World*.[28]

It is impossible to engage with evolutionary science without being confronted with the age-old problem of evil. Contemporary science brings a new intensity to the ancient problem, making it abundantly clear that the costs of evolution are built into the process—they are intrinsic to the emergence of life. Life evolves by processes that involve not only cooperation, but also competition for resources, predation, death, and extinction. Like many others, I had long been struggling with this hardest of all theological issues. It was an immense help to me when in September 2005, CTNS and the Vatican Observatory cosponsored a conference on the problem of natural evil at Castel Gandolfo.[29] I learnt a great deal from the scientists, philosophers and theologians gathered from around the world, and my own essay, reassessed in the light of the critical reflections of other scholars, became the beginning of the book *How God Acts*. Although I did the writing, this book is the fruit of a dialogue with Bill Stoeger. It is a project that was greatly helped by my time as a research fellow at Durham University and by the hospitality of Professor Paul Murray. I am conscious of the limits, and the partial nature, of my response in this book to the costs of evolution, to the problem of suffering more broadly, and to the theological issue of the nature of divine action, but I see struggling with these issues in this book as an important moment in my theological journey.

Celia Deane-Drummond is a long-standing colleague who has helped me to think more deeply about animal suffering by inviting me

---

28. Denis Edwards, *Jesus and the Natural World* (Melbourne: Garratt Publishing, 2012).
29. See Nancey Murphy, Robert John Russell and William R Stoeger, *Physics and Cosmology: Scientific Perspectives on the Problem of Natural Evil* (Vatican: Vatican Observatory; Berkeley: Center for Theology and the Natural Sciences, 2007).

to write on it when she was editor of *Ecotheology*,[30] and to engage with others on this topic at a conference in Wales.[31] In her own more recent work she has explored what she calls a liminal theology that explores what links humans together with other animals in evolutionary and ecological relationships,[32] and this led me to focus particularly on our evolutionary relationship with our nearest living relatives, the great apes, and bringing this relationship into dialogue with the early Christian tradition of humans as made in the image of God.[33]

Another important colleague in recent years has been Ernst Conradie, a Reformed theologian of the University of the Southern Cape. He led an international, ecumenical group that worked collaboratively on ecological theology, particularly on the issue of the relationship between creation and salvation, beginning in 2007 and culminating in a research conference at Stellenbosch, South Africa, in 2012, resulting in a series of publications.[34] The conclusion that emerged from this cooperative project was that a Christian ecological theology for the twenty-century needs to be grounded not simply in creation theology, but in the whole action of God in creation and salvation in Christ, that reaches its fulfilment in the transformation of all things in Christ.

In this period, as I focused on the meaning of the incarnation for the natural world, I found myself being drawn back to the theology of Athanasius, to his theological conviction that the Word in whom all things are created is also the Word of the incarnation, the Word

---

30. Denis Edwards, 'Every Sparrow that Falls to the Ground: The Costs of Evolution and the Christ-Event', in *Ecotheology*, 11/1 (March 2006): 103–123.

31. See Celia Deane-Drummond and David Clough, *Creaturely Theology: On God, Humans and other Animals* (London: SCM, 2009).

32. Celia Deane-Drummond, *The Wisdom of the Liminal: Evolution and Other Animals in Human Becoming* (Grand Rapids, Michigan: Eerdmans, 2014).

33. Denis Edwards, 'Humans, Chimps, and Bonobos: Towards an Inclusive View of the Human as Bearing the Image of God', in *Turnings: Theological Reflections on a Cosmological Conversion; Essays in Honor of Elizabeth A Johnson*, forthcoming from Liturgical Press.

34. See the two volumes edited by Ernst Conradie, *Creation and Salvation, Volume 1, A Mosaic of Selected Classic Christian Theologies* (Zurich: LIT, 2012); *Creation and Salvation, Volume 2, A Companion on Recent Theological Movements* (Zurich: LIT, 2012); *Christian Faith and the Earth: Current Paths and Emerging Horizons in Ecotheology*, edited by Ernst M Conradie, Sigurd Bergmann, Celia Deane-Drummond and Denis Edwards (London: Bloomsbury, 2014).

on the Cross. In his thought, creation and transforming renewing incarnation are deeply linked in a dynamic trinitarian theology. As he famously puts it: 'the Father creates and renews all things through the Word in the Holy Spirit'.[35] I am convinced that such a ttheology can ground a contemporary understanding that the Wisdom/Word's embrace of flesh involves not just the humanity of Jesus, and not just the wider human community, but the whole natural world in its evolution and its groaning.

I have found the concept of 'deep incarnation' helpful in an evolutionary and ecological context. It was introduced by Danish theologian Niels Gregersen and has since been taken up by other theologians in different ways, including Elizabeth Johnson and Celia Deane Drummond, as well myself.[36] Gregersen writes that 'the incarnation of God in Christ can be understood as a radical or 'deep' incarnation, that is, an incarnation into the very tissue of biological existence, and system of nature'.[37] He sees the cross as God's identification with creation in its evolutionary emergence, and as a microcosm of God's redemptive presence to all creatures in their suffering and death. I am particularly grateful to have had the chance to attend a research conference on deep incarnation with a wonderful mix of scholars in Helsingor, Denmark, in 2011, a conference funded by the John Templeton Foundation and hosted by Neils Gregersen and Mary Ann Myers. The book that springs from this conference is an important resource for incarnational theology in an ecological context.[38]

---

35. Athanasius, *Letters to Serapion*, 1.24.6, in Mark DelCogliano, Andrew Radde-Gallwitz and Lewis Ayres, trans., *Works on the Spirit: Athanasius and Didymus: Athanasius's Letters to Serapion on the Holy Spirit and Didymus's On the Holy Spirit* (New York: St Vladimir's Seminary Press, 2011), 91.

36. Niels Henrik Gregersen, 'The Cross of Christ in an Evolutionary World', in *Dialog: A Journal of Theology*, 40 (2001): 205; Niels Henrik Gregersen, 'Deep Incarnation: Why Evolutionary Continuity Matters in Christology', *Toronto Theological Journal* 26/2 (2010): 173–88; Elizabeth Johnson, 'An Earthy Christology: "For God so Loved the Cosmos"', in *America*, 200/12 (April 13, 2009): 27–30; Celia Deane Drummond, *Christ and Evolution: Wonder and Wisdom* (Minneapolis, MN: Fortress Press, 2009), 128–55; Edwards, *Ecology at the Heart of Faith*, 58–64.

37. Gregersen, 'The Cross of Christ', 205.

38. Niels Henrik Gregersen, editor, *Incarnation: On the Scope and Depth of Christology* (Minneapolis, MN: Fortress Press, 2015).

In recent times, I have brought Athanasius's ancient theology and the recent concept of deep incarnation into a new trinitarian theology of the natural world, in a book called *Partaking of God*,[39] which presents the Spirit as the Energy of Love and the Word of God as the Attractor, in the evolution and final transformation of the universe of creatures. In the last section of the book I explore the place of human beings as part of one profoundly interrelated community of creation before God, and as called to ongoing ecological conversion, in thinking, seeing, feeling, acting and living.[40]

About the same time a long-standing colleague, Elizabeth Johnson, brought out an inspiring theological vision of the natural world developed in dialogue with the thought of Charles Darwin, in her *Ask the Beasts*.[41] In the last six months I have been giving much of my time to speaking about Pope Francis's *Laudato si'* and his theology of the natural world, highlighting above all three convictions that emerge from the encyclical: that other creatures have intrinsic value; that they reveal God us; and that they form, with us, a sublime communion in God. This reflection on my own journey leads to a deep sense of gratitude for the chance to be part of a wider theological community rediscovering the profound interconnection between ourselves and the rest of the natural world, before God.

39. Denis Edwards, *Partaking of God: Trinity, Evolution and Ecology* (Collegeville, Minnesota: Liturgical Press, 2014).
40. My current work is on a book on the history of the theology of creation, to be published by Fortress Press in their Historical Trajectory Series, edited by Denis Janz.
41. Elizabeth Johnson: *Ask the Beasts: Darwin and the God of Love* (London: Bloomsbury, 2014).

In Memoriam

Denis Edwards (1943–2019)

As many of the essays in this volume attest, James "Denis" Edwards was a fine, internationally acclaimed theologian. His insights and writings profoundly influenced local, national and international theological thinking and pastoral practice. In many ways, he was a theologian before his time, anticipating in his own research and writings decades earlier the key issues that would be central to ecclesial life.

Denis' fifteen books focused on ecclesiology, inclusive ministerial practice, the relationship between science and religion, and the gift which theology could offer those seeking to bring the mystery of God into dialogue with the natural world, its beauty and struggles. It is this last theological theme for which Denis is most remembered and perhaps his greatest contribution. His passion to offer an authentic Catholic theological approach to the ecological crisis sprang from his desire to present an alternative to the popular post-Christian perspective critical of Catholic biblical and theological interpretations perceived as endorsing environmental dominance and destruction.

Denis wrote profoundly, yet with simplicity. He was able to communicate authentic Catholic theological insights in non-technical language that allowed ordinary people to appreciate the mysteries he was communicating. This touch of 'ordinariness', an ability to be and speak with ordinary people seeking to understand the heart of faith and their experience of God, found its origins in his earliest years.

Denis was born at Port Pirie, in the mid-North of South Australia, in 1943 at a time of social unrest brought about in the final years of World War II. This social complexity engaged the young Denis through his schooling and seminary formation and finally after his priestly ordination in 1966. His earliest years of ministry saw him involved in adult education, catechesis and youth formation with various appointments as assistant priest to parishes in the Archdiocese of Adelaide before he finally studied at Fordham University, New York in 1973 and, later, at Catholic University of America at Washington DC, completing his Doctorate in Theology ("Summa cum Laude") in 1976.

His post-ordination studies were influenced by a mystic and a theologian: John of the Cross and Karl Rahner. Avery Dulles, his principal doctoral supervisor, encouraged him to pursue a dialogue between the mystical theology of John of the Cross and Rahner's transcendental theology. Denis' thesis title expressed the intellectual and spiritual quest that accompanied him throughout the rest of his life, "The dynamism in Faith: The interaction between experience of God and explicit faith." This experience of God lay at the heart of everything that he thought and wrote about, and in the way he acted.

A few years before his doctoral engagement with John of the Cross and Rahner, Denis found a collaborator in his concern for the poor and the marginalised in the writings of the Peruvian theologian, Gustavo Gutierrez. Denis' doctoral thesis later grounded him in a method of theological dialogue which carried over in his numerous writings on the relationship between science and God. His earlier attraction to the works of Gutierrez, though, deepened his concern for the poor and the ordinary, marginalised by systems of oppression. This found its expression in his writings on the Australian Church, lay leadership and ministry and, finally, in the theological focus of his final years, the natural world and God's creation. Gutierrez's insights also shaped Denis' living context.

On his return from doctoral studies and while developing programs of theological education at professional and lay levels in the Archdiocese, he took up residence in a public housing situation, in Mansfield Park, a suburb north of Adelaide where many socially and economically disadvantaged lived. In the spirit of Gutierrez, Denis wanted to connect to the poor. It is here, also, that I, after completing my own post-ordination studies, was invited to live with him in an intentional community. And here, too, I came to know Denis at a deeply human and spiritual level as we grew in friendship and reflected upon our pastoral and teaching ministries as Diocesan priests. We lived simply, prayed together weekly and discussed our respective academic interests over shared meals and a glass or two of wine.

From this communal experience that I enjoyed for several years I learnt much about and from Denis. These learnings could be the subject of a much longer précis of his life. However, one overarching characteristic about him stays with me from those years. Denis was a deeply humble man.

While in his later writings he engaged with the works of great theologians like Basil, Irenaeus, Athanasius, Augustine, Hildegard of Bingen, Thomas Aquinas, Bonaventure, Luther, Teilhard de Chardin, Sallie McFague and Elizabeth Johnson, their insights into those aspects of theology that he was studying and writing about deepened his spirit of humility. Whether in discussions with colleagues of the Adelaide College of Divinity or, later, faculty members of the Australian Catholic University, or guiding his doctoral students in their studies, or in advising Archbishop Faulkner and his pastoral team as consultant theologian (1986–2001) or in ecumenical meetings— Denis was the longest serving member of the Australian Lutheran-Roman Catholic Dialogue (1983–2016)—or as founding member of the *International Society for Science and Religion,* Denis always acted with humility. This characteristic defined his relationship to others, his scholarship and his commitment to the local church of Adelaide.

And it is this that I shall always remember about him.

The last words of his penultimate work on creation reflect the way his humble spirit penetrated his theological acumen and allowed him to love and advocate for God's community of creation. These words sum up Denis' life:

> Humans are to see other creatures as kin, within a community of creation before God, where each creature has its own intrinsic value. They are to see themselves as called by God to love and respect other creatures and their habitats, and to see Earth as our common home. They are called to act to protect the planetary community of life, and to support the well-being and flourishing of other species.[1]

Michael Trainor
October 2020

---

1. Denis Edwards, *Christian Understandings of Creation: A Historical Trajectory* (Minneapolis: Fortress Press, 2017), 303–304.

From Deep Incarnation to Deep Divinisation

Is the Universe a Sacrament? Denis Edward's Contribution to Sacramental Thinking

Niels Henrik Gregersen

> At a more fundamental level still, Jesus of Nazareth is the fundamental
> sacrament of God in the world. He is the radical expression of, and
> mediation of, divine self-bestowal.
> Denis Edwards.[1]

Abstract: The article discusses Denis Edwards' expansion of sacramental thinking into the view of a deep sacramental presence of Christ in the world of nature. Edwards uses Karl Rahner's theology as a matrix for his own thinking but I argue that he adds important new aspects to Rahner's sacramental theology. First, he prioritizes a deep Christology over the sacramental view of the church; second, he emphasizes a corresponding deep pneumatology, in which the Spirit of God opens up human minds for experiencing grace in our interactions with nature. Edwards' view of the sacramentality of nature is in line with the Encyclical *Laudato si'* from 2015, which sees the world of creation as 'a sacrament of communion' but his emphasis on the interaction between human beings and nature leads him to a more concrete approach to events of grace within that communion.

Keywords: Denis Edwards; Karl Rahner; Paul Tillich; *Laudato si'*, deep incarnation; sacramental theology

'Do we experience God in our encounters with birds, animals, tree, forests, mountains, deserts and beaches?' Denis Edwards raises this question in an essay on human experiences of Word and Spirit in the world of nature,[2] and he responds in the affirmative, based on

---

1. Denis Edwards, 'Exploring How God Acts', in *The Natural World and God: Theological Explorations* (Adelaide: ATF Press, 2017), 224.
2. Denis Edwards, 'Experience of Word and Spirit in the Natural World', in Edwards, *The Natural World and God: Theological Explorations*, 187–201, here at 187.

theological arguments derived from Athanasius and Karl Rahner. Edwards brings in his own spiritual experiences with engrossing landscapes and rivers on the Australian continent too. He is not a Romanticist with a rosey view of nature, however, for he is fully aware of the ambiguities of nature. Since all life is lived at the expense of other life, mother Earth is not only a space for positive experiences of wonder and beauty but also a space of pain and suffering. 'The natural world is both unspeakably beautiful and also a place of competition and violence.'[3] While already empirical observations point to the mixture of joy and woe in nature, evolutionary theory shows its inescapability. Since God is the source of all that is, theology too has to acknowledge that joy and pain are interconnected in the development of living organisms. In the uncompromising words of the Danish philosopher-theologian KE Løgstrup, 'the Creator has coupled development and decay together in His creation . . . God's act of creation is terrifying in its splendor and annihilation; it exceeds our intellectual and emotional apprehension.'[4]

The fact that nature is indeed a mixed package seems to foreclose any reference to the nature as a sacrament. Indeed, Edwards nowhere declares that nature is a sacrament in the strict sense of the term, fully in parallel to the sacraments of the church, which are accompanied by an unambiguous divine promise of salvation. Yet Edwards insists that people sometimes do encounter God—even the gracious presence of God the Father, Son and Spirit—in their everyday encounters with nature. And he is arguing that since the co-suffering of Christ is present in the midst of our cruciform creation, there is a sacramental presence of Christ also in states of decay and pain.

So, what is the difference between saying that nature simply *is* a sacrament, and saying that we need to extend our sacramental thinking so that we can receive the grace of God in our encounters with nature too, in joy as well as in woe? What is the difference between *being* a sacrament and having the potential of *becoming* a sacrament? What are the differences and continuities between the sacramental potentials of nature, and the sacraments of the church? These are the questions to be explored in this essay.

---

3. Edwards, 'Experience of Word and Spirit in the Natural World', 198.
4. KE Løgstrup, *Metaphysics. Volume I-II* [1976–1984]. Translated by Russell L. Dees (Milwaukee: Marquette University Press, 1995), Volume 1, 271–272.

Denis Edwards' View of Sacramentality: The Inspiration from Athanasius

In his sacramental thinking, Denis Edwards often goes along with two of his principal theological sources, bishop Athanasius of Alexandria (c 298–373) and Karl Rahner, SJ (1904–1984). Athanasius has played a growing role in Denis Edwards' work, as can be seen in many essays from recent years.[5] Yet the theology of Karl Rahner has been the companion of Denis Edwards throughout, and I will therefore go into more detail with his reception of Rahner, noting what he is takes in from Rahner, what he does not receive, and what he adds of his own to Rahner's work. As I will argue, only the encyclical *Laudato si'*, issued by Pope Francis at Pentecost 2015, provides the broader perspective for Denis Edwards' view of the sacramentality of the world of creation.

With Athanasius, Edwards underlines the immediacy of God's Wisdom/Word to each creature individually, and in sustaining the body of the world at large.[6] In Athanasius' anti-Arian theology, there exists no intermediary buffers between the Triune God and the world of creation; rather, the deep unity between God's creation of the cosmos and God's saving presence in the incarnate Word and through the divine Spirit is the fundamental Christian assumption. The Father's love of humanity (*philanthropia*) can only be *mediated only by the immediacy of God Godself*, that is, by the incarnation of the same divine Logos by which the world was brought into being from the beginning. In God's incarnational reach, God's own Son, Word or Wisdom, comes down to earth to live with and for the creatures, and through full re-connection of the divine Logos with the whole of creation, the Spirit of God lifts up the world of creation into participation with the Triune God. 'Every creature on Earth, every whale, every sparrow and every earthworm exists by participation in the Father through the Son and in the Spirit—not one of them is forgotten in God's sight (Lk 12:6).'[7]

---

5. See Denis Edwards, *Deep Incarnation: God's Redemptive Suffering with Creatures* (Maryknoll, NY: Orbis Books, 2019), chapter 3 (55–80), and the reprinted essays in *The Natural World and God: Theological Explorations,* 381–466.
6. Denis Edwards, 'Experience of Word and Spirit in the Natural World', 188–195, with reference to Athanasius, *Against the Arians*, 2.78.
7. Edwards, 'Where on Earth is God? Exploring an Ecological Theology of the Trinity in the Tradition of Athanasius', in *The Natural World and God: Theological Explorations,* 445–466, here at 452.

Sacramentality and Deep Incarnation: Karl Rahner and Denis Edwards

With Karl Rahner, Edwards shares the emphasis on the 'mysticism of everyday life'.[8] Rahner's view of the self-endowment of the transcendent God in the world of creation may be said to undergird Edwards' understanding of the universe as having a *potential sacramental value* for human beings, that is, a potential for becoming an effective medium of divine grace by the divine Spirit.

Let us now take a look at Denis Edwards' own understanding of the sacraments: 'In Christian theology, a sacrament is a visible sign and agent of divine self-bestowal'.[9] The underlying thrust of Denis Edwards' Rahner-inspired thinking may be rendered as follows: Since (1) the transcendent God is radically present in the world by the divine self-bestowal, and since (2) no natural event is without the grace of the self-giving God, (3) no theologian is entitled to say that natural events cannot become embodied carriers of divine grace for human beings. I here phrase this underlying argument cautiously, since it only says that there no barriers to the access of grace, no divine self-withdrawal involved in God's self-giving, even though the world of nature, as we saw above, remains ambiguous. Therefore, I suggest to make distinction between affirming the *sacramental potentials* of nature while *not equating* the sacramental potentials of nature with the sacraments of the church. For only the latter are accompanied with the divine promise, or donor intention, that the grace of God is offered in the message and sacraments of church in unambiguous form.[10] While the divine grace is omnipresent in Rahner, it is not omnimanifest, we may say.

Denis Edwards, too, takes his point of departure in the concrete sacraments before discussing the sacramental presence of Christ in the universe. The prime instances of sacrament are to be found in

---

8. Edwards, 'Experience of Word and Spirit in the Natural World', 195–198, here at 196.
9. Edwards, 'Exploring How God Acts', in *The Natural World and God: Theological Explorations*, 205–226, here at 223.
10. The view of the sacramental potentials of all reality is furthermore undergirded by Rahner's anthropological assumption that human beings are constitutively open to God due to their self-transcending sense of mystery. As we will see below, however, Edwards points to the work of the Spirit of God when referring to the opening up of human beings in particular situations.

the midst of the life of Christian communities, like Baptism and the Eucharist. These are the sacraments in the proper sense, since they are accompanied by the promise of the self-donating God that will be present there *for us*. On this basis Edwards presents the Roman-Catholic view that 'the church itself has a sacramental nature. It is a sign and agent of communion with God and of human community, called to be the universal sacrament of salvation'.[11] This is fully in line with Rahner too, but it is worth noting some subtle differences of emphasis. First, Rahner consistently writes the Church with capital letters with reference to the hierarchical body of the Roman-Catholic Church, while Edwards omits any reference to the church as having a particular social shape with a particular 'juridical composition', as Rahner puts it.[12] Second, Edwards refers to the 'calling' of the church to be a sacrament for all people, rather than simply stating a given fact. Third, and in the same line, Edwards omits any reference to Rahner's view that the sacraments of the Church are visible and efficient means of grace that are at work *ex opere operato*, that is, valid prior to and independently from the individual reception of grace. Fourth, and most importantly: While Rahner views the Church as the 'primary sacrament of the grace of God',[13] Edwards is very clear in stating that it is Christ who is the primary sacrament:

> At a more fundamental level still, Jesus of Nazareth is the fundamental sacrament of God in the world. He is the radical expression of, and mediation of, divine self-bestowal. As the incarnate Word and Wisdom of God, he is the sacrament of divine self-bestowal in the world. He is the real symbol of God, in which God is manifested and acts in a world of matter and flesh.[14]

Edwards here appropriates Rahner's concept of the 'real symbol' about Christ though Edwards emphasises Christ as the foundation of the Church rather than the church as the historical continuation of Christ. This Christ-centredness comes to the fore in Denis Edwards'

---

11. Edwards, 'Exploring How God Acts', 223–224.
12. Karl Rahner, 'The Theology of the Symbol', in Rahner, *Theological Investigations IV: More Recent Writings* (London: DLT, 1974), 224–242. Here quoted from *A Rahner Reader*, edited by Gerald A McCool (New York: Crossroad 1989), 120–130, here at 128.
13. Rahner, 'The Theology of the Symbol', 128–129.
14. Edwards, 'Exploring How God Acts', 224.

commitment to deep incarnation. Chapter 5 of his last book, *Deep Incarnation* from 2019, carries the title 'The Cross: Sacrament of God's Redemptive Suffering with Creatures'. In this chapter, Denis affirms the view of deep incarnation that the cross of Christ is 'an *icon* of God's redemptive co-suffering with all sentient life as well as with the victims of social competition'. And since Christ bears the painful costs of evolution, he is 'the microcosm in which the suffering of the macrocosm is represented and lived out'.[15] The overall argument may be rendered as follows: The actual compass of the historical church is always *de facto* limited in scope (though called to be a universal medium of grace for all people on the Earth). By contrast, the scope of Christ is universal by his divine nature and by the assumption of all flesh in the incarnation, so that 'all flesh' is co-constitutive for the human nature of Christ in the process of incarnation. In this sense, the divine Logos/Wisdom encompasses the entire world of God's creation: quarks and electrons, soil and water, grass and trees, animals and humans, with all their active and passive potentialities.[16] So Edwards:

> Precisely as created, and as interconnected with evolutionary history, with all flesh, Jesus is the irreversible historical expression of God's self-bestowal and the sacrament of salvation for our world.[17]

Only if Christ himself is the primary and fundamental sacrament can we speak about experiencing God in the splendors of nature as well as in the decay and disruption that characterizes the evolution of life. Just as the structuring power of the divine Logos manifests Christ 'in, with and under' the developmental growth of organisms (active in reshaping ever new lifeforms on planet earth), so the crucified and resurrected Christ redeems suffering creatures together with the

---

15. Edwards, *Deep Incarnation*, 117–118, *cf* 3–4 referring to my essay in Gregersen, 'The Cross of Christ in an Evolutionary World', in *Dialog: A Journal of Theology*, 40/3 (Fall 2001), 192–207, here at 203.
16. See further Rebecca Copeland, *Creative Being: An Inclusive Creedal Christology* (Waco, TX: Baylor University Press, 2020, forthcoming). Copeland argues that the human nature of Christ in the Chacedonian Definition (451) involves the entire 'created *ousia*', the cosmos in its creative as well as passive character.
17. Edwards, 'Exploring How God Acts', 224.

vivifying and re-creative Spirit of God, who will weave together a new world out of decaying structures.

Rahner's Concept of the 'Real Symbol' and Edwards' View of Sacramental Continuity

It is in the context of this sacramental view of cross of Christ that Edwards uses Rahner's concept of 'the real symbol' (*Realsymbol*), defining it as follows: 'A real-symbol, or sacrament, is the self-expression of what is signified, and it is effective. It not only represents, but it also brings out what is signified.'[18]

In Rahner's theology, the concept of the symbol is part of his basic ontology—an ontology shaped by his interpretation of the Triune God as essentially self-communicating and with ramifications for his view of the sacraments of the church.[19] According to Rahner, 'all beings are by their nature symbolic, because they necessarily 'express' themselves in order to attain their own nature'.[20]. This can be viewed as an updated version of Thomism, in so far activity expresses a prior being while no being exists without its proper self-expression. Rahner is aware that 'all beings (each of them, in fact) are multiple'; and in this sense each being may express something other than itself in its 'plural unity'.[21] Even so, however, oneness retains the primary ontological status in Rahner's ontology. Unity is a so-called 'transcendental', and Rahner endorses 'the profound principle of St Thomas' that there can be no union of things which are themselves merely multiple: *non enim plura secundum se uniuntur.*[22] All beings are, so to speak, given as individual beings *prior* to their relations.

Yet Rahner adds a second assertion on the status of the symbol that in some sense inverts, or at least broadens, his earlier emphasis on unity and oneness: 'The symbol strictly speaking (symbolic reality) is the *self-realization of a being in the other, which is constitutive of its essence.*'[23] In this sense, the relation of a being to other beings may become co-constitutive of its own being—exactly the emphasis in

---

18. Edwards, *Deep Incarnation*, 119.
19. Rahner, 'The Theology of the Symbol', 120–130.
20. Rahner, 'The Theology of the Symbol', 121.
21. Rahner, 'The Theology of the Symbol', 122.
22. Rahner, 'The Theology of the Symbol', 123.
23. Rahner, 'The Theology of the Symbol', 125; Italics added.

Denis Edwards in his reception of Rahner's concept of the *Realsymbol* in his Christology.

Allow me here to give a few comments on Rahner's use of the ontology of the symbol in his trinitarian theology: The Logos is the perfect self-expression of the Father, at one and the same time 'of the same essence as himself' (the *homoousios* in the Nicene Creed) yet also a divine person other than the person of the Father. Moreover, the *internal* self-expression of the Father in the Son as his image, imprint and radiance lies behind the logic of the Word of God being the *outward* self-expression of divine nature. So Rahner:

> It is because God 'must' express himself inwardly that he can also utter himself outwardly; the finite, created utterance *ad extra* is a continuation of the immanent constitution [that is, within the Triune life, nhg] of 'image and likeness'—a free continuation, because its object is finite—and takes place in fact 'through' the Logos (Jn 1:3).[24]

Now, given that God has indeed wanted to create the finite world of creation (the first article of faith), the Logos 'must be thought of as exteriorizing itself'[25] so that the Logos becomes the *raison d'être* as well as the grounding agency of the person of Jesus Christ. It is this divine agency, which is continued in the Church as the body of Christ. More precisely, it is the *humanity* of Christ and the socio-historical *body of the Church* that according to Rahner constitute the media of divine self-communication to human beings.

In Rahner's work, we thus see a very particular focus on the humanity and historicity of the Church in human culture. It is only in this ecclesiological mediation that Rahner speaks of God as the incarnate Logos who becomes the effective sign of grace for human beings today: '*As* God's work of grace on man is accomplished (incarnates itself), it enters the spatio-temporal historicity of man as sacrament, and *as* it does so, it becomes active with regard to man, it constitutes itself.'[26]

I have here quoted some central (but also cumbersome passages) from Rahner in order to show that his Christology has its focus on

---

24. Rahner, 'The Theology of the Symbol', 126–127.
25. Rahner, 'The Theology of the Symbol', 127.
26. Rahner, 'The Theology of the Symbol', 129; italics in original.

humanity, and so also his sacramental thinking. Since the sacraments have been given over to the Church irrevocably, Rahner speaks with the Roman-Catholic tradition of the *opus operatum* of the sacrament. That is, the seven Catholic sacraments have conclusively been given over to the Church, being the primary sacrament, and the sacraments are valid prior to, and independently of any individual reception thereof. As we will see below, this is the aspect of Rahner's theology of the sacraments that Denis Edwards does not continue.

Nonetheless, it would not be correct to describe Rahner as anthropocentric and ecclesiocentric theologian, for his view of the sacraments is carried by a theocentrism based on his trinitarian view of God as self-communication and self-giving love. Moreover, Rahner was one of the early Roman-Catholic theologians to take seriously the evolutionary context of Christology. In his long essay, 'Christology of within an Evolutionary View of the World', he argues that 'spirit and matter have more things in common (to put it this way) than things dividing them', and that 'the Incarnation appears as a necessary and permanent beginning of the divinization of the world as a whole'.[27] As shown by Edwards in Chapter 4 of *Deep Incarnation*, aspects of Rahner's work does approach the view of deep incarnation. He can say, for example, that 'becoming material' is the most basic statement of Christology, and that in Jesus, 'the Logos bears the matter no less than the soul, and this matter is part of the reality and the history of the cosmos'.[28] Still, there is some abstractness to Rahner's reference to the material world, and he clearly views evolution in a teleological perspective.

In my view, Denis Edwards has done a great service to Rahner's legacy by emphasising the spatial aspects of Rahner's work more than the time-and history oriented view that in fact dominates Rahner's many references to Christ as the 'climax of development' and 'the climax of the history of the cosmos', which is subsequently continued in the historical, social and juridical body of the Catholic Church within 'the new epoch'.[29] What Edwards has done is to reemphasise Rahner's pastoral and mystical writings. Every human being is

---

27. Karl Rahner, 'Christology of within an Evolutionary View of the World', in *Theological Investigations V: Later Writings* (London: DLT, 1984), 157–192, here at 161.
28. Rahner, 'Christology of within an Evolutionary View of the World', 176–177.
29. Rahner, 'Christology of within an Evolutionary View of the World', 176 and 178.

surrounded by mystery, within oneself as well as in relation to reality as symbol. Similarly, Rahner argued that '*everything* has been assumed' in the incarnation, since Christ 'truly lived a human life in all its breath and height and depth'.[30]

Going beyond the human perspective, Edwards reminds of the early essay by Rahner, 'A Faith that Loves the Earth' (1950), in which he speaks of Christ as 'the very heart of all the lowly things on the earth that we are unable to let go of and that belongs to the earth as mother'. And Rahner continuous: 'He is at the heart of the nameless yearning of all creatures, waiting—though perhaps unaware that they are waiting—to be allowed to particulate in the transfiguration of his body'.[31] Here is where Edwards speaks of the sacramental presence in the universe of the co-suffering Christ who promises of a cosmic transformation of all created reality within the everlasting life of God.

It is this wide-scope view of the incarnation (the life, cross and resurrection of Jesus Christ) that Edwards refers to as the primary sacrament, also more fundamental and more comprehensive than any actual shape of the Christian church(es). Edwards has the courage to speak of experiencing God in the lowlands, heights and depths of natural events even beyond the scope of the historical church, thus opening up for sacramental encounters with nature, in which both its wonders and its cruciform shape can be seen as infused by a divine presence. Rahner can say something very similar, speaking of the 'quasi-sacramental' nature of any concrete being. For as we saw above, in Rahner's ontology all things are divinely-created symbols *including* their co-constitutive relations to other beings within the interconnected world of creation. In this vein, Rahner can say that 'any grace-giving event has a quasi-sacramental structure and shares in Christ's character as both divine and human'.[32]

I have so far focused on how Denis' full commitment to deep incarnation shapes his sacramental thinking. But there is also a

---

30. Karl Rahner, *Mission and Grace: Essays in Pastoral Theology II* (London: Sheed and Ward, 1963), 42, here quoted from Edwards, *Deep Incarnation*, 85.

31. Karl Rahner, 'A Faith that Loves the Earth', in *The Mystical Way in Everyday Life: Essays and Prayers: Karl Rahner, SJ*, edited by Annemarie S Kidder (Maryknoll, NY: Orbis Books, 2010), 52–58, here at 56. See also Edwards, *Deep Incarnation*, 86–89.

32. Karl Rahner, 'The Church and the Sacraments' in *Inquiries* (New York: Herder and Herder, 1964), 191–299. Quoted from *A Rahner Reader*, 278–299, here at 281.

corresponding deep pneumatology at work in Edwards' work. The fundamental sacrament of the living Christ is not only something present 'out there' which works automatically, *ex opera operato,* to put it in traditional terms. Being addressed and transformed by what we see and encounter in God's wider world of creation, only becomes real *to us* by the callings and challenges of the Spirit of God. The in-principle openness of the human mind and heart to the divine Spirit is what Edward's takes in from Rahner. But Denis Edwards emphasizes that the Spirit of God breaks in upon everyday life, and thereby creates sacramental situations in which grace is given to humans as individuals. Natural events already have an intrinsic value. Yet they gain a life-changing value for us when they *become* sacraments that embody the divine grace as presented *to us.* Grace can come to us in any moment, Edwards argues, and the Spirit of God can be experienced both in radical intimacy and in disruption, yet always mediated by embodied by created words, events, and persons—'secondary causes', in Denis Edwards' use of Thomistic terminology.

In Edwards, there is thus *a continuity between the sacraments of the church and the quasi-sacramental encounters with worldly events.* In both cases, the Spirit of God opens up human minds, thereby eliciting a spiritual sense of being encouraged as well as challenged by grace in multiple forms, including ethically appeals, joyful experiences of being uplifted and the likewise passive experience of being led into stillness and meditation:

> Grace can come to us in any moment. We are challenged by an encounter with a homeless person, and forced to ask hard questions about our use of wealth and our collusion in systems that damage people. We are entranced by the song of a single bird and led beyond it for a moment to the Source of all music: In a quiet moment in the celebration of the Eucharist we are led to stillness before God. The experience of the Spirit can be an experience of radical intimacy or disruption, but in either it is an experience mediated by our engagement with created words, events and persons.[33]

---

33. Edwards, 'Exploring How God Acts', in *The Natural World and God: Theological Explorations,* 219.

In Rahner's work, we do not find a similar continuity between the sacraments of the Church in the strict sense and the sacramental encounters with fellow creatures in nature and human societies. This has to do, I think, with another difference between Rahner and Edwards. While Rahner speaks of the sacraments as an *opus operatum* (that is, something already accomplished by God in the Church), Edwards emphasizes that experiences with God in the encounters with nature are not generic experiences with God but particular experiences of Christ and Spirit.[34] The activity of the Spirit is related to the creation of life as the 'giver of life' (the Nicene Creed) but the special role of the Spirit in sacramental theology is related to opening up and changing the mindsets and life-orientation of human beings, when they suddenly experience and embrace grace 'in, with and under' natural and social events.

Risking the danger of over-systematization, we might say that Denis Edwards' commitment to *deep incarnation* entails that Christ is being there for us (and for all other created beings as well), also prior to human awareness. His corresponding commitment to a similarly *deep pneumatology* is that the Spirit is constantly at work opening up human minds to become aware—consciously or below the threshold of clear consciousness—of the callings of the Spirit of Christ in mundane as well as in extraordinary events. Thus, by virtue of being part of God's world of creation, conjoined with the suffering and elevated Christ in all that is, every single material event has the *potential of becoming* a sacrament. But only if it is apprehended as such by a human mind under the inspiration of Spirit of God, it will *actually become* a sacrament.

Denis Edwards, *Laudato si'*, and the Interactivity Between Nature and Humanity

What a relief it must have been for Denis Edwards to see the publication of the Encyclical Letter of Pope Francis, *Laudato si'*, issued at Pentecost in 2015. Here, for the first time at this magisterial level, the pope addressed shared ecological problems such as pollution, climate change, loss of biodiversity and of water resources, while at the same

---

34. See Edwards' critical note on Rahner in 'Experience of Word and Spirit in the Natural World', 198.

time pointing out that our present ecological situation creates a social predicament with deep and long-ranging consequences for human societies. Pointing to the particular theological resources in Eastern Orthodoxy and the tradition of St Francis, the pope also addresses the need to bring in the voices of scientists alongside philosophers, theologians, and civil groups. Such collaborative work should inform the teaching of the Church in its care for the planet as our common home (§ 7).

As Edwards notes, it is the interconnectedness of all that exists that that underlies the theological and ethical viewpoints of *Laudato si'*.[35] 'This is the basis of our conviction that, as part of the universe, called into being by one Father, all of us are linked by unseen bonds and together form a kind of universal family, a sublime communion which fills us with a sacred, affectionate and humble respect' (§ 89).

At prominent place, *Laudato si'* also affirms the *sacramentality of the world*. After all God and humanity meet in the details as well as in the whole of the created order down to the planetary dust from which the Earth is formed: 'As Christians, we are also *called to accept the world as a sacrament of communion*, as a way of sharing with God and our neighbours on a global scale. It is our humble conviction that the divine and the human meet in the slightest detail in the seamless garment of God's creation, in the last speck of dust of our planet.' (§ 9; italics added.).

It is furthermore argued that the larger ecosystems have an 'intrinsic value independent of their usefulness', just as 'each organism, as a creature of God, is good and admirable in itself'. It is on the background of the intrinsic value of nature that *Laudato si'* also speaks of a 'sustainable use' of nature by human beings, whereby due consideration must be given to each ecosystem's regenerative ability (§ 140).

What we see in *Laudato si'* are many of the concerns expressed in the work of Denis Edwards and other ecotheologians. The 'intrinsic value' of organisms and ecosystems requires similar ethical considerations as the dignity of human person, insofar as an ethic of self-restraint is required of human societies, including the sense of wisdom and tenderness no less than the search for technological solutions. The 'susteainable use' of natural resources requires considerations of the

---

35. Edwards, "Everything is Interconnected": The Trinity and the Natural World in *Laudato si'*, in *The Natural World and God: Theological Explorations*, 119–133.

long-term conviviality between human societies in tandem with the regenerative powers of the ecological systems of nature.

Where does this leave the 'sacramental use' of nature? Unfortunately, there is no detailed reflection on the sacraments and the sacramentality of nature in *Laudato si'*. This is a pity, since the friendly interplay between natural elements (such as clean water, flour and grapes) and human culture (bread-baking and winemaking) plays a strong role in the main sacraments of Baptism and Eucharist. However, *Laudato si'* confirms Edward's view of the continuity between the sacraments of the church and the sacramental potentials of nature, when the encyclical speaks of the need to accept the world of creation as a 'sacrament of communion' (§9), shared by God, humans and fellow creatures. Indeed, a sacramental use of nature is a prime exemplification of an intense *interactivity between humanity and nature* that values nature for what it already is: a medium of divine self-communication, and for what it may become: a shared communion of humanity and nature to be unfolded in the everlasting life of God.

The important perspective of René Girard is revealing in the context of the sacraments too. Since its beginnings, the Christian religion eliminated ritual slaughters and animal offerings from its repertoire, and the church thereby took distance of violent uses of nature in religious life.[36] 'Unlike the other highpriests, he [Christ] has no need to offer sacrifices day after day, first for his own sins, then for those of the people; this he did once and for all when he offered himself', as stated in the Letter to the Hebrews (8:27).

This does not mean that offerings play no role in the Christian religion, however, for there is still a reciprocal interaction between God and humanity, beginning with the blessings of God and followed up by human thanksgiving. Incidentally, both the Hebrew and the Greek words for 'blessing' (*baruch* respectively *eulogeomai*) also refers to thanksgiving on the human part. Blessing, thanksgiving, praise, prayer, honest lament, and a tender heart towards people and co-creatures belong to the flow of grace, initiated by the prior divine generosity.[37]

---

36. René Girard, *Violence and the Sacred* (Baltimore: The John Hopkins University Press, 1979), 39–67.
37. Niels Henrik Gregersen, 'Radical Generosity and the Flow of Grace', *in Word-Gift-Being: Justification-Economy-Ontology*, edited by Bo Kristian Holm and Peter Widmann (Tübingen: Mohr Siebeck, 2009), 117–144.

Compare with the walk through the Flinder Ranges that Denis uses to exemplify the experience of in the human encounter with nature. Such a walk leaves only a minimal ecological footprint but it is potentially rich in spiritual interactions with nature. Denis particularly mentions the Brachina Gorge as stunning in itself, as a natural formation, but his experience was further enriched by the remembrance of the spiritual connections with nature in the company with members of Adnyamathanha people, who have been celebrating there for immemorial times. Finding peace, quiet joy, inner freedom, as Denis points out, leads to an extension of the human mind. Spiritual experiences with natural and religious-cultural sites such as the Brachina Gorge is a friendly and respectful way of being part of the world as a sacramental communion.[38] It may even lead to a considerable ethical re-orientation and meekness of the heart as result of the expansion of heart.

On (Not) Numbering the Sacraments: Concluding Ecumenical Perspectives

Paul Tillich (1886–1965) is a Protestant theologian that would have shared central concerns in Edwards' view of nature. As Tillich makes clear, the attempt to reduce the Christian media to that of spoken words inevitably leads to an inner impoverishment and to a corresponding neglect of potentially enriching relations to the world of nature:

> It is one of the shortcomings of the churches of the 'word,' especially in their legalistic and exclusively personalistic form, that they exclude, along with the sacramental element, the universe outside humanity from consecration and fulfilment. But the Kingdom of God is not only a social symbol; it is a symbol which comprises the whole of reality.[39]

This is Tillich's criticism of his own neo-Protestant heritage. Tillich wanted to combine 'the Protestant principle' that rightly criticised religious institutions for putting their own institution in front of Christ, with what he called the 'Catholic substance' that retains the enlivening relations to the sacraments as media for what he called the Spiritual Presence.[40]

---

38. Edwards, 'Experience of Word and Spirit in the Natural World', 198–199.
39. Paul Tillich, *Systematic Theology, Volume 3* (London: SCM Press, 1964), 377.
40. Tillich, *Systematic Theology, Volume 3*, 122.

We are here back to the theology of the symbol. Like Rahner, also Tillich argues that the sacramental material is not just 'sign' pointing towards backwards or forwards to God but a 'symbol', which in itself encapsulates the divine presence that the sacraments refer to. Sacraments are real symbol, as Rahner put it. However, Tillich took distance to the inherited Catholic view of the *opus operatum* that we found in Rahner's view of the sacraments of the Church. The traditional Protestant objection has been that hereby the sacraments are turned into non-personal acts of a semi-magical character. This allegation is unfounded, at least in relation to contemporary Catholic thinking, and Tillich was aware of that. But Tillich retained his criticism that the sacraments should not be seen as being in the possession of the Church. Rather, the churches are to be seen as particular rooms for the presence of Christ in word and sacrament. In this view, the being of the church is constituted by Christ, and the sacraments of the church rest on the general divine promise that 'where two or three are gathered in my name, I am there among them' (Matt 18:20). More specific promises are related to the sacraments of Baptism (Matt 28:18–20) and the Eucharist (1 Cor 11:23), and perhaps for other sacraments of the church. The point is that such sacraments are accompanied by an unambiguous divine promise that we do only rarely find in the world of creation. In this sense, 'the word comes to the elements and makes the sacrament', as phased by Augustine, and repeated by both Thomas and Martin Luther.[41]

However, the table can also be turned around so that elements of nature 'speak' to us. In such cases, encounters with nature can indeed become sites for experiencing God. In the Christian tradition—from the Middle Ages over the age of the Reformation to modernity—we find steady references to the 'Book of Nature' as a parallel to the 'Book of the Bible'.[42] This metaphor gives a sense of human beings as part of the wider alphabet of God's world of creation, in which all parts of nature have a say of their own. In Martin Luther's *Commentary on Genesis* we find one such example of seeing co-creatures as divine

---

41. Augustine, *Commentary on the Gospel of John*, 80.3 (on Jn 15:3), cited with approval by Thomas Aquinas, *Summa Theologiae* III, q 60 a 6 (*accedit verbum ad elementum et fit sacramentum*), and multiple times also by Martin Luther and other Reformers.

42. Olaf Pedersen, *The Book of Nature* (Vatican: Vatican Observatory Publications, 1992)

words: 'sun, moon, heaven, earth, Peter, Paul; I, you etc—we are all words of God, in fact only a singly syllable or letter by comparison with the entire creation'.[43] We are here indeed placed on par with, and together with our co-creatures, all of which are small divine words derived from the Word of God. In the same vein, Luther can say in his *Commentary on the Sermon of the Mount* that 'we have as many teachers and preachers as we have small birds up in the air'. They laugh at our worldly concerns, but they also bring the gospel to us, as in the singing of a single nightingale.[44] In this view, natural events do have the potential to become sacramental agents of grace, if God so wills. If we do not acknowledge this possibility, we think too petty about God's capacity to give Godself to human beings; we would also distrust the deep presence of Christ in all that is, and not respect the inventiveness of the Spirit of God in finding ways to open us up, and turning us around.

Let me end this essay by sharing a memory with the late Stephen Sykes, the former Anglican bishop of Ely and former Professor of theology at Cambridge University. At the Nordic-Baltic Conference in Estonia 1992, he made an intervention during a discussion on the sacraments. 'The Catholics know that there are seven sacraments, and you Lutherans believe that there are only two sacraments. We Anglicans do not how many sacraments there are.' I guess that Denis would agree with Stephen Sykes, perhaps with some modifications. But at least he would smile!

---

43. *Martin Luther's Works*, edited by Jaroslav Pelican (Minneapolis: Fortress Press, 1958), volume 1, 22–23.
44. *Martin Luther's Works*, edited by Jaroslav Pelican (Minneapolis: Fortress Press, 1965), volume 21, 186–209.

From Deep Incarnation to Deep Divinisation?

Ernst M Conradie

'*Deep incarnation* means that the 'divine Logos' . . . has assumed not merely humanity, but the *whole malleable matrix of materiality.*'[1]
Niels Henrik Gregersen

Abstract: 'This contribution engages with Denis Edwards' understanding of deep incarnation. It notes that any notion of deep incarnation has implications for the interplay between all six the classic Christological symbols (incarnation, cross, resurrection, ascension, session and parousia). This is affirmed by Edwards especially as far as cross and resurrection is concerned, speaking of 'deep resurrection'. However, instead of the symbol of parousia he emphasises an Athanasian view on divinisation. It is argued that this emphasis creates a tension between his affirmation of the whole creation as implied in deep incarnation Christology and his affirmation of that which is material, bodily and earthly. This move has become dangerous in the Anthropocene where humans have indeed become divine—as the 'God-species'.

Key Terms: Anthropocene, Deep incarnation, Denis Edwards, divinisation, ecotheology, *theosis,*

Is a coincidence God's way of remaining anonymous (Einstein)? Perhaps that is a theory of divine action that Denis Edwards could warm to! In 2003 I walked into Catholic Bookshop in Cape Town, South Africa, and browsed through the shelves. I found a copy of the volume *Earth Healing—Earth Revealing* (Liturgical Press, 2001) that Denis Edwards edited. It was exorbitantly expensive. To my

---

1. Niels Henrik Gregersen, 'Deep Incarnation: Why Evolutionary Continuity Matters in Christology', in *Toronto Journal of Theology,* 26/2 (Fall 2010): 173–187, here at 176, Gregersen's italics.

amazement I received a ninety per cent discount on the volume, promptly worked through it and discovered that this volume is addressing the same kind of challenges that I was engaging with, namely the need for a more or less orthodox (and therefore radical!) reinterpretation of the content and significance of the Christian faith in the light of ecological concerns and scientific insights.

Although buying the book in this way could not have happened through Amazon.com, the internet did come to my help: I did not know anything about Denis at the time, but found his email address and started corresponding with him. He then invited me to a conference in Adelaide in January 2004 where I also met Celia Deane-Drummond. The rest as they say is history. Denis visited South Africa in 2012 for the culminating conference of the Christian Faith and the Earth project and we collaborated in multiple ways subsequently.[2]

We last met during an ecotheology conference in Serafino near Adelaide in March 2015.[3] We often walked together, both appreciated mature red wine and shared a theological commitment to what is material, bodily and earthly. We both approached ecotheology with a deeply trinitarian intuition but from contrasting positions—Catholic and Reformed—albeit that Denis was always reforming the (Roman) Catholic Church in which he served, while I seek to work in a spirit of catholic (ecumenical) cooperation.

Deep Incarnation Only?

In seeking to address contemporary ecological concerns and learn from emerging scientific insights Denis Edwards typically drew from his wealth of knowledge of Patristic Christianity and from Karl Rahner, his main twentieth century conversation partner. His

---

2. See *Christian Faith and the Earth: Current Paths and Emerging Horizons in Ecotheology,* edited by Ernst M Conradie, Sigurd Bergmann, Celia E Deane-Drummond and Denis Edwards (London: T&T Clark, 2014), including an essay by Denis Edwards entitled 'Where on Earth is God? Exploring an Ecological Theology of the Trinity in the Tradition of Athanasius' (11–30).

3. The outcome was a volume entitled *The Nature of Things: Rediscovering the Spiritual in God's Creation,* edited by Graham Buxton and Norman Habel (Eugene: Pickwick, 2016), including an essay by Denis Edwards entitled 'Experience of Word and Spirit in the Natural World' (13–26), drawing especially from Athanasius and Karl Rahner, as was typical of his later work.

oeuvre adopts a Trinitarian pattern since he used the Trinity as a lens to address such challenges. One may mention his books *Jesus the Wisdom of God: An Ecological Theology* (Orbis, 1995), *The God of Evolution: A Trinitarian Theology* (Paulist, 1999), and *Breath of Life: A Theology of the Creator Spirit* (Orbis, 2004). This pattern is also clear in *Ecology at the Heart of Faith* (Orbis, 2006), *Partaking of God: Trinity, Evolution, and Ecology* (Liturgical Press, 2014), *Christian Understandings of Creation* (Fortress, 2017) and *Deep Incarnation: God's Redemptive Suffering with Creatures* (Orbis, 2019). Finally, in the last year of his life Denis contributed an essay on 'The Triune God and Climate Change' to the *T&T Clark Handbook on Christian Theology and Climate Change* (T&T Clark, 2019) that Hilda Koster and I edited.

In this contribution I will focus on Edwards' Christology and more specifically his endorsement of the notion of 'deep incarnation' as proposed by Niels Henrik Gregersen and others.[4] I will relate this to Denis' affirmation of an Athanasian notion of divinisation. I will take him up on the latter, asking whether his notion of divinisation is deep enough, namely whether it can sustain an unwavering, eschatological commitment to God's creation in the sense of *creatura*, to that which is material, bodily and earthly.

Let me explain my intuition in this regard with reference to a core insight derived from the renowned South African missiologist David Bosch. In his book *Witness to the World* (1980) Bosch explored the tension between so-called 'evangelicals' and so-called 'ecumenicals' that dominated world Christianity in the 1960s and 1970s.[5] In response he stressed that mission has to hold together the witness (*marturia*) of Christians as proclamation (*kerygma*), service (*diakonia*), fellowship (*koinonia*) and also worship (*latreia*).[6] In his magnum opus *Transforming Mission* (1991) Bosch moved away

---

4. See especially the volume edited by Niels Henrik Gregersen, *Incarnation: On the Scope and Depth of Christology* (Minneapolis: Fortress, 2015) with an essay by Denis Edwards entitled 'Incarnation and the Natural World: Explorations in the Tradition of Athanasius' (157–176).

5. David J Bosch, *Witness to the World: The Christian Mission in Theological Perspective* (Atlanta: John Knox Press, 1980).

6. These insights have been developed for Christian ecotheology in *The Church in God's Household: Protestant Perspectives on Ecclesiology and Ecology,* edited by Clive Ayre and Ernst M Conradie (Pietermaritzburg: Cluster Publications, 2016).

from this analysis to trace paradigm changes in the theology of mission, while discerning an emerging ecumenical paradigm. In the concluding chapter he astutely observes confessional differences in an emphasis on the core Christological symbols.[7] In generalised terms: Catholics and Anglican typically favour the symbol of incarnation, Lutherans the cross, the Orthodox the resurrection, Pentecostals the Ascension (to make room for Pentecost), Reformed churches the rule of Christ, sitting at the Father's right hand and Adventists the so-called 'second coming' (Parousia) of Christ. Bosch maintains that any adequate theology of mission needs to juggle all six these symbols, keeping them in 'creative tension' with each other.

One may say the same about the need for a creative tension between all the aspects of God's work—creation, ongoing creation, providence, salvation, church, mission and consummation. In *The Earth in God's Economy* I suggested the image of a juggler to guard against distortions that result from focusing on one aspect only.[8] This is easier said than done as a series of edited volumes on creation and salvation, to which Denis Edwards contributed essays on Athanasius and on Karl Rahner, demonstrate.[9]

Likewise, one may insist that a deeply trinitarian theology is required but that it is also easier said than done to affirm all three perspectives on God's identity and character.[10] With others Denis Edwards recognizes that a deep Christology requires a deep Pneumatology. It is the inhabitation of the Spirit who brings

---

7. David J Bosch, *Transforming Mission: Paradigm Shifts in Theology of Mission* (Maryknoll, NY: Orbis Books 1991).

8. Ernst M Conradie, *The Earth in God's Economy: Creation, Salvation and Consummation in Ecological Perspective* (Berlin: LIT Verlag, 2015).

9. See Denis Edwards, 'Athanasius: "The Word of God in Creation and Salvation"', in *Creation and Salvation, Volume 1: A Mosaic of Essays on Selected Classic Christian Theologians*, edited by Ernst M Conradie (Berlin: LIT Verlag, 2011), 37–52; 'Karl Rahner (1904–1984)—The Divine Self-Bestowal' in *Creation and Salvation, Volume 2: A Companion on Recent Theological Movements*, edited by Ernst M Conradie (Berlin: LIT Verlag, 2012), 61–65.

10. See my article 'Only a fully Trinitarian theology will do, but where can that be found?', in *Ned Geref Teologiese Tydskrif*, 54/1&2 (2013): 1–9, drawing on a famous essay by Arnold van Ruler, "The necessity of a Trinitarian theology", in *Calvinist Trinitarianism and Theocentric Politics: Essays towards a Public Theology*, edited by John Bolt (Lampeter: Edwin Mellen Press, 1989), 1–26.

about the incarnation.[11] Likewise, a radical understanding of God's transcendence is required, radical enough so that God becomes open to the suffering of creatures.

So here is my question: If one affirms with Gregersen and others an emphasis on deep incarnation—which I certainly welcome[12]—what implications would that have for the interplay with other Christological symbols?

One may speak about a 'deep' notion of the cross, to appreciate that Godself was crucified—which raised much controversy regarding secular theology following John Robinson's theology of the death of God and Jürgen Moltmann's *The Crucified God*.[13] What about 'deep' resurrection? This clearly raises long-standing debates since the advent of the Enlightenment on the so-called 'bodily' resurrection of Christ, where the pernicious dualisms of spirit and matter, soul and body, brain and mind, have wreaked havoc.

And 'deep' Ascension? Calvin for one, maintained that the Ascension has to be understood as being as physical as the resurrection and that our salvation depends on that (or else Christ cannot be everywhere (*contra* Luther).[14] 'Deep' session may be easier to contemplate, albeit that the material impact of Christ's perceived reign over "every square inch of society" has a disastrous track record in the history of Christianity, not least in South Africa. That leaves eschatological questions about the depth of an understanding of Christ's Parousia amidst numerous millennial misunderstandings. Can this also be maintained without falling in the traps of either literalist or spiritualising views on the 'return' (better 'coming') of Christ (the Messiah)?

---

11. See Denis Edwards, *Deep Incarnation: God's Redemptive Suffering with Creatures* (Maryknoll, NY: Orbis, 2019), 106–110.

12. 'Deep incarnation' is typically related to 'deep time' on the basis of scientific insights on evolutionary history. There is a need to explore the links between deep incarnation, 'deep ecology' and 'deep economy', but this cannot be offered here. On 'deep economy' see Hans Dirk van Hoogstraaten, *Deep Economy: Caring for Ecology, Humanity and Religion* (Cambridge: James Clarke & Co, 2001).

13. See John AT Robinson, *Honest to God* (London: SCM Press, 1963); Jürgen Moltmann, *The Crucified God* (New York: Harper, 1974).

14. For a discussion, see my essay 'Darwin's Ambiguous Gift to Reformed Theology: The Problem of Natural Suffering and Calvin's Meditation on Future Life', in *Restoration through Redemption: John Calvin Revisited*, edited by Henk van der Belt (Leiden: Brill, 2013), 95–112.

Denis Edwards on Deep Incarnation Christology

In Denis' last book *Deep Incarnation: God's Redemptive Suffering with Creatures* it is clear from the outset that he does not restrict the notion of deep incarnation to the symbol of incarnation only. Instead, he insists that incarnation 'does not refer simply to the birth of Jesus, but to the whole event of the Word becoming flesh, to every aspect of Jesus' material and bodily existence, and to his whole life and ministry that culminates in his death and resurrection'.[15] The incarnation is no Plan B in that it merely responds to the predicament of human sin.[16] God becomes incarnate so that God can best be known by God's creatures. His own position becomes clear in the last chapter of the book but then on the basis of his conversations with especially Irenaeus of Lyons, Athanasius of Alexandria (a theologian on whom he contributed several essays since 2012[17]) and Karl Rahner. His views are clearly articulated in the final chapter under five rubrics so that there is no need for a detailed description here.[18] Let me then comment only on how deep incarnation is related to the other five Christological symbols.

a) With Gregersen Edwards maintains that 'Christ cannot be thought of as the Word incarnate apart from ecological and cosmic interconnections'.[19] Therefore, 'Social, ecological, and cosmic relationships are not add-ons to the Word made flesh. They are constitutive of the Word made flesh'.[20] He also affirms the significance of deep incarnation for suffering creatures, suffering that is deeply embedded in the evolutionary process (death, extinction, predation, disselection) irrespective of human sin. Godself becomes incarnate

---

15. Edwards, *Deep Incarnation*, xvii.

16. Edwards, *Deep Incarnation*, 53.

17. More or less the same argument is found in *How God Acts*, 107–127; 'Athanasius'; *Partaking of God*, 37–53; 'Where on Earth is God'; 'Incarnation and the Natural World'; 'Experiences of Word and Spirit in the Natural World'; *Christian Understandings of Creation*, 45–64; and *Deep Incarnation*, 55–80.

18. The headings read 'The Holy Spirit brings about the incarnation', 'Cosmic, evolutionary and ecological relationships as constitutive of the Word made flesh', 'God can be said to suffer with suffering creatures', "The cross as sacrament of God's redemptive suffering with creatures', and 'Resurrection: A promise of healing and fulfilment that embraces all creatures'.

19. Edwards, *Deep Incarnation*, 111.

20. Edwards, *Deep Incarnation*, 113.

in the very tissue of biological existence. With Gregory of Nazianzus Edwards captures the significance of this insight: what has not been assumed, cannot be healed.[21] With Rahner Edwards insists that the whole of creaturely reality is assumed so that the whole universe of creatures might participate in salvation.[22] Indeed, 'all things are assumed in Christ so that all things might be liberated (Rom 8:21), reconciled (Col 1:20) and recapitulated (Eph 1:20) in him'.[23] Creaturely humanity is ascribed to the Word, it is 'made Word', or 'Worded'.[24]

Edwards opts for a radicalised notion of transcendence, namely where God can freely and lovingly enter into the pain of creation. That God can pour Godself out in love does not diminish God but constitutes the very identity and character of God.[25] This reveals a more fully transcendent God than one who is unable to do this.[26] In this way God transcends God's own transcendence.[27] God's greatness is thus understood in terms of God's love. God is unknowable by creatures in terms of greatness but so loves creatures as to find a way to be known by them.[28]

b) This presence of God is radicalised in the cross where God's participation in such suffering becomes most evident (xvii). Edwards affirms that God can be said to suffer with suffering creatures. Does this make any difference? For Edwards such participation in suffering is redemptive, as the subtitle of his book also indicates. However, is incarnation by itself salvific for the whole creation because of the 'loving self-identification of the crucified Christ with creation' (as Edwards following Bauckham seems to suggest)?[29] How, then, is the cross the cause of our salvation?[30] With Rahner Edwards affirms the cross as symbol of divine mercy and forgiving love. He explains this redemptive co-suffering as God's 'loving accompaniment', 'redemptive

---

21. Edwards, *Deep Incarnation*, 84.
22. Edwards, *Deep Incarnation*, 85.
23. Edwards, *Deep Incarnation*, 113.
24. Edwards, *Deep Incarnation*, 68.
25. Edwards, *Deep Incarnation*, 117.
26. Edwards, *Deep Incarnation*, 114.
27. Edwards, *Deep Incarnation*, 115.
28. Edwards, *Deep Incarnation*, 49.
29. Edwards, *Deep Incarnation*, 111. Edwards does add 'and because the risen Christ draws the whole creation with him into the eschatological newness of resurrection' (111).
30. Edwards, *Deep Incarnation*, 118.

embrace' and 'strengthening presence'.[31] Indeed, an embrace is by itself a form of forgiveness and reconciliation, but does that address forms of suffering other than guilt and resentment? Edwards is keen to emphasise that such compassionate presence of God applies to all creatures in an evolutionary world.[32] There is indeed some consolation if suffering is shared although one would hope for more, namely that the suffering will also be overcome, especially for the victims of injustice. What about the victims of predation? For Edwards it is indeed not enough to say that God is lovingly present with suffering sentient creatures.[33] This is why an extension of the depths of the cross to deep resurrection is necessary.

c) Edwards follows Karl Rahner and Elizabeth Johnson in proposing that a theology of deep incarnation requires a theology of 'deep resurrection'.[34] Resurrection is a promise of God that not only involves humanity, the whole of humanity, but also the whole creation. Because Christ is raised in the body, he remains profoundly connected to all that is bodily.[35] His resurrection is like the first erupting of a volcano. The risen Christ does not abandon the earth but is radically present to all creatures in their longing.[36] All creatures participate in the promised transformation of all things. With Irenaeus Edwards maintains that the resurrection of Christ 'involves the fulfillment and transformation of "all things"—the whole visible, material, biological and human world'.[37] There is a symmetry between the God who creates all things and the God who saves all things.

This emphasis on deep resurrection is crucial but also open to diverging interpretations. For Gregersen it is the risen Christ (with an extended body) that co-suffers with all creatures. If so, the presence of the incarnate Word is itself saving. As paraphrased by Edwards, 'Salvation is the communion between God and creatures brought about through the Word and in the Spirit'.[38] What difference does such communion make to suffering creatures? Does solidarity

---

31. Edwards, *Deep Incarnation*, 121–122.
32. Edwards, *Deep Incarnation*, 123.
33. Edwards, *Deep Incarnation*, 123.
34. Edwards, *Deep Incarnation*, 8.
35. Edwards, *Deep Incarnation*, 87.
36. Edwards, *Deep Incarnation*, 88.
37. Edwards, *Deep Incarnation*, 53.
38. Edwards, *Deep Incarnation*, 23.

in suffering suffice or does the presence of the risen Christ make a material difference to such suffering, beyond consolation? What does it mean that creation will be set free from its bondage to decay (Rom 8:18–25)? Does this include only the suffering of sentient forms of life or also finitude (mortality), beyond the corruption caused by sin? What transformation does the presence of the risen Christ make possible? Is there not a danger, if resurrection is treated as ubiquitous, touching on every moment and each epoch in history,[39] that there is no temporal transformation, so that only the idea of transformation remains? Edwards is cognisant of such caveats (regarding Gregersen's position) and thus emphasises the significance of deep resurrection for the reconciliation of all things in Christ. This is a hope, based on God's promises and God's character, not an accurate comprehension of the future of the universe.[40]

One may therefore conclude that deep incarnation is shorthand for the three Christological symbols of incarnation, cross and resurrection so that the latter two is regarded as an extension of the significance of incarnation. With Celia Deane-Drummond Edwards affirms Von Balthasar's notion of a theo-drama, so that the various Christological symbols are weaved together within a narrative framework that offers a dramatic and transformative re-description of the scientific account of the history of the universe.[41] There is one economy of creation, salvation and consummation, united in one divine intention, but this takes place and becomes evident only in history.[42]

d) Edwards does recognise the significance of Christ's ascension for discourse on deep incarnation. With Rahner he affirms the notion of God's self-bestowal. The incarnation is necessary for the self-bestowal of God to the world of creatures and for creatures to accept such self-bestowal.[43] He then adds that in the resurrection and the ascension of the risen Christ, creaturely reality is taken fully into God and irrevocably adopted as God's own reality, as the beginning and the pledge of the transfiguration of the whole creation.[44]

---

39. Edwards, *Deep Incarnation*, 24.
40. Edwards, *Deep Incarnation*, 127.
41. Edwards, *Deep Incarnation*, 9–13.
42. Edwards, *Deep Incarnation*, 125.
43. Edwards, *Deep Incarnation*, 94.
44. Edwards, *Deep Incarnation*, 94.

e) Edwards does not address the symbols of session or the parousia on the basis of deep incarnation. Instead, with Athanasius he speaks consistently of divinisation and juxtaposes that with the terms transfiguration, reconciliation and recapitulation. My sense is that the replacement of the symbol of parousia with that of *theosis* has far-reaching implications. The parousia suggests that Christ returns (better: 'comes', 'turns') to this world so that God's home in on earth (Rev 21:3), while the notion divinisation almost inevitably suggest that we are to follow Christ's ascension into heaven to be with God. It is therefore necessary to consider Edwards' understanding of deep divinisation in more detail.

Edwards on Deep Divinisation

It is clear from his whole oeuvre over the last two decades that Denis Edwards regards divinisation, alongside liberation, as one of two concepts that have a unique potential to enable new generations of Christians to see the meaning of Christ for our world.[45] As far as I can see he uses the terms deification and the preferred divinisation or deifying transformation[46] as synonyms.

Edwards typically juxtaposes these with the Irenaean term recapitulation, the notion of transfiguration, the Pauline emphasis on transformation, the liberation of all things from the bondage of sin and corruption, the Johannine notion of glorification and the reconciliation of all things in Christ. In one instance he speaks with Irenaeus of 'the whole creation as being restored to its primeval condition and placed under the dominion of the righteous'.[47] His intention is clear, namely that these terms may complement each other to gain a glimpse of the mystery expressed in the hope for eschatological consummation. This is also the meaning of recapitulation, namely a summary statement (used in rhetoric), bringing things together under one heading.[48] Edwards emphasises with Irenaeus of Lyons that recapitulation in Christ involves all things and that eschatological redemption involves

---

45. Edwards, *Partaking of God*, 38. It is interesting to note that the term divinisation (or *theosis*) does not appear in the index of *Jesus the Wisdom of God*. There are only three paragraphs on Athanasius (54–55).
46. See, for example, *How God Acts*, 118–126.
47. Edwards, *Deep Incarnation*, 44.
48. Edwards, *Deep Incarnation*, 37.

the whole creation. On the basis of Ephesians 1:10 he holds that the recapitulation all things in Christ suggests one economy of incarnation and consummation: 'In his death and resurrection the incarnate Word recapitulates, saves, and brings to fulfilment, all things,'[49] including visible and corporeal things.[50] None of these terms can be captured in conceptually precise language since they are symbols that point well beyond what can be captured. With Andrew Louth Edwards speaks of two arches in the divine economy, a lesser one involving sin and salvation and a greater one from creation to deification. The lesser arch is required because humanity has failed to participate in the greater arch of the divine economy.[51]

In his own summary statement of the hope for eschatological consummation Edwards describes the fullness of redemption in Christ as the deifying transformation of created reality at three levels. First, deep incarnation and deep resurrection symbolises the beginning of the transfiguration of the universe at the material level.[52] How this is understood given the connections between matter and energy ($E=mc^2$) is not clear (to me), so that such transfiguration remains open to neo-Platonic forms of idealism, that is matter is transfigured into the idea of matter.

Second, the recapitulation and reconciliation of all things include biological life in unforeseeable ways, pertaining to each species and each individual creature. How the creature can then remain a creature—with all its implications for predatory species—is again not clarified.

Third, at the human level divinisation includes for Edwards the forgiveness of sin and the indwelling of the Holy Spirit.[53] God embraces the flesh of Jesus of Nazareth so that creatures of flesh may be transformed and taken fully into communion with the living God. Edwards adds that it is safe to argue that such transformation will be appropriate to each creature and each species. The flesh that is transformed includes each kangaroo, each dolphin, each sparrow, each bilby, in ways that are appropriate to each.[54] But does it remain flesh, subject to eating, defecating, reproduction and death?

---

49. Edwards, *Deep Incarnation*, 41.
50. Edwards, *Deep Incarnation*, 42.
51. Edwards, *Partaking of God*, 47.
52. Edwards, *Deep Incarnation*, 127.
53. Edwards, *Deep Incarnation*, 127.
54. Edwards, *Deep Incarnation*, 127.

My sense is that the best way to explain Edwards' position on divinisation is in terms of participating in the trinitarian community. As the body of Christ and through the inhabitation of the Holy Spirit all creatures may participate in the communion between Creator, Word and Spirit without ceasing to be what they are. He typically describes such participation in terms of 'partaking'. 'Partaking of God' is also the title of one of his recent books.[55] Participation means that the creature remains a creature and does not actually become divine. With Athanasius Edwards maintains that 'Through the incarnation God is joined to creaturely reality in a radically immediate and internal way, for the sake of brining creatures into the intimacy of the divine trinitarian life'.[56] All things exist through the Word and by participation in the Word of God, they partake of the Word of God as bringing into existence, governing, establishing, leading, providing for and ordering creation.[57] In musical imagery, 'The wisdom of God, holding the universe like a lyre, draws together a variety of created things, producing in beauty and harmony a single world and single order within it'.[58]

Such participation in the triune communion does lead to a renewal, a transformation of the creature given the benefits that such participation entails. What this transformation implies is hard to capture but Edwards describes this in biblical metaphors such as liberation from bondage, reconciliation and forgiveness. The renewal of the world is effected by the Word who created it from the very beginning.[59]

The transforming effect of incarnation is described by Edwards as deification (*theopoiēsis*) or deifying transformation. He insists that the Word of God is not deified since Christ is fully divine. However, the bodily humanity of Jesus is indeed deified by its union with the Word, and it is this that enables the deification of humanity.[60] The whole of creation is included in the Christ's resurrection, uniting

---

55. See Edwards, *Partaking of God: Trinity, Evolution, and Ecology* (Collegeville: Liturgical Press, 2014).

56. Edwards, *Deep Incarnation*, 67.

57. Edwards, *Deep Incarnation*, 58.

58. Edwards, *Deep Incarnation*, 59.

59. Edwards, *Deep Incarnation*, 59.

60. Edwards, *Deep Incarnation*, 69.

and reconciling the whole creation with the Father.[61] In the Spirit the Word divinises all that has come into existence.[62] There is no division between the creative Word and the deifying Word. In a summary statement Edwards paraphrases Athanasius (and expresses his own view), namely that 'The Word is made flesh that humans might be forgiven, deified, and adopted as beloved sons and daughters and that the rest of creation might be transformed in Christ in its own proper way'.[63] The wider creaturely world is therefore 'explicitly and unambiguously included in the eschatological transformation and deification of all things in Christ'.[64]

The Divinisation of that Which is Material, Bodily and Earthly?

Denis Edwards was one of the leading Christian eco-theologians of his time. His commitment to God's beloved creation is unwavering and beyond any doubt. In numerous instances he expresses a concern for each individual creature as beloved by God. I do want to raise the question here whether his emphasis on divinisation is not at odds with doing justice to what is material, bodily and earthly. Can one still maintain life in all its substructures if creatures become 'divine', that is gain some divine characteristics by participating in the triune communion? With Athanasius Edwards take deification to entail a 'radical ontological transformation in creature reality'.[65] This does entail an 'ethical aspect' (growth in holiness) and Edwards emphasise the 'interior' of God's self-giving,[66] but he is clearly also concerned about those aspects of creaturely reality that suffer from natural causes. The problem is not only sin or the impact of sin but natural suffering in an evolutionary world.

With Rahner Edwards affirms that Christians are inherently materialists. Deep incarnation implies that God is forever a God of matter and flesh; 'matter and flesh are irrevocably taken into God and embedded in the divine Trinity', but this is now 'radically transfigured'.[67]

---

61. Edwards, *Deep Incarnation*, 70.
62. Edwards, *Deep Incarnation*, 70.
63. Edwards, *Deep Incarnation*, 71.
64. Edwards, *Deep Incarnation*, 78.
65. Edwards, 'Incarnation and the Natural World', 164.
66. Edwards, *Partaking of God*, 44.
67. Edwards, 'Incarnation and the Natural World', 168.

The transformation of the material world remains a mystery but this does not imply a disregard for what is material. Despite his emphasis on a 'radical ontological transformation', Edwards insists that 'The deification of humanity is not about changing human nature into something other than it is, but about becoming fully human in a way that is faithful to God' intention'.[68] Does this transformation imply more than a divine memory of what was material?[69] Edwards argues that Christians are committed to the idea that matter will last forever and be glorified forever in Christ and on the basis of the hypostatic union of his human (bodily) and divine natures, that remain distinct (not mingled as monophysists maintain). This transfiguration of matter has already begun in Christ and is ripening and developing to that point where it will become manifest.[70] What then about the uniqueness of Christ? Are humans to imitate Christ also by gaining some of his divine characteristics? Does that also apply to all other forms of life?

Put differently, what is the underlying problem that has to be addressed through divinisation? If it is primarily the impact of human sin, then only a restoration of God's beloved creation is required so that evolutionary history can get back on track without the corruption associated with human sin.[71] If the problem is not only injustices and oppression but also pain, suffering, sickness, ageing and death, how is that to be imagined? If death is the sting of God's otherwise good creation, then there may be a need to overcome death but how is that possible without also overcoming predation, evolutionary disselection and the limited life-cycle of cells? Is eating still possible without death, or is eating itself to be overcome?[72] Can

---

68. Edwards, *Partaking of God*, 44.
69. See Edwards, *Ecology at the Heart of Faith*, 122: redemption may occur in creatures 'being taken up, loved, and celebrated eternally in the living memory of the Trinity and the communion of saints. It may occur in other ways that we cannot yet imagine or envisage.'
70. Edwards, *Deep Incarnation*, 98.
71. For Edwards' position on sin, see especially *The God of Evolution*, 60–70. He distinguishes clearly between natural evil and social evil without making natural evil the cause of social evil. Nature is damaged by human sin and therefore in need of redemption but is not itself fallen.
72. I have addressed such questions in a series of articles, including, most recently 'Could Eating other Creatures be a Way of Discovering their Intrinsic Value?', in *Journal of Theology for Southern Africa*, 164 (2019): 26–39.

one imagine life without eating; is it still life? Does eating not assume death, if not necessarily killing? What could be meant by a God of life (one who promotes life) or indeed a living God (one who is alive) if multi-cellular life depends on absorbing other forms of life?[73] If any form of finitude in space, time and knowledge is to be overcome, does this not imply an erasure of the very distinction between Creator and creature?

For Athanasius the primary purpose of the incarnation is to overcome death. In Edwards' paraphrase, 'God's response was unthinkably generous: The Word in whom all are created would come in the flesh to bring about forgiveness of sin and to enter into death and overcome it in the power of resurrection.'[74] For Athanasius death in a biological sense is the consequence of sin. If this assumption is no longer tenable in an evolutionary world (as Edwards often notes[75]), Athanasius views cannot be readily adopted to solve (through 'ontological transformation') a problem that is primarily biological in nature, a flaw in God's otherwise good creation. If other creatures are included in salvation, which Edwards warmly endorses, the same question arises: Are they included because of the impact of human sin on other creatures or because such an ontological transformation is needed irrespective of human sin? If the latter, can the goodness of what is material, bodily and earthly still be affirmed?

Denis may be forgiven for not finding adequate answers to these questions but they do illustrate the difficulties that are confronted on the route to affirming a form of divinisation. I have argued elsewhere that there are four dominant concepts employed in Christian theology to explain the relationship between proton and eschaton, namely restoration, elevation, replacement and recycling.[76] None of these are really adequate and each are plagued with intractable problems. The neo-Calvinist notion of restoration tends to underplay evolutionary history. The Catholic and Orthodox notion of elevation

---

73. The Christian affirmation that God is a God of life is far less obvious than it may appear at first sight since the genitive is not clear. See, for example, my 'The God of Life: A counter-intuitive confession', *The Ecumenical Review,* 65/1 (2013): 3–16.

74. Edwards, 'Where on Earth is God?', 21.

75. Edwards, *Partaking of God,* 39. Here Edwards believes, irrespectively, that Athanasius' reasons for the incarnation still holds.

76. See especially Chapter 6 of *The Earth in God's Economy.*

tends to undervalue that which is material, bodily and earthly (nature is good but culture is better). The Anabaptist notion of replacement (a radically new creation) cannot affirm the continuity between creation and eschaton and therefore undermines the consolation of Christian hope. The ecofeminist notion of endless recycling allows for the continuation of life but leaves little role for God and does not really address distortions associated with sin except insofar as interruptions of the recycling process are concerned. This debate remains unresolved. As argued above, my sense is that notions of *theosis* hardly escape from the limitations associated with typically Catholic strategies of elevation. How I would love to discuss this further with Denis Edwards.

There is worse to come. In the context of discourse on the Anthropocene Athanasian orthodoxy has received a radical reinterpretation. With the advent of the 'God-species', the indicative is changed into an imperative: humans must become gods. In the often quoted words of Stewart Brand, 'We are as gods and HAVE to get good at it'.[77] To which Mark Lynas adds an 'Amen to that'! In the words of Yuval Harari, 'having raised humanity above the beastly level of survival struggles, we will now aim to upgrade humans into gods, and turn *Homo sapiens* into *Homo deus*'.[78]

Jung Mo Sung argues that the belief that because God became human, we humans can become divine is indeed the foundational myth of the modern West.[79] If the attempt to overcome human limits was previously regarded as hubris, in modernity it is regarded as a virtue since there can be no limits to human development. Moreover, although modernity has rested upon the denial of divine transcendence, this has been expressed in terms of its inverse, namely the denial of human limitations, while the quest for the divinization of

---

77. Quoted in Mark Lynas, *The God Species: Saving the Planet in the Age of Humans* (Washington: National Geographic Society, 2011), 22. The reference is to Brand, *Whole Earth Discipline: An Ecopragmatist Manifesto* (New York *et al*: Viking, 2009), epitaph on page 1.

78. See Yuval Harari, *Homo Deus: A Brief History of Tomorrow* (London: Vintage, 2017), 24.

79. See Jung Mo Sung, 'Greed, Desire and Theology', in *The Greed Line: Tool for a Just Economy*, edited by Athena Peralta and Rogate Mshana (Geneva: WCC, 2016), 43–54 (53).

humans and the building of heaven on earth remains intact. For Sung the underlying problem remains treating what is finite as infinite.

In the context of the Promethean dreams to control the Earth's climate, the Enlightenment critique of religion, namely that humans create their gods in their own image, according to their needs, desires and aspirations, becomes radicalized. As Ludwig Feuerbach already asserted, 'The turning of history will be the moment when man becomes aware that the only God of man is man himself. *Homo homini Deus!*'[80] The prophet of such Promethean aspirations was Friedrich Nietzsche: God had to be declared dead so that the *Übermensch* can come to fruition—nowadays in the shape of the cosmopolitan consumer.[81] We become gods when we are able to create 'God' in our own image.

This is no longer meant as a critique of religion but as a celebration of human ability. We can not only 'make' God but custom engineer God to ensure that there is a space for a system-compatible God![82] This becomes a matter not only of 'playing God' but of becoming divine, with godlike attributes. Athanasian orthodoxy is radicalised: God in Jesus Christ became human so that we can become divine (instead). To gain human autonomy, it is not enough to imitate or abandon God; God must be killed so that we can become divine. This is then symbolised by Christ's death.

In my view latter-day followers of Athanasius, the Nicene champion of orthodoxy, would need to guard against heretical distortions of their soteriological views on *theosis* in the Anthropocene. With discourse on the God-species, it seems that Athanasius has gained quite a secular following although he will surely be horrified by that! As was the case in Patristic theology, a heresy may become manifest in the person of Christ, but the reason why that heresy had to be denounced was and remains of a soteriological nature. It is our salvation that is at stake.

---

80. Quoted in Bob Goudzwaard and Craig B Bartholomew, *Beyond the Modern Age: An Archaeology of Contemporary Culture* (Downers Grove: IVP Academic, 2017), 61.
81. See Peter Sloterdijk, *In the World Interior of Capital: For a Philosophical Theory of Globalization*. (Cambridge: Polity Press, 2014), 209.
82. See Clive Hamilton, *Earthmasters: The Dawn of the Age of Climate Engineering* (New Haven: Yale University Press, 2013), 111.

Did the Natural World Go Wrong?

Christopher Southgate

'Every sparrow, every frog, the members of every threatened species—each is 'the object of the Father's tenderness', and each is enfolded with God's affection.'[1]
– Denis Edwards

Abstract: This chapter considers a range of explanations of the disvalues in the non-human world. It goes on to explore how an explanation lacking a fall-event or rebellion against divine intentions can be integrated into a Christian narrative of creation and redemption. En route to this destination we compare and contrast scholars such as Denis Edwards, Niels Henrik Gregersen, Neil Messer, Celia Deane-Drummond, Paul Fiddes, Ernst Conradie, Ted Peters, John Haught, and Robert John Russell.

Keywords: creation; evolution; suffering; original sin; theodicy; Fall; eschatology; atonement, Denis Edwards, Niels Henrik Gregersen, Neil Messer, Celia Deane-Drummond, Paul Fiddes, Ernst Conradie, Ted Peters, John Haught, and Robert John Russell.

It is both a pleasure and a great honour to contribute to this collection remembering Denis Edwards. Denis and I were at many academic meetings together. His infallible courtesy and quiet kindness left a deep impression on me, as did his ever-humble, ever-searching enquiry into the things of God and the world. In August 2012 a group of us walked most of the way up a South African mountain—Denis making fine pace despite less than ideal equipment. Only when it came on to snow did he judiciously point out that we were without map, food or mobile phone and it might be wise to settle for reaching the waterfall. With Denis there was always wisdom and judiciousness,

---

1. Denis Edwards, *The Natural World and God: Theological Explorations* (Adelaide, Australia: ATF Press, 2017) 69.

and there was always a waterfall—the healing torrent of his strong sense of the compassion of God and the strength of the Holy Spirit.

I want to honour Denis Edwards by picking up an old exchange of ours, and using it to develop my current thinking in dialogue with his work. Some years ago we were at a colloquium on ecological issues and a colleague remarked, almost in passing, that whatever formulations were attempted, there always had to be a fall-event at the centre of the narrative. Denis and I smiled quietly to one another, because in both our minds was a sense that the dominant Western Christian position—that a primal human sin disorders the whole creation—is no longer sustainable, and that an ecological theology must be developed out of an evolutionary narrative that can find no place for such a sudden, late-onset disordering of the cosmos into its Darwinian state.[2] We will pick up the conversation with this thesis.

The Origin of Nature's Disvalues

Where then can lie the origin of the disvalues in a Darwinian creation such as violence between creatures, suffering caused by predation, parasitism and disease, and the extinction of almost all species that have ever existed?[3] Michael Lloyd comes to the conclusion that the only satisfactory account is one based on the rebellion of angels before

---

2. See Denis Edwards, *The God of Evolution: A Trinitarian Theology* (New York: Paulist Press, 1999) for a durable account of the possibilities and challenges of this sort of theology. Also Christopher Southgate, 'Cosmic Evolution and Evil' in *The Cambridge Companion to the Problem of Evil*, edited by Chad Meister and Paul K Moser (Cambridge: Cambridge University Press, 2017), 147–164. In this regard it is interesting to note Stanley Rosenberg's recent re-reading of Augustine, in which he suggests that Augustine's prelapsarian world, 'very good' and under the providence of the sovereign God, already includes thorns and poisonous snakes. It may not after all be necessary for Augustinians to perform somersaults in order to assign all apparent disvalues in creation to human sin. Rosenberg, Stanley, 'Can Nature be 'Red in Tooth and Claw' in the thought of Augustine?' in *Finding Ourselves after Darwin: Conversations on the Image of God, Original Sin, and the Problem of Evil*, edited by Stanley Rosenberg, Michael Burdett, Michael Lloyd and Benno van den Toren (Grand Rapids, MI: Baker Books, 2018), 183–196.
3. See Christopher Southgate, *The Groaning of Creation: God, Evolution and the Problem of Evil* (Louisville, KY: Westminster John Knox Press, 2008), chapter 1, for a justification of this list.

the creation of the present universe.[4] That account suffers from two major problems: first, the power that has to be accorded to the angels to frustrate the intentions of the Creator of all things *ex nihilo*; second, the inescapable scientific conclusion that it is the *same* process of evolution by natural selection that gives rise both to creaturely diversity, beauty, and ingenuity of adaptation and to the disvalues listed above.

Much more challenging for *fall-free* accounts of an evolving creation[5] are the proposals of Neil Messer, invoking Karl Barth's 'Das Nichtige'[6] and Celia Deane-Drummond, drawing on Sergius Bulgakov's language of 'Shadow Sophia'.[7] Both invoke a mysterious constraint on divine activity in creation. A great deal turns on the nature of this constraint on God's capacity to create a world where there is creaturely flourishing without creaturely struggle, competition and violence. If the constraint is construed as a spiritual force, then old concerns that exercised the early Christian theologians about dualistic formulations resurface. A God who, from the beginning, has been in a battle with contrary spiritual forces powerful enough to radically alter the character of any creation to which God might give rise, is no longer the sovereign Lord of the cosmos whose ontological priority and absolute goodness guarantees the goodness of creation. If on the other hand the constraint on God's creative action is not an opposing agency but some form of logical constraint, how can the logic be demonstrated?[8]

A Spectrum of Accounts for Disvalue in Nature

I identify a spectrum of formulations in the recent literature. Lloyd's angelic fall sits at one end of the spectrum, as the position most

---

4. Michael Lloyd, 'The Fallenness of Nature: Three Non-Human Suspects' in *Finding Ourselves after Darwin*, 211–224.
5. Such as Bethany Sollereder has formulated in her *God, Evolution and Animal Suffering: Theodicy Without a Fall* (London: Routledge, 2018).
6. Neil Messer, *Science in Theology* (London: Bloomsbury, in press), see also his 'Evolution and Theodicy: How (Not) to do Science and Theology', in *Zygon*, 53/3 (2018): 821–835.
7. Celia Deane-Drummond, 'Perceiving Natural Evil through the Lens of Divine Glory?', in *Zygon*, 53/3 (2018): 792–807.
8. This is in effect Lloyd's challenge to me in his summary of the debate, *Finding Ourselves after Darwin*, 261.

explicitly informed by a sense of the rebellion of identifiable freely-choosing beings. Next I would place Nicola Hoggard Creegan, for whom the disvalues in creation are like the 'tares' in the parable of the wheat and the tares in the Gospel of Matthew (Matt 13:24–30 KJV).[9] The appearance of the tares of disvalue is ultimately mysterious, but the parable's witness that they are sown by an 'enemy' (Matt 13:25), suggests that Hoggard Creegan too invokes a consciously rebellious force.

In the middle of our spectrum we might place Messer, working from Barth, and Deane-Drummond, working from Bulgakov. The constraint on God's perfect freedom is a mystery, not a conscious resistance. As I have suggested,[10] this position is metastable— when the appeal to mystery on which they rest is subject to closer questioning, these approaches would necessarily collapse either into a conscious opposing spiritual force, or a form of logical constraint.

Perhaps the instincts of Paul Fiddes belong next on our spectrum. Fiddes after a very careful analysis of the 'non-being' tradition, which he traces back to Plotinus, seeks to avoid the conclusion that natural evil is a logical necessity. He writes:

> Some overall vision of the 'responsiveness' and 'resistance' of creation to the Spirit of God is needed for a doctrine of creative evolution, for a proper theodicy, and certainly for the claim . . . that God suffers conflict with a non-being which is alien to him. It may be that process thought is pointing in a direction whose destination we do not yet have the conceptual tools to map.[11]

For Fiddes the resistance is not logically necessary, nor is it malevolent, but it is inevitable.[12] One could place here also process theologians and others influenced by process thought such as John Haught.

---

9. Nicola Hoggard Creegan, 'Theodicy: A Response to Christopher Southgate', in *Zygon*, 53/3 (2018): 808–820.

10. Christopher Southgate, 'Response with a Select Bibliography', in *Zygon* 53(3) (2018):909–930.

11. Paul S Fiddes, *The Creative Suffering of God* (Oxford: Clarendon Press, 1991), 228.

12. 'Not necessary but inevitable' is also a formulation to which Deane-Drummond is attracted, see 'Perceiving'.

At the far end of this spectrum of positions would be *a forthright acceptance that the world unfolding through the processes of Darwinian evolution is the world God intended to make.* The evolutionary theologian has a choice here. Is this decision of God's an unconstrained decision to create disvalue along with value? That would drive the interpreter of creation back towards an appeal to mystery, though also to texts in the Hebrew Bible such as 'See now that I, even I, am he; there is no god besides me. I kill and I make alive; I wound and I heal; and no one can deliver from my hand.' (Deut 32:39), 'The Lord kills and brings to life; he brings down to Sheol and raises up.' (1 Sam 2:6) and Deutero-Isaiah's description of God as the author of 'weal and woe alike' (Isa 45:7).

It is at least worth considering whether centuries of philosophical reflection on the doctrine of God have taken Christian thought too far from these formulations. They survive within liturgy in protest and lament after disaster, as I have recently explored.[13] They survive in a depersonalised form in the influential and persuasive thought of Wesley Wildman, with his appeal to an interreligious understanding of God as the (non-personal) ground of being.[14]

But for those who want to regard God as both 'not less than personal', in Philip Clayton's phrase,[15] and benevolent towards God's creatures (caring for every sparrow that falls, to use an image beloved of Denis Edwards[16]), the presumption must be that God's creation of disvalues results from an intrinsic constraint as to the field of possibilities in creation. Such a view would hold that if God could have created an alternative world with a balance of value against disvalue (actual or potential) tilted more in favour of value, God would have done so. Robin Attfield concludes that there is no evidence that such

---

13. Christopher Southgate, 'In spite of all this, we will yearn for you' in *Tragedies and Christian Congregations: The Practical Theology of Trauma,* edited by Megan Warner, Christopher Southgate, Carla A Grosch-Miller and Hilary Ison (London: Routledge, 2020), chapter 7.

14. Wesley J Wildman, *In our own Image: Anthropomorphism, Apophaticism and Ultimacy* (Oxford: Oxford University Press, 2017).

15. Philip Clayton, and Steven Knapp, *The Predicament of Belief: Science, Philosophy, Faith* (Oxford: Oxford University Press, 2011), 22.

16. Denis Edwards, 'Every Sparrow that Falls: The Cost of Evolution and the Christ-Event', in *Ecotheology,* 11/1 (2006): 103–123.

an alternative world exists.[17] Robert John Russell is concerned that it might, and therein lies his concern about putting too much weight on the 'only way' argument'—that the evolutionary process was the only, or at least the optimal, way to give rise to the array of values we observe in the world (including those past values now disappeared).[18] But this concern of Russell's seems to me to underrate the force of the argument from God's benevolence.

Two other formulations of fallenness should be noted at this point. Ernst Conradie in his careful and ecologically aware explorations of the doctrine of sin explores the possibility of a 'minimalist' version of the Fall. He writes of a position that would hold that:

> things may not be perfect, but that this is the best that could be expected. This is a modification of Leibniz's best of all possible worlds argument, now framed in evolutionary history as an upward trajectory from brutish savages to civilised common humanity. While this view is quite common, it does not exclude a critique of the present in the sense that moral progress could have been further advanced than it is.[19]

This for Conradie would be the minimum basis for a discussion of the way the world is. Note the careful language—things could have been better than they now are.

Where Did Nature Go Wrong?

Compare Conradie with Ted Peters in a response to my recent reflections on divine glory. Peters says this:

> The more coherent route, in my judgment, is the one taken by [those] . . . who synthesize creation with redemption. Accordingly, the suffering we see in the disvaluing of evolutionary processes are signs of the world's alienation, estrangement, fallenness. One need not locate Adam and Eve in biological history to recognize that the world within

---

17. Robin Attfield, *Creation, Evolution and Meaning* (Aldershot: Ashgate, 2006), chapter 7.
18. Robert J Russell, 'Southgate's Compound Only-Way Evolutionary Theodicy: Deep Appreciation and Further Directions', in *Zygon* 53/3 (2018): 711–726.
19. Ernst Conradie, unpublished paper, quoted with permission.

which we live is not the creation promised in biblical symbols such as the Peaceable Kingdom or the New Creation. What is broken needs repair. What is alien needs to be brought home. What is estranged needs to be reconciled. What hurts needs to be healed. Only when redeemed, will our world be created.[20]

Note the language here: alienation, estrangement, brokenness—familiar imagery to describe the view not just that 'things could be better than they are' but that 'the world is broken'.

Against Peters, I contend that the creation as it has evolved over billions of years has been full of values of actual or potential beauty, creativity and ingenuity, full too of creaturely flourishing, accompanied by the competition, suffering and extinction that *necessarily* accompanies those values in a Darwinian world. *Much about the human world has 'gone wrong' and manifested alienation, estrangement and brokenness, but the non-human world, while it manifests great disvalue in the form of creaturely suffering and extinction, does not manifest alienation or brokenness, except where humans have begun to inflict irreversible damage upon it.*

This view, then, supposes that there is a decisive difference between self-conscious, freely-chosen acts of selfishness, violence, and cruelty, humans knowing the right and choosing to resist it, and the instinctive behaviours of other animals. So the classic single-act version of original sin can be modified to suggest that the multiplication of those conscious wrongs over time acts as a cumulative drag on the human spirit. Has the Fall thereby returned to the centre of the narrative? No, because this accumulation of human choices develops only towards the very end of the history of the natural world up to the present, and does not affect the fundamental character of that world.

Peters however slips into that so tempting view that the disvalues in evolution show that something went wrong with the divine plan, and he calls as witnesses Barth's *Nichtige* and Tillich's 'resistance of non-being'.[21] I note above that it is not clear what these resistances amount to, but if they are powerful enough to frustrate God's plan they pose severe problems for the Christian confession of a God who made absolutely everything out of absolutely nothing. Denis

---

20. Ted Peters, 'Evolution, Suffering and Redemption: Sollereder, Southgate, and Russell on Theodicy', in *Theology and Science*, 17/2 (2019): 195–208.

21. Ted Peters, personal communication.

Edwards' own instincts are I believe more secure here. He writes: 'The divine act of creation can be understood as an act of love, by which the trinitarian Persons freely make space for creation *and freely accept the limits of the process*.'[22]

This is a very important formulation, freeing us as it does both from the picture of God frustrated at not being able to create straw-eating lions,[23] and the cosmic-sadist caricatures of the God of evolution offered by atheist commentators.[24]

The Fall-Free Account

Nevertheless Peters identifies a key point. The most important challenge for new formulations of evolutionary theology is not to try and rescue some form of 'mysterious fallenness' to account for the apparent 'alienation' of the natural world, but rather to look at the Christian narrative afresh on the basis that this is indeed the sort of world God intended to create. How then is the drama of redemption to be set in register with that understanding of creation? I believe that that is the sort of quest Denis Edwards would have strongly endorsed and I am glad to be pursuing it in his memory.

In a review of my recent work, Jonathan Chappel comments that:

> [t[he fact that creation requires 'redemption' surely undermines Southgate's claim that the world as we see it now is as God originally intended it to be. For, if nothing has ever 'gone wrong' with creation, why does it need Christ to 'redeem' it? Is Christ 'saving' the world from the negative consequences of the system that He (as God) originally put in place? And why should humans strive to act in non-violent ways, when the use of violence has been sanctioned by God Himself?[25]

22. Edwards, *God of Evolution*, 41–42, italics mine.
23. Christopher Southgate, 'Re-reading Genesis, John and Job: a Christian's response to Darwinism', in *Zygon* 46/2 (2011): 370–395.
24. For example David L Hull in 'The God of the Galapagos', calling the God of evolution 'careless, wasteful, indifferent, almost diabolical', in *Nature* 352 (August 1992): 485–486.
25. Jonathan Chappel, 'Review of *Theology in a Suffering World: Glory and Longing*', in *Science and Christian Belief*, 31/2 (2019): 213–216, quotation on 215.

Here we see well expressed the other aspect of the work that Fall-events do in so much Christian theology. Not only do they give accounts of a world apparently alienated from God, but they also explain the necessity of the rescue act that God performs in the Incarnation, Cross and Resurrection of Christ. So a necessary element of a 'fall-free' theology is a different type of formulation of the whole Christian narrative.

On a fall-event-based scheme, sin and evil frustrate God's attempt to create heaven (as symbolised by the myth of Eden). Jesus' death and resurrection, by one of the mechanisms postulated in centuries of reflection on the atonement, breaks the opposing power and makes possible the reconciliation of all things (Col 1:20). On a fall-free scheme, in which God creates, under constraint, the only sort of world capable of realising the values God desires, a world that is not 'broken', it is harder at first sight to see what work the Christ-event is doing.

On this I take the view, which goes back at least to the twelfth century,[26] that the Incarnation can be thought of not as a rescue act of a wholly corrupted world but as planned by God from 'before the foundation of the world' (*cf* Rev 13:8) to make possible a new stage in the unfolding of the divine plan. The exact role of Christ's atoning work on the Cross remains an area of major debate.[27] But my approach finds a place for two profoundly important models. First for Christ's example of utterly free human action, free because unconstrained by anything but the paths of love, and therefore truly 'the image of God' (2 Cor 4:4), as the model for all human growth into freedom. Second, for Christ's Cross and Resurrection as the triumph over 'the powers' (Rom 8:38; Col 1:16; Eph 6:12), or 'Sin' (Rom 3:9; 5:21), which derive their influence over human action precisely from myriad un-free choices made by human beings over the millennia.[28]

---

26. So Marilyn McCord Adams, *Christ and Horrors: the coherence of Christology* (Cambridge: Cambridge University Press, 2006), chapter 7.

27. Importantly added to by Eleanore Stump, *Atonement* (Oxford: Oxford University Press, 2018).

28. I would also want to include a sense of God's taking personal, and infinitely costly, responsibility for the disvalues in creation. See Southgate, *Groaning*, chapter 4, and Frances Young, *God's Presence: A Contemporary Recapitulation of Early Christianity* (Cambridge: Cambridge University Press, 2013), 247.

Such a new formulation is also needed to answer what Robert Russell, writing about my compound theodicy, identifies as the most difficult and underexplored question raised by my approach, 'why did God not just create heaven?'[29] If God can give rise, eventually, to a reconciled and suffering-free creation, why did God not simply do so without the need for myriad instances of creaturely suffering? And as Russell and I both acknowledge,[30] there is a danger of such a scheme as mine seeming 'broken-backed', indeed crypto-Gnostic, in that the first creation is seen as flawed, such that it needs to be escaped from into a heavenly realm of existence.[31] This is precisely what the early Christian theologians sought to reject in their insistence on a 'very good' creation *ex nihilo*, and, as the logical culmination of that position, original sin as the source of all disvalue.

Russell picks up on my response to this problem, which is that 'our guess must be that though heaven can eternally preserve those [creaturely] selves, subsisting in suffering-free relationship, it could not give rise to them in the first place'.[32] In other words, the 'only way' argument needs to be boldly extended. An *eventual* reconciled cosmos required the era of struggle and suffering that is the first or 'old' creation, in order that it might give rise to the creaturely selves that can undergo transformation.

Russell refers to this as 'the "heaven requires earth" argument' and continues:

> I believe it is an *essential*, and not just an ancillary, argument to Southgate's overall theodicy . . . with this new element, Southgate's theodicy insists that 'heaven and earth' are held together as the domain of God's creating and redeeming Spirit in which 'all will be well.' . . . 'Heaven requires earth' is, as best I know, an almost unique insight in the field of natural theodicy, and in natural and moral theodicy as a whole. It's extraordinarily profound yet utterly simple claim is, to me at least, astonishing, liberating, and compelling . . . I suggest . . . the seventh argument 'heaven requires earth' brings a deeper,

29. Robert J Russell, 'Moving ahead on Christopher Southgate's Evolutionary Theodicy', in *Theology and Science* 17/2 (2019): 185–194.
30. Russell, 'Moving Ahead'; Christopher Southgate, *Theology in a Suffering World: Glory and Longing* (Cambridge: Cambridge University Press, 2018),
31. Russell' 'Moving Ahead'.
32. Southgate, *Groaning*, 90.

more satisfying, and coherent completion to Southgate's 'only way' approach to evolutionary theodicy . . .[33]

Another aspect of this extension of the 'only way' argument is that one of the values that (it may be presumed) God desires the old creation to possess is 'redeemability'.[34] The evolved world has to be such that an event starting with an incarnation of the divine Word could inaugurate a process of transformation leading to a new creation in which God 'will be all in all' (1 Cor 15:28).

Given the difficulty of formulating an account of the *origins* of disvalue in the natural world, it is not surprising that a range of figures emphasise instead eschatology, God's ultimate redemptive purposes for this world. Four examples (differently motivated) are Russell;[35] Peters;[36] Edwards;[37] and Messer.[38]

The Eschatological Component

Here again we can see a range of views of the transition by which God will give rise to the eschaton. There would be those who would emphasise the apocalyptic passages in the New Testament (especially in the Synoptics and Revelation) to insist that God's consummating action, God's final struggle with the powers leading the Last Judgment, will be sudden and soon. A period of terrible and bitter struggle gives way rapidly to the Parousia. The opposite emphasis would be found in those process thinkers who see the long persuasive work of God on the panpsychic flow of events in the universe as stretching out

---

33. Russell, 'Moving Ahead'.
34. Robert J Russell, *Cosmology: from alpha to omega* (Minneapolis, MN: Fortress Press, 2008), 308.
35. On the basis that only eschatological redemption can guarantee a satisfactory theodicy. Russell, *Cosmology*, chapter 8.
36. Out of his sense of the ontological priority of the future, see Ted Peters, *God: The World's Future*, 3rd edition (Minneapolis, MN: Fortress Press, 2015).
37. Because of his very strong sense of the compassion of God for all creatures. Edwards, 'Every Sparrow'.
38. I include him because he emphasises the eschatological vision of Isa 11 as indicative of the true purposes of God, and therefore rejects any view in which God is the author of violence within creation. Neil Messer, 'Natural Evil after Darwin' in *Theology after Darwin* edited Michael Northcott and RJ Berry (Carlisle: Paternoster Press, 2009), 139–154.

into the future with no dramatic transformation at all, perhaps not even any guarantee of the ultimate triumph of good over evil. John Haught has eloquently combined insights from process thought with the influence of Teilhard de Chardin in insisting that it is early days in the universe project. No dramatic transformation is in immediate view, only the slow outworking of the divine purpose towards a greater 'rightness'. Haught writes,

> Theologically speaking, creation is still awakening—haltingly and not without setbacks—to rightness. The newly emergent sensitivity to life's suffering . . . is all part of a single narrative of cosmic awakening. This recent conscious awakening to rightness must be taken into account whenever we ask what the universe is really all about.[39]

For Russell, as also for John Polkinghorne, the transformation to a final harmonious state must be radical, because it involves the instantiation of new laws of nature, or a new destiny for matter (of which the Resurrection of Jesus may be seen as the prolepsis).[40] Working as much from the considerations of physics as of theology, they argue that the transformation will involve profound elements of discontinuity with the present ordering of the universe.[41] Russell has laid particular stress on the second law of thermodynamics as the physical principle that would need to be transformed if there is to be a state from which all struggle has been eliminated. In an analogous way Jürgen Moltmann has argued that evolution must stand in need of redeeming transformation, explicitly criticising both Teilhard and Rahner for supposing that evolutionary processes can lead to the eschaton.[42]

Gradual Transformation

Denis Edwards, following Rahner rather than Moltmann, wants to insist that the divine transformation of the cosmos will be as

---

39. John Haught, 'Faith and Compassion in an Unfinished Universe', in *Zygon* 53/3 (2018): 782–791, quotation on 789.
40. Russell, *Cosmology*, chapters 9–10; John Polkinghorne, *The God of Hope and the End of the World* (London: SPCK, 2002).
41. See for example Russell, Cosmology, chapter 10.
42. Jürgen Moltmann, *The Way of Jesus Christ: Christology in Messianic Dimensions* translated by Margaret Kohl (London: SCM Press, 1990), 292–305.

gradual as possible.[43] This I take to be because of Edwards' emphasis (characteristic of an ecotheologian as opposed to a theologian of physics) on the immanent presence of God in the world, informing all its processes, also perhaps because of his desire to retain an evolutionary unity to the overall narrative.

My own position wants to combine different elements from across this spectrum of views. On the one hand, my scientific training tells me that Russell and Polkinghorne must be correct that the ultimate transformation of the fabric of the universe must be a radical one. On the other hand Edwards must be right in insisting that this transformation is not wrought by a God who is altogether 'outside' the cosmos, but rather by a God who immanently empowers its processes while all the while longing for the time when this immanence will acquire a new dimension—God 'all in all'.

Haught is right to stress, with process thinkers, the long patience of God as the universe unfolds. And I have sympathy too with the much-criticised thought of Teilhard when he pictures a 'noösphere' in which human intelligence floods the world and is everywhere influential, as the penultimate state of the creation.[44] The terrible current consequences of this extent of human influence, dramatically illustrated by plastic in the oceans and the intensification of hurricanes and forest fires by anthropogenic climate change, need no elaboration here. But I have long been struck by St Paul's extraordinary insight in Romans 8:19–22, that the current state of the creation, groaning in the labour pains of the birthing of something beyond the present, awaits 'the freedom of the glory of the children of God' (v 21 NRSV).

This can be read as suggesting that the interim phase in the eschatological redemption of all things, the phase preceding the final radical transformation involving the laws of physics themselves, is a phase most to do with the transformation of the human spirit, the discovery in human beings of what true freedom consists of. For that the non-human creation is made to wait.

So for all the importance of the 'deep incarnation movement', starting with the work of Niels Gregersen and taken forward by

---

43. Denis Edwards, *How God Acts: Creation, Redemption and Special Divine Action* (Minneapolis, MN: Fortress Press, 2010), 155–159.
44. I bracket out considerations of extra-terrestrial civilisations and their possible need for redemption. As we still lack any evidence that these exist, I frame my theology for the present in terms of what we do know about the cosmos.

Denis Edwards in his last writings—for all the importance of Christ's identification with 'all flesh', indeed all matter—the crucial influence of incarnation and atonement on the Christian narrative proves to be on human beings. A fine and precious thread of authentic, Christ-like freedom is offered whereby humans can be led out of the labyrinth of limit, guilt and shame that has so characterised human experience.[45]

This is, as Edwards has so importantly emphasised, the work not of some magical-miracle-working external God, but of the immanent Spirit. Here I am able to make a link with Denis' most recent writing. It is gratifying that his 'theological response' (rather than 'theodicy') in respect of the problem of evolution includes many of the same elements as mine. And when Denis demurs from the 'only way' argument as the first step in the construction of an evolutionary theodicy, he makes in effect the same step as I make in my most recent reflection on the subject, admitting a greater element of negative theology into the response to suffering, and therefore making a less bold theodical response.[46] I agree with Denis moreover that the heart of the human vocation in Spirit-given freedom must be that '[h]uman beings are called to participate in God's love and action towards the wider creation in an ecological commitment to the healing and flourishing of the planetary community of life'.[47] The terrible urgency of this is now all too clear, and tragically evident in Denis' own land of Australia, in the grip as I write this of catastrophic mega-fires.

Conclusion

To summarise, then, the shape of this Christian story in dialogue with evolution is as follows: There have been three great phases in God's action in the world. First, the creating, sustaining, and protecting from ultimate catastrophe of the 'old creation', which operates with the physical laws with which we are familiar, and the biological process of Darwinian evolution. Among the products of this process are self-conscious freely-choosing organisms with an (admittedly flawed) God-consciousness, *Homo Sapiens Sapiens*. Humans, evolving in a

---

45. *Cf* Paul S Fiddes, *Freedom and Limit: a dialogue between literature and Christian doctrine* (Basingstoke: Palgrave Macmillan, 1991); also Stump, *Atonement*.
46. Christopher Southgate, *Theology in a Suffering World*, 3–4.
47. Edwards, *Deep Incarnation*.

vastly long (and necessary) evolutionary process, and inheriting from their evolution a mixture of drives including both the altruistic and the cruel, violent and selfish, could have their freedom of will brought to authentic fruition only by the second of God's great actions.

In this, God offered out of pure self-giving love the perfect example of the Incarnate Son. That example, and the Son's victory, through pure persistence in his Passion and divine deliverance in his Resurrection, over the powers of sin and death, transforms the scope of human possibility. However, the transformation of the world, though profound, is not immediately apparent. The processes of the old creation go on. Christ's victory has to grow 'soul by soul and silently' in the long process by which the intensified immanence of the Spirit[48] works with human wills to make that authentic freedom a reality. And that enigmatic Pauline passage from Romans 8 on which I have drawn suggests that, for whatever reason in the mystery of the divine economy, the radical transformation of the cosmos by which it will attain its final harmonious state, awaits this human growth into freedom, 'the freedom of the glory of the children of God'.

Only then, so this model supposes, will come the third great action of God, the radical transformation of the physical universe, some laws retained and others, such as the second law of thermodynamics, suspended, such that (resurrected) bodily existence is possible without suffering or struggle. In this final state God is present to creatures in a yet more intense way, but without depriving them of individuality.

Note that the second phase is impossible without the first, and the third without the second. This is a narrative without a human fall from perfection as the source of all creaturely suffering. But I suggest that it is at least as consistent with Scripture and reason as the classic U-shaped evangel of the Western tradition. It belongs within a family of such positions to which Denis Edwards' work has been and will continue to be a distinguished contribution. I am deeply thankful to have known him.

---

48. Made possible by the Christ-event, and by the Resurrection and Ascension, *cf* Jn 16:7.

Deep Incarnation:
from the Hypostatic Union to the Universe
in the Image of the *Image*

Alexei V Nesteruk

'At the centre of this theology is the Christian claim that the resurrection of Jesus Christ is the promise and the beginning of the final healing and divinisation of the whole of creation.'[1]
– Denis Edwards

Abstract: This paper offers four critiques of the idea of *Deep Incarnation* in Denis Edwards and others from an Eastern Orthodox Christian perspective. 1) Because of the vast and causally disconnected structure of the universe, humanity at best is consubstantial to the four per cent of matter in the *visible* universe so that the claims for the relevance of the historical Incarnation to the whole creation are not plausible. 2) By *de facto* equating the transfigured flesh of Christ (through the hypostatic union), with the rest of creation, thus depriving the process of deification of the human person and transfiguration of the *visible* universe of its temporal dimension, deep incarnation goes contrary to the Orthodox stance on deification as a personal endeavour not implanted into the logic of the natural world. 3) Deep incarnation is a trivial statement if it would concern only the necessary conditions for the historical Incarnation, which are cosmological. 4) More positively, the idea of deep incarnation can be treated as contributing to the old *makroanthropos* idea, related to humanity as a mediating agency between divisions within creation and between creation and God. Humanity remains the centre of disclosure and manifestation of the universe, being hypostasis of the universe imitating the incarnate Logos-Christ hypostatic union.

Key words: Christ, cosmology, creation, humanity, hypostasis, incarnation, Logos, mediator, theology, universe.

---

1. Denis Edwards, *The Natural World and God: Theological Explorations* (Adelaide, SA: ATF Press, 2017) 150.

The idea of deep incarnation so attractive to Roman Catholics and Lutherans is off-putting to an Eastern Orthodox theologian. Why? I will answer this question in what follows.

Deep Incarnation Christology according to Denis Edwards

In his last book titled *Deep Incarnation. God's redemptive suffering with creatures*,[2] Denis Edwards provides a systematic account of the recent theological developments in the field of Christology under the name 'Deep Incarnation'. Edwards links deep incarnation with the Patristic heritage of Irenaeus of Lyons and Athanasius of Alexandria, as well as with the Christology of Karl Rahner. One of Edwards's major preoccupations in deep incarnation is described by him as a necessity of further development of Christian ecological theology, namely by extending the scope of the Western theology of redemption towards non-human realms of the world, the universe in its entirety, so that 'faithful to the biblical promises of a new heavens and new earth, salvation can be seen to involve the whole creation'.[3]

Edwards' second point is related to the recent advance in understanding that the biological evolution on this planet involved an incredible loss, pain and death, leading to the question 'How can we think of the good, generous and loving God of biblical faith in relationship to the costs of evolution?'[4]. This question, according to Edwards and some other contemporary theologians, attempts to relate the event of the historical Incarnation of God in Jesus of Nazareth to the general entrance of God in the material conditions of the physical world. Roman Catholic Edwards follows Lutheran Niels Henrik Gregersen by adopting the language of deep incarnation, meaning that the Incarnation of God in human flesh of Jesus Christ entailed a certain subordination of all natural creation to the conditions of its very possibility.[5]

The Cross in this view is identified with creation in its evolutionary emergence, 'and as an icon an microcosm of God's redemptive presence

---

2. Denis Edwards, *Deep Incarnation: God's Redemptive Suffering with Creatures* (Maryknoll, NY: Orbis Books, 2019).

3. Edwards, *Deep Incarnation*, xvi.

4. Edwards, *Deep Incarnation*, xvii.

5. Niels Henrik Gregersen, 'Deep Incarnation: Why Evolutionary Continuity Matters in Christology', in *Toronto Journal of Theology*, 26/2 (Fall 2010): 173–187.

to all creatures in their suffering and death'.[6] Thus the fundamental alteration in the order of nature effected in the Easter Resurrection of Christ (impossible without the Incarnation), being an initial step in transfiguration of the universe, is efficacious for the whole creation.

In the final chapter of his book Edwards gives his own contribution to the theology of deep incarnation by formulating five theological positions, one of which we are going to discuss in this paper. This position claims that cosmic, evolutionary, and ecological relationships are constitutive of the Word made flesh, and that the Incarnation, being a transcendent *event* related to the Divine-human relationship, was nevertheless prepared by the whole development of the physical universe and biological evolution on this planet. We undertake a reflection upon this Edwards' stance on deep incarnation, in conjunction with other modern and Patristic views, with a purpose of providing an Eastern Orthodox theological, philosophical and scientific assessments of some of his and others' ideas.

An Eastern Orthodox Theological Narrative of the Incarnation, and Deep Incarnation

Christology in virtually every Christian tradition considers the historical event of the Incarnation of the second person of the Holy Trinity, the eternal Word-Logos of God in Jesus of Nazareth in whom the Word 'became flesh' for the purpose of salvation of humanity, as a primary and fundamental phenomenon laid in the foundation of all further theological developments in understanding the sense of human life and its destiny in the universe.

The Incarnation meant the union between the Divine and the created in the hypostasis of the Logos of God: Jesus Christ was fully divine as 'the Son of God, the only-begotten of the Father, begotten before all ages' and fully human ('and was made man'). The phrase 'begotten before all ages' implies that from eternity the Logos was prepared to become incarnate in humankind meaning that the humanity of Jesus was forever the part of God's way of existence. The latter assertion points towards the connection between creation and the Incarnation, where the Incarnation becomes implanted into the logic of the creation aiming to bring the world to union with God.

---

6. Edwards, *Deep Incarnation*, xviii.

According to Maximus the Confessor the creation of the world contained the goal for which all things were created: 'For it is for Christ, that is, for the Christic mystery, that all time and all that is in time has received in Christ its beginning and its end.'[7]

By linking the motive of the Incarnation to the logic of creation, Orthodox theology extends the scope of the Incarnation beyond the opposition Fall-Redemption, towards a wider span in the plan of salvation related to the deification of humankind and bringing the whole creation to the union with God. The lesser arch of the Fall-Redemption becomes a tool in restoring the greater arch Creation-Deification.[8] If the world was created in order to attain the union with God, it is humanity which is granted the means of such an attainment through a special call. The possibility of such an attainment effectively contributes to the definition of the human: only in communion with God the human becomes 'himself' or 'herself'.[9] In this sense the human, in spite of being consubstantial to the *visible* creation,[10] is a special creation whose essence requires *grace*, the mechanism of acquiring of which proceeds through the Incarnation.

The integrity of the human commitment to acquisition of grace and transfiguration of the world was expressed by Maximus the Confessor advocating the mediating role of the human being in overcoming the moral tensions between different parts of creation[11], including, one can suggest, different biological species as well as, may be, inorganic creation. 'Man [sic] is the "microcosm" who sums up, condenses, recapitulates in himself the degrees of the created being and because of this he can know the universe from the inside.'[12] Correspondingly,

---

7.   Maximus the Confessor, *Questions to Thalassius*, 60.
8.   A Louth, 'The place of *Theosis* in Orthodox theology', in *Partakes of the Divine Nature: The History and Development of Deification in the Christian Traditions*, MJ Christensen and JA Wittung (Madison: Fairleigh Dickinson University Press), 34–35.
9.   J Zizioulas, *Communion and Otherness* (London: T&T Clark, 2006), 248.
10. One cannot affirm any link of humanity with the ninety-six per cent of the matter of the universe (Dark Energy and Dark Matter) which is not physically consubstantial to the terrestrial environment.
11. See, for example, L Thunberg, *Microcosm and Mediator: The Theological Anthropology of Maximus the Confessor* (Chicago: Open Court, 1995), 387–427.
12. O Clément, 'Le sense de la terre' *Le Christ terre des vivants. Essais théologiques. spiritualite orientale*, n 17, (Bégrolles-en-Mauges: Abbaye de Bellfontaine, 1976), 90; see also his *On Human Being. A Spiritual Anthropology* (London: New City Press, 2000), 109.

if God's plan 'consists in deification of the created world' (some parts of which require salvation), its plausibility is rooted in the conviction that the human person is ontologically united (that is consubstantial) with the created nature. Correspondingly the human person is created propensities placed in the framework of his Divine image would be sufficient to transfer the aim of creation, revealed through the Incarnation, to those parts of creation, including organic and inorganic creatures, which need salvation. Maximus the Confessor refers to the human created in the image of God as a key to understanding creation in the process of divinisation when the human person may elevate it to the supreme level of its full soteriological comprehension, so that the universe is called to become the 'image of the image'.[13] Since the historical Incarnation recapitulates the visible universe on the level of *consubstantiality*, its proper sense can be directly related to the constitution and meaning of the cosmos.[14] The existence of Earth and human beings allows one to claim that the *necessary* conditions for the Incarnation are fulfilled in the entire *visible* cosmos.

However, the movement from creation to deification through the Incarnation is not a 'natural process' inherent in the fabric of creation. Created things participate in God through the fact of their existence, that is through 'being in communion'. However, when Maximus enquires in the human capacity of deification, he stresses that it does not belong to the human's natural capacity.[15] This is the reason why Maximus claims that the aeon after the Incarnation corresponds to a contrary movement of the human being to God, whose very possibility was effected by the Incarnation. By separating the aeons before and after the Incarnation Maximus makes a difference between the participation in God which is bestowed to the man being by creation and that participation which is bestowed by deification. The

---

13. As was expressed by O Clément, 'The indefinitiveness of the world is . . . situated in sanctified humanity and becomes the symbol of the "deep calling the deep"', *On Human Being*, 111. Discussing the sense of human person Vladimir Lossky describes it as if 'each human person can be considered as hypostasis of common nature, an *hypostasis of the whole of the created cosmos* or, more accurately, of earthly creation' (V Lossky, In the Image and Likeness of God (Crestwood: St Vladimir's Seminary Press, 1985), 188 (emphasis added)).

14. See, for example, L Thunberg, *Man and the Cosmos* (Crestwood: St Vladimir's Seminary Press. 1985), 76 referring to Maximus' *Questions to Thalassius 35*.

15. Maximus the Confessor, *Ambigua 20* [ET: Constas, 411].

latter requires *grace* which is not implanted in the natural conditions of existence, but which is bestowed by God on the grounds of the human being's personal extent of perfection.[16] This grace can be acquired by the man being and used for the transfiguration of the universe, including all other life forms and inorganic matter.

The Incarnation aims to link the Divine with the created. How this can be understood philosophically: what is the meaning of the union between two non-consubstantial essences? Theology, based on ideas of pre-Christian philosophy, makes a distinction between essence and hypostasis in Christ, where the latter, after the Council of Chalcedon is associated with the personhood of the Logos of God. If the Logos creates the world, whose essence is different in comparison with that of the Logos himself (but the world yet is linked to the Logos as its creator), this can only mean that the Logos as Hypostasis (Person) enhypostasises the world, that is the shape of the world which is non-consubstantial to the essence of the Logos, is determined by the volitions and intentions of the Logos as Hypostasis. In this sense to express the Divine presence in the world is equal to say that the world is dependent upon God and exists only in the Hypostasis of the Logos. The world itself is not hypostatic, but is enhypostasised.[17]

Seen in this perspective the body of Jesus of Nazareth, as part of created world, was also enhypostasised by the Logos. But the crucial difference with all other human beings whose bodies and whose created hypostases have been also enhypostasised by the Logos is that the hypostasis of Jesus Christ, was the uncreated Hypostasis of the Logos. In this sense the link between the Divine and human natures in Christ was only *hypostatic* and uncreated, whereas for ordinary human beings and all other creatures, their link with the Divine was only *en-hypostatic*. When theology affirms the Divine image in the

---

16. L Thunberg, with reference to Maximus, asserts: 'There is in man [sic] no natural power that can deify him, but there exists on the other hand a reciprocal relationship between God and man that permits him to become deified to the degree in which the effects of the Incarnation are conferred on him' (Thunberg, *Man and the Cosmos*, 55).

17. See details in A Nesteruk, 'The Universe as Hypostatic Inherence in the Logos of God. Panentheism in the Eastern Orthodox Perspective', in *In Whom We Live and Move and Have Our Being: Reflections on Panentheism in a Scientific Age*, edited by Philip Clayton and Arthur Peacocke (Grand Rapids, MI: Eerdmans, 2004), 169–183.

human person, it effectively asserts that the *enhypostatic hypostasis* in the human being, is the image of the uncreated Hypostasis of the Logos. Correspondingly, the human flesh as well as human intelligence in the Incarnate Logos-Christ was brought to communion with God in the already deified manner, when the flesh of Christ, being fully human and not confused with the Divine nature, was already transfigured by the Logos-Christ. Shortly, the flesh of Christ, being in a hypostatic union with God, and in the conditions of removing of all moral tensions between the created and its creator, is not exactly the same flesh of the world which exists enhyposatically through being created by God. Since, according to Maximus the Confessor, the divine embodiment and human deification in Christ necessarily take place at the same time, so that deification is simply the other side of the Incarnation, one rather speaks of the flesh which is deified. If in Christ this is effected through the Incarnation of the Logos and the mediation between creation and God effected in his ascension to the Father, for human beings, a deification and transfiguration of their flesh is still a task which never ceases to be applicable and which covers the whole of human existence and the whole of creation, but in potentiality.

Then the question, which arises in the context of the idea of deep incarnation, is whether this transfigured flesh of Christ can be somehow linked to the flesh of the rest of the world in order to claim that Christ's incarnation is efficacious for the whole creation (not through an enhypostatic creation by the Logos) as an already transfigured by this Logos.

In other words, can one claim that the transfiguration of flesh through the historical Incarnation in Jesus Christ could be 'transferred' to the whole universe? Seen in this perspective, the idea of deep incarnation attempts to remove the process of deification or transfiguration of all created matter as extended in time to the already accomplished fact legitimising the incomprehensibility of the human physical existence in the universe, all injustice and pain of its and other creatures' suffering, as already being transfigured (and hence redeemed). Philosophically and scientifically, if the human beings exercise their limited capacity to comprehend things logically and reasonably, the incommensurable scales of the empty and hostile universe create a serious doubt with respect to the deep incarnation's implicit suggestion that its structure is related to the already transfigured consubstantial flesh of Christ.

Modern scientific cosmology, accentuating the extent of the physical insignificance of humanity in the universe contributes, according to our view, to a further theological insistence on the necessity to renormalise the human view of the universe, as extended and disconnected in space and time, through the process of *personal deification* when the human being will be able to achieve the state of its flesh transfigured to the same extent as it was in the Incarnation of Christ and hence to 'see; the universe through the eyes of the Logos-Christ as 'all in all' (Eph 4:6) of good creation by the good God. In this sense the idea of deep incarnation can be justified by assigning to it an eschatological sense related to the Divine task given to humanity to transfigure the whole creation and thus to bring all its parts (human, organic non-human, inorganic) to union with God by imitating Christ in his Resurrection and his Ascension.

The crucial difference between humanity and all non-human creatures is that humanity is gifted with the capacity of imitating the hypostatic union in the Logos-Christ and employ it for the transfiguration of the whole created world whereas the non-human (and hence non-hypostatic) forms of existence can receive communion with the Hypostasis of the Logos only through the human being. This is the reason why Maximus the Confessor asserted the world not as micro-Logos, but *macro-anthropos* (a human enlarged), that is as the image of the anthropos ('image of the image'[18]) as that a world which acquires the features of humanity constantly effecting its own incarnation, for example through knowledge of the universe and all organic and inorganic nature in the image of the Logos made flesh.[19]

Cosmological Assessment of the Idea of Deep Incarnation: Can the Unity of Creation and Critique of Anthropocentrism be Sustained?

In order to make a transition to the cosmological implications of the idea of deep incarnation, one has to look at the event of the historical

---

18. Cf Gergory of Nyssa, *On the Making of Man*, 12.
19. Maximus the Confessor, *Mystagogy*, 7.

Incarnation from the point of view of its intrinsic presence in the concept of creation of the world.

It was in early Patristic times that Origen and Athanasius of Alexandria first reflected upon a certain topological paradox which appears if one treats the Incarnation as the descend of God in the midst of the world. On the one hand the Logos assumed human flesh and was in the conditions of space and time, on the other hand, as God, He was on the right of the Father and thus present hypostatically in the whole universe since the latter was created by Him and through Him. Here an analogy with the hypostatic union of the two natures in Christ can be used. Indeed, it is because of the hypostatic union between the divine and the natural (human) in Christ that one can argue that the interplay between the space and time of the universe and its uncreated ground is also upheld hypostatically by God in the course of his 'economy' in relation to the world. The fulfilment of this economy took place in the eternal anticipation of the Incarnation when the link between the humanity of Christ (in space) and his divinity as the Logos (beyond space) was established at the 'beginning' of the world. Thus the universe in its spatio-temporal extension manifests its Christologically specific hypostatic inherence in the Logos.

As was expressed by TF Torrance: 'The world, then is made open to God through its intersection in the axis Creation-Incarnation.'[20] Torrance goes even further suggesting that the space-time extension of the universe as a whole is relational upon the Logos' enhypostatic presence in this universe and the Logos' hypostatic presence in Christ (in a way similar to the relationality between space-time and matter in General Relativity). He writes:

> The interaction of God with us in the space and time of this world sets up . . . a coordinate system between two horizontal dimensions, space and time, and one vertical dimension, relation to God through His Spirit. This constitutes the theological field of connections in and through Jesus Christ who cannot be thought of simply as fitting into the patterns of

20. TF Torrance, *Space Time and Incarnation* (Oxford: Oxford University Press, 1968), 74–75. According to Torrance the universe is uniformly *theogenic* (God is present everywhere) thus effectively making the location of the Incarnation theologically equivalent to all possible locations in the universe.

> space and time formed by other agencies, *but organising them round Himself and giving them transcendent references to God in and through Himself.*[21]

What this statement implies is that the structure of the physical universe is *organised round Christ* in what concerns his human embodied condition. The universe must be such that his body (as well as the body of his Mother (Virgin Mary)) could exist. This requirement cascades down to all human race and the biosphere, as well as to the astronomical and cosmological conditions. In this sense, if one links the Incarnation to the logic of creation, the creation of the universe is not entirely contingent but subjected to the *necessary* conditions which are required for the historical Incarnation.

As to the *transcendent references to God*, they are dwelling exactly in that contingency of the Incarnation which is not neutralised by the *necessary* conditions and related to its *sufficient* conditions which originate from beyond the natural world and point to the participation of the Holy Spirit (who is beyond space and time) in the event of the Incarnation.

As we mentioned above, in order for God to assume human flesh, there *must* be this flesh, so that the entire created universe *must* have *necessary* conditions for the embodied intelligent humanity to appear. Cosmologically, physically and biologically this entails that the universe must be at least ten billion years old. Correspondingly the necessary conditions for the Incarnation are present in the reversed history of the universe.[22] Then the entire created universe must contain the traces of the initial intent of God to create a very special universe in which human body and the Incarnation would be possible. In this sense, the idea of the Incarnation is 'deep' since it cascades down to all structural levels of the universe predetermining its evolution and preparing the conditions for emergence of biological life on this planet. But if the 'deepness' of the Incarnation could be

---

21. Torrance, *Space Time and Incarnation*, 72 (emphasis added). The dimension of space d=3, for example, is responsible for the stability of atoms and hence all astrophysical objects, such as solar system, cascading ultimately to the necessary conditions of existence of life on Earth, and of the Incarnation.
22. These conditions are summarised in various versions of the Anthropic Principle (AP), which detects consubstantiality of the physical stuff of the universe and human corporeal beings.

reduced only to the necessary conditions, the idea of deep incarnation would be trivial, since the *necessary* conditions for the Incarnation affect all material stuff in the *visible* universe (ninety-six per cent of the universe' stuff is *invisible* (Dark Matter, and Dark Energy) and not consubstantial to any known physical matter and hence living forms).

However, the statement of the *necessary* conditions for the historical Incarnation of Christ does not entail any further *necessity* for this Incarnation to actually happen (the sufficient conditions are independent from the necessary ones). This is also related to all other forms of matter which allegedly involved in "preparation" of the historical Incarnation. However, it is hardly to be comprehensible what would be the meaning of the traces of the Incarnation in Dark Matter and Dark Energy which have nothing to do with physics of the terrestrial world and its biological life-forms. Here the deep incarnation proposal as a universal assertion of the link between the historical Incarnation and the entire creation becomes philosophically and scientifically problematic because this proposal implicitly assumes a sort of unity of the created universe. Modern cosmology, however, points to the fact that it is only four per cent of the observable matter of the universe which is explicitly related to the conditions of the historical Incarnation of God in flesh. This means that the linking the Incarnation to the logic of creation of the universe is only to that part of the universe which gave rise to its visible part, but not to creation in its entirety!

The deep incarnation assumption, implicitly based on the old theological formula 'What has not been assumed has not been healed' entails that 'what has been assumed in the flesh taken by the Word is the whole of creature reality'[23]: said philosophically, there is the unity of the created world whose centre is Logos-Christ the incarnate. However, in view of what we have said about the universe, the claims of deep incarnation's advocates for the relevance of the historical Incarnation of the Logos-Christ in terrestrial flesh to the whole creation seem to be scientifically and philosophically implausible. The situation rather can be described through rephrasing the abovementioned theological formula: 'There is something in the universe which has not been assumed (for example Dark Matter and Dark Energy) and hence has not been healed.' Correspondingly, the

---

23. Edwards, *Deep Incarnation*, 112.

proposal for deep incarnation Christology, in order to have sense, *must be reduced* only to those forms of matter with which humanity can interact and which it can comprehend.[24] In other words, the idea of the deep incarnation is *epistemologically bounded* by the conditions of the *human* access to the universe.

The assumption of the idea of deep incarnation that human evolutionary history on Earth is literally related to all cosmological levels, let say only of the visible universe, does not either hold on the ontological level, because physically the universe is fragmented, it is huge and not limited to its visible part (that is consisting of many causally disjoint regions whose sense can only by guessed), it is empty and infertile in most of its space and time. Correspondingly, the underlying idea of the unity of all creation represents a *mental* 'instantaneous synthesis of the universe' in which the human being imitates the Logos-like propensity of being the co-creator of the universe through its articulation. In this sense, the claim of the proponents of deep incarnation transferring through the antecedent conditions the specifically human qualities to the fundamentally non-human and dead forms of matter seems to be unjustified.

What is forgotten in such a claim is the fundamental difference between humanity as hypostatically conscious formation and the rest of the world. This is a major philosophical defect of any theories of the human place in the universe which forget a simple truth that whatever place in the universe humanity assigns to itself (significant or insignificant, consubstantial to creation or not), it is only through its conscious faculty that any speculation about this place can be exercised. Humanity remains at the centre of disclosure and manifestation of the universe and that is why any attempt to place its hypostatic consciousness in the metaphysics of some underlying substance (that is reducing to the epiphenomenon of the material) is philosophically futile. It is humanity (not animals or particles) which acts as hypostasis of the universe by asserting the universe's

---

24. In this sense the assertion that 'in Christ, God enters into the biological tissue of creation in order to share the fate of biological existence' (NH Gregersen, 'Introduction', in *Incarnation. On the Scope and Depth of Christology*, edited by NH Gregersen [Minneapolis, Fortress Press, 2015], 18) is open to discussion, but at least it does not enter into the conflict with the limitations of the human cognitive faculties, whereas its extension towards non-living and non-consubstantial matter seem to be philosophically contradictory.

presence in the style of Maximus' *makroanthropos* idea through the continuing transferral of its qualities of the Divine image to the universe. In this sense that the idea of deep incarnation can be treated as a continuation of that infinite task, posed to humanity by God, of overcoming the moral divisions between different parts of creation (organic creatures and inorganic matter) thus transfiguring creation and bringing it to the union with God in the manner of the hypostatic union in Christ. As a moral move towards taking responsibility for the whole of creation, the idea of deep incarnation (as a human idea) has a simple theological justification in the central position of humanity whose task is to follow Christ in his bringing the whole creation to the seat of God through the Resurrection and Ascension. But any ontological claim of deep incarnation theorists, equating the modus of the presence of the Logos-Christ in the flesh of Jesus of Nazareth with all living creatures or even the created world as a whole, represents another level of the allegedly neutralised anthropocentrism, imposing on creatures the propensities of their communion with God which are beyond their natural capacity.

Now even if we accept a point that one can reasonably relate the conditions of the Incarnation only to four per cent of the observable matter of the universe, the idea of deep incarnation can be subjected to further scrutiny. It will be based on a subtle distinction between the *necessary* and *sufficient* conditions of the possibility of the historical Incarnation. Let us start, as a matter of analogy, with life in general. Even if the *necessary* conditions for existence of life are fulfilled on Earth and other exoplanets, there is no straightforward sufficiency in them for life to actually emerge.

Indeed, the *necessary* physical conditions on this planet, do not automatically entail the appearance of life forms, a cell for example. Biology at this stage of development is not capable of producing a living cell from an inorganic matter. The very evolution turns out to be so incredibly complex and fine-tuned that scientists anticipate that if nature on Earth would have to start it again, its very repetition would probably not be possible at all and if this would happen, its outcome hardly to be the same. Modern science does not understand mechanisms which launched the process of life on this planet, that is it does not know the *sufficient* conditions which are required to produce life, in particular life of *Homo Sapiens* leading ultimately to the possibility of the Incarnation.

The *sufficient* conditions for existence of life and for the historical Incarnation are not in the causal chain of the natural events and any attempt to equate the *necessary* conditions with the *sufficient* ones, which is implicitly supposed in the idea of deep incarnation,[25] places the Dogma of the Incarnation in the framework of theories of immanent presence of God in the world, risking to make the historical Incarnation a new type of a metaphysical doctrine. The participation of flesh of all biological existence and even quantum particles in the Logos through being *enhypostasised* by this Logos (the necessary conditions), must not be mixed up with the hypostatic union of the same Logos with the flesh of Jesus of Christ (the event of the Incarnation, that is the realisation of the sufficient conditions).

The unknowability of the sufficient conditions for the Incarnation to take place in space-time[26] indicates that the actual happening of the Incarnation is not a natural process which would be prepared through the endless theophanies in the history of humanity on Earth, but *the event* in the sense that the Incarnation, the Christ-event, as an empirical contingent happening in human history is not predetermined by the material laws and worldly necessities. Saying philosophically the Incarnation has an event-like phenomenality so that the *sufficient* conditions for it to happen do not belong to that realm where the *necessary* conditions operate. The event-like truth of the Incarnation places it in the class of those phenomena whose intuitive saturation invokes an infinite hermeneutic of its appropriation and, in accordance with Torrance, provides some transcendent references.

One can conjecture that the unknowability of the sufficient conditions for the Incarnation of the Logos-Christ is of the same origin as the unknowability of one's own origin through physical birth. The mystery of the Incarnation resides in human thought at the same level as the mystery as one's own birth (in which the historical Incarnation of Christ becomes a certain archetype of that how to approach existentially one's own phenomenologically concealed

25. *Cf* R Cole-Turner, 'Incarnation Deep and Wide: A response to Niels Gregersen', *Theology and Science* 11/4 (2013): 427.

26. In spite of a possible thorough account of all historical circumstances which can be treated as the signs of the advent of the Incarnation (see a profound analysis of these signs in NH Gregersen, '*Curs Deus caro*: Jesus and the Cosmos Story', *Theology and Science* 11/4 [2013]: 379–381).

origin.[27]) In spite of not knowing the sense of its origin but being the image of God and acting as its archetype, that is the Logos-Christ the incarnate, humanity articulates the universe thus co-enhypostasising it through knowledge and thus exercising the function of its own hypostasis. In this sense the idea of 'Deep incarnation', if it is seen as a hermeneutical tool of explicating the human condition, is contributing to such an enhypostasisation (articulation) by the human being of his own presence in the universe which closely links it to the whole terrestrial physical and biological world thus extending the sense of the historical Incarnation of the Logos-Christ in human flesh towards everything which is consubstantial to this flesh and needs salvation. However, such an epistemological anti-anthropocentrism, transferring the Incarnation beyond humanity, still remains anthropocentric in virtue of the fact that it is being proclaimed from within a specifically human embodied consciousness made in the archetype of the Logos-Christ the incarnate. In spite of the fact that it is understood that this is being done on purely moral grounds related to the sympathy and solidarity with the rest of the organic world as well as ecological concerns, such a transmission can be admissible theologically only if it is placed in the context of the old *makroanthropos* idea, understood as the human being's mediation between different parts of the created world bringing them to moral harmony with God. Humanity remains here epistemologically central in the created universe thus exercising the Logos-given quality of being *hypostasis of the universe*. The deep incarnation idea can thus be seen as a regulative infinite task of humanity of renormalizing its vision of the universe as split in fragments and disharmony towards the 'all and all' of the Logos-Christ's vision of this universe.

Conclusion

The idea of deep incarnation contributes to an open-ended hermeneutic of the human condition in the universe, in particular human relatedness to the surrounding terrestrial biosphere, as well as to the cosmic environment at large. Its distinctive picture is to balance

---

27. See, for example, A Nesteruk, *The Sense of the Universe* (Minneapolis: Fortress Press, 2015), 323–334.

the ambivalent position of humanity in the universe (being its centre of disclosure and manifestation, as well as a tiny part of it) by creating an archetypical Christology, in which Christ, being distinctively the unique hypostatic union between God and the human being, somehow transfers his qualities to the whole creation which is thus closely involved in the underlying logic of the historical Incarnation. Here we envisage some problems with this idea.

1) We point out that because of the vast and causally disconnected structure of the universe, humanity at best has access to its *visible* (causally connected with us as observers) part and it is consubstantial only to four per cent of matter allegedly comprising the whole universe. Correspondingly, the claims of 'Deep Incarnation's' advocates for the relevance of the historical Incarnation of the Logos-Christ in terrestrial flesh to the whole creation seem to be scientifically and philosophically implausible. The 'Deep Incarnation' idea has sense only in relation to the consubstantial part of the universe, that is to that part of the whole created reality to which humanity has access.

2) The 'Deep Incarnation' reference to an effective entailment from 'assumption' to 'healing' in application to the whole creation *de facto* equates the transfigured flesh of the Logos-Christ (through the hypostatic union) with the rest of creation thus depriving the process of deification of the human being and transfiguration of the *visible* universe of its temporal dimension, that is of making it as an already accomplished fact. This goes contrary to the Orthodox stance on deification as a personal endeavour based in ascetic struggle and contemplation and not implanted into the logic of the natural world.

3) Deep Incarnation is a trivial statement if it would concern only with the necessary conditions for the historical Incarnation, which are cosmological. However, the sufficient conditions of the Incarnation as an *inaugural event* cannot be placed into the fabric of the material world (here comes a pneumatological aspect of the Incarnation). Since in tendency the 'Deep Incarnation' idea identifies the necessary conditions with the sufficient ones, the historical Incarnation is deprived of its event-like phenomenality and thus is positioned as a new metaphysical doctrine contributing to theories of immanent presence of God. It is exactly the unknowability of the sufficient conditions for the Incarnation (as well as for other natural inaugurating events) that provides us with its transcendent references, pointing to its non-natural, non-worldly essence.

4) The idea of 'Deep Incarnation' can be treated positively as contributing to the old *makroanthropos* idea, related to the stance on humanity a mediating agency between divisions in creation, and between creation and God. In this sense the idea of 'Deep Incarnation' can be treated as a new expression of the moral mediation between creation and God already exercised by Christ through his Resurrection and Ascension.

Finally, in spite of its anti-anthropocentiric overtones, the idea of 'Deep Incarnation', positioning humanity in solidarity with the rest of the consubstantial creation, remains a human production implicitly placing humanity in the centre of disclosure and manifestation of the universe. Humanity retains its status as hypostasis of the universe through imitating the incarnate Logos-Christ's hypostatic union between creation and God.

Deep Incarnation and the Redemptive Suffering of Christ for all Creation

Mark Worthing

'I have thought it important to keep creation and incarnation together as aspects of God's loving self-giving to creatures, and to see redemption, or salvation in Christ, as embracing not just human beings but the whole of creation. So the kind of ecological theology that I have worked on in these essays is one that seeks to embrace the natural world within a fully Trinitarian theology of creation and incarnation.'
– Denis Edwards[1]

Abstract: The concept of deep incarnation, first introduced into the theological discussion by Niels Gregersen, was taken up enthusiastically by Denis Edwards, among other theologians. Edwards immediately saw the implications for the science and faith dialogue, but even more so for the emerging eco-theology to which he had fully committed. Even more than this, he saw the implications for the redemptive suffering of God for all creation, into which God had fully entered in the incarnation.

Key words: Deep incarnation, suffering, theology of the cross, atonement.

When Denis Edwards read Danish theologian Niels Gregersen's article on 'The Cross in an Evolutionary World,' he was struck by his use of the term 'deep incarnation' to describe the depth of God's identification with the pain and suffering of an evolutionary world. Denis had long been a keen student of the classic incarnational theologians, and had written widely on God's place within an evolutionary world, or perhaps that should be an evolutionary world's place within God. The concept of God's identification with all suffering was another enduring theme of his thinking and writing.

---

1. Denis Edwards, *The Natural World and God: Theological Explorations* (Adelaide: ATF Press, 2017), 9.

So the concept of deep incarnation resonated strongly with his theological concerns and he began incorporating the idea into many of his books and papers. Indeed, Edwards was finishing a book on the subject of deep incarnation, based upon his Duffy lectures at Boston College, at the time of his death.

But what exactly is meant by deep incarnation? And what new insights does it shed on God's relationship to the physical world and its creatures that has attracted such strong interest, especially from theologians active in the science-faith conversation and in eco-theology? Gregersen sought to portray the radical implications of the incarnation for all creation. He proposed that 'the incarnation of God in Christ can be understood as a radical or 'deep' incarnation, that is, an incarnation into the very tissue of biological existence, and system of nature.'[2] As Edwards explained, Gregersen saw 'the cross as God's identification with creation in its evolutionary emergence, and as an icon and microcosm of God's redemptive presence to all creatures in their suffering and death.'[3] Deep incarnation, therefore, means not just the penetration into the 'very tissue of biological existence' but also the transcendent God entering into the pain and suffering of this existence. Again, as Edwards put it: 'A God who can freely and lovingly enter into the pain of creation and feel with suffering creatures is actually more truly and fully transcendent than the concept of a God who is unable to do this.'[4] This is deep incarnation. It is God taking on flesh, becoming a part of the creation so thoroughly and deeply that God suffers for and with the creation. As a result, all creatures and all creation find redemption in God's presence among us.

To understand why the concept of deep incarnation is finding such traction, we need to recall something of the recent history of the doctrine. For much of the twentieth century discussions of the doctrine of the Incarnation focused largely on the perceived problem of a human being (Jesus of Nazareth) being at the same time God. The discussion was perhaps best epitomised by *The Myth of God Incarnate*, edited by John Hick and the various responses to it, as for example George Carey's *God Incarnate*, which appeared later that

---

2. Niels Henrik Gregersen, 'The Cross of Christ in an Evolutionary World', in *Dialog: A Journal of Theology*, 40 (2001): 205.
3. Denis Edwards, *Deep Incarnation: The Cross as Sacrament of God's Redemptive Suffering with Creatures* (Maryknoll, NY: Orbis Books, 2019), xviif.
4. Edwards, *Deep Incarnation*, 113f.

same year.[5] What these various writings all had in common was a focus on the issue of the divinity of Christ and the problems this posed for the modern mind. The implications for a physical world characterised by suffering of God taking on flesh was largely off the agenda. The emergence of the concept of deep incarnation has taken up a key aspect of the doctrine long overlooked. It asks just how far the implications of the incarnation extend for and into the physical world.

The shared assumptions of those taking up the theme of deep incarnation might be characterised as follows: The incarnation is unlimited in scope; it is not restricted to a particular species (or portion thereof in the case of humanity); it has implications for how human beings view and treat the rest of creation; and it embeds God within the suffering of all creation. It is this last point that strikes perhaps the most poignant chord with many today. Deep incarnation underscores the true power of the Christian message, at the centre of which is the crucified God.

This attraction to the God who suffers is well illustrated by Christos Tsiolkas in his recent novel *Damascus*. He describes the conversion of the character Lydia and the appeal of the early Christian message in terms of God's identification with those who suffer. Paul says to Lydia, who has recently had her first child, a baby girl, taken away from her and left to die: 'Only those who've suffered will be there—those who've been enslaved, those who've endured cruelty and evil. Only they are promised to the kingdom to come.' Lydia, thinking on these words, reflects: 'His [Paul's] God grieved for my daughter and I was suddenly stunned by the enormity of such unthinkable compassion.'[6] It is a reminder of the power to be found in a God who suffers not only for, but also with creation.

It was the power of the suffering God that attracted Denis Edwards, a Roman Catholic theologian, to Luther's theology of the cross. In over a decade serving together with Denis on the Australian Lutheran-Roman Catholic dialogue one of my most vivid memories is of Denis' frequent and friendly reminders to me: 'But you are forgetting Luther's theology of the cross!' A true incarnational theology will always also

---

5. John Hick, editor, *The Myth of God Incarnate* (London: SCM Press, 1977); George Carey, *God Incarnate: Meeting the Contemporary Challenges to a Classic Christian Doctrine* (Downer Grove: IVP, 1977).
6. Christos Tsiolkas, *Damascus* (Sydney: Allen and Unwin, 2019), 84f.

be a theology of the cross. And the idea of deep incarnation, springing as it did from an article by a Lutheran theologian linking evolution and the theology of the cross, was certain to resonate strongly with a theologian such as Edwards.

The Confluence of Deep Incarnation with an Evolutionary Worldview

The Christian doctrine of the incarnation has long played a positive role in the affirmation of the material world and the knowledge of that world. Within the philosophical milieu of ancient Hellenism the value of the physical world was often relegated to secondary importance or even seen as an evil compared to the value and reality of the spiritual realm. The idea that God as a pure spiritual being would take on human flesh was simply preposterous, even scandalous. Long battles were fought within early Christianity against attempts by various forms of Gnostic and docetic movements to reject the idea that God could or would take on human flesh. The central affirmation of the incarnation which prevailed was not only a victory for orthodox Christian belief, but also for the appreciation of the physical world. If God takes on human flesh, then the physical world has value. The incarnation dignifies the physical. It makes the physical something worth valuing, worth redeeming . . . and worth understanding.

The doctrine of the Incarnation is at heart an affirmation of the value and knowability of the physical world, in all of its evolutionary complexity. Combined with the Christian affirmation of God as Creator, it forms the theological foundations for both nature and a natural theology. It is no accident that the two concepts are so closely related in the prologue of John's gospel. Thomas F Torrance expressed this well when he wrote:

> There must be a close coordination between theological concepts and physical concepts; which is, after all, the inescapable implications of the Christian doctrines of creation and incarnation and the inescapable relation between logos and being which they establish. This being the case, an essential place must be found for so-called 'natural theology,' if only out of recognition of the fact that the interaction of

God with the world grounds our conceiving of him within the
relation of God to the world and of the world to God.[7]

Importantly, deep incarnation points to the evolutionary
interconnectedness of all life. An understanding of deep incarnation
within an evolutionary context brings with it the recognition that
the incarnation is not simply a divine-human event. In *Ecology at
the Heart of Faith,* Edwards explains that incarnation 'includes the
whole interconnected world of fleshly life and, in some way, includes
the whole universe to which flesh is related and on which it depends
. . . Flesh points beyond the humanity of Jesus and beyond human
community embraced by God in the incarnation to the biological
world of living creatures.'[8] In this earlier work, one of the first in
which Edwards took up the concept of deep incarnation, he clearly
saw that the incarnation was vital not only for how we understand
God's relationship to the physical world, but also for how sense
human beings value and respect the non-human physical world.

The Radical Focus of Deep Incarnation on the God who Suffers

The idea that God entered incarnationally into an evolutionary world
leads necessarily to a recognition of the deep connection of this
incarnational God with human suffering. As Edwards reminds us, this
was recognised clearly by Karl Rahner who, he explains, saw 'human
beings in one interconnected world, existing only in evolutionary
and ecological interrelation with the biological and material world in
which they evolve'.[9] As Rahner put it: 'An Incarnation of the Logos in
the true sense, which attains to and commits itself to matter itself as
such—in other words the radical potentiality of the world as such—is
why the total reality of the world is . . . touched to its very roots by
the incarnation of the Logos precisely in virtue of the fact that matter

---

7. TF Torrance, *Reality and Scientific Theology* (Eugene, Oregon: Wipf & Stock, 2001), 36f.
8. Denis Edwards, *Ecology at the Heart of Faith: The Change of Heart that Leads to a New Way of Living on Earth* (Maryknoll, NY: Orbis, 2006), 58.
9. Edwards, *Deep Incarnation*, 90.

must be conceived fundamentally and from the outset as one.'[10] It is precisely because of this oneness of matter that the incarnation is so profound. When God became flesh, the entirety of matter was embraced, and embraced in its evolutionary processes. And at these processes lies Darwin's principle of the survival of the fittest. Suffering and death are an inherent part of the physical world and this too— indeed, especially this—is embraced in the incarnation.

Edwards concludes his book *Deep Incarnation* with his thoughts on the doctrine's implications for the suffering of all creatures. This is, after all, what deep incarnation is about at its most profound level. The theology of deep incarnation leads us to conclude, as Edwards points out, that 'God can be said to suffer with suffering creatures; the cross of Christ is the sacrament of God's redemptive suffering with creatures; and the resurrection is a promise of healing and fulfilment that embraces all creatures.'[11]

Again, this is nothing entirely new. These key insights, as Edwards reminds us, are faithful to the Christian tradition, as seen in Paul's letter to Romans.[12] The apostle writes:

> The creation waits with eager longing for the revealing of the children of God; for the creation was subjected to futility, not of its own will but by the will of the one who subjected it, in hope that the creation itself will be set free from its bondage to decay and will obtain the freedom of the glory of the children of God. We know that the whole creation has been groaning in labor pains until now; and not only the creation, but we ourselves, who have the first fruits of the Spirit, groan inwardly while we wait for adoption, the redemption of our bodies (Rom 8:19–23).

This text does not diminish the centrality of Christ's suffering on the cross, but rather implies that divine suffering extends beyond the cross and is linked to the suffering of the whole of creation. The hope of salvation and an end to suffering for humanity and the whole of creation are inescapably bound together through the suffering of God in Christ on the cross.

---

10. Karl Rahner, 'Christology in the Setting of the Modern Man's Understanding of Himself and His World,' in *Theological Investigations* 11, translated by David Burke (London: Darton, Longman & Todd, 1974), 219.
11. Edwards, *Deep Incarnation*, 105.
12. Edwards, *Ecology at the Heart of Faith*, 59.

This is a challenging perspective for a tradition that has tended to limit its thinking about the scope of the atonement to human beings, and then often to a very select portion of human beings. As a further challenge to our traditional thinking about the scope of atonement and reconciliation, the whole of creation in this text has broader reference than just to the animal kingdom. The concept of deep incarnation helps us to consider this text from a very different perspective. We should ask, for instance, how we might conceptualise the suffering of plants, oceans, mountains, the atmosphere we breathe? Traditionally only sentient beings are seen as capable of suffering as only sentient beings can experience pain. Even then, there are questions about whether so-called lower forms of fauna experience as much pain as higher forms. Can a spider experience as much pain as a fish, a fish as much as a dog, a dog as much as a chimpanzee, a chimpanzee as much as a human?[13] But in the light of a God who takes on flesh and becomes a part of the suffering of the whole creation, these questions become moot. And this view is backed up by the science as well.

We learn from comparative ethology that such presumed hierarchies of the capacity of various sentient life forms to experience suffering is problematic. Darwin himself, in *The Descent of Man*, concluded that 'the difference in mind between . . . [humans] and the higher animals, great as it is, certainly is one of degree and not kind.'[14] The implication is that pain and suffering are experienced far beyond the confines of the human. Simple observation suggests to us that animals indeed experience suffering in ways similar to humans. As Peter Singer observed: 'Nearly all the external signs that lead us to infer pain in other humans can be seen in other species . . . The behavioural signs include writhing, facial contortions, moaning, yelping or other forms of calling, attempts to avoid the source of the pain, appearance of fear at the prospect of its repletion, and so on.'[15]

---

13. *Cf* Maria Stamp Dawkins, 'Scientific Basis for Assessing Suffering in Animals', in *In Defense of Animals. The Second Wave*, edited by Peter Singer (Oxford: Basil Blackwell, 2006), 28ff. See also the discussion of this and the related question of intelligence in Worthing, 'Human and Animal Intelligence: A Difference of Degree or Kind', in *God, Life, Intelligence and the Universe*, edited by Terrence Kelly and Hilary Regan (Adelaide: ATF Press, 2002), 85ff.

14. Charles Darwin, *The Descent of Man and Selection in Relation to Sex* (London: Murray, 1871), 128.

15. Peter Singer, *Animal Liberation*, 2nd edition (New York: Avon Books, 1990), 11.

Studies in ethology and comparative psychology have supported the view that however great the quantitative distinction between humans and other animals may be—it is just that—a quantitative and not a qualitative distinction. Studies such as those by Hauser, *The Evolution of Communication*; Euan Macphail, *The Evolution of Consciousness*; and the several works by Donald Griffin, including *The Question of Animal Awareness, Animal Thinking*, and *Animal Minds*, suggest that the demarcation between animals and humans may be less clear cut than we are accustomed to assume.[16] Theologically, only the attribute of the image of God in humans sets us apart—but this is not something we possess by virtue of some special innate human abilities, but is a gift of the creator. Therefore, also from the Christian point-of-view, there is great difficulty with insisting on a difference of kind in the areas of intelligence, consciousness, and ability to experience suffering.[17] This fits well with the concept of deep incarnation.

From a theological perspective, the biblical creation account, traditionally used to demonstrate the uniqueness of humans, must be considered from the perspective of the solidarity of humanity with other animals. Again, we see the importance of the interconnectedness of all creation as underscored in the concept of deep incarnation. Both humans and animals are made from the earth (Gen 2:7, 19), literally the dirt of the ground, the same ground out of which all plants grow (Gen 2:9). Both animals (Gen 2:7) and humans (Gen 1:30) are described as being 'living souls'. There is an inescapable boundness of human beings to the rest of God's creation. The discovery that all things living share the same building blocks of DNA serves as a further reminder of this millennia-old theological truth.

This puts Paul's teaching that all of creation experiences suffering into a very concrete context. This suffering includes traditional ideas of pain, but also subjection to futility, which might be described as

---

16. Marc Hauser. *The Evolution of Communication* (Boston: MIT Press, 1996); Euan Macphail, *The Evolution of Consciousness* (Oxford: Oxford University Press, 1998); Donald Griffin, *The Question of Animal Awareness* (New York: Rockefeller University Press, 1976): *Animal Thinking* (Boston: Harvard University Press, 1984); and *Animal Minds: Beyond Cognition to Consciousness* (Chicago: University of Chicago Press, 2001).

17. This raises significant and unavoidable issues concerning the inherent value and rights of animals and their ethical treatment that we are not able to explore in the context of his discussion.

loss or distortion of purpose; and decay, which calls to mind the inescapable reality of the second law of thermodynamics. In the context of this passage, suffering must be understood as something broader and more intertwined than simply the experience of pain of individual sentient beings.

In light of the relatively recent re-discovery of the idea of divine suffering, and the rise in awareness of the inherent value of the non-human created order within theological discussions, the question of the connections between divine, human and whole creational suffering merits fresh consideration. The suffering of God, humans and fauna are all distinct, yet they are somehow bound together in both their causes and their resolution. The whole of creation exists in necessary relationship to its creator (Col 1:16f). Christ holds all creation together. He is bound to creation, and we to him.

The fact that all of creation suffers along with us (and with God) is also a clear inference from the Old Testament eschatological visions of the lion and lamb lying down with one another (Isa 11:6–9). The fact that the benefits of the hoped for New Age extend to all creation also bears witness to the fact that the whole of creation presently suffers.

A restoration of the human-divine relationship brings with it a healing that extends to the non-human creation. As the Psalmist writes: 'You save humans and animals alike, O Lord' (Ps 36:6). Paul's reflections in Romans, therefore, do not arise in isolation from the context of the Hebrew biblical tradition. We should not be surprised to hear the Apostle argue that just as the whole of creation suffers, so also it shares in the benefits of the atoning work of Christ. As biblical scholar James Dunn pointed out with relation to this text: 'Paul's vision of God's saving purpose drives him beyond any idea of a merely personal or human redemption. What is at stake . . . is creation as a whole.'[18]

This brings the question of the scope of the incarnation and the atonement firmly into the discussion. Elizabeth Johnson, in her recent book, *Ask the Beasts*, suggests something of the extent of the rethink needed in our thinking about the atonement in light of the concept of 'deep incarnation'. Johnson writes: 'God's own self-expressive Word

---

18. James Dunn, *Romans 1–8: Word Biblical Commentary* (Dallas: Word Books, 1988), 487.

personally joins the biological world as a member of the human race, and via this perch on the tree of life enters into solidarity with the whole biophysical cosmos.' It is this perspective that allows her to conclude that the 'logic of deep incarnation gives a strong warrant for extending divine solidarity from the cross into the groan of suffering and the silence of death of all creation.'[19]

The concept of deep incarnation is especially significant at this juncture. It has become a means of expressing theologically the magnitude of God's involvement with the creation. Gregersen, in light of biological evolution, described the incarnation as an 'incarnation into the very tissue of biological existence, and system of nature.' Significantly, for consideration of the Romans 8 text, he claimed that when seen in this way 'the death of Christ becomes an icon of God's redemptive co-suffering with all sentient life . . .'[20] Denis Edwards took the implications of deep incarnation even further when he argues that the flesh embraced by God is not limited to humanity but 'includes the whole interconnected world of fleshy life and, in some way, includes the whole universe to which flesh is related and on which it depends.'[21]

A similar point was made by Matthew Fox in his *The Coming of the Cosmic Christ*. Fox argued that 'those who indulge exclusively in their personal salvation and their personal Savior do so in direct contradiction to the entire teaching of the Cosmic Christ crucified for all. Salvation must be universal in the sense of a comprehensive healing of all the cosmos' pain, or it is not salvation at all.'[22] Again, Fox pointed out, that 'since the pain, suffering and sin are cosmic–bigger than we can control and far more complex in space and time than we can imagine—the redemption must be cosmic as well.'[23]

The evolutionary theme of new life out of suffering and death is paralleled in the theological insights of deep incarnation, which points to the suffering of humans and of all creation and our finding of common healing and new life through the suffering of God in Christ.

19. Elizabeth Johnson, *Ask the Beasts: Darwin and the God of Love* (London: Bloomsbury, 2014), 198.
20. Gregersen, 'The Cross of Christ in an Evolutionary World', 205.
21. Edwards, *Ecology at the Heart of Faith*, 58.
22. Matthew Fox, *The Coming of the Cosmic Christ* (Melbourne: Collins Dove, 1988), 151.
23. Fox, *The Coming of the Cosmic Christ*, 152.

The point is significant. A God who creates all things, suffers with all things, and finally redeems all things. God's act of becoming flesh as well as God's act of vicarious death of the cross, have universal implications. Although humans are seen to occupy a special place in this nexus of creation, suffering and reconciliation, no part of creation is excluded. As Sallie McFague put it: 'Creation is not one thing and salvation something else . . . Salvation is for all of creation. The liberating, healing, inclusive ministry of Christ takes place *in* and *for* creation.'[24]

God's suffering on the cross is universal in the sense that it is unrestricted. Nothing is withheld, nothing excluded. So, too, the significance of this divine suffering is universal just as the incarnation was universal in its impact. Paul goes so far as to declare that through Christ and his suffering 'God was pleased to reconcile himself to all things, whether on earth or heaven; by making peace through the blood of the cross' (Col 1:20). An anthropocentric understanding of the incarnation and atonement has long caused us to begin and conclude our reflections on what God accomplished through the incarnation and the death of the Incarnate One. The biblical texts make it clear that we are not the exclusive focus of Christ's atoning work. The cross brings healing to all of creation in ways we cannot yet fully comprehend just as the incarnation underscores the interconnectedness of all creation in ways that we are only now discovering.

Only a God who suffers and who suffers fully and completely can defeat suffering. As Dietrich Bonhoeffer expressed it from his prison cell: 'The Bible directs us to God's powerlessness and suffering: only a God who suffers can save us.'[25] From the moment of the Incarnation, suffering is exactly what Christ came among us to do. As Hans Urs von Balthasar expressed it: 'Suffering is in fact the pinnacle of Jesus' achievement on earth.'[26] God redeems our suffering and makes it no longer pointless, not with some rational explanation for our suffering, but by freely embracing the fullness of suffering within his own being.

---

24. Sallie McFague, *The Body of Christ: An Ecological Theology* (Minneapolis: Fortress Press, 1993), 182.

25. Dietrich Bonhoeffer, *Letters and Papers from Prison*, edited by E Bethge (New York: Macmillan, 1971), 361.

26. Hans Urs von Balthasar, *Gott und das Leid*, Antwort des Glaubens 34, Informationszentrum Berufe der Kirche (Freiburg: Informationszentrum Berufe der Kirche, 1992), 10.

God's suffering makes us at one with God. God defeats death with death, suffering with suffering. The death of Christ signals the end of death, just as the suffering of Christ signals the end of suffering. The redemptive quality of God's suffering is at the core of our being made 'at one' with God. Just as the death of Christ signals the end of death, the suffering of Christ signals the end of suffering. Japanese theologian Kazoh Kitamori put it this way: 'What heals our wounds is the love rooted in the pain of God.'[27] And this process of God's love being embedded with and through God's pain begins not with the cross, but with the incarnation.

Conclusion

In many ways the concept of deep incarnation is a very old idea, thoroughly embedded in traditional Christian understandings of the incarnation. But it is also a new idea inasmuch as it returns the focus of the incarnation to the implications of God becoming flesh for the creation. It deliberately opens this discussion to include the whole creation, and it does this in full light of current scientific understandings of the place of suffering within the physical realm. Denis Edwards saw this clearly, and was eager to join voices like those of Niels Gregersen, Celia Deane-Drummond, Elizabeth Johnson and others in exploring the depths of God's act of becoming flesh for all humanity, for all life, and for all creation.

---

27. Kazoh Kitamori, *Theology of the Pain of God* (Louisville, KY: John Knox Press, 1965), 64.

Life in the Cosmos:
Deep Incarnation in Deep Space

Ted Peters

> 'The whole of the world's industrial, aesthetic, scientific and moral
> endeavour serves physically to complete the Body of Christ,
> whose charity animates and recreates all things.'
> Pierre Teilhard de Chardin[1]

Abstract: How might *Deep Incarnation Christology* apply to deep space?
Both Niels Henrik Gregersen and Denis Edwards have eloquently articulated
the implications of God's incarnation in the historical Jesus for all physical
existence on Earth, demonstrating the internalisation of creaturely
experience within the trinitarian perichoresis. What remains as a theological
assignment is the application of deep incarnation to deep space, including
extraterrestrial life. This task should be given to today's astrotheologian.
Here is this article's hypothesis: the historical incarnation of the divine Logos
in Jesus of Nazareth on Earth is constituted by the exchange of divine and
creaturely attributes, the *communicatio idiomatum*; and, when *communicatio
idiomatum* is combined with a proleptic understanding of God's promised
new creation, we can accompany the entire material history of all galaxies and
all extraterrestrial creatures into the eternal perichoresis of God as Trinity.

Key Terms: deep incarnation, astrotheology, astrobiology, Trinity,
perichoresis, Denis Edwards, Niels Henrik Gregersen, Karl Rahner, Robert
John Russell.

What are the implications of *deep incarnation*? To date, deep
incarnationist theologians have advanced three important points:
first, the Logos (λóγος) in the flesh incorporates all physical reality
into the trinitarian life of God. Second, because all physical reality

---

1. Pierre Teilhard de Chardin, *The Future of Man*, translated by Norman Denny
    (New York: Harper, 1964), 24.

is taken into the divine life, then God suffers with every creature in its own suffering. Third, this shared suffering is redemptive, at least according to the deep incarnation school of Christology. Because shared suffering is redemptive, it follows that this divine sharing resolves the theodicy problem: God is the victim of suffering, not the perpetrator.[2] One can imagine constructing an entire systematic theology that coherently links all the *loci* based on only one principle, deep incarnation.

So, I would like to ask: what are the implications of the concept of deep incarnation for our growing grasp of the immensity of the universe? Does deep incarnation apply to deep space? To extraterrestrial life?

It is one thing to claim that in the historical Jesus the entire materiality of his existence—biochemistry, DNA, molecules, and atoms—is taken up into God's experience. It is another thing to acknowledge that these very same physical and perhaps even biological processes occur also on exoplanets in the Milky Way and in supernovas at distances measured in billions of light years. What is the connection, if any, to the Logos present in Jesus' fleshly biography and the chemistry of Andromeda?

The God of Israel is not the God of Israel alone. There is nothing in this vast creation that does not owe its existence to this Creator. *Creation* applies not only to microbes in Jesus' intestines but also to every event occurring in a trillion or more galaxies. If our term *creation* is this inclusive, is *incarnation* equally inclusive?

Denis Edwards would answer affirmatively.

> A fully Christian approach to the natural world cannot be limited to the theology of creation in isolation, but must also involve salvation in Christ. The theological meaning

---

2. It's not clear just how divine sharing in creaturely suffering is redemptive. Key to the Christian gospel is the promise of resurrection. 'Ultimately, the response that I would make as a Christian to suffering in humanity and in the natural world, is to interpret the whole history of life on earth as a process of redemption which points directly to eschatology. The suffering of God on the cross leads, praise God, to the resurrected God of Easter—otherwise you have a God who suffers with us forever.' Robert John Russell, *Cosmology, Evolution, and Resurrection Hope: Proceedings of the Fifth Annual Goshen Conference on Religion and Science,* edited by Carl S Helrich (Kitchener, Ontario: Pandora Press and Adelaide, Australia: ATF Press, 2006), 34.

of mountains, seas, animals, plants, and the climate of our planet, the Milky Way Galaxy, and the observable universe will involve the whole story of God's self-bestowal to creatures in creation, incarnation, and final transfiguration.'[3]

Wherever we find physical existence, there is God acting in creative, incarnate, and eschatological modes.

Yet, I wonder if there remains a task yet to be undertaken. Traditionally the *logos* is identified with Jesus' divine nature, while the flesh is identified with the human nature. For the theologian to assert the ubiquity of the divine Logos throughout the cosmos is an easy move; it's consonant with the scientific worldview according to which all physical reality is organised mathematically. The same mathematically formulated laws of nature apply everywhere in the cosmos. Yet, the deep incarnationists ask for more. They assert the ubiquity of the fleshly nature of the incarnate Logos. Is this coherent?

The point of deep incarnation Christology is to assert that the physical history of creation is, by virtue of God's action in Jesus Christ, internal to the trinitarian perichoresis or *circumincessio*. I find this coherent. I also find this to be good news: our once alien world is now at home again in God.

What risks incoherence, however, is ascribing the universality belonging to the divine hypostasis or logos to the particularity of each and every physical or fleshly entity that expresses that Logos. Can we make this coherent? And can we apply it coherently to the furthest reaches of outer space? In what follows, we will test the illuminative power of deep incarnation Christology by drawing out its implications for the scientific grasp of our immense cosmos.

All this leads to the following hypothesis: the historical incarnation of the divine Logos in Jesus of Nazareth on Earth is constituted by the exchange of divine and creaturely attributes, the *communicatio idiomatum*; and, when *communicatio idiomatum* is combined with a proleptic understanding of God's promised new creation, we can accompany the entire material history of all galaxies and all extraterrestrial creatures into the eternal perichoresis of God as Trinity. In what follows we will put this hypothesis to the test.

---

3. Denis Edwards, *Deep Incarnation: God's Redemptive Suffering with Creatures* (Maryknoll NY: Orbis, 2019), xvi.

The Basic Tenets of Deep Incarnation Christology

The Pied Piper of deep incarnation is Niels Henrik Gregersen, a systematic theologian at the University Copenhagen. His piped tune is hummed and sung by theologians such as Elizabeth Johnson, Celia Deane-Drummond, Richard Baukham, Kristin Johnston Largen, Robert John Russell, Jamie Fowler, and, of course, Denis Edwards. This choir does not sing in unison. Rather, each sings a different note although in harmony with the others.

Incarnation strikes a theological chord with three notes. First, the *strict sense* of incarnation applies to the biography of Jesus and, in addition, to the Church as the Body of Christ. Second, the *broad sense* of incarnation applies to Jesus' sharing in the human and extra-human dimensions of geo-biological reality. Third, the *soteriological* dimension of incarnation reveals that in Christ God 'co-suffers with and for all suffering creatures' while working for their salvation through the power of the Holy Spirit.[4] Like a *basso profundo*, the second and third take us into deep incarnation.

'What we hear in the *deep incarnation* refrain is that 'the divine Logos . . . has assumed not merely humanity, but the *whole malleable matrix of materiality*.'[5] Here is Gregersen's succinct theological recitative.

> Deep incarnation is the view that God's own Logos (Wisdom and Word) was made flesh in Jesus the Christ in such a comprehensive manner that God, by assuming the particular life story of Jesus the Jew from Nazareth, also conjoined the

---

4. Niels Henrik Gregersen, '*Cur deus caro*: Jesus and the Cosmic Story', in *Theology and Science* 11/4 (2013): 381–391, here at 386. 'In a biological view of reality, we cannot think of the human without thinking of our evolutionary dependence on the creatures that have gone before us and of our interdependence with the biological systems of our planet. In the Christ-event, God enters into the heart of creation, embracing finite creaturely existence from within. In the Word made flesh, God embraces not only the human but also the evolutionary pattern of life that is intrinsic to and constitutive of human existence. God-with-us in Christ is to be understood as God-with-all-living-things. Niels Gregersen calls this *deep incarnation*.' Denis Edwards, *The Natural World and God: Theological Explorations* (Adelaide, Australia: ATF Press, 2017), 56.
5. Niels Henrik Gregersen, 'Deep Incarnation: Why Evolutionary Continuity Matters in Christology', in *Toronto Journal of Theology*, 26/2 (Fall 2010): 173–187, here at 176, Gregersen's italics.

material conditions of creaturely existence (all flesh), shared and ennobled the fate of all biological life forms (grass and lilies), and experienced the pains of sensitive creatures (sparrows and foxes) from within. Deep incarnation thus presupposes a radical embodiment that reaches into the roots (*radices*) of material and biological existence as well as into the darker sides of creation: the *tenebrae creationis*.[6]

Edwards responds with a recitative of his own. 'God embraces "flesh" in Jesus of Nazareth, that flesh might be transformed and deified. This flesh, I am arguing, includes each wallaby, dog and dolphin.'[7] Jesus' humanity marks a juncture in the physical world where all materiality becomes represented and sanctified.

The melody of deep incarnation was already intoned during the patristic era with recapitulation and deification in mind. Already with Irenaeus of Lyons (130–200), for whom *recapitulation* belonged to the lyrics, we heard this song. 'It was necessary for Adam to be recapitulated in Christ, that mortality might be swallowed up in immortality.'[8] Or, Athanasius (296–373), God 'became human that we might become divine'.[9]

Today's recapitulationists and deificationists rely on the principle that what was materially present in Adam's body is materially present throughout the universe. Incorporating Adam's body into Jesus' resurrection redeems not just Adam but all materiality. 'This concept

---

6. Niels Henrik Gregersen, 'The Extended Body of Christ: Three Dimensions of Deep Incarnation', in *Incarnation: On the Scope and Depth of Christology,* edited by Niels Henrik Gregersen (Minneapolis: Fortress Press, 2015), 225–251, here at 225–226. Gregersen has his critics. 'We require a still more precise account of the union between Word and flesh, whether that flesh be understood as the human life of Christ or the realm of material existence more broadly.' Joseph Lenow, 'Christ, the Praying Animal: A Critical Engagement with Niels Henrik Gregersen and the Christology of Deep Incarnation', in *International Journal of Systematic Theology,* 20/4 (October 2018): 554–578, here at 556.

7. Edwards, *Natural World and God,* 39.

8. Irenaeus, *The Demonstration of the Apostolic Preaching,* 33; cited by Edwards, *Deep Incarnation,* Chapter 2. 'Wherefore also He [Jesus] passed through every stage of life, restoring to all communion with God', in Irenaeus, *Against Heresies* 3.18.7 (ANF, 1:448).

9. Athanasius, *De Incarnatione* 14, cited by Edwards, 'Incarnation and the Natural World: Explorations in the Tradition of Athanasius', in *Incarnation,* 157–176, here at 163.

of deep incarnation', cantillates Kristin Johnston Largen, editor of *Dialog, a Journal of theology,* 'reminds us that, in Christ, God entered into the whole of creation and united all beings with God, redeeming the entire material universe in the process."[10]

The event of deep incarnation is itself redemptive. According to Oxford's Celia Deane-Drummond's lyrics, deep incarnation is 'the *transformative and dramatic movement* of God in Christ'[11] Denis Edwards joins this chorus.

> I think Gregersen is right to say, then, that being related to the whole universe of creatures is co-constitutive of the Word made flesh. If one were to think of the Word as made flesh simply as an isolated individual, then one would miss the deep truth of incarnation. By the divine intention, the flesh assumed in the incarnation is that of Jesus of Nazareth in all its internal relationality with other human beings, with the community of life on our planet, and with the universe itself in all its dynamic processes. The flesh of Jesus is made from atoms born in the processes of nucleosynthesis in stars, and shaped by 3.7 billion years of evolution on Earth. Social, ecological, and cosmic relationships are not add-ons to the Word made flesh. They are constitutive of the Word made flesh.[12]

'Being related to the whole universe' is co-constitutive of the 'Word made flesh', chants Edwards in agreement with Gregersen. Robert John Russell, who accompanies the deep incarnation chorus on the theological equivalent of a Bösendorfer Disklavier, emphasizes how the divine reach extends beyond our human biology down into basic physics itself, and beyond our Milky Way to the physics of every galaxy.[13]

---

10. Kristin Johnston Largen, 'Un/natural death and distinction', in *Dialog* 57/4 (December 2018): 279–286, here at 282.

11. Celia Deane-Drummond, *A Primer in Ecotheology: Theology for a Fragile Earth* (Eugene OR: Cascade Books, 2017), 87.

12. Edwards, *Deep Incarnation,* 113. Whereas Gregersen emphasizes that the divine Logos always takes incarnate form, Edwards demurs. Edwards leaves room for Logos without the flesh, *asarkos*. Edwards, *Deep Incarnation,* 125.

13. Robert John Russell, 'Jesus: The Way of all Flesh and the Proleptic Feather of Time', in *Incarnation,* 331–353, here at 332.

Even though the Logos made flesh took place in a particular location at a single point in terrestrial history, it is universal and cosmic in efficacy. Because all matter is materially connected by a single cosmic history from the Big Bang to the present moment, the divine presence in Jesus becomes simultaneously the incarnate presence everywhere and everywhen. This seems to be the melody sung by the deep incarnationist choir. This seems to be the key to the coherence of the deep incarnationist fugue.

It is the single history of physical reality—Big Bang cosmology is actually a physical history of the universe—that supplies the glue binding all discreet physical entities into a single physical hypostasis, making it just as universal as the Logos hypostasis is.[14] This underlying unity of physical history helps us demonstrate just how the deep incarnationist moves from the historical flesh of Jesus to the biochemistry of deep sea extremophiles on Earth and the physics of the Whirlpool Galaxy.

Theological Background: Incarnation as Creation

It is the divine Word—the *Logos*—which is responsible for the creation of a world that is other to God. The creation is not divine; it is not the product of an emanation from God's own being. God creates *de novo, ex nihilo*. Before we creatures became something, we were nothing.

Wolfhart Pannenberg can aid our discussion here, because he anchors temporal creation in the eternal perichoresis of the Trinity; and this provides an embarkation port for deep incarnation. When the Son differentiates himself from the Father, the Son makes possible the creation of a world that is not divine.

> For if the eternal Son, in the humility of his self-distinction from the Father moves out of the unity of the deity by letting the Father alone be God, then the creature emerges over against the Father, the creature for whom the relation to the Father and Creator is fundamental, i.e., the human creature. With

---

14. 'As [the Big Bang] story of the universe makes clear, everything is connected with everything else; nothing is isolated.' Elizabeth A Johnson, 'Jesus and the Cosmos: Soundings in Deep Christology', in *Incarnation*, 133–156, here at 137.

> this creature, however, the existence of the world is posited,
> for it is the condition of the possibility of this creature.[15]

A kenosis takes place within the divine life that results in perichoresis. The eternal Son, the Logos, self-differentiates from the first person of the Trinity. This kenotic move includes the Son ceding divinity to the Father alone. Then, when the creation comes into existence ordered according the ubiquitous Logos, the creation becomes non-divine. Looking forward we ask: how then can the physical creation ordered by the Logos become re-sanctified, re-divinised?

Let's trace this path from creation to redemption again. The kenosis of the Son divesting himself of divinity cedes to the Father exclusive divinity, thereby making the second person of the Trinity along with a non-divine world possible. 'In the self-distinction of the eternal Son from the Father . . . he is not united to the Father [so he becomes] the principle of all creaturely existence.'[16] Creation is the product of the trinitarian perichoresis, the dynamic of differentiation and reunion, dividing and uniting, disintegrating and reintergrating. It is the Holy Spirit who is responsible for the unity in love shared by God as Father and God as Son.[17]

This is a theological explication of Genesis 1 and John 1; and it places us on the doorstep of deep incarnation. But it does not quite cross all the way over the threshold. Where Pannenberg leaves us is with a universal Logos present in all physical and spiritual existence; but this Logos has been secularized, so to speak. What remains is to re-divinize the creation through divine presence. This is accomplished by the two natures Christology, by the exchange of attributes, by the *communicatio idiomatum*.

---

15. Wolfhart Pannenberg, *Systematic Theology,* tranalted by Geoffrey W Bromily, 3 Volumes (Grand Rapids MI: Eerdmans, 1991–1998) 2:22–23.

16. Pannenberg, *Systematic Theology*, 2:196. Christopher Southgate, like Pannenberg, locates the alien or otherness condition of the creation in the trinitarian perichoresis. 'Otherness in the Trinity is the basis for the otherness of creation.' Christopher Southgate, 'Creation as "Very Good" and "Groaning in Travail": An Exploration in Evolutionary Theodicy', in *The Evolution of Evil*, edited by Gaymon Bennett, Martinez Hewlett, Ted Peters, and Robert John Russell (Göttingen: Vandenhoeck & Ruprecht, 2008), 53–85, here at 64.

17. See Ted Peters, *God as Trinity: Relationality and Temporality in Divine Life* (Louisville KY: Westminster John Knox, 1993).

Can the human Jesus take on the attributes of God and remain human? Can God take on human attributes and remain divine? Deep incarnationists answer in the affirmative to both.

What all this adds up to is the inextricable tie between creation and redemption. While creating, God is also redeeming. While God is creating a world, God is present everywhere in the non-divine world as the Logos. What is clear is that the divine Logos is universal. As Logos the second person of the Trinity is as ubiquitous as the physical universe. But, the deep incarnationists make an additional claim: the fleshly presence of the Son is equally ubiquitous. How can this position be justified?

What remains to date underdeveloped within the school of deep incarnationalism is God's ubiquitous presence in the flesh, in the world's materiality. Deep incarnationists have asserted this presence, but have they sufficiently explained just how the human Jesus has become ubiquitous? Have they sufficiently explained the connection between Jesus' individual incarnation and the breadth of physical creation?

The prevailing deep incarnationist position needs to be buttressed, I believe, with a greater investment in history and eschatology. 'The act of creation had an origin such that it continues to the eschatological finale, itself an act of new creation. Creation is history, natural history,' declares Paul Hinlicky rightly.[18] It's the history of creation consummated in its eschatological redemption that renders incarnation efficacious.

Regardless of my doubts here, let's presume that the position developed by deep incarnationist theology is sound. Then let's test its illuminative power by examining its implications. Let's ask: what are its implications for the cosmos, especially the cosmos as explicated for us by the natural sciences? Specifically, by astrobiology?

Theological Foreground: Theology of Nature

To proceed to answer this query, we must appeal methodologically to a *Theology of Nature*. Within the more comprehensive field of Theology and Science, a theology of nature interprets the natural world as scientists see it in light of a theological perspective.

---

18. Paul R Hinlicky, *Beloved Community: Critical Dogmatics after Christendom* (Grand Rapids MI: Eerdmans, 2015), 751.

Nature can itself provide a source for theological reflection. Russian Orthodox physicist, Alexei Nesteruk, feels nature's invitation to love God's creation. 'To enquire into the sense of the universe means not only to know it, but to be in communion with it, to love it.'[19]

Yet, even with the natural world as a source, a theology of nature relies upon special revelation for its norm. 'A theology of nature is appropriate as long as it is suitably qualified by proper attention to revealed theology', avers Deane-Drummond.[20] Through the lenses of biblical revelation, the theologian of nature re-assesses what scientists see through their telescopes and microscopes. In what comes next in our discussion, it's what we see through telescopes.

In a theology-of-nature recital, the theologian need not merely sing the scientist's song. The theologian may compose distinctively theological lyrics. Yet, discord between theology and science should be avoided when possible. Rather, it is consonance theologians pursue. Complete harmony is not necessary; only consonance is. 'There must be consonance between the assertions of science and theology about the world in which we live', asserts the hybrid physicist and theologian, John Polkinghorne.[21]

Theologians dare not hire scientists as subcontractors to renovate doctrinal theology. But theologians can borrow scientific building materials for their own construction. When possible, a theology of nature should exhibit some level of consonance with the scientific worldview. This applies especially to astrotheology, to which we now turn.

Constructing Astrotheology on a Deep Incarnation Base

In what follows we will see if we can construct an astrotheology on a deep incarnation base. Although he did not use the term, *astrotheology*, Edwards himself engaged the question of extraterrestrial life.

19. Alexei V Nesteruk, *The Sense of the Universe: Philosophical Explication of Theological Commitment in Modern Cosmology* (Minneapolis: Fortress Press, 2015), 6.

20. Celia Deane-Drummond, *Christ and Evolution: Wonder and Wisdom* (Minneapolis: Fortress Press, 2009), xvi.

21. John Polkinghorne, *One World: The Interaction of Science and Theology* (Princeton NJ: Princeton University Press, 1986), 78.

Theologians cannot know exactly how God might freely act with regard to extraterrestrials. But if God's creation includes such creatures, we have good reason to trust that God also gives God's self to them in the Word and in the Spirit, with the same generous and extravagant love we encounter in our own experiences of incarnation and grace.[22]

Astrotheology as a solo within the larger theology-of-nature chorus includes theological reflection on astrobiology and related space sciences. And more. Here is the definition of *astrotheology* the scholars at CTNS in Berkeley work with.

Astrotheology is that branch of theology which provides a critical analysis of the contemporary space sciences combined with an explication of classic doctrines such as creation and Christology for the purpose of constructing a comprehensive and meaningful understanding of our human situation within an astonishingly immense cosmos.[23]

With this definition in mind, we will ask about the implications of deep incarnation for three astral concerns: how does deep incarnation apply (1) to inanimate physical and chemical processes located at unconquerable distances elsewhere in the universe? (2) to microbial or non-intelligent life within our solar system or elsewhere in the Milky Way galaxy? (3) to intelligent life elsewhere in the Milky Way? Because galaxies beyond the Milky Way are speeding away at such high rates of speed, and even accelerating, we cannot imagine any two-way communication beyond our own immediate galaxy. We may be able to develop an interactive relationship with exoplanets within the Milky Way, but it's theoretically impossible beyond. For the sake of realism, the second and third questions will be galactic, while the first one will be extra-galactic and cosmic in scope.

---

22. Edwards, *Deep Incarnation,* 101–102.
23. Ted Peters, 'Introducing Astrotheology', in *Astrotheology: Where Science and Theology Meet Extraterrestrial Life,* edited by Ted Peters, Martinez Hewlett, Joshua Moritz, and Robert John Russell, (Eugene OR: Cascade, 2018) 3–26, here at 23–24, italics in original.

The Logos, the Cosmological Principle, and the Copernican Principle

How many galaxies are in our universe? Scientific estimates keep changing, changing upward. University of Arizona astrobiologist Chris Impey and Hayden Planetarium director Niel DeGrasse Tyson estimate one hundred billion galaxies.[24] Recently, estimates by other astronomers have jumped to a trillion and then two trillion.[25]

If we live among two trillion galaxies, how many stars? If the Milky Way hosts four hundred billion stars, and if this is typical of other galaxies, the universe is filled with a lot of real estate for God's omniscience to supervise.

Do the stars and planets in each of those galaxies operate according to the same laws of physics and chemistry as we study here on Earth? Scientists must assume that this is the case, otherwise astrophysics as a science would be unthinkable. The assumption that the universe is homogenous seems to get confirmed as researchers learn more and more. This assumption has a name: the *Cosmological Principle*. According to Harvard astronomer Owen Gingerich, the Cosmological Principle says 'that the universe should be homogeneous and uniform not only in space, but also in time'.[26]

A corollary of the cosmological principle is the Copernican Principle. According to physicist turned astrobiologist at Arizona State University, Paul Davies, the *Copernican Principle* "says that our location in space isn't special or privileged in any way, so that what happens in our part of the universe should happen elsewhere too."[27] Because the laws of nature obtain both at home on Earth as well as on a planet orbiting a star in the farthest galaxy, we earthlings have

---

24. Chris Impey, *Humble Before the Void* (Conshohocken PA: Templeton Press, 2014), 154–155; Neil DeGrasse Tyson, *Astrophysics for People in a Hurry* (New York: WW Norton, 2017), 62.

25. Christopher J Conselice, 'Our Trillion-Galaxy Universe', in *Astronomy* 45/6 (2017): 8; Ted Peters, 'Oh No! Not More Galaxies!', in *Theology and Science*, 15/2 (May 2017): 133; Ted Peters, 'Oh No! Still More Galaxies!', in *Theology and Science*, 15/3 (August 2017): 219.

26. Owen Gingerich, *God's Planet* (Cambridge MA: Harvard University Press, 2014), 112.

27. Paul Davies, *The Eerie Silence: Renewing Our Search for Alien Intelligence* (Boston: Houghton Miflin Harcourt, 2010) 205.

no claim at being special. At least, no scientific claim. What about a spiritual claim?

It has been said frequently that the Copernican Principle is responsible for a spiritual revolution in Western culture. In the face of heliocentrism and deep space, we modern earthlings feel small, marginalised, de-centered. Here is how former Vatican Observatory astronomer José Funes articulates the spiritual implications of Copernicus.

> A 'Copernican Revolution', in spiritual terms, means going out, leaving our own convictions, our well-known land and culture to change our mindset if necessary, not being auto-referential . . . We can ask ourselves: What is the place of humankind in this huge Universe of billions of galaxies, each of them with billions of stars, and billions of worlds? This question opens our hearts and minds to another deeper question full of wonder as put it by the Psalm 8: 'What are humans that you are mindful of them, mere mortals that you care for them?' (Ps 8, 5)[28]

Despite this interpretation of cultural history, the astrotheologian should attend primarily to the scientific version of the Copernican Principle, not the alleged spiritual revolution. Astrotheology responds first to astrobiology, not to debatable interpretations of Western culture.

Here is what is important: these two astrophysical principles—the Cosmological and the Copernican—look a lot like what theologians know as the Logos, the rational structure within the trinitarian perichoresis upon which the structure of the creation is established.

Scientists tend to mathematize the Logos. Marcelo Gleiser, astronomer at Dartmouth College, declares: "No question about it: There is order in the universe and much of science is about finding patterns of behavior—from quarks to mammals to galaxies—that we translate into general laws . . . [We] build mathematical or conceptual

---

28. José G Funes, SJ, "The Road Map to Other Earths: Lessons Learned and Challenges Ahead," *Astrotheology*, 56–73, here at 64. "Human beings are not the centre of the universe. In fact, it is the human belief that we are the centre of all things that the Bible calls sin . . . .. God is the centre of all things, and we are creatures given status by his love." David Wilkinson, *Science, Religion, and the Search for Extraterrestrial Intelligence* (Oxford: Oxford University Press, 2013), 148.

models to understand it better."[29] Such treatment of nature's laws leads Drew theologian Catherine Keller to connect scientific cosmology with Logos cosmology. "Primal themes, like $E=mc^2$ and the law of gravity, seem to express the law or *logos* of this universe."[30] What theologians have learned from Holy Scripture about God's Word seems consonant with the Cosmological Principle, with the confirmed assumption that the most distant galaxies operate according to the same principles we see exhibited here on Earth.

This should suffice to establish consonance between the theological concept of the Logos, on the one hand, and scientific modeling of the cosmos, on the other. The divine Logos is just as much at home in the Whirlpool Galaxy as it is in the Milky Way.[31]

But does this suffice to establish deep incarnation on planets in the Whirlpool Galaxy? No. Because the concept of deep incarnation does not rely on the Logos alone, on Christ's divine nature alone. Rather, deep incarnation relies on the hypostatic union, the presence of Christ's human nature and the exchange of attributes between the human and the divine. How can we know whether the Logos is *physically* present in off-Earth sites, bodily present under the conditions of finite time and space?

For deep incarnationism to apply to off-Earth locations especially at great distances, we need a bridge premise. One candidate for the office of bridge premise would be the *communicatio idiomatum*. How can the communication of attributes taking place in the personal biography of Jesus apply to off-Earth histories which may never converge with Jesus' terrestrial history? Until such a connecting premise is constructed, theologians will have to be satisfied with the ubiquity of the Logos but shy away from commitments to deep incarnation.

We will return to the *communicatio idiomatum* later. In the meantime, we need to assess challenges to the concept of deep incarnation arising from astrobiological speculations about extraterrestrial life.

---

29. Marcelo Gleiser, 'How Much Can We Know?', in *Nature*, 557:7704 (10 May 2018) S20–S21, here at S21.

30. Catherine Keller, *On the Mystery: Discerning God in Process* (Minneapolis: Fortress, 2008), 60.

31. "The Logos-Christ expresses Himself in the logoi of every created nature of animals, insects, plants, minerals . . ." Maximus the Confessor, *On Difficulties in the Church Fathers: the Ambigua* 1:8; edited and translated by Nicholas Costas (Cambridge MA: Harvard University Press, 2014), 269.

What about Microbes and other Critters?

Astrobiologists customarily distinguish between non-intelligent life and intelligent life. I have argued to the contrary that this is a misleading distinction. I contend that all life, regardless of how simple, is intelligent.[32] What is empirically observable is that intelligence comes in degrees, with *Homo sapiens* relatively more intelligent than wombats; and wombats relatively more intelligent than amoebas. Despite the persuasiveness of my argument, I have failed to date to convince the world's space scientists to erase the distinction between intelligent ET and non-intelligent ET. The conventional distinction still obtains in astrobiological literature. Sigh! So, rather than fight convention, we will work here with the scientific distinction between microbial life and intelligent life.

The consensus among space scientists is that no intelligent life lives within the solar system, except on Earth. Even though no off-Earth life has yet been discovered, astrobiologists are hopeful they will find microbial life on Mars or a moon of Saturn or Jupiter. Microbial life, but not intelligent life. That's the most we can hope for. The search goes on.

Let's ask: what would be the Christological or soteriological implications of discovering microbial life on Mars, Titan, Europa, or Enceladus? Would the divine Logos be present? Yes, indeed. What about the incarnate Christ? This is an as yet underdeveloped question.

We may safely assume, according to the Cosmological Principle, that the physical, chemical, and most likely the biological processes we know on Earth will apply to off-Earth sites as well. And we may safely assume that the divine Logos is equally homogenous and ubiquitous. Yet, we must ask: does the Cosmological Principle in itself count as support for deep incarnation? Will God share in microbial suffering off-Earth just as God does on-Earth? Will this shared suffering be redemptive as well? If so, how do theologians explain this?

---

32. Ted Peters, 'Where There's Life There's Intelligence,' in *What is Life? On Earth and Beyond*, ed., Andreas Losch (Cambridge UK: Cambridge University Press, 2017), 236–259.

The ETI Myth: A Slight Detour

To date astronomers have confirmed more than four thousand exoplanets within the Milky Way, some of which qualify as earthlike.[33] To be earthlike a planet should be rocky and within a temperature range to accommodate liquid water. This temperature range places the planet in the habitable zone, or Hz. In time, astrobiologists are confident the number of Hz confirmed planets in our galaxy will number in the billions.

Before drawing out the implications of so many Hz planets, let's take a slight detour into an important assumption at work in the science of astrobiology, namely the assumption that evolution is progressive, progressing from the simple toward the complex, from the non-intelligent to the intelligent. To assume that evolution is progressive is questionable if not doubtful, in my judgment; yet we must proceed. This assumption includes corollary assumptions such as this one: where pre-biotic conditions favorable to life exist, such as on an earth-sized planet in the habitable zone, life will begin as simple organisms. After a period, simple life will evolve into complex life, leading over time to intelligent life.

This progressive evolutionary assumption continues with an additional corollary: should life on another planet have evolved longer than it has on Earth, then that life will be more intelligent than terrestrial life. This means that the beings who live today in such an extraterrestrial environment will be more advanced in science and technology. This is a very self-serving assumption, obviously; it is widely held by scientists who like to think they themselves represent the highest stage of evolution on our home planet thus far. This line of thinking has all the earmarks of a myth told to celebrate the status of the myth-teller, to enhance the status of the terrestrial space scientist.[34]

Like telling a story with the story-teller as the superhero, Paul Davies dramatizes the logic of this ETI myth. "There will be communities of beings who may have reached our stage of development millions of years ago. Those beings are likely to be far ahead of us not only scientifically and technologically, but ethically too. Quite possibly they will have used genetic engineering to eliminate grossly criminal or

---

33. As of Valentine's day, February 14, 2020, NASA confirmed 4126 exoplanets. https://exoplanets.nasa.gov/.

34. See Ted Peters, 'Extraterrestrial Salvation and the ETI Myth', *Astrotheology*, 347–377.

antisocial behaviour. By our standards they would be truly saintly."[35] Advanced science and technology will destine our ETI neighbors to ethical sainthood, just as terrestrial science and technology are currently saving us on Earth from ignorance and sin. This is quite a myth![36]

This ETI myth suffers from two drawbacks. First, science does not back it up. Most evolutionary biologists deny that evolution is directed by any progressive teleology. The late Stephen Jay Gould, Harvard paleontologist and evolutionary biologist, denies even the direction toward increased complexity. 'We are glorious accidents of an unpredictable process with no drive to complexity.'[37] Therefore, we should conclude that even if life should begin on an exoplanet, there is little or no likelihood that it will progress toward complex organisms and intelligence as it did on Earth. So, there is no sound scientific basis to speculate that extraterrestrial life evolving millions of years longer will produce a more advanced civilization.[38]

The theologian need not, therefore, hum the progressive evolutionist's song, says Richard Baukham. 'There is no one direction of development favored by evolution.'[39]

The second drawback is that we have zero empirical evidence that extraterrestrial life exists in either microbial or intelligent form, so scientists are unable to put such assumptions to the test. This leaves plenty of room for alternative scenarios to be raised. Here's one we'll call the *microbe hypothesis*: microbial life is prevalent in the universe, even though highly intelligent life is rare. Here's a second one we'll call the *art and beauty hypothesis*: a more highly advanced extraterrestrial civilization exists; but it has elected to perfect art and beauty rather than science and technology. A third alternative is the *zoo hypothesis*: at

---

35. Davies, *Eerie Silence*, 189.
36. Simon Conway Morris speaks of 'evolutionary myths. Not fairy-tales, of course, but areas of received wisdom that might benefit from a re-examination, or if you prefer a really good kicking'. Simon Conway Morris, 'If the Evolution of Intelligence is inevitable, then what are the Metaphysical Consequences?', in *The Science and Religion Dialogue: Past and Future*, edited by Michael Welker (Frankfurt am Main: Peter Lang GmbH, 2014), 218.
37. Stephen Jay Gould, *Full House* (New York: Three Rivers Press, 1996).
38. Davies actually knows that importing progress into evolutionary biology is not scientific. 'Unfortunately, the popular view of evolution as progress is at best a serious oversimplification, at worst, just plain wrong', *Eerie Silence*, 68.
39. Bauckham, 'The Incarnation and the Cosmic Christ', *Incarnation*, 25–58, here at 47.

least one extraterrestrial civilisation treats Earth and all its inhabitants as a zoo, watching us but preventing us from seeing them. We are not yet ready to confirm or disconfirm any such hypotheses.

Despite these drawbacks and unconfirmed hypotheses, I recommend that the astrotheologian tentatively though conditionally accept the ETI myth as our astrobiologists tell it. At least the progressive evolution component, but certainly not the pseudo-soteriology associated with the confidence that 'science saves'.

Why should the theologian address progressive evolution? Astrotheology is constructive theology, and construction requires disciplined imagination. Pursuing hypothetical consonance with the space sciences could lead to fertile speculation about the implications of deep incarnation. By pressing research agendas drawn from astrobiology on to deep incarnation Christology, we can test the deep incarnation thesis for its applicability, coherence, and illuminative power. This would count as a thought-experimental at work.

While waiting for the confirmation or disconfirmation of the ETI myth through contact with creatures more intelligent and more advanced than Earth's *Homo sapiens,* we can now project two scenarios. The first is biological. We can imagine aliens who are biological organisms with intelligence, consciousness, and technology sufficiently advanced to communicate. The second scenario imagines post-biological ETI. We can imagine an extraterrestrial civilization so technologically advanced that mind has escaped the body and now resides digitally in the computer cloud. The first fits deep incarnation Christology, but the second seems to falsify it.

An intelligent mind without a biological body. That's what we're talking about. Transhumanists call this *Substrate Independent Mind* or SIM.

> If we can carry out the function of a mind both in a biological brain and in a brain that is composed of computer software or neuromorphic hardware . . . then that mind is substrate-independent. The mind continues to depend on a substrate to exist and to operate, of course, but there are substrate choices.[40]

---

40. Randal A Koene, 'Uploading to Substrate-Independent Minds', in *The Transhumanist Reader,* edited by Max More and Natasha Vita-More (Oxford: Wiley Blackwell, 2013), 146–156, here at 146.

Here is the issue. If scientists either here on Earth or on a more highly advanced exoplanet were to develop non-biological or disembodied intelligence, would this nullify the *incarnate* dimension of the incarnation? Would the divine Logos which appeared as the divine hypostasis in Jesus' incarnation eliminate the carnal or physical access to divine presence? Would the eternal Logos merge directly with the disembodied consciousness of our posthuman design? Let's explore this.

What about Disembodied Intelligence on Exoplanets?

Techno-prognosticators here on Earth anticipate that today's humanity will evolve into something higher, posthumanity. The transhumanists (called Human Plus or H+) among us picture themselves as leading the transition from the human to the posthuman.[41] Our consciousness will get uploaded into a computer, they forecast; and then we will live in the cloud, bodiless, indefinitely. Soon we earthlings will cross the threshold of the Singularity, when machine intelligence will supersede the biologically dependent intelligence we've known.

One relevant goal of the H+ movement on earth is to shed our biology in favor of electronic existence through whole brain emulation, through uploading. Ray Kurzweil anticipates uploading our intelligence to the computer cloud. 'Uploading a human brain means scanning all of its salient details and then reinstantiating those details into a suitably powerful computational substrate. This process would capture a person's entire personality, memory, skills, and history.'[42]

---

41. 'As a philosophy transhumanism deals with the fundamental nature of reality, knowledge, and existence. As a worldview, it offers a cultural ecology for understanding the human integration with technology. As a scientific study, it provides the techniques for observing how technology is shaping society and the practice for investigating ethical outcomes. Its social narrative emerges from humans overcoming odds and the continued desire to build a world worth living in. These processes require critical thinking and visionary accounts to assess how technology is altering human nature and what it means to be human in an uncertain world.' Natasha Vita-More, 'History of Transhumanism', in *The Transhumanism Handbook,* edited by Newton Lee (Heidelberg: Springer, 2019), 49–62, here at 49.

42. Ray Kurzweil, *The Singularity is Near: When Humans Transcend Biology* (New York: Penguin, 2005), 198–199.

Once uploaded into the computer cloud, our digitised minds would no longer be subject to physical death. We would become immortal. 'Post-human minds will lead to a different future and we will be better as we merge with our technology . . . humans will be able to upload their entire minds to The Living Cyberspace and BECOME IMMORTAL.'[43]

This digital techno-utopia will liberate us from our fleshly bodies. '*As humanism freed us from the chains of superstition, let transhumanism free us from our biological chains*', we find in the Transhumanist Manifesto.[44] If transhumanists accomplish their goals, our future descendants will live solely in the domain of Logos, unencumbered by the flesh. Might this nullify the accomplishment of the hypostatic union?

From the transhumanist vision it is a small step to imagine that our new space neighbors will have already made this advance. At least according to Paul Davies.

> In a million years, if humanity isn't wiped out before that, biological intelligence will be viewed as merely the midwife of 'real' intelligence—the powerful, scalable, adaptable, immortal sort that is characteristic of the machine realm . . . And at that stage, the self-created godlike mega-brains will seek to spread across the universe.[45]

Machine intelligence, whether terrestrial or extraterrestrial, will live in the computer cloud, not in a fleshly body. What are the implications of disembodied intelligence for deep incarnation?

Self-identified *Christian* Transhumanists voice a need to protect the role of the body within the story of salvation. 'The body is part of God's good creation, described as the temple of the Holy Spirit for those who are redeemed, and Jesus' bodily incarnation, resurrection and ascension demonstrate the value God places on the physical human body. So then, should we. And yet, it is not the body that is to

---

43. Henrique Jorge, 'Digital Eternity', *Transhumanism Handbook*, 645–650, here at 650.

44. Simon Young, *Designer Evolution: A Transhumanist Manifesto* (Amherst, NY: Prometheus Books, 2006), 32, italics in original.

45. Davies, *Eerie Silence*, 161. See Ted Peters, 'Outer Space and Cyber Space: Meeting ETI in the Cloud', in *International Journal of Astrobiology* doi:10.1017/S1473550416000318 © Cambridge University Press 2016.

be worshipped nor is this flesh-suit eternal.'[46] On the one hand, some secular transhumanists seek cybernetic immortality in the form of disembodied machine consciousness. On the other hand, Christian transhumanists reaffirm the normative place of the fleshly body in human existence.

As we draw out the implications of posthuman consciousness living in the computer cloud, we see friction with the Christian notion of redemption of the flesh. A disembodied intelligence no longer subject to physical death would already have attained a near equivalent of the eternal Logos, so it would not need resurrection. This means it's difficult to conceive of how the Christian promise of resurrection-of-the-body would apply to an already disembodied intelligence.

One deep incarnationist refrain is that the Logos is perpetually incarnate in material reality. What will happen, then, if we hear intelligible voices mumbling from an extraterrestrial computer cloud in a disembodied state? How will the enfleshment of the Logos apply? Will digitised immortality provide a substitute salvation superior to resurrection of the body?

Here is my preliminary judgment. Whether our mind belongs to a biological or non-biological substrate, deep incarnation would apply. Deep incarnation theology does not necessarily privilege biochemistry over abiotic chemistry or even physics. If any life belongs to the creaturely world, it is included in the body of the Logos.

One Deep Incarnation or Many?

Another among the questions the astrotheologian must confront is this: *If multiple societies of extraterrestrial intelligent beings on exoplanets exist, can we forecast that God will or already has provided a species-specific incarnation for each planet parallel to God's incarnation in Jesus Christ on Earth?* Some theologians respond affirmatively and tout multiple incarnations, while other theologians contend that God's single incarnate history in Jesus of Nazareth on Earth is efficacious for the entire cosmos. What happens to this question when we introduce deep incarnation?

---

46. Carmen Fowler LaBerge, 'Christian? Transhumanist? A Christian Primer for Engaging Transhumanism', *Transhumanism Handbook,* 771–776, here at 774 .

Arguing on behalf of multiple incarnations we find theologians such as Robert John Russell, Ilia Delio, and John Polkinghorne. Russell's argument begins with the *problem of distance.* We must factor in the almost unimaginable enormity of the visible universe, which is ~46 billion light years in size. We must also factor in the physical limitations on communication between us and distant solar systems by the finite speed of light. For example, it would take 3.4 years for signals from Earth just to reach the nearest star, Alpha Centauri; and it would take some 2.5 million years to reach the nearest galaxy, Andromeda. So, Russell asks, how could we communicate the terrestrial revelation of Jesus to the countless species of ETI strewn across the immeasurable distances of space? Needless to say, without such communication ET could not come to have faith and participate in the ecclesial community of those who belong to Jesus' history on Earth. Therefore, concludes Russell, 'God provides multiple incarnations wherever ETI has evolved.'[47] For Russell, what we learn from science about the distances in space provides the data for rendering a theological judgment.

Ilia Delio makes a theological rather than a scientific argument on behalf of multiple incarnations. Delio, like Edwards following Karl Rahner, sees incarnation as divine self-bestowal. We can, therefore, expect multiple divine self-bestowals on multiple planets as long as an extraterrestrial intelligence is ready to receive it. 'Incarnation on an extraterrestrial level could conceivably take place, as long as there is some type of intelligence within the extraterrestrial species to grasp the Word of God through knowledge of the divine embodied Word. ... many incarnations but one Christ.'[48] Or, as John Polkinghorne puts it colorfully, 'God's creative purposes may well include "little green men" as well as humans, and if they need redemption we may well think that the Word would take little green flesh just as we believe the Word took our flesh.'[49]

---

47. Robert John Russell, 'Many Incarnations or One?', *Astrotheology*, 303–317, here at 303.

48. Ilia Delio, *Christ in Evolution* (Maryknoll NY: Orbis Books, 2012), 169. 'In view of the immutability of God in himself and the identity of the Logos with God, it cannot be proved that a multiple incarnation in different histories of salvation is absolutely unthinkable.' Karl Rahner, 'Natural Science and Reasonable Faith', in *Theological Investigations*, 22 volumes (London: Darton, Longman, and Todd, 1961–1976; New York: Seabury, 1974–1976; New York: Crossroad, 1976–1988), 21: 16–55, here at 50.

49. John Polkinghorne, *Science and the Trinity: The Christian Encounter with Reality* (New Haven CT: Yale University Press, 2004), 177.

Arguing for the opposing position—the cosmic sufficiency of God's action in the one incarnation on Earth—we find Joshua Moritz, Mark Worthing, and George Coyne. Moritz, managing editor of *Theology and Science,* makes the position clear: 'the one incarnation of God in Christ is efficacious for all sentient creatures [the animals, the Neanderthals, and ET] wherever and whenever they live.'[50] Similarly, Adelaide theologian Mark Worthing posits a single cosmic Christ implying the single-incarnation view. 'If there is other intelligent life in the universe then God relates to it through Christ—the same Christ through whom God reconciles us to Godself. I do not believe Christian theology can posit a multiplicity of Christs and remain Christian theology.'[51]

The late George Coyne, SJ, director of the Vatican Observatory from 1978 to 2006, factors deep incarnation into astrotheogical speculation; and deep incarnation seems to support a single historical incarnation rather than multiple.

> How could he be God and leave extraterrestrials in their sin? After all he was good to us. Why should he not be good to them? God chose a very specific way to redeem human beings. He sent his only Son, Jesus, to them and Jesus gave up his life so that human beings would be saved from their sin. Did God do this for extraterrestrials? . . . There is deeply embedded in Christian theology . . . the notion of the universality of God's redemption and even the notion that all creation, even the inanimate, participates in some way in his redemption.[52]

In sum, what happened on Earth when God became incarnate in Jesus of Nazareth is efficacious for the redemption of creatures regardless of their respective planet, star, or galaxy.

Now let's ask: what are the implications for deep incarnation Christology prompted by this debate within astrotheology? All parties

---

50. Joshua M Moritz, 'One *Imago Dei* and the Incarnation of the Eschatological Adam', in *Astrotheology,* 330–346, here at 343.
51. Mark Worthing, 'The Possibility of Extraterrestrial intelligence as Theological Thought Experiment', edited by Terence Kelly and Hilary Regan, *God, Life, Intelligence and the Universe* (Adelaide, Australia: ATF Press, 2002) 61–84 here at 83.
52. George V Coyne, SJ, 'The Evolution of Intelligent Life on Earth and Possibly Elsewhere: Reflections from a Religious Tradition', in *Many Worlds,* edited by Steven Dick (Radnor PA: Templeton Press, 2000), 177–188, here at 187.

will grant the ubiquity of the divine Logos. As Logos, Christ is present everywhere and everywhen. To be incarnate, however, requires divine presence in a particular time and a particular location. The historical Jesus is singular; he belongs to one span of time and one geographical location. Must this be duplicated again and again within the time and place of each intelligent civilization? In my judgement: no, this does not follow. I expect a deep incarnationist to take the following position: one single historical incarnation event suffices to establish the incorporation of temporal materiality within the eternal perichoresis that is the divine life. Once is for all.

In the single historical event we know as the life of Jesus, a communication of attributes took place. This exchange of attributes suffices to establish that the once non-divine creation has now been taken up into the divine life; and the non-divine creation is now a home for that divine life. God takes up residence in the world, and the world takes up residence in God. Our trinitarian God relates to Godself through the creation everywhere and everywhen, on Earth and in our heavens.

Communication of Attributes

I suggest that the astrotheologian relying on deep incarnation could benefit from a bridge premise developed from the *communicatio idiomatum*.

The ancient concept of the communication of attributes or *communicatio idiomatum* refers to the exchange of properties between the two natures of Jesus of Nazareth, the divine and the human. The human receives the attributes of majesty such as eternity or sovereignty, while the divine receives the attributes of humiliation such as sin, suffering, and death. In the Lutheran tradition, this exchange takes place in reality, *vere et realiter,* 'so that suffering and death can be predicated of God and sovereignty over the world can be predicated of the babe in the manger'.[53]

---

53. Notger Slencska, 'Communicatio Idiomatum', in *Religion Past and Present,* edited by Hans Dieter Betz; Don S Browning; Bernd Janowski; and Eberhard Jüngel; English translation of *Religion in Geschichte und Gegenwart,* 14 volumes (Leiden and Boston: Brill, 2007–2014), 3:302–303.

Ignatius of Antioch (35–107) had already implicitly answered in the affirmative when writing against the Gnostics. He would speak of 'the blood of God' or use antinomies such as 'God existing in the flesh; true life in death; both of Mary and of God'.[54] The concept of the *communicatio idiomatum* was further developed by the Alexandrian theologians, according to whom the flesh of Jesus shares in the properties of the Logos while remaining flesh. Conversely, the Logos shares in the properties of the flesh while remaining Logos. The particular and the universal interpenetrate. Theologian Ingolf Dalferth applies trinitarian perichoresis to the hypostatic union of two natures, where he finds 'mutually interpenetrating perichoresis that constitutes the intercommunication between his divine and his human nature'.[55]

Among these shared or exchanged properties, we may ask: is sin, suffering and death included? Yes, and no. Fifth century Chalcedonians tried to protect divine impassability by limiting sin, suffering and death to the human nature of the second person. The two natures (Φύσει, *substantiae*), though united in one person (*unio personalis*), remain without confusion, without change, without division, without separation (ἀσυγχύτως, ἀτρέπτως, ἀδιαιρέτως, ἀχωρίστως). Though suffering was admitted to the perichoresis within the life of the Trinity, the eternity and immutability of the first person of the Trinity could, in principle, remain protected. God the Father cannot suffer, even if the human Jesus can suffer. That's the dogma of Chalcedon.

Deep incarnationists, however, risk raising the ire of contemporary Chalcedonians by affirming theopassianism, by affirming suffering within God's life. In the incarnation, God suffers with the creatures. 'The transcendent God has the capacity to enter into the limits and suffering of creaturely existence.'[56] Does this violate the traditional commitment to divine impassibility? God as Father, according to Chalcedon, is immutable and cannot suffer. God as Trinity, including the Son with a human hypostasis, can incorporate the historical suffering of Jesus into the perichoresis.

---

54. Ignatius of Antioch, *Epistle to the Smyrneans*, 8 (ANF, 1:90).
55. Ingolf U Dalferth, *Crucified and Resurrected: Restructuring the Grammar of Christology*, translated by Jo Bennett (Grand Rapids MI: Baker Academic 1994), 145.
56. Edwards, *Deep Incarnation*, 117.

Perhaps we can further clarify by distinguishing between suffering within the trinitarian perichoresis, theopassianism, from the suffering of the first person specifically, patripassionism. Chalcedonians were particularly concerned about protecting the divine Father from pollution by fleshly suffering and death. Is there wiggle room? Might divine suffering apply to the trinitarian perichoresis without compromising the first person as person?

According to *theopassianism*, God genuinely suffers. This is not the same as *patripassianism*, according to which God in the person of the Father would suffer. Might the deep incarnationist affirm theopassianism while denying patripassionism and still remain Chalcedonian? Should the theopassianist squirm between the Scylla of patripassionism, on the one side, and avoid the Charybdis of total divine immutability, on the other?

Perhaps the theological squirming and squeezing of Jürgen Moltmann might be instructive. On the one hand, Moltmann makes it clear that in the cross of Jesus we see God as Godself absorbing the slings and arrows of creaturely sin and suffering.

> The Son suffers and dies on the cross. The Father suffers with him, but not in the same way. There is a Trinitarian solution to the paradox that God is 'dead' on the cross and yet is not dead, once one abandons the simple concept of God.[57]

On the other hand, the divine participation in creaturely suffering takes place *in* the trinitarian life of God, *not in* the person of the Father. 'Jesus death cannot be understood "as the death of God", but only as death *in* God.'[58] Theopassianism, yes. Patripassianism, no. At least according to Moltmann.

Now, I ask: is all this theological wiggling and squirming in Chalcedon's corner necessary? What needs to be affirmed is this: the entire history of the material cosmos is taken up into the perichoresis of the divine life through the material event we know as Jesus the Christ. Regardless of whether we need to protect the first person of

---

57. Jürgen Moltmann, *The Crucified God,* translated by RA Wilson and John Bowden (New York: Harper, 1974), 203.

58. Moltmann, *The Crucified God,* 207, Moltmann's italics.

the Trinity from temporal change, we need not protect the trinitarian life from dynamism, movement, and even change.[59]

This is certainly the song composed by Karl Rahner and sung by Denis Edwards. Rahner rejects the view that in the incarnation change occurs only in the creaturely humanity of Jesus and not in the eternal Logos of God. Rahner holds that an anti-theopassianist position would require that 'all change and history, with all their tribulation, remain on this side of the absolute gulf which necessarily sunders the unchangeable God from the world of change and prevents them from mingling.'[60] Such an anti-theopassianist view would be inadequate, contends Rahner, because it fails to show that what happened in Jesus is precisely the history of the very Word of God. The eternal Logos has a history, Jesus' history plus the history of all creation.

> If anything was not assumed, neither was it redeemed . . . But *everything* has been assumed, for Christ is true human being, true son of Adam, truly lived a human life in all its breadth and height and depth. And hence, everything, without confusion and without separation, is to enter into eternal life; there is to be not only a new heaven but a new earth. Nothing, unless it be eternally damned, can remain outside the blessing, the protection, the transfiguration of this divinization of the whole, which, beginning in Christ, aims at drawing everything that exists into the life of God himself, precisely in order that it may thus have eternal validity conferred upon it. This is the reality of Christ, which constitutes Christianity, the incarnate life of God in our place and our time.[61]

Deep incarnation Christology is the leitmotif in the antiphon I dub, *Rahner's Rule:* the immanent Trinity is the economic Trinity, and the economic Trinity is the immanent Trinity. Rahner calls this his basic axiom, *Grundaxiom.*

---

59. For Luther and the Lutherans, 'the whole doctrine of the *communicatio* in all its genera makes sense only if it employs an understanding of God that is Trinitarian from the outset', Dalderth, *Crucified and Resurrected,* 14. Tacitly, today's deep incarnationists seem to presuppose this five century old position on the *communicatio idiomatum.*

60. Karl Rahner, "On the Theology of the Incarnation," *Theological Investigations,* 4: 105–120, here at 113.

61. Karl Rahner, *Mission and Grace: Essays in Pastoral Theology II* (London: Sheed and Ward, 1963), 39–42.

> The Father is the incomprehensible origin and the original
> unity, the Word his utterance into history, and the Spirit the
> opening up of history into the immediacy of this fatherly
> origin and end. And precisely this Trinity of salvation history,
> as it reveals itself to us by deeds, is the immanent' Trinity.[62]

Let me note that Rahner himself does not draw an implication of Rahner's Rule to support either side in the debate between single incarnation versus multiple. In a separate discussion, Rahner speculates that many events of revelation might occur on extraterrestrial planets; but these revelatory events need not necessarily count as incarnations.

Here is the significance of Rahner's Rule for our discussion: the temporal history of the cosmos becomes the medium through which the incarnate Son interacts with the eternal Father, bound together by the uniting love of the Holy Spirit. Or, in other words, the material history of the temporal cosmos becomes the medium through which the three persons of the Trinity relate to one another in the perichoresis.

My hypothetical conclusion is this: reliance on the *communicatio idiomatum* within deep incarnation Christology supports the notion that the single historical incarnation in Jesus of Nazareth suffices to establish the redeeming relationship between the non-divine creation and the perichoresis within God's trinitarian life. Beyond the Christ event on Earth, no further special incarnational events would be required for the redemption of creation.

In no way does this preclude events of special revelation or other mighty acts of God within the parallel histories of extraterrestrial civilizations.

The bridge notion of the *communicatio idiomatum* improves the explanatory adequacy of deep incarnation Christology. It ameliorates our explanation of the relationship between the universality of the Logos and the particularity of the Jesus of terrestrial history.

Yet, this bridge is not yet sturdy enough to support theological let alone scientific traffic. Establishing God's physical presence in the creation's materiality does not, in itself, explain the redemptive power of deep incarnation. For towers sturdy enough to stabilise the *communicatio idiomatum* bridge, we must turn to eschatology.

---

62. Karl Rahner, *The Trinity*, translated by Joseph Donceel (New York: Herder and Herder, 1970), 46–47.

Adding the Eschatological Stanza

As I have remarked frequently, incarnate presence of the Logos all by itself falls short of redeeming living creatures. In Jesus' incarnation, God experiences not only physicality but also the shadow side of existence, the unredeemed side of nature and history. In the trinitarian perichoresis, God experiences sin and evil. 2 Corinthians 5:21: 'For our sake he made him to be sin who knew no sin, so that in him we might become the righteousness of God.' Divine presence includes presence in sin, evil, and death. Incarnation as divine presence alone does not transform, redeem, or save.

Redemption is yet outstanding. Hinlicky makes clear that incarnation requires eschatology to be what it is. 'The Incarnation is inaugurated, not completed eschatology.'[63]

Redemption is achieved through the Easter resurrection of Jesus combined with God's promise of an eschatological new creation. Romans 6:5: 'For if we have been united with him in a death like his, we will certainly be united with him in a resurrection like his.'[64]

Redemption is achieved through the Easter resurrection followed by the eschatological new creation. Or, perhaps it's the reverse. God's future new creation reaches back into our temporal span and blesses us with that redemption in anticipation. It is through this anticipation that the material world becomes one and undergoes what Edwards dubs 'transfiguration' and 'deification'.[65]

It is the theological seed of prolepsis planted by Moltmann and Pannenberg and cultivated by Russell that anchors the supporting columns of the *communicatio idiomatum* bridge. Let me adumbrate.

First, the astrotheologian along with the deep incarnationist should recognise the inextricable connection between the eschatological new creation, Easter, and transformation. 'Eschatology entails a transfiguration of the entire cosmos based on the bodily resurrection

---

63. Hinlicky, *Beloved Community,* 475.
64. The Christian faith confesses the resurrection of Jesus Christ as an eschatological saving event simply because it proves that not even death prevents God from maintaining living fellowship with those whom he wants to be together: it determines unequivocally and irrecovably the life-giving power of God's desire for fellowship and his love for his creation.' Dalferth, *Crucified and Risen,* 28.
65. Edwards, 'Incarnation and the Natural World', 176.

of Jesus at Easter such that all of nature is taken up by God and made into the New Creation', exclaims Russell.[66]

Second, prolepsis:

> The Christ event is a prolepsis or connection with ordinary time in which the eschatologically transformed new creation extends back into time at Easter. I am proposing that we extend this concept such that the prolepsis normatively revealed in Easter is available and happens *at each moment* in the history of the universe, and thus *at the moment of death of all creatures.* In this way, every creature at its death experiences the real presence of the risen Lord taking it up directly into the new creation.[67]

The eternal new creation will not only transform the temporal history of the universe, it become available ahead of time at the moment of each creature's death just as it did in the case of Jesus.

To repeat: the eschatological new creation reaches back into the present moment, confronting each creature with the ultimacy of cosmic transformation. Total transformation is as close to us as the next moment, inspiring us through confrontation and anticipation.

Third, the new creation applies to the entire cosmos, to all that is biological, physical, and even in the computer cloud. 'The proleptic character of resurrection, while grounded normatively in the Easter event and intended primarily for the redemption of humanity, can be thought of as extended to and efficacious for all living creatures.'[68] All living creatures, and all the chemistry and physics that constitute living creatures, according to Russell.

Fourth, the eschatological new creation unifies all that exists now and ever has existed in the one history of the universe from the Big Bang on to its final future. All that has been becomes what it truly is only at the moment of its renewal in the new creation. Eschatological renewal retroactively re-defines and hence defines in the first place every event and every entity that has been. God's ongoing creation will not be completed until it is redeemed.

---

66. Robert John Russell, *Cosmology from Alpha to Omega: The Creative Mutual Interaction of Theoloyg and Science* (Minneapolis: Fortress Press, 2008), 293.

67. Russell, 'Jesus: The Way of all Flesh and the Proleptic Feather of Time', *Incarnation*, 351.

68. Russell, 'Jesus: The Way of all Flesh and the Proleptic Feather of Time', *Incarnation*, 345–346.

Fifth, the proleptic anticipation of God's new creation ahead of time in Jesus' Easter resurrection relies on the *adventus* rather than the *futurum* dimension of time. *Futurum* foresees a future as development from the past, an evolution. *Adventus* foresees a future as an abrupt and decisive transformation, as an act of God's grace without precedent in previous natural history. The 'new' in 'new creation' includes a genuinely 'new' component, even as it fulfills all that has come before.

Reliance on the *adventus* component to temporality leads to reluctance on the part of the theologian to endorse progressive evolution or transhumanist promises of utopia, and certainly not the ETI myth. Implicit reliance on *adventus* leads theologian Richard Baukham to reject the progressivism built into the evolution of nature touted by Teilhard de Chardin. Bauckham, like Russell along with Moltmann and Pannenberg, touts an eschatological in-breaking of the new creation. 'In the case of the new creation, *all creatures* are taken up and transformed within a *universally comprehensive* new whole that at the same time preserves the distinctive creaturely being of each.'[69]

Conclusion

Our thesis has been this: the historical incarnation of the divine Logos in Jesus of Nazareth on Earth is constituted by the exchange of divine and creaturely attributes, the *communicatio idiomatum*; and, when *communicatio idiomatum* is combined with a proleptic understanding of God's promised new creation, we can celebrate the incorporation the entire material history of all galaxies and all extraterrestrial creatures into the eternal perichoresis of God as Trinity.

The refrain in the deep incarnation oratorio emphasises that all material and psychic reality—all molecules and minds—become incorporated into the dynamics of God's trinitarian life. Once internalized into the trinitarian perichoresis, the three persons of the Trinity relate to one another through the cosmos. The economic Trinity has entered the immanent Trinity, and the immanent Trinity is co-extensive with the economic Trinity.

---

69. Richard Bauckham, 'The Incarnation and the Cosmic Christ', *Incarnation*, 25–58, here at 54.

What remains to be added is eschatology, God's promise of personal resurrection and cosmic redemption. God's creation is slated for transformation, renewal, healing. Should Denis Edwards offer us a *madrigale arioso*, it might sound like Russell's crescendo: 'Eschatology entails a transfiguration of the entire cosmos based on the bodily resurrection of Jesus at Easter such that all of nature is taken up by God and made into the New Creation.'[70]

---

70. Russell, *Cosmology from Alpha to Omega*, 293.

Ecological Theology:
From Dialogue to Symposium

Stephen Downs

Abstract: Ecological theology has achieved much, notably an emerging Christian understanding of the natural world that is informed by and compatible with the accounts of natural science. Challenges remain, however, for both the Christian vision of life and for an effective and shared response to the global environmental crisis. This paper argues that by engaging with a broader range of perspectives, including new plant studies, Indigenous and secular spiritualities and the arts, ecological theology might further contribute to these challenges.

Key Terms: anthropocentrism, biocentrism, creation-centred, integral ecology, spirituality.

Ecological theology has achieved much in its relatively short history of forty plus years. One of its most significant contributions to contemporary theology has been its dialogue with the natural sciences. It has demonstrated that Christians today can maintain their belief in both the major tenets of their faith and the proposals of modern science, most notably 'big bang' cosmology and evolutionary theology. In recent years it has shown that Christianity shares many of the interests and concerns of ecological science, notably on the challenges of climate change. In the process it has contributed to the development of such major Christian doctrines as: Creation, Trinity, the Holy Spirit, Christology, the Eucharist, spirituality, divine action, miracles, the Resurrection and salvation.[1]

Impressive as these achievements are, there is yet more work to be done by ecological theology. This includes further consideration of

---

1. Examples of all these can be found in Denis Edwards, *The Natural World and God: Theological Explorations* (Hindmarsh: ATF Press, 2017).

Christian doctrine and practice informed by reflection on and dialogue with the sciences. Theology failed to do this for too long, leading to misunderstandings by many Christians. The inherent revisability of the sciences makes this task very challenging. Still I dare to suggest further work that I hope ecological theologians will consider. Behind my suggestions are several issues, emerging or persisting, that I think ecological theology can (further) help us address.

First, despite the cogent arguments of ecological and other theologians, the view that religious belief is incompatible with modern science is an enduring feature of contemporary Western society. As philosopher Charles Taylor argues, it is not that science has refuted religion; though some loud voices make just this claim.[2] Rather the worldview of modern science—of a wholly material world, governed by impersonal and purposeless forces—has become the default or commonsense position for a growing number. And this seems to conflict with the Christian worldview, which 'relates us to a personal Creator-God'[3], and which explains our personal situation in terms of this relationship. A second challenge is the need to change the way we think and live in the light of climate change. Ecological theology has certainly addressed this issue.[4] But the urgency of the task is more apparent than ever; its effects seem to be affecting us sooner than expected; and we are falling behind in our efforts to avert disaster. In some parts of the world, including Australia, resistance to the premise of human-induced climate change still rages. Third, in Australia, and elsewhere, there is a growing recognition in both secular and religious circles that we have much to learn about our world and how to live in it from Indigenous peoples.

In this paper I encourage ecological theologians to expand the range of dialogue partners in their enterprise. I am aware of engagement with a broader range of scientific disciplines, such as astrophysics and neuroscience, and with climate science, economics and social theory. But to this sympathetic theological observer dialogue with one or other scientific discipline seems to be their

2. Charles Taylor, *A Secular Age* (Cambridge, Mass: Belknap Press of Harvard University Press, 2007), 361–369.

3. Taylor, *A Secular Age*, 362.

4. See, for example, Denis Edwards, 'Celebrating Eucharist in a Time of Global Climate Change', and 'Climate Change in the Theology of Karl Rahner: A Hermeneutical Dialogue', in *The Natural World and God*, 157–172 and 361–380.

principal methodology. And I think a more expansive approach might better enable ecological theology to engage with the broad range of ecologically-minded people in our society; and to be more inclusive for its diverse readers and supporters. The 'symposium' of my title alludes to both the academic consideration of a subject with a number of participants and also, from Plato, the convivial discussion of issues after a banquet. As examples of new conversation partners, I suggest recent critical studies of plants; Indigenous, religious and secular spiritual perspectives; and insights from music, art and literature.

In referring to works of ecological theology, I sometimes cite works by my late friend and colleague Denis Edwards where I might have referred to others. This is partly to recognize and honour his contributions on a diverse range of topics. And because of this I think he would have been broadly sympathetic to my suggestions.

Plants and Biocentrism

One set of guests that I would like to invite to the ecological symposium is a movement in contemporary scholarship and thought that is re-considering the world of plants and our relationship with them. I will refer to it as 'new plant studies', noting that it includes scientific, philosophical and literary perspectives.[5] In the sciences 'recent studies have shifted the paradigm from a mechanicist approach to vegetable life, reduced to its constituent parts, to a perspective attributing greater agency to plants in dynamic relation to their environment'.[6] Adopting an integrated and ecological approach, this new approach presents and understands plants more in their own terms: not as merely passive and reactive but rather as complex, active and communicative organisms. Like Erasmus Darwin in the eighteenth century these scholars highlight the continuity between human and plant existence.[7] In like vein some contemporary philosophers are re-thinking the very concept of nature, the language we use to talk about the natural world and where plants fit into it. Some literary scholars consider 'the representation of the intelligence, behavior,

---

5. Monica Gagliano, in *The Language of Plants: Science, Philosophy, Literature*, edited by John R Ryan, and Patricia Vieira (Minneapolis: University of Minnesota Press, 2017). The overview in the Introduction is especially helpful for this paper.
6. Gagliano and others, xiii.
7. Gagliano, xi–xiii.

and subjectivity of the vegetal world in works of poetry and prose, fiction and non-fiction.[8]

At the heart of the movement is a critique of traditional Western hierarchical thinking about reality and the living world especially. According to the 'scale of nature', inherited from ancient philosophy, plants are positioned below animals that are in turn ranked beneath humans. Although it suggests a continuity of life forms, this view has encouraged the belief that those lower down the scale are inferior to those above. For example, only the higher life forms have the capacity for (self) consciousness and language. Modern biological science continues to challenge these beliefs. But a bias towards the human lingers in the practice of science and in Western culture more generally.[9] It is supported by a deep-seated anthropocentrism; the idea that the human as human is 'the measure of all things' and consequently 'every form of life appears to be deficient by comparison with it'. This sort of thinking, it is argued, skews our understanding of the different 'orders' of being and ultimately alienates human beings from the rest of the natural world.[10]

A distinctive and controversial feature of the new plant studies takes this critique a step further. It accuses the sciences, philosophy, and contemporary Western culture of zoo-centric thinking, of unjustifiably focusing on animal life and effectively excluding vegetal life from consideration in its own right. It cites the disproportionate quantity of animal research, the structuralism of biology and 'plant blindness', that is, the inability to recognize and appreciate the importance of plants in the biosphere and their impact on the environment. Zoo-centrism (and anthropocentrism more generally) fosters instrumentalist attitudes: lower life forms are recognized and valued for the benefits they might afford higher life forms. The new plant studies would rather we view all living things, including plants, as part of the environment that we all inhabit and share. They advocate biocentrism.[11]

Ecological theology is broadly sympathetic to this critique of the Western intellectual tradition. Catholic theologians at least will be familiar with theological expressions of the hierarchy of being. For example, the view that the vertical scale reflects the relative

---

8. Gagliano, xvi.
9. Gagliano, xiv–xv.
10. M Marder, 'To Hear Plants Speak', in Gagliano and others, 104; xii, xxix.
11. Gagliano, xi--xix.

likeness and closeness to God of the different orders of being; and the 'ecclesiastical hierarchy' devised by Pseudo-Dionysius in the late fifth century that the church is still struggling to overcome today.[12] Ecological theologians and Christian ethicists have expressly criticized anthropocentric and instrumentalist attitudes and identified them as having contributed to the present ecological crisis.[13] It might be thought their frequent insistence on the special dignity of human beings constitutes a modified form of anthropocentrism; given their equal insistence on the inherent dignity of every created being, I do not think so. But the point is worthy of discussion.

I suspect ecological theology would also largely accept the judgement of bio-centrist Matthew Hall and others that hierarchic and anthropocentric thinking have been widely accepted because they have been authorised by the dominant religious tradition of the West.[14] The biblical texts and key teachings of Augustine and Aquinas that Hall cites in support of his judgement will be familiar to them; they cite them in their own criticisms of the Christian tradition. Other claims will generate useful debate. For example, Hall's view that even when the biblical tradition includes a more horizontal understanding of relationships among living things, it generally involves at least an animal-plant hierarchy; similarly, where plants seem to be presented positively in the Bible, they are 'used as symbols of life and are not actually and explicitly recognised as being alive'.[15] On these texts, and his reading of biblical texts in general, I do not think Hall engages sufficiently with 'ecological hermeneutics', though he is aware of it. Theologians, and certainly ecological theologians, acknowledge that theology is a work in progress, willing and able to learn new things. The 'word of God' is a living word; and the Christian tradition as a whole is always being reinterpreted.

---

12. John Marenbon and DE Luscombe, 'Two medieval ideas: eternity and hierarchy', in *The Cambridge Companion to Medieval Philosophy*, edited by AS McGrade (Cambridge University Press, 2003), 60–62.

13. See, for example, Edwards, 'Climate Change in the Theology of Karl Rahner', 366–367; and Thomas Massaro, *Living Justice: Catholic Social Teaching in Action*. Second Classroom edited by Lanham (Maryland: Rowman & Littlefield Publishers, 2012), 165–172.

14. See the work cited in Gagliano, Matthew Hall *Plants as Persons: A Philosophical Botany* (Albany: State University of New York Press, 2011), cc 3–4.

15. Hall, *Plants as Persons*, 56–57.

It may be that the concerns with zoo-centrism expressed by Gagliano, Hall and others do not become as widely held as opposition to anthropocentrism. Still I think it useful to ask: is Christianity inherently zoo-centric? In fact, theological interest in non-human animals is relatively recent and still dismissed by many.[16] But as there are changes in the ways science is being practised, so too in theology. Deep Incarnation theology, for example, is based on the conviction that the central event of Christian faith, the death and resurrection of Jesus, is significant for the whole of the universe, not just humans. Admittedly its focus on the Cross and the suffering of sentient beings is problematic in this context. But at least some theologians are clear: the 'creatures' saved by Christ include grasses and trees, all biological life forms in fact. They too support a more ecological perspective which acknowledges the relationship between and interdependence of all species.[17]

Further discussion would centre on Hall's recognition of the shift made by contemporary eco-theologians: from the longstanding 'dominion model' in which humanity exists apart from, above and with rights over the rest of creation, to the 'stewardship model' in which human beings care for creation, as God's agents. Hall readily accepts that the latter model is preferable. But it remains instrumentalist.[18] He seems unaware, however, of the more recent and popular 'creation-centred' or eco-centric model that is neither instrumentalist nor anthropocentric. In the words of Pope Francis, who has embraced and promotes this model: 'Nature cannot be regarded as something separate from ourselves or as a mere setting in which we live. We are part of nature, included in it and thus in constant interaction with it . . . called into being by the one Father, all of us are linked by unseen bonds and together form a kind of universal family, a sublime communion which fills us with a sacred,

---

16. See, for example, John Berkman and Celia Deane-Drummond, 'Catholic Moral Theology and the Moral Status of Non-Human Animals', in *Journal of Moral Theology*, 3/2 (2014): 1–10.

17. Denis Edwards, *Deep Incarnation: God's Redemptive Suffering with Creatures* (Maryknoll, NY: Orbis Books, 2019). The reference to 'grasses and trees' is from a section on Elizabeth Johnson, 5–6.

18. Hall, *Plants as Persons*, 55–56.

affectionate and humble respect."[19] The pope is also influenced by the revival of the spiritual tradition of St Francis of Assisi and he makes a small but telling reference to the saint's instruction that 'the friary garden always be left untouched, so that wild flowers and herbs could grow there, and those who saw them could raise their minds to God, the Creator of such beauty'.[20] For Christians the final perspective is God's. Further conversation might well show (or confirm) that the biocentric approach of secular ecologists is compatible with the Christian theocentric view.

One aspect of the Christian tradition's special concern for the human, one that I think will add something to the conversation with thinkers like Hall, is treated at length by Pope Francis in *Laudato si*; namely, that today we face a twin interrelated crisis: environmental degradation and global inequality. A true ecological approach, the Pope holds, must integrate questions of justice in our concern for the environment; it must hear "both the cry of the earth and the cry of the poor".[21] I am sure this is shared by many people. For Christians, belief in God helps sustain this belief. Can the same be said for an independent biocentric approach?

Religious, Spiritual and Personal Perspectives

Another set of conversation partners can be found by looking beyond the natural sciences. One reason for doing so is recognised by some scientists and philosophers of science. They maintain that science has a 'blind spot' that means its account of the world will never be complete, will always be lacking something. It has come to light in attempts to explain the most fundamental aspects of reality such as the nature of matter, time and consciousness. Complete certainty and objectivity have eluded the sciences. The underlying problem is the assumption that physical reality is all there is. What's missing is the human dimension. Without reference to human experience a full account of reality is not possible. A scientific account of time, for example, will never be complete because it cannot include our lived

---

19. Pope Francis, *Laudato Si—On Care for Our Common Home*, 2015, paragraph 139. http://www.vatican.va/content/francesco/en/encyclicals/documents/papa-francesco_20150524_enciclica-laudato-si.html

20. *Laudato si'*, paragraph 12.

21. *Laudato si*, paragraph 49 and chapter 4.

experience of time, which is what gives time meaning. It seems the best science can do is construct accounts that are at least consistent with our 'inner' experience.[22]

In their search for the most appropriate behavior in a time of ecological collapse some secular ecologists think we should consider what religious and spiritual traditions have to offer. Despite its historical shortcomings the Christian tradition deserves to be in this conversation. But like others, I also think Indigenous perspectives warrant consideration. Not for any scientific insights they might have but rather their ontological perspectives, moral ideals and human experience of relating to the natural world.[23]

We can start by noting relatively recent studies that dispel long-held beliefs about Australian Aboriginal culture. Building on less widely known scholarship the historian Bruce Pascoe has questioned the long-held view of Aborigines as nomadic hunter-gatherers. There is overwhelming evidence of pre-colonial Aboriginal people irrigating and harvesting the land; constructing houses and thriving in large villages. They also established sophisticated aqua-cultural systems.[24] This work demands honest reflection on how we came to hold such false understandings. Another recent study reveals that nineteenth century European knowledge of the Australian environment was in fact greatly dependent on the profound understanding of Indigenous people.[25] Such studies are also relevant for our present environmental

---

22. Adam Frank, Marcelo Gleiser and Evan Thompson, 'The Blind Spot', *Aeon*, 08 January, 2019. https://aeon.co/essays/the-blind-spot-of-science-is-the-neglect-of-lived-experience Accessed 4 December 2019.

23. Hall, *Plants as Persons*, 5, cites the work of Eliot Deutsch and Freya Matthews in support of his own work on this. See also Edwards, 'Planetary Spirituality: Exploring a Christian Ecological Approach', in *The Natural World and God*, 174–177.

24. Bruce Pascoe, *Dark Emu: Aboriginal Australia and the Birth of Agriculture*, new edition (Broome, Australia: Magabala Books, 2018), 7. Although an award-winning bestseller, the central claims of the book, and Pascoe's own Aboriginal identity, have been challenged in some sections of the Australian media. Most historians believe Pascoe's general findings (re Aboriginal agriculture and aquaculture) are sound. For a review of Pascoe's work and its reception by a distinguished academic historian see Tom Griffiths, 'Reading Bruce Pascoe', *Inside Story*, 26 November 2019: https://insidestory.org.au/reading-bruce-pascoe/ Accessed 28 January 2020.

25. Anna Clark, Review of *Australia's First Naturalists: Indigenous People's Contribution to Early Zoology*, by Penny Olsen and Lynette Russell, *Australian Book Review*, August 2019, 18–19.

concerns. Pascoe suggests we might learn from Indigenous agricultural practices, and from the attitudes to nature that underpinned them, ways of repairing some of the damage done to this country since colonization and develop strategies that will enable us to survive here.

Reflection on firsthand accounts of Aboriginal people and scholars who have spent years living with them reveals attitudes to the natural world fundamentally different from those dominant in Western culture. One is a sense of universal kinship. In the Dreaming stories of the creative beings that shaped the Australian landscape, humans and all beings are kin based on their common origin, the earth.[26] Another is the Indigenous Australian view of humans as embedded within a local landscape, commonly referred to as 'country'. Itself a subject, country provides nourishment, gives and receives life. As Bruce Pascoe expresses it: 'Aboriginal people are born of the earth, and individuals within the clan had responsibilities for particular streams, grasslands, trees, crops, animals, and even seasons. The life of the clan was devoted to continuance.'[27]

Some Christian traditions seem at least compatible with and possibly consistent with these non-hierarchical Indigenous attitudes to nature. The great hymn of St Francis of Assisi, for example, "reminds us that our common home is like a sister with whom we share our life and a beautiful mother who opens her arms to embrace us. 'Praise be to you, my Lord, through our Sister, Mother Earth, who sustains and governs us, and who produces various fruit with coloured flowers and herbs' . . . our very bodies are made up of her elements, we breathe her air and we receive life and refreshment from her waters.' So too the consequences of our mistreatment of our shared home, which we can feel: 'God has joined us so closely to the world around us that we can feel the desertification of the soil almost as a physical ailment, and the extinction of a species as a painful disfigurement.'[28] Feeling personally connected to particular places is possibly an even more challenging attitude in our urbanised and cosmopolitan culture. An ecological spirituality might assist us.

---

26. Hall, *Plants as Persons*, 104, 160.
27. Pascoe, *Dark Emu*, 209.
28. *Laudato sí*, paragraphs 1, 2, 89.

More detailed Christian engagement with Indigenous perspectives is emerging; slowly perhaps because the dominant Christian tradition, as part of Western culture, was so successful in suppressing them. In a recent reflection Gaston Kibiten recalls his childhood in rural Philippines where 'people had a mutual and respectful regard for other things around'.[29] Farmers naturally addressed their rice fields and gardens encouraging them to grow, asking trees their permission to cut them and bandaging the wounds caused. Having abandoned such attitudes following his Christian instruction, Kibiten now calls for 'radical inculturation, integration of indigenous deities and spirits, and shaping up an indigenous-Christian ecological ethos'.[30] Creation theology and ecological theology surely have a role to play. In the Australian context this should include engagement with Aboriginal Australians and their perspectives.

One of the attractions of Indigenous perspectives like this for our increasingly secular society is that they provide motivation for personal change. They help people discover what might be called their own spirituality of nature. There is a growing recognition that the environmental crisis is also a cultural and spiritual crisis.[31] This is another aspect of experience that ecological theology has in common with otherwise secular people today. Denis Edwards, for example, has shared several instances of experiencing the sacred in the natural world. He relates them to his reading of Athanasius and Rahner. But these thoughtful reflections on time spent in the Flinders Ranges, his sense of peace on looking at the rolling hills he views while working at his theological studies, and the personal connection he feels with an old river red gum he encounters in a park on the edge of suburbia will resonate with many readers, not just those interested in the Christian tradition.[32]

---

29. Gaston Kibiten, '*Laudato si*'s call for dialogue with indigenous peoples: a cultural insider's response from the Christianized indigenous communities of the Philippines', in *Solidarity: The Journal of Catholic Social Thought and Ethics*, 8. https://researchonline.nd.edu.au/solidarity/vol8/iss1/4/ Accessed 7 December 2019.

30. Kibiten, Abstract in '*Laudato si*'s call for dialogue'.

31. See, for example, Freya Matthews, 'We've had forty years of environmental ethics—and the world is getting worse', https://www.abc.net.au/religion/weve-had-forty-years-of-environmental-ethics-and-the-world-is-/10214334 Accessed 4 July 2019.

32. Denis Edwards, 'The Natural World and God: Theological Explorations', in *The Natural World and God*, 198–201.

Here I think ecological theology might converse with the very recent essays of Australian writer Sophie Cunningham.[33] Although they include nature, travel and personal memoir writing, most of the essays investigate, report and reflect on ecosystems, trees and animals—and human relations with them. They are explicitly set in the context of global climate change and are well-informed by both history and ecological science. Most obviously there is a consistent reference to trees, clearly the object of Cunningham's personal interest, concern and love: she posts the photo of a tree on Instagram each day @sophtreeofday. Whole essays are devoted to the live oak, moonah (melaleuca), cypress, gingkos, eucalypts (coolibah, river red gum), the olive tree, the Moreton Bay fig, Mexican fan palm and American yellowwood. Significantly, it is only when writing about her encounters with trees that Cunningham feels the need to employ spiritual language, in what is otherwise a secular book. When she writes about the giant sequoia she likens being in their presence to 'being in the presence of qualities Christianity ascribes to God . . . If one of these trees started a religion that is the religion I would join . . . you find yourself [on] higher, more expansive ground. They make anything seem possible.'[34] And again when Cunningham recounts her time with the largest tree in Victoria, a mountain ash given the name Ada. Seventy-five metres in height, with a girth of fifteen metres and some four hundred years old, Ada has a majesty that Cunningham approaches with 'reverence'. But also with a great deal of knowledge, including the wanton destruction of vast numbers of even older trees, and all the life forms that live in them, in the production of woodchips. When she finally comes to stand before the regal tree Cunningham confesses: 'I drop to my knees, say a prayer, swear an oath'; a commitment, it seems to Ada, 'to this city—to our planet—of trees'.[35] In these passages at least Cunningham expresses the desire and need for something more than scientific knowledge of the natural world, more than a philosophical understanding of it, and certainly more than a socio-political system that would permit its destruction for profit. It is a cry shared by growing numbers in Western societies

33. Sophie Cunningham, *City of Trees: Essays on Life, Death and the Need for a Forest* (Melbourne: Text Publishing, 2019).
34. Cunningham, 'Giant Sequoia (*Sequoiadendron giganteum*)', *in City of Trees*.
35. Cunningham, 'Mountain Ash (*Eucalyptus regnans*)', in *City of Trees*.

and it includes the need for action.[36] It is also shared with ecological theologians, who rightly seek to engage with all who hold them.[37]

The Natural World in the Arts

My final suggestion for expanding the conversation of ecological theology is music, art and literature—the works themselves and our engagement with them. For many people today they provide more than entertainment; they are sources of meaning and insight. Major studies by sociologist Robert Wuthnow have shown that they are among the most important of our 'spiritual practices'.[38] This is true for those who still participate in organized religion and the growing number who do not. The acclaim given to the novels of Marilynne Robinson's 'Gilead' novels and Tony Kushner's plays *Angels in America*, for example, demonstrates that this can still include works that deal with religious themes.[39] Clearly many artists, like the rest of us, are deeply interested in the natural world, how we relate to it, what science might teach us and with the global environmental crisis.

Music is sometimes considered too difficult to consider in this way—because it so strongly involves our feelings, emotions and moods. But surely these are relevant in our reflections on our place in the natural world. And as philosopher Lawrence Kramer argues, in interpreting the feelings music generates we reason with them. They shape the way we see and understand the world; they motivate us.[40] A wonderful recent example is Australian Nigel Westlake's 'Spirit of the Wild', a concerto for oboe and orchestra.[41]

---

36. See Matthews, 'We had forty years of environmental ethics'.
37. See, for example, *Laudato si*, paragraph 2; and Edwards, 'Planetary Spirituality' which develops and advocates a Christian 'mysticism of ecological praxis', 184.
38. Robert Wuthnow, *Creative Spirituality: The Way of the Artist* (Berkeley, Los Angeles, London: University of Los Angeles Press, 2001); and *all in sync: How Music and Art Are Revitalizing American Religion* (Berkeley, Los Angeles, London: University of Los Angeles Press, 2003).
39. Marilynne Robinson, *Gilead* (London: Virago, 2005). *Home* (2008) and *Lila* (2014) followed. Tony Kushner, *Angels in America: A Gay Fantasia on National Themes*. Revised and complete edition (New York: Theatre Communications Group, 2013).
40. Lawrence Kramer, *Expression and Truth: On the Music of Knowledge* (Berkeley and Los Angeles: University of California Press, 2012).
41. *Spirit of the Wild*: Diana Doherty—oboe, Sydney Symphony Orchestra conducted by Nigel Westlake. ABC Classics: ABC481 7899 (Together with: Steve Reich's *The Desert Music*).

From the opening fanfare the listener is led on a sonic tour that reveals a place that is wild, rugged and spirited. The listener feels it brimming with life. But there are also plaintive passages suggesting a vulnerability. And sections that convey a sense of wonder, mystery and awe. If an introduction to the piece is provided, Australian listeners at least will not be surprised to learn that the inspiration for the work was a trip Westlake shared with environmental activist, Bob Brown (founder of the Australian Greens political party), to Tasmania's Bathurst Harbour. Westlake himself has said of the place: 'Almost completely devoid of modern human intrusion, the area was the home of the Needwonnee people for many thousands of years, and is accessible only by boat, plane or foot . . . It is a magical patchwork of button-grass moorlands, heathlands, and estuaries, bordered by jagged peaks, wild rivers and rugged coastlines.'[42] As Cunningham and Edwards both felt towards the trees they encountered, listeners will likely feel very protective of the wild place this music evokes and be convinced that it must be kept safe. Recognising the importance of experiencing the natural world, firsthand if possible but also via the work of composers and other artists, is to be encouraged in ecological theologians, especially if it aims to influence our behaviour.

The visual arts also continue to assist us in our quest for meaning, even if most Western art has long followed its own path separate from the church with which it was intertwined for so long. Janet Laurence, for example, is an Australian artist who has been drawing attention to the fragility of the natural world for over thirty-five years. Understandably her work has become even more fraught in recent years.[43] In *Heartshock* (2008) parts of the giant branch of a tree, dead from drought, are bandaged like a human limb, as if this might rescue it. I am reminded of Kibiten's Filipino farmers bandaging their still living crops. In *Deep Breathing: Resuscitation for the Reef* (2015) a room with projected blue walls and watery reflections is filled with large Perspex boxes containing coral, sea creatures, turtles, cephalopods,

42. http://musictrust.com.au/loudmouth/spirit-of-the-wild-westlake-the-desert-music-reich/ My commentary draws on a review: https://www.australian musiccentre.com.au/workversion/westlake-nigel-spirit-of-the-wild/31852. Accessed on 15 November 2019.

43. 'Janet Laurence: After Nature', at the Museum of Contemporary Art, Sydney, 1 March—10 June 2019. https://www.mca.com.au/artists-works/exhibitions/829-janet-laurence/ Accessed 20 March 2019.

shellfish. The creatures are beautiful to behold, until one notices the vials and tubes of 'blood' around them are keeping them alive. This is an undersea hospital—made necessary by human behaviour. Her most recent work is *Forest (Theatre of Trees)*, 2018–19, an epic installation of five-metre high fabric drops made of silk, gauze and reflective fabric that mimic the rings of a tree trunk, brought alive by projections and screen-printed photographic images. Walking through this creation one enters a different world, the vegetal world, where time is slowed down.[44] It is exactly what several of the writers in Gagliano's collection of new plant studies ask us to do. Surrounding the *Forest* are three rooms with old and new botanical books, laboratories and elixirs, each representing (instrumental) scientific studies of trees. Laurence sees herself as having a dual nature, passionate artist and quiet activist, whose work furthers an urgent cause. In this time when so much of our world is sick, it is equally legitimate and necessary for ecological theologians to be activists as well as academics. The feelings engendered by *Forest* just might lead some visitors to change their behavior.

Finally, I want to argue that ecological theologians should include literature and writers in their conversations, as Gagliano's collection of new plant studies includes articles on novels and poetry. The popular genre of Climate Change Fiction ('Cli-Fi'), which 'offers ways of thinking about something we desperately do not want to think about: the incipient death of the planet'[45] seems an obvious partner. Barbara Kingsolver's *Flight Behaviour*[46] is a good example: written by someone trained in ecology and evolutionary biology and with an interest in the worldviews of religion and science. The central character, Dellarobia Turnbow, a young woman living in rural America, witnesses what first appears to be a miracle of great beauty. But she soon discovers that it is in fact an ecological tragedy in the making. Because of the destruction of their traditional winter habitat, due to climate change, migrating monarch butterflies take refuge in the less hospitable Appalachian

44. Prudence Gibson, 'Janet Laurence: After Nature sounds an exquisite warning bell for extinction', in *The Conversation*, March 11, 2019 https://theconversation.com/janet-laurence-after-nature-sounds-an-exquisite-warning-bell-for-extinction-112942 Accessed 20 March 2019.

45. Katy Waldman, 'How Climate-Change Fiction, or "Cli-Fi," Forces Us to Confront the Incipient Death of the Planet', https://www.newyorker.com/books/page-turner/how-climate-change-fiction-or-cli-fi-forces-us-to-confront-the-incipient-death-of-the-planet?verso=true Accessed on 1 December 2018.

46. Barbara Kingsolver, *Flight Behaviour* (London: Faber and Faber, 2012).

mountain region.[47] How Dellarobia and others in the community respond to this situation is the principal concern of the novel.

Desperately wishing to escape the frustrations of her marriage and restrictions of small-town life, Dellarobia is immediately attracted to the worldview of the scientists who arrive to study and hopefully save the butterflies. Smart as she is, learning the language of science and its limitations, especially in relation to a complex issue like the causes and effects of climate change, does not come easily. I am sure this is also true for those Christians attracted by the insights of ecological theology. It is further complicated by factors that have little to do with the principles of entomology or ecology, particularly her relationships with family and community. Still becoming her own person, Dellarobia is forced to make life-changing choices. There are clear parallels with the Christian vocation. For some in Dellarobia's community, despite their evangelical faith and Pastor Ogle's insistence on the biblical injunction to respect and love God's creation, the presence of the butterflies is a potential source of income; as time passes, it becomes an obstacle to land clearance and the needed income it will generate. As Dellarobia tells the chief scientist, communities like hers cannot afford to worry about the environment. At the same time, these are people, like Dellarobia's mother-in-law and great adversary, who have a knowledge of and intimacy with the local environment; and who feel that the 'miracle' is a sign from God. There is much to be gained by reflecting on such 'real-life' accounts of the challenges of climate change. Pope Francis and ecological theologians are surely right to insist that economic factors must be part of an 'integral ecology'.[48]

An internet search quickly reveals that *Flight Behaviour* has been a popular choice for reading groups and book clubs, which I imagine resemble the symposia of Plato's time; where all the guests are able to discuss the things that concern them. In this paper I have argued that works like this, along with others in the arts, as well as emerging scientific studies, Indigenous cultural perspectives and diverse works of secular writers and commentators be included as conversation partners of ecological theology. Interest in and concern for the environment is a growing movement and ecological theology should do its best to be part of it.

---

47. There is a brief account of this scientifically recorded phenomenon in Cunningham, 'I Don't Blame the Trees', *City of Trees*.
48. *Laudato sí*, paragraphs 137–146.

From Evolution to Eucharist to Ecology

Denis Edwards, Teilhard de Chardin, and Karl Rahner

John F Haught

'The big bang and the expansion of our universe from a small dense hot state 13.7 billion years ago, and the evolution of life since its beginning on Earth 3.7 billion years ago—this whole story exists within the vision of the divine purpose.'[1]
– Denis Edwards

Abstract: Denis Edwards's theology was influenced by the Jesuit scientist Pierre Teilhard de Chardin. Denis' reading of Teilhard, however, was shaped in some measure by his expertise in the thought of Karl Rahner, especially Rahner's Christology. Neither Rahner nor Edwards, however, was a Teilhard scholar. Rahner had apparently read some of Teilhard's works, but he makes few formal references to his fellow Jesuit's writings. Nevertheless, a never fully acknowledged Teilhardian 'atmosphere' enveloped Rahner's Christology, especially after 1965. Similarly, a hope-filled Teilhardian spirit—with its sense that the whole universe shares in the resurrection of Jesus—animates Denis' Christology. Neither Rahner nor Edwards, however, participates fully in the radical metaphysical reconfiguration of Catholic thought that Teilhard envisioned.

Key Terms: Denis Edwards, Teilhard, Karl Rahner, metaphysics, evolution, future, Omega.

Denis Edwards was one of a very few English-speaking theologians to have integrated the religious thought of the Jesuit priest, geologist, and paleontologist Pierre Teilhard de Chardin into his own theological

---

1. Denis Edwards, *The Natural World and God: Theological Explorations* (Adelaide, Australia: ATF Press, 2017), 15.

work.[2] Other theologians have made passing references to Teilhard's thought, and a few of them have read Teilhard's best-known work, *The Human Phenomenon*. But most theologians today are unfamiliar with books such as Teilhard's *Writings in Time of War*, *The Heart of Matter*, *How I Believe*, *Hymn of the Universe*, *The Future of Man*, *Human Energy*, *Activation of Energy*, *Christianity and Evolution*, as well as other collections of essays and letters to friends. Denis' reading of Teilhard was wide and deep. Still, I think it was primarily in terms of theologian Karl Rahner's theological vision that he read Teilhard.[3]

Rahner, it appears to me, had familiarized himself with Teilhard's worldview, but Rahner makes few formal references to his fellow Jesuit's writings. Nevertheless, a never fully acknowledged Teilhardian 'atmosphere' envelopes Rahner's Christology, especially after 1965. Similarly, a hope-filled Teilhardian spirit—with its sense that the whole universe shares in the resurrection of Jesus—animates Denis' Christology. Neither Rahner nor Edwards, however, participates fully in the radical metaphysical reconfiguration of Catholic thought that Teilhard envisioned.

Teilhardian Evolution without a Catholic Revolution

I have had the opportunity to referee scholarly papers for theological journals that deal with aspects of Teilhard's thought, but most of them manifest little acquaintance with writings of Teilhard other than the *Phenomenon*. As a result, they sometimes miss the religious depth of Teilhard's evolutionary vision of emergent transformation, since Teilhard's theological understanding is revealed only in part toward the end of the *Phenomenon* (a work that is now available in

---

2.   Pierre Teilhard de Chardin, *The Human Phenomenon*, translated by Sarah Appleton-Weber (Portland, Ore: Sussex Academic, 1999); *Writings in Time of War*, translated by René Hague (New York: Harper and Row, 1968); *The Heart of Matter*, translated by René Hague (New York: Harvest, 2002); *The Divine Milieu* (New York: Harper and Row, 1962); *Human Energy*, translated by JM Cohen (New York: Harvest/Harcourt Brace Jovanovich, 1962); *The Future of Man*, translated by Norman Denny (New York: Harper and Row, 1964); *How I Believe*, trans. René Hague (New York: Harper and Row, 1969); *Activation of Energy*, translated by René Hague (New York: Harcourt Brace Jovanovich, 1970).

3.   Denis Edwards, 'Teilhard's Vision as Agenda for Rahner's Christology', in *The Natural World and God: Theological Explorations*, 757–790.

a fresh English translation).[4] Some religious critics chastise Teilhard for being too materialist, others for being too naive about 'progress'; and some biologists have criticised Teilhard for being Lamarckian, or a 'Spencerian', or for conceding too much to secular modernity, and so on.[5]

Having spent half a lifetime studying the works of Teilhard, I can only judge the picture of his thought as presented by most philosophers and theologians to be lacking in precision and focus. This is so mostly, though not only, because most commentaries leave out the very heart of Teilhard's synthesis—namely, his christocentrism.

The word 'Christ' does not appear in most secular assessments of Teilhard's significance. I understand why philosophers are often reluctant to bring the figure of Christ into their scholarly writings, but in the case of Teilhard, leaving Christ out of any representation of his thought, including those of secular critics, is comparable to leaving mention of Abraham Lincoln out of a book on American history. This omission only perpetuates the caricatures that have clouded interpretations of Teilhard's writings for decades, including the opinion that Teilhard's body of work is just one more modern capitulation to naïve secularist progressivism. Yet, if one looks carefully at Teilhard's writings one cannot help noticing that his main concern is always to re-express for our times the apostle Paul's vision of a universe converging on Christ. It is not secular optimism but Christian hope— quite a different thing—that animates Teilhard's religious writings.

Denis Edwards was especially aware of Teilhard's christological focus. Since, for Teilhard, Christ is the goal of the *natural* evolution

---

4. *The Human Phenomenon*, translated by Sarah Appleton-Weber (Portland, Ore: Sussex Academic, 1999).
5. For details see my article, 'True Union Differentiates: A Response to My Critics', in *Science & Christian Belief*, 17/1, 57–70. Respected authors such as NT Wright, J Moltmann, J Maritain, Arthur Peacocke, and many Thomistically oriented Catholic philosophers have typically read only a limited number of Teilhard's writings and then extrapolated a portrait—often fortified by misguided secondary sources—that exaggerates and distorts Teilhard's overall intentions (as I indicate below). In no way do I consider Teilhard's writings unflawed, for they all need updating in many respects. Reading only one or two works of Teilhard, however, even if it includes plowing one's way bravely through the *Phenomenon*, is insufficient to establish expertise. For more information see my book *Making Sense of Evolution: Darwin, God, and The Drama of Life* (Louisville: Westminster/ John Knox Press, 2010), 140–148.

of the universe, theology must always be interested in science and cosmology. The appropriate way to read Teilhard's writings, apart from his purely geological and other scientific papers, however, is not as philosophy, science, or natural theology, but as a theology of nature, as Ian Barbour rightly recommends.[6] My sense is that Denis agreed with Barbour.

Creation, Incarnation, and Redemption

Even though Teilhard was not professionally a theologian, his writings and especially his Christology, are composed in the spirit of the Eastern Fathers and Duns Scotus. That is, Teilhard tends to merge the themes of creation, incarnation, and redemption with his experience as a contemporary cosmologist. For Teilhard—as for the Eastern Fathers—the word of God is present at the creation of the universe. The meaning of creation is revealed in the resurrection, of course, but the creative and promising word of God is formative of the universe from the start.

In the Eastern and Scotist interpretations, God intends from all eternity to become incarnate in the world. In Christ—the incarnate word of God—the universe is created, redeemed, and divinized in one unbroken outpouring of love. Unlike the Western theologians Augustine, Anselm, and Aquinas, who understand the incarnation predominantly as an *ad hoc* response to, or expiation for sin, the Eastern Fathers, Duns Scotus, and more recently Karl Rahner, understand the Christ-event as both creative and redemptive. Much of Denis' theology of evolution is composed in this same spirit.[7]

Teilhard, as I read him, however, was looking for a whole new metaphysics to contextualise his Christology and, indeed, the whole of Catholic thought. His thought begs to be removed from under the pervasive influence of the classical Eastern and Western 'metaphysics of the eternal present' which 'clips the wings of hope'.[8] Theology after Darwin and Einstein must be placed in a new setting, one that Teilhard

---

6. Ian Barbour, 'Five Ways to Read Teilhard', *The Teilhard Review*, 3 (1968): 3–20.

7. Here I am making use especially of Denis' collection *The Natural World and God: Theological Explorations* and particularly the chapter entitled 'Teilhard's Vision as Agenda for Rahner's Christology', 757–790.

8. Pierre Teilhard de Chardin, *Christianity and Evolution*, translated by René Hague (New York: Collins, 1969), 79.

never clearly identifies but which I like to call a 'metaphysics of the future'. In any case, unlike Rahner and Edwards, Teihard avoided the typical theological project of looking for the 'right philosophy' to express the meaning of his faith in Christ. He wanted to begin with the unmediated cosmic story that *scientists*—not philosophers—have laid bare.

The Universe as an Unfinished Story

The most important insight Teilhard takes from scientific thought is that the universe is an unfinished story 'still aborning'. In fact, he was one of the first scientists in the 20th century to see clearly that nature is narrative to the core, and that the universe is a story still going on.

For Teilhard it is the narrative quality of nature rather than a ready-made metaphysics that provides the appropriate point of intersection of science and theology. He was suspicious of any portrayal of nature that failed to present it as a seamless, unfinished story rooted in the empirical sciences of geology, biology, and cosmology. He sought to express his religious thought directly in terms of the new scientifically based cosmic story rather than through Platonic, Aristotelian, Hegelian, Thomistic, materialist, vitalist or any other brand of metaphysics. If there is any metaphysical dimension to Teilhard's thought it is what I would call a 'metaphysics of the future'. Such a metaphysics is implicit in Teilhard's succinct claim that the world 'rests on the future . . . as its sole support'.[9] His understanding of Christ is decidedly futuristic and cosmic. For Teilhard, Christ does not call us out of the universe or away from nature. Instead Christ is the goal of the *natural* evolution of the universe, and we fail to encounter him if we separate him—by way of a classical, often otherworldly, metaphysics from the physical cosmos.[10]

Whereas theology traditionally has employed one metaphysical system or another in order to provide a field of discourse on which conversation between theologians and scientists can occur, for Teilhard it was sufficient to look at theology and science as two

9. Teilhard de Chardin, *Activation of Energy*, translated by René Hague (New York: Harcourt Brace Jovanovich), 239.
10. See especially Pierre Teilhard de Chardin, *The Heart of Matter,* translated by René Hague (New York: Harvest, 2002).

different ways—or two distinct levels—of 'reading' what is going on in the one story of an unfinished universe (or of a multiverse if relevant). Teilhard feared, understandably, that any traditional metaphysical discourse would ignore or suppress the narrative quality of nature and the God who is enfleshed in the cosmic story.

Consequently, telling the story of biological evolution in the context of the new and larger cosmic story became for Teilhard the essential prelude to an expansive understanding of God, Christ, and the work of redemption. For the Protestant twentieth century theologian Paul Tillich the purpose of theology was to address the question of human finitude and how to find 'the courage to be',[11] but for Teilhard the point of theology should be to address the question of how to read and interpret a universe story that remains unfinished.

For Teilhard we should now take advantage of the fact that the totality of events, including the Christ-event, falls within a single cosmic *story*. Like any story, our new scientific cosmic story has multiple levels of depth whose content is accessible to many disciplines and methods of inquiry including both scientific and theological ways of reading it. It is only recently that Christian thought such as Teilhard's has been able to differentiate science from theology as two distinct levels of reading a single story. This is because it is only recently that learned thought has been able to understand the cosmos as essentially narrative or dramatic in its fundamental constitution.

In previous ages, by contrast, the universe did not seem to be going anywhere itself. Instead, the natural world was a point of departure for the spiritual journey as well as a stage for the human drama of sin and redemption. At times the universe seemed to be nothing more than a squirrel-cage for practicing the virtues considered necessary to the working out of one's personal salvation.[12] Teilhard, however, reaches out directly into the empirically grounded scientific *cosmic*

---

11. Paul Tillich, *The Courage To Be* (New Haven: Yale University Press, 1952).

12. Pierre Teilhard de Chardin, *Activation of Energy*, translated by René Hague (New York: Harcourt Brace Jovanovich, 1970), 229–244. The emphasis in Teilhard's thought on our need to 'build the earth' has, ironically, provided much of the substance of the second Vatican Council's main document 'The Pastoral Constitution on the Church in the Modern World', a document that the Catholic theologian Henri de Lubac noted '. . . accomplished exactly what Teilhard had intended'. See my book *Resting on the Future: Catholic Theology for an Unfinished Universe* (New York: Bloomsbury Press, 2015), 29–44.

story to locate the meaning of Christ for today. His objective is to provide a contemporary Christian vision of what is really going on in the physical universe that science has recently revealed to us. He is distrustful of any theology that is mediated by a metaphysics that abstracts from the narrative disposition of the universe, especially any metaphysics that had its origin long before Darwin and Einstein.

Metaphysics and Evolution

Denis, like Rahner, is more reluctant than Teilhard to leave classical metaphysics out of his evolutionary vision. Denis' understanding of Teilhard has been deeply influenced by, or filtered through, the metaphysical theology of the famous twentieth Century Catholic theologian Karl Rahner. Because of the pervasive influence of Rahner on the shaping of Denis' theology, there is a slant to the latter's interpretation of Teilhard that renders it somewhat abstract when compared to the empirically based understanding of nature that Teilhard espoused. Rahner's theological interpretation of Teilhard is sophisticated, but it is one that lacks the revolutionary spirit of Teilhard's call for a drastic renewal of Catholic thought in the twentieth century.[13] Denis, a Catholic priest and sometime seminary professor, is more at home with Karl Rahner the Jesuit systematic theologian than he is with Teilhard the Jesuit geologist and evolutionist.

This is not a criticism, but an observation. There is a place for the kind of metaphysical theology that Rahner and Denis have made their lives' work. The result, however, is that Teilhard's disillusionment with Thomistic theology does not come through either in Denis' writings, or in Rahner's.[14] One reason for this omission, I believe, is that Denis' fierce loyalty to Athanasius and other Platonically influenced early Christian writers tends, almost by definition, to blunt the narrative thrust of Teilhard's cosmological rethinking of the meaning of Christianity after Darwin and Einstein.

As for Rahner, his sense of obligation to the Roman Catholic Thomistic turn in the early twentieth Century remained constantly

---

13. I have devoted a whole book to a discussion of Teilhard and what his renewal of Catholic thought would entail: *Resting on the Future: Catholic Theology for an Unfinished Universe* (New York: Bloomsbury Press, 2015).

14. See for example, Karl Rahner, SJ, *Hominization: The Evolutionary Origin of Man as a Theological Problem,* translated by WT O'Hara (Freiburg: Herder, 1965).

present. Such a metaphysics can serve as a distraction from looking at evolution up close. It is important to remember here that throughout most of his theological career, Rahner (like other Catholic theologians of the twentieth Century) had felt obliged to follow faithfully his Church's instruction to adhere to the thought of Thomas Aquinas. This commandment came directly from Pope Leo XIII who in 1903 warned against the extremes of modern thought that might confuse Catholic scholars. In his turn-of-the-century encyclical *Aeterni Patris* the Pope had sought to combat the swirling confusion of late nineteenth and early twentieth Century Western thought by telling Catholic thinkers to return to the seemingly more stable system of Thomas Aquinas, the thirteenth Century Aristotelian philosopher.

For Teilhard, on the other hand, it is not easy for a Thomistic metaphysics to capture what is going on in the story of life and an emergent universe. Any attempts to use other philosophical systems than Thomism, however, could lead theologians to be silenced and even threatened with excommunication if they could not pull off the synthesis of evolution and faith to the Church's liking.

Thomism Today

Today, as far as I can tell, a good number of Catholic theologians and philosophers still attempt to make Thomistic philosophy the comprehensive framework of their writings on God, Christ, human distinctiveness, and divine action. Following Rahner, Denis is no rigorous Thomist, but he still takes for granted the value of a loosely Thomistic metaphysics. As a result, his theology of divine action in the world, including his reflections on how God relates causally to the evolution of life, is understandably quite cautious. This hesitancy comes out clearly when Denis interprets divine influence in the natural world—including God's influence on the evolution of life—in accordance with the distinction Thomas made between primary and secondary causation.[15]

---

15. Denis Edwards, *How God Acts: Creation, Redemption, and Special Divine Action* (Minneapolis: Fortress Press, 2010), 62. In this work Edwards also experiments with other ways of thinking about divine action. This volume is a very good introduction to the whole question of divine action in the age of science.

To be clear, I admire Denis' concern to keep his theological attention on earlier ages of Christian thought, including both medieval and ancient, as he sets about in search of a theology of evolution. These sources are part of Christian theological tradition, and Denis' efforts to summarize the thought of the early church writers is in my view his most important contribution to Catholic scholarship. Furthermore, one can only applaud his efforts to hold together the philosophical ideas of early Christianity and the drastically different world of contemporary scientific thought. To those contemporary theologians who are intimidated by the work of integrating science and faith, Denis provides an informed, though still quite traditional, synthesis that may suffice for most contemporary Catholic theologians.

Yet it seems to me that there are limits to any attempts to synthesise Catholic metaphysical tradition on the one hand with contemporary evolutionary and cosmological understanding on the other. It is hard for a metaphysics of being (*esse*) to make full sense of a world of process and becoming. Hence, I doubt that Teilhard himself would have been fully satisfied with either Denis' or Rahner's attempts to link a metaphysics of being with a world of becoming. What is missing in both Edwards and Rahner's attempts at such a synthesis is the earth-filled, cosmic, messy, but hopeful, futurist, and sometimes iconoclastic thrust of Teilhard's thought.

Teilhard is not concerned to synthesise the juiciness of evolutionary science directly with the Thomistic metaphysics of being that Pope Leo preferred. My impression in reading his books of essays and especially his collections of letters to friends, is that he considered medieval philosophy a distraction from, rather than a means of making sense of, what is going on in the story of life and the universe. Teilhard is content, it seems to me, simply to link the ancient promissory, Abrahamic and Pauline understanding of faith in the future directly to the dramatic, narrative portrait of nature as depicted by biology and cosmology after Darwin and Einstein.[16] As I noted earlier, theology and science in that case are two distinct ways of reading the single drama of an awakening universe.

---

16. For development of this point see my books *Resting on the Future* and my forthcoming volume *God after Einstein: What's Really Going on in the Universe* (Yale University Press, forthcoming 2021).

To Teilhard, scientific cosmology cannot be intelligibly translated into Aristotelian and Thomistic terms without losing something important in the process. Furthermore, the natural world, as seen in the light of science, does not have to be reinterpreted metaphysically in order for educated people today to appreciate the relevance of the biblical theme of promise or the meaning of Christ's incarnation to understanding an unfinished universe. Following Rahner, Denis understands what is going on in the universe as God's self-bestowal to the cosmos and the universe's acceptance of this divine self-gift in the life, death, and resurrection of the man Jesus. This interpretation is certainly necessary if we are to relate God to the cosmos, but it fails to accentuate sufficiently that God is *goal* and not just governor of our emergent universe.

Theology of Nature

Denis' theology of nature, I believe is open to a futurist interpretation, but it does not make a clean break from the Thomistic metaphysical tradition. Denis does a wonderful job of clarifying Rahner's theology for a large, mostly Catholic audience, and this is one of the truly great accomplishments of his theological career. Nevertheless, because of Rahner's own Thomistic leanings, Denis' writings on science and theology express his attraction to the rather immobile pre-evolutionary metaphysics of being that Teilhard sought to transcend by speaking of creation not in terms of being (*esse*), but in terms of *uniri* (to be united).

For Teilhard creation is always in the process of 'being brought into unity' with the cosmic goal that Teilhard calls God-Omega. *Uniri* means, therefore, that in some sense the universe is not-yet. It is not yet fully intelligible because it is not yet completely *one*. The cosmos, mostly, remains to be actualized. Since it is still coming into being, theology should turn its attention toward the future rather than toward the fixed past or the eternal present. The search for the universe's intelligibility requires that we approach it with bridled expectancy, with long-suffering hope and with superhuman patience. The metaphysics of being (*esse*), by contrast, is ready-made for the disposition, not of faith and hope, but of impatience.[17]

---

17. I make this point at length in my book *Resting on the Future*.

The Thomistic understanding of creation and being does not leave enough room for a hope that includes the future of the universe. I suspect that Denis' dalliances with Thomism are supported by the Thomistic orientation of his friend, the late Jesuit astronomer William Stoeger. Their joint adherence to Thomistic metaphysics and method is understandable and interesting, but this approach cannot capture the dynamic, experimental, and futurist theological orientation underlying Teilhard's own impressive synthesis.

The allegiance to Thomism comes out also in Denis' theology of divine action in evolution.[18] Here he follows the traditional Thomist distinction between God as the primary cause, and natural selection as the secondary cause of speciation. I suspect that employing the distinction between primary and secondary causation raises serious questions about divine complicity in the suffering and cruelty of the Darwinian evolutionary process.

In Denis' encounters with the thought of Niels Gregersen, Christopher Southgate, and Elizabeth Johnson he shows that he is sensitive to the issue of life's suffering.[19] Still he stops short of developing a futurist understanding of the universe and God in a manner that corresponds to a metaphysics of the future wherein God is not so much the First cause or the Eternal Present but the world's Future.[20] I believe that Teilhard was striving for something like a metaphysics of the future when he insisted that, after Darwin and Einstein, we need a *new* God.

One finds in the works of Rahner a synthesis of many sources, including several vague allusions to some works of Teilhard, but it is not easy to say where he came by this or that idea. Rahner does admit that his reading of Teilhard was influenced also by Henri de Lubac's books defending Teilhard's orthodoxy, but De Lubac too leaned toward

---

18. Edwards, *How God Acts.*
19. Edwards, *Deep Incarnation: God's Redemptive Suffering with Creatures* (Maryknoll: Orbis, 2019).
20. Both Rahner and Edwards referred to God as 'Absolute Future', signaling their familiarity with the promissory visions of the Protestant theologians of the future. See Karl Rahner, SJ, *Theological Investigations,* volume 6, translated b y Karl Kruger and Boniface Kruger (Baltimore: Helicon, 1969), 59–68. For the theological turn to the future in Protestant theology, see Wolfhart Pannenberg, *Faith and Reality,* translated by John Maxwell (Philadelphia: Westminster Press, 1977); and Ted Peters, *God: The World's Future: Systematic Theology for a New Era,* 2nd edition (Minneapolis: Fortress Press, 2000).

a Thomistic metaphysics of the eternal present in such a way as not to have seen clearly the radical revision of Christianity that Teilhard was seeking. Rahner found in Teilhard's science-friendly religious worldview an intellectually respectable framework for facilitating a conversation of faith and science, at least in principle. But, because Rahner was constantly trying to rethink the Catholic Thomistic tradition in terms of modern philosophies of Kant and Hegel, he missed the vital futurist leaning that had become increasingly central to Teilhard's thought.

Apologetic Theology

Here we need to recall that a little after the middle of the twentieth century what Paul Tillich called 'apologetic theology' was more fashionable than it is today. And so, like the Protestant Rudolf Bultmann, Rahner wanted to make sure that there were no false intellectual stumbling blocks to having scientifically educated people embrace the message of Christianity.

This meant that theology had to come to grips with evolutionary science, and undoubtedly Rahner found in Teilhard a scientist who could assist him in the apologetic mission of the Church. Rahner's own turn toward Eastern Christianity also allowed him to read Teilhard favorably. Since Teilhard had been influenced by Eastern Christianity and was also aware of the theology of Duns Scotus, Rahner had little trouble integrating what he took to be the theological tone of Teilhard's religious sense of sin, redemption, and Christ.

To magnify the figure of Christ after Darwin Teilhard needed an alternative to the traditional Catholic metaphysics of being to which Rahner clung and to which Denis also remained devoted. Teilhard thought that the materialist metaphysics assumed by so many of his fellow scientists blinded them to what is really going on in life's evolution. He also understood that a materialist metaphysics is inadequate to the full reality of life and mind. Instead of leading scientists to see what is really going on in evolution and cosmic process, materialism actually prevents them from grasping the most important feature of evolution, namely, the novelty that is continually coming into the cosmic story from out of the future. The thinking of most evolutionists is determined in great measure by an unreflective commitment to materialist metaphysics, but Thomism is not a successful alternative.

Teilhard was looking for an alternative metaphysics but he could not find it in the traditional Thomist metaphysics of which he began to become weary even when he was a student. Teilhard writes:

> Like a river which, as you trace it back to its source, gradually diminishes till in the end it is lost altogether in the mud from which it springs, so existence becomes attenuated and finally vanishes away when we try to divide it up more and more minutely in space or—what comes to the same—to drive it further and further back in time. The grandeur of the river is revealed not at its source but at its estuary.

> Pierre Teilhard de Chardin, *Hymn of the Universe,* trans. Gerald Vann (New York: Harper Colophon, 1969), 77.

Summary and Conclusion

Although it is true that toward the end of his life, Rahner began to refer to God as 'Absolute Future', he never worked out the radical implications of this interesting variation in theological language. Denis approved of Rahner's shift of language here, but the metaphysical framework of both of these theologians remained one in which God is still thought of more as the Eternal Present or as *Esse* than as somehow *not-yet*.

As Teilhard acknowledged explicitly, Catholic thought has been dominated by a metaphysics of *esse* (or 'being') that has obscured the obvious fact of nature's constant 'becoming' and its persistent movement into the future. The metaphysics of 'being' that we find in Plato and Aristotle had been taken over in one form or another by Christian, Jewish, and Islamic theology, including by Thomas, and it still remains the official intellectual setting of much Catholic theology, including (in my opinion) that of Denis Edwards.

A metaphysics of *esse* is inadequate to the reality of evolution. An exclusivist preoccupation with 'being' may have been adequate as long as the cosmos seemed stationary. But evolutionary science is such a radical revolution in humanity's experience and understanding of nature that in order to render it intelligible we must now entertain a proportionately radical revolution in our understanding of God and cosmos. Theology in the age of science needs to emphasize the priority of the future—of what is not-yet. I do not believe that the

Catholic philosophical tradition alone is sufficient to provide such a worldview. Nor did Teilhard.

I believe it was a 'metaphysics of the future' that Teilhard was searching for. Such an Abrahamic worldview would allow space not only for the hopes of religious believers but also for the ongoing drama of the universe. Teilhard called his proposed alternative a 'metaphysics of *uniri*', a conception of reality in which all things are drawn perpetually toward deeper (dramatic) coherence— by an ultimate force of attraction, by a 'God who has future as his very essence', in the words of the Marxist philosopher Ernst Bloch. Evolution, to put it as directly as I can, seems to require a divine source of being that resides not in a timeless present located somewhere 'up above', but in the future, essentially 'up ahead', as the goal of a world still in the making.[21]

Teilhard called this force of attraction Omega abstractly, but he identified it with the cosmic Christ concretely. The term 'God' must mean for us the transcendent future horizon that draws an entire universe, and not just human history, toward an unfathomable fulfillment yet to be realised. Teilhard agreed that God is both Alpha and Omega. Where he seems to differ from Denis and most other Catholic thinkers is in his belief that God must become for us *less* Alpha than Omega.[22]

---

21. See Jürgen Moltmann, *The Experiment Hope*, edited and translated by M Douglas Meeks (Philadelphia: Fortress Press, 1975); Ernst Bloch, *The Principle of Hope*, volume 1, translated by Neville Plaice, Stephen Plaice, and Paul Knight (Oxford: Basil Blackwell, 1986).

22. Teilhard, *Christianity and Evolution*, 240. Although the Protestant Wolfhart Pannenberg is known for having developed something akin to what I am calling a metaphysics of the future, his thought has not significantly influenced my own argument in the present essay. I believe that Teilhard discovered the metaphysical priority of the future long before Pannenberg, Moltmann and other theologians of hope, although he is seldom given credit for having done so.

Theology of Nature or Relational Holism?
Building on Teilhard 's Vision

Ilia Delio, OSF
Villanova University

'God freely creates in a way that respects the limits and integrity of creaturely processes. This means that we can think of God as waiting upon the proper evolutionary unfolding of these finite processes.'
– Denis Edwards[1]

Abstract: This chapter seeks to describe a new paradigm of relational holism where mind, matter and God are perichoretic realities. Relational holism places a new emphasis on the knowing subject as integral to the cosmic process of evolving life. We humans emerge from nature; we are part of nature and thus human knowledge must begin on the level of nature and redound on the whole of nature, both in science and religion. The writings of Teilhard de Chardin deepen relational holism by illuminating a self-engaged, dynamic God who is rising up in and through evolution as the power within and the future on which evolution rests. Teilhard speaks of the knower as an artisan of the future, for without human knowledge God cannot realize God's vision of wholeness and unity.

Key Terms: Teilhard de Chardin, consciousness, cosmotheandrism, ecopoiesis, theogenesis, holism

Introduction

The efforts to bring science and religion into a unified field of knowledge have given rise over the last few decades to a theology of nature in a way that seeks to respect the current science of evolution

---

1. Denis Edwards, *The Natural World and God: Theological Explorations* (Adelaide, Australia: ATF Press, 2017), 19.

and quantum physics.[2] A number of notable theologians, including the late Denis Edwards, have written thoughtful systematic treatises on God and evolution, offering new ways to understand the God-world relationship and divine action. As laudable as these efforts have been, they have also stifled the imagination of a thoroughly new paradigm of science and religion, one that moves beyond an implicit anthropocentric theology.

While current trends in science are acknowledged, theology continues to be done against the background of medieval cosmology and philosophy. The persistent metaphysics of Thomas Aquinas and his notion of primary and secondary causality are often used to describe the God-world relationship and divine action. There is a type of cognitive dissonance that takes place, as scholars strive to fit this medieval metaphysics into a contemporary scientific worldview, weaving his illuminative Aristotelian notion of Being with concepts of quantum physics and evolution. I sincerely doubt Thomas himself would have done such a thing because he paid close attention to the natural philosophy of his day and sought to understand theology in light of an Aristotelian philosophy received largely through the Islamic commentators, especially Avicenna. I have to admit that scholars do work out their paradigms in such a way that they are reasonable and intellectually attractive, but this type of theology is deeply problematic. Thomas adapted his metaphysics to a static, fixed, hierarchical and geocentric cosmos, not a Big Bang universe.

I have long wondered why efforts to bridge science and religion have failed to produce any significant results or provide a robust theology of nature, one that could inspire a new ethic of planetary life. I have finally come to the conclusion that we are asking the wrong question. The construct of science and religion as a discipline of study is, in a sense, contrived, created by the human subject. We address the question of science and religion from a Kantian perspective, the knower in search of meaning. It is a one-dimensional paradigm, exalting the subject who, using logical and rational procedures, progressively approaches and gains control over an external object (for example, a model of science and religion). The subject makes

---

2. A *theology of nature* 'must take the findings of science into account when it considers the relation of God and [humanity] to nature, even though it derives its fundamental ideas elsewhere'. Ian G Barbour, *Issues in Science and Religion* (New York: Prentice Hall and Harper, 1966), 415.

every effort to establish an appropriate method, which in itself is already a technique of possession, mastery and transformation.

What is the problem with this Kantian paradigm? It contradicts the basic principles of nature, as science now discloses them. If the aim of true knowledge is to be in harmony with nature, then the starting point for knowing anything, including religion, must be nature. In this respect, our epistemological models must change both in science and religion. We humans emerge from nature; we are part of nature and thus our knowledge must begin on the level of nature and redound on the whole of nature, both in science and religion.

The Australian philosopher Arran Gare has taken up the question of a new naturalism from a philosophical perspective, critiquing the western philosophical tradition. Gare proposes a new worldview grounded in the philosophy of nineteenth century idealists, especially Frederich Schelling, indicating that such idealism effected a third Copernican Revolution (following Kant's second revolution of the 'turn to the subject'.) In Gare's view, the German philosophers' 'turn to nature' conceived nature in such a way that living beings, including humans, could be seen as evolving within a creative process. In this view, nature precedes humans and finds in human consciousness a new creative power. The human spirit rises in and through nature, and the maximisation of spirit, particularly in human thought and imagination, gives rise to ultimate meaning for the cosmic process.

Gare calls this new naturalism a 'speculative naturalism', since it begins with respect for the processes of nature, in contrast to scientific materialism and reductionism which seek to control nature. His paradigm is a step in the right direction; but it does not go far enough to render a meaningful paradigm shift. For one, use of the term 'naturalism' signifies that we have not left the nineteenth century; it objectifies the very thing we are trying to identify with, more so, that we now know ourselves to be integrally part of, and thus continues a type of naturalism where consciousness is marginalised and religion is exempt. I agree with the direction Gare is taking but I think a better approach is to begin with the dynamic relational whole of infinite depth and movement, as described by aspects of quantum physics.

Pierre Teilhard de Chardin was interested in quantum physics and the new understanding of matter. He offers a new paradigm, in which nature is an ongoing construct of complexified wholeness, where consciousness is part of the emerging wholeness. The evolutionary story inclusive of human consciousness is a comprehensive story stretching from Alpha to Omega. As Denis Edwards puts it, 'The big bang and the expansion of our universe from a small dense hot state 13.7 billion years ago, and the evolution of life since its beginning on Earth 3.7 billion years ago—this whole story exists within the vision of the divine purpose.'[3] Teilhard's emergent wholeness is a *poiesis* of nature; nature creates itself (*poiesis*) through creative processes integral to evolution empowered by an infinite depth and presence that cannot be wholly identified with nature. Teilhard calls this empowering presence Omega. Since God is part of the emerging wholeness of nature, God too is becoming more whole in and through nature. This chapter seeks to explore a new God-world relationship, a relational holism, through Teilhard's ideas on mind, matter, evolution and God.

The Emergence of Knowledge

The new post-Kantian holism I advocate incorporates an evolutionary epistemology that includes both matter and mind, object and subject. '*Evolutionary Epistemology*', says Wentzel van Huyssteen, 'refers to an evolutionary theory of cognition and knowledge, and thus to the fact that human knowledge, even in its most sophisticated forms, like scientific knowledge, is a direct result of organic evolution.'[4] This evolutionary epistemology is best developed, in my judgment, by Teilhard de Chardin.

In his magnum opus, *The Human Phenomenon*, Teilhard described himself as more naturalist than physicist, as he set out to understand evolution as the operative process to explain reality. He asks: 'Is evolution a theory, a system or a hypothesis? It is much more: it is a general condition to which all theories, all hypotheses, all systems must bow and which they must satisfy henceforward if they are to be thinkable and true.'[5] If all systems of knowledge fall under the rubric of evolution then no system of knowledge is exempt from change and complexification, including theology. In this respect one can no longer speak of 'theology' and 'nature' or 'God and evolution'

---

3. Edwards, *Natural World and God*, 15.
4. J Wentzel van Huyssteen, *Duet or Duel? Theology and Science in a Postmodern World* (Harrisburg PA: Trinity Press International, 1998), 136, italics added.
5. Pierre Teilhard de Chardin, *The Phenomenon of Man*, translated by Bernard Wall (New York: Harper Row, 1959), 219.

as two separate (static) areas of knowledge; now one must begin with evolution as the basis of all knowledge and understand science and religion as part of the whole of evolution: 'religion and science are the two conjugated faces or phases of one and the same complete act of knowledge—the only one which can embrace the past and future of evolution as to contemplate, measure and fulfill them.'[6]

In his essay on 'The Position of Man in Nature and the Significance of Human Socialization', Teilhard indicated that intelligent life cannot be considered in the universe any longer as a superficial accident;[7] rather the universe orients itself toward intelligent, conscious, self-reflective life. He declared 'man discovers that he is nothing else than evolution become conscious of itself . . . The consciousness of each of us is evolution looking at itself and reflecting upon itself.'[8] The human person rises from evolution and, in turn, can reflect on evolution, a knowledge that redounds on the very processes that make knowledge possible. Knowledge is a function of evolutionary emergence; not the structures of the human mind alone but the dynamic structures of evolution. Whereas the modern Kantian is a knower in a world of phenomena, in Teilhard's paradigm the knower and known are integrally related in the process of evolution; that is, the knowing process emerges from evolution and in turn affects evolution: 'How indeed could we incorporate thought into the organic flux of space-time without being forced to grant it the first place in the process? How could we imagine a cosmogenesis reaching right up to mind without being thereby confronted with a noogenesis?'[9] The mind creates by perceiving the phenomena of reality and, in doing so, continues the fundamental work of evolution. 'To discover and know is to actually extend the universe ahead and to complete it', Teilhard wrote.[10] The knower is an artisan of evolution; 'each time the mind comprehends something it unites the world in a new way.'[11] Knowledge is in the service of unity, a position consonant with

---

6. Teilhard de Chardin, *The Phenomenon of Man*, 285.
7. Teilhard de Chardin, 'The Position of Man in Mature and the Significance of Human Socialization', in *The Future of Man*, 211–217.
8. Teilhard de Chardin, *Phenomenon of Man*, 221
9. Teilhard de Chardin, *Phenomenon of Man*, 221.
10. Thomas M King, *Teilhard's Mysticism of Knowing* (New York: Seabury Press, 1981), 35.
11. King, *Mysticism of Knowing*, 36.

Teilhard's law of complexity-consciousness in which consciousness and relationships rise in evolution. Teilhard's insights on mind in evolution distinguished his paradigm from Darwinian evolution.

Relational Holism and Consciousness

Although Darwin showed how natural selection could account for species variation, he could not explain the appearance of mind or consciousness. As a result, 'mental qualities were either squeezed out of existence or dismissed as mere causally inefficacious and epiphenomenal by-products of brain processes'.[12] Wolfgang Pauli found this troublesome since scientific theories themselves were 'products of the psyche'.[13] More recently philosopher Thomas Nagel wrote that the mind has eluded physical explanation because 'the great advances in the physical and biological sciences excluded the mind from the physical world'.[14]

Hence Darwinian evolution can explain material complexity but it treats consciousness as a later phenomenon that appears at higher levels in the process. In the early twentieth century, Einstein's special theory of relativity changed our understanding of matter and energy. Instead of seeing matter and energy as two separate properties, Einstein posited that mass is a property of energy and energy is a property of mass. As a consequence of the wave-like aspects of reality, the constituents of matter, the elementary particles, are *not* in the same sense real as the real things that they constitute. Left to themselves they exist in a world of possibilities, 'between the idea of a thing and a real thing', as Werner Heisenberg wrote.[15]

Because electrons are waves and particles, their wave aspects will interfere with each other; they will overlap and merge, drawing the electrons into an existential relationship whereby their actual inner

12. Peter B Todd, *The Individuation of God: Integrating Science and Religion* (Wilmette, IL: Chiron Publ, 2012), 61.

13. Todd, *The Individuation of God*, 61.

14. Thomas Nagel, 'The Core of "Mind and Cosmos"'. http://opinionator.blogs. nytimes.com/2013/08/18/the-core-of-mind-and-cosmos/?_php=true&_ type=blogs&_r=1.

15. Lothar Schäfer, 'Quantum Reality and the Importance of Consciousness in the Universe', 82 http://bdigital.ufp.pt/bitstream/10284/770/1/81-102Cons-Ciencias%2002-8.pdf.

qualities such as mass, charge and spin, as well as their position and momentum, become indistinguishable from the relationship among them. All properties of the electrons are affected by the relationship; in fact, they cease to be separate things and become parts of a whole. The whole will possess definite properties of mass, charge and spin, but it is completely indeterminate as to which constituent electrons are contributing to this whole. Indeed, it is no longer meaningful to talk of the constituent electrons' individual properties, as these continually change to meet the requirements of the whole. This kind of internal relationship exists only in quantum systems and has been called 'relational holism'.[16]

David Bohm and Karl Pribam each speculated on wholeness in nature and developed theories to explain wholeness as a function of consciousness. Bohm said there are two ways of seeing the universe. The first is the mechanistic order, in which the universe is seen as a collection of entities existing independently in time and space and interacting through forces that do not cause any change in the essential nature of these entities. This is the Newtonian perspective, following fundamental laws of classical physics, in which each atom, molecule, cell, organism or entity acts according to classical physical laws of motion.

The second perspective is based on quantum reality and cannot be accounted for by the mechanistic order. In quantum reality, movement is generally seen as discontinuous. An electron can move from one spot to another without going through any of the space between. Particles, like electrons, can show different properties depending on the environment they are in: in some places they are particles while in other places they are waves. Finally, two particles can show 'non-local relationships' which means they can be separated by vast distances but react as if they are connected to each other.[17]

Bohm recognised that these new features of quantum theory require the entire universe be considered as an unbroken whole, with each element in that whole demonstrating properties that depend on the overall environment: 'Thus, if all actions are in the form of discrete quanta, the interactions between the different entities (for example,

---

16. Danah Zohar, *The Quantum Self* (New York: William Morrow, 1991), 99.
17. David Bohm, *Wholeness and Implicate Order* (London: Routledge & Kegan Paul, 1980), 175.

electrons) constitute a single structure of indivisible links, so that the entire universe has to be thought of as an unbroken whole.'[18] He called this unbroken wholeness 'implicate order' meaning that enfolding takes place in the movements of various universal fields, including electromagnetic fields, sound waves, and others.[19] The enfolded order is the basis of the explicit order that we perceive in the unfolded state. For example, if you take a piece of folded paper and pierce it and then unfold the paper, the spots will appear random, separate and unrelated. However, if the paper is folded back into its initial position, all the holes come together into the single spot that was pierced through.[20]

Science is an elusive discipline that makes epistemological claims about materiality in such a way that the claims are described as 'objective'. However, new studies in the area of consciousness have challenged the scientific reductionistic paradigm. In the early twentieth century physicist Max Planck spoke of consciousness as fundamental to matter, that is, we cannot consider matter apart from consciousness. He wrote:

> All matter originates and exists only by virtue of a force which brings the particle of an atom to vibration and holds this most minute solar system of the atom together. We must assume behind this force the existence of a conscious and intelligent mind. This mind is the matrix of all matter.[21]

Physicist Erwin Schrödinger, like Planck, thought that consciousness is absolutely fundamental to matter and always experienced in the singular; everything begins with consciousness which itself is immaterial.[22] The philosopher Bertrand Russell said, 'we know nothing about the intrinsic quality of physical events except when these are mental events that we directly experience'.[23] These insights

18. Bohm, *Wholeness and Implicate Order*, 175.
19. Bohm, *Wholeness and Implicate Order*, 178.
20. Marjorie Hines Woollacott, *Infinite Awareness: The Awakening of a Scientific Mind* (Lanham: Rowman & Littlefield, 2015), 76.
21. Susan Borowski, 'Quantum Mechanics and the Consciousness Connection', *AAAS* (July 16, 2010) https://www.aaas.org/quantum-mechanics-and-consciousness-connection
22. Erwin Schrodinger, *What is Life?*, translated by Verena Schrodinger reprint edition (Cambridge: Cambridge University Press, 2012), 93–95.
23. Bertrand Russell, 'Mind and Matter', 1950 https://russell-j.com/19501110_Mind-Matter.HTM

have led to 'the hard problem of matter', namely, we cannot talk about matter apart from consciousness.[24]

In the 1950s astrophysicist James Jean wrote: 'The universe looks more like a great thought than a great machine. Mind no longer appears as an accident intruder into the realm of matter . . . The quantum phenomena make it possible to propose that the background of the universe is mindlike.'[25] Since consciousness is absolutely fundamental to matter, everything seems to begin with consciousness which itself is immaterial.[26] No one really knows what consciousness is or how it arises; what is known is that it is fundamental to existence itself. Nothing can said about anything apart from consciousness. Philosopher Gaylen Strawen describes this as the 'hard problem of matter'. 'Consciousness is not the fundamental mystery', he states, 'matter is'.[27]

Two principal positions on consciousness and matter have been at the heart of discussions in the twentieth century: the first known as monism or *panpsychism* claims that both physical and mental are ontologically equal parts of reality and that one cannot be reduced to the other. Physicist Max Tegmark holds to a radical panpsychism whereby there is a fundamental realm of matter, which is consciousness.[28] Philosopher Phillip Goff, author of *Galileo's Error*, explains that panpsychism is the best explanation for our current understanding of physics. He writes:

> Physical science doesn't tell us what matter *is*, only what it *does*. The job of physics is to provide us with mathematical models that allow us to predict with great accuracy how matter will behave. This is incredibly useful information; it allows us to manipulate the world in extraordinary ways, leading to the technological advancements that have transformed our society beyond recognition. But it is one thing to know the *behaviour*

---

24. Gaylen Strawson, 'Consciousness Isn't a Mystery. Its Matter', *New York Times* (May 16, 2016) https://www.nytimes.com/2016/05/16/opinion/consciousness-isnt-a-mystery-its-matter.html
25. James Jeans, *The Mysterious Universe* (New York: Macmillan, 1931), 158.
26. Erwin Schrödinger, *What is Life?*, translated by Verena Schrödinger reprint edition (Cambridge: Cambridge University Press, 2012), 93–95.
27. Strawson, 'Consciousness Isn't A Mystery'.
28. Max Tegmark, 'Consciousness as a State of Matter', in *Chaos, Solitons & Fractals*, 76 (July 2015): 238–270. Tegmark gives the name 'perceptronium' to this fundamental state of matter which is consciousness.

of an electron and quite another to know its *intrinsic nature*: how the electron is, in and of itself. Physical science gives us rich information about the behaviour of matter but leaves us completely in the dark about its intrinsic nature. In fact, the only thing we know about the intrinsic nature of matter is that some of it—the stuff in brains—involves experience. We now face a theoretical choice. We either suppose that the intrinsic nature of fundamental particles involves experience or we suppose that they have some entirely unknown intrinsic nature. On the former supposition, the nature of macroscopic things is continuous with the nature of microscopic things. The latter supposition leads us to complexity, discontinuity and mystery. The theoretical imperative to form as simple and unified a view as is consistent with the data leads us quite straightforwardly in the direction of panpsychism.[29]

The second position known as 'dual-aspect monism' states that the mental and the material are different aspects or attributes of a unitary reality, which itself is neither mental nor material. They are both properties of one neutral substance x, that is neither physical nor mental. Wolfgang Pauli, who was one of early pioneers of quantum physics, said 'it would be most satisfactory if physis (matter) and psyche (mind) could be conceived as complementary aspects of the same reality'.[30] This view is known as 'dual-aspect monism'. By way of definition, 'Two or more descriptions are complementary if they mutually exclude one another and yet are together necessary to describe the phenomenon exhaustively'.[31]

Dual-aspect monism excludes reductionism of either an idealist (the primacy of consciousness or panpsychism) or materialist nature (inert matter and mind) while being necessarily incompatible with dogmatic physicalism and scientific materialism. Similarly, Carl Jung proposed a view of basic reality which does not consist of parts but is one unfragmented whole, the *unus mundus*, based on the complementarity of mind and matter. David Bohm spoke of mind and matter *as different aspects of one whole and unbroken movement*

---

29. Philip Goff, 'Panpsychism is Crazy, but it is also most probably true', *Aeon* https://aeon.co/ideas/panpsychism-is-crazy-but-its-also-most-probably-true.

30. Harald Atmanspacher, '20th Century Variants of Dual-Aspect Thinking', *Mind and Matter*, 12/2 (2014): 245–288.

31. Atmanspacher, '20th Century Variants', 252.

(emphasis added). Harald Atmanspacher writes: 'Conceiving the psychophysically neutral domain holistically rather than atomistically, reflects the spirit of a corresponding move in quantum theory, which started out as an attempt to finalize the atomistic worldview of the 19th century and turned it into a fundamentally holistic one.'[32] According to Atmanspacher, the Jung-Pauli dual-aspect monist position corresponds to a philosophical insight implicit in quantum theory, namely, that mind and matter form a complementary whole, which cannot be reduced to parts.[33]

Teilhard de Chardin was aware of the problem of consciousness and held to a dual-aspect monist position to explain evolution. Life, he wrote, is 'a specific effect of matter turned complex; a property that is present in the entire cosmic stuff'.[34] He considered matter and consciousness not as 'two substances' or 'two different modes of existence, but as two aspects of the same cosmic stuff'.[35] From the Big Bang onward there is a 'withinness' and 'withoutness', or what he called, radial energy and tangential energy.[36] Consciousness is the withinness or 'inside' of matter and attraction is the 'outside' of matter; hence, matter is both attractive (tangential) and transcendent (radial). The complementarity of mind and matter helps explain both the rise of biological complexity and the corresponding rise of consciousness.

Human consciousness and selfhood transcend the material substrate from which we have emerged. Like Teilhard, Edwards holds that 'the 'self' in self-transcendence means that the evolutionary capacity is truly intrinsic to creaturely reality. It comes from within the natural world . . . it exists only because of God's creative act. God's presence in self-bestowing love enables creatures to exist, to interact, and to evolve.'[37]

By including consciousness as part of the material world, Teilhard opened up a place for religion within nature, transcending the abstraction of supernaturalism and reframing religion as the depth and breadth of evolution. Religion is an emergent dimension of matter

---

32. Atmanspacher, '20th Century Variants', 285.
33. Atmanspacher, '20th Century Variants', 285.
34. Pierre Teilhard de Chardin, *Man's Place in Nature*, translated by Noel Lindsay (New York: Collins, 1966), 34
35. Teilhard de Chardin, *Phenomenon of Man*, 56–64.
36. Teilhard de Chardin, *Phenomenon of Man*, 56–64.
37. Edwards, *The Natural World and God: Theological Explorations*, 18.

itself and hence of evolution. He wrote: 'To my mind, the religious phenomenon, taken as a whole, is simple the reaction of the universe as such, of collective consciousness and human action in process of development.'[38] Although religion is manifested in individual thought or self-consciousness, if we are to evolve, we must release ourselves from religious individualism and confront the general religious experience, which is cosmic and evolutionary, and involve ourselves in it.[39]

A Metaphysics of Love

Teilhard recognised a fundamental force of attraction throughout all levels of cosmic life, leading to greater levels of complexification and consciousness. Based on what he knew from quantum physics, he sought a core energy that satisfied the requirements of dual-aspect monism, a type of energy that includes both consciousness and attraction. Love is the unitive energy of attraction, transcendence and personalisation. He identified love energy as the most mysterious energy in the universe, present at all levels of life though indistinguishable from molecular forces: 'But even among the molecules, love was the building power that worked against entropy, and under its attraction the elements groped their way towards union.'[40]

On the level of cosmic life, love is both the impetus and the term of the process of development: 'This creative love interiorizes and transforms each individual unit while uniting it to the whole.'[41] While love-energy may not explicitly show itself on the level of the pre-living and the non-reflective, it is present inchoately as the unifying principle of wholeness. Love amplifies itself by way of union. Teilhard wrote: 'Love is the most universal, the most tremendous and the most mysterious of the cosmic forces';[42] further on he states, 'the physical structure of the universe is love.'[43]

---

38. Pierre Teilhard de Chardin, 'How I Believe', in *Christianity and Evolution*, translated by René Hague (New York: William Collins & Sons, 1971), 118–119.
39. Teilhard de Chardin, 'How I Believe', 118.
40. King, *Teilhard's Mysticism of Knowing*, 104–105.
41. Ewert H Cousins, 'The Evolving Cosmos: Teilhard de Chardin and Bonaventure', in *Cord*, 16 (1966): 131–136.
42. Pierre de Chardin, *Human Energy*, translated by JM Cohen (New York: Harcourt Brace Jovanovich, 1969), 32.
43. Teilhard de Chardin, *Human Energy*, 72.

The core energy of love in the universe impelled Teilhard to consider a new metaphysics, beyond the static metaphysics of Being. Considering that love is dynamic relationship and cosmic life is intrinsically relational, Teilhard posited that, from a philosophical perspective, being is not the principle of existence. He wrote: 'What comes first in the world for our thought is not "being" but "the union which produces this being."'[44] Union is the primary principle or cause; to be is to be united. Being is the outflow of union and union is always toward more being. If being is intrinsically relational then nothing exists independently or autonomously. Rather, 'to be' is 'to be with'. Reality is 'being with another' in a way open to more union and more being. Since being is existence towards another, being is relational and exists for the sake of giving. I do not exist in order that I may possess; rather I exist in order that I may give of myself, for it is in giving that I am myself.

By reversing the classic Aristotelian notion of being and union, Teilhard described relationality as the principle of being and suggested that a metaphysics of union (or love) is the principle of existence. Union is always towards more being. The principle of 'more life', therefore, is not support from below but from the future, impelling Teilhard to reframe the notion of metaphysics as 'hyperphysics'. Life is oriented to more life, making the future the absolute principle of life itself.

Creative Union

Teilhard's metaphysics provides the basis of his relationship between God and world. Thomas King described Teilhard's God as a God of matter: 'God is not found through opposition to matter (anti-matter) or independent of matter (extra-matter) but through matter (trans-matter).'[45] We take hold of God in the finite; God is sensed as 'rising' or 'emerging' from the depths of physical evolution, born not in the heart of matter but *as* the heart of matter.[46] Such an understanding of God and materiality is deeply incarnational. God is within physical evolution in a discreet way such that lower level entities become

44. Teilhard de Chardin, *Christianity and Evolution*, 227.
45. King, *Teilhard's Mysticism of Knowing*, 66–67.
46. King, *Mysticism of Knowing*, 103.

higher-level entities, with a persistent emergence of novelty. While in the case of a static world, Teilhard wrote, the creator is structurally independent of his work; in an evolutive world the contrary is true. God is not conceivable except in so far as God coincides with evolution without being lost in the center of evolutionary convergence or cosmogenesis.[47] In this process of evolution, multiplicity is dependent on unity and on some final unity which does not need any principle beyond itself to unify it, since it is the 'already One'. This ultimate unity is God Omega.

Although Teilhard did not provide a systematic treatment of God, he does indicate that God is Trinity.[48] God's relationality begins with the Father who vitalizes and engenders, the Son and Word who centers, and the Spirit who is the energy of love. Teilhard's God is a communion of love engaged in the development of the world. Michael Meerson wrote:

> God's ultimate reality cannot be located in substance (what it is in itself) but only in personhood: what God is toward another . . . Since love produces communion among persons, love causes God to be who God is.[49]

The dynamic divine life is 'trinitizing' the universe, drawing all things from multiplicity into unity.

Teilhard described God and world as an interrelated pair. He held to a genuine 'complementarity' between God and the world. God and world are a coincidence of opposites and exist in mutually affirming union. The optimal way to understand God and world is to perceive God as different from the world but personally linked to it in a relationship of mutual complementarity, in such a way that neither God nor world cannot adequately exist without the other.

This God-world relationship may be more aptly described by concepts from quantum physics, such as 'quantum entanglement', where change in one dimension affects the other. The God-world relationship is like a complex dynamical system in that God and world cannot be considered separately but must be considered in relation to

---

47. Teilhard de Chardin, *Christianity and Evolution*, 239–240.
48. Teilhard de Chardin, *Christianity and Evolution*, 157.
49. Michael Aksionov Meerson, *The Trinity of Love in Modern Russian Theology* (Quincy, IL: Franciscan Press, 1998), 4.

each other. Without creation, something would be absolutely lacking to God, considered in the fullness not of his being but of his act of union. Christopher Mooney writes: 'Teilhard wants to do away once and for all with the idea that God's continuous act of creation is one of absolute gratuity.'[50] He spoke of creative union as an act of immanent unification; the world is in process of being created by the gradual unification of multiplicity. In his *'Mon Univers'* he wrote:

> The theory of creative union is not so much a metaphysical doctrine as a sort of empirical and pragmatic explanation of the universe. This theory came to birth out of my own personal need to reconcile, within the confines of a rigorously structured system, the views of science respecting evolution (which views are accepted here as being definitively established, at least in their essence) with an innate tendency which has driven me to seek out the presence of God, not apart from the physical world, but rather through matter and in a certain sense in union with it.[51]

Teilhard sees God as dynamically engaged in materiality; God is rising up in and through evolution. Christopher Mooney wrote, 'if God did not fully engage in evolution something would be absolutely lacking to God, considered in the fullness not of his being but of his act of union'.[52] He opposed the idea of an absolutely gratuitous creation because it makes creation independent of God, that is, no real relation.[53] Evolution towards greater unity rests on the involvement of God in creation. The world is coming to be and God is coming to be; God makes nature and nature makes God. The verb 'make' here follows the Hebrew word *bara*, 'to bring into existence'.[54] God brings nature into existence and nature brings God into existence. Hence, creation is not the 'beginning' of the world but its 'end'. Creation is

---

50. Christopher Mooney, SJ, *Teilhard de Chardin and the Mystery of Christ* (New York: Harper & Row, 1966), 174–175.

51. Donald P Gray, *The One and the Many: Teilhard de Chardin's Vision of Unity* (London: Burns and Oates, 1969), 34.

52. Christopher Mooney, SJ, 'Teilhard de Chardin and the Christological Problem', *The Harvard Review*, 58/1 (1965): 91–126.

53. Gray, *The One and the Many*, 127.

54. See Jürgen Moltmann, *God and Creation: A New Theology of Creation and the Spirit of God*, translated by Margaret Kohl (Minneapolis: Fortress, 1993), 73.

that which is coming to be, as multiplicity proceeds toward unity and the formation of a universe.[55]

Teilhard's metaphysics of love and his doctrine of creative union suggest that God, cosmos (nature) and human are intertwined. The term 'cosmotheandrism' was coined by Raimon Panikkar to describe the inextricable, perichoretic realities of cosmic—human—divine realities.[56] To separate out one reality over and against the other is to distort all three realities. They must be held together. Teilhard's paradigm is a cosmotheandric paradigm of ecopoeisis, the ability of nature to make itself, to become something more than what it is because God is the infinite depth and power of love at the heart of nature.

The complementarity of the created and the uncreated means that the two terms are brought together, each in its own way, and have an equal need both to exist in themselves and to be combined with each other so that the absolute maximum union may be effected *in natura rerum*. He states:

> We are inevitably making our way to a completely new concept of being: God completely other in nature than the world and yet unable to dispense with it. The two movements of God and world are intertwined in such a way that the emergence of new being is the emergence of a new cosmotheandric wholeness, where cosmos, theos, anthropos share in the maximization of consciousness.[57]

Nature's dynamic becoming is God's dynamic becoming; as nature becomes something new so too God becomes new. Teilhard wrote: 'All around us and within our own selves, God is in process of 'changing,' as a result of the coincidence of his magnetic power and our own thought.'[58] God is creating the world and the world is creating God by giving birth (theogenesis) to God: 'God fulfills himself, he in some

---

55. Teilhard de Chardin, *Christianity and Evolution*, 176.
56. Raimon Panikkar, *The Rhythm of Being: The Guifford Lectures* (Maryknoll, NY: Orbis, 2010), 191. The idea of '*theandrism*' is found as far back at Maximus the Confessor (c. 580–662). It is an ancient theme in Christian theology, reflecting an understanding of the Incarnation as a cosmic event.
57. Teilhard de Chardin, *Christianity and Evolution*, 227.
58. Teilhard de Chardin, *Hymn to Matter*, 53.

way *completes* himself, in the pleroma.'[59] To ask how God 'acts in nature', therefore, is not a question for Teilhard. God does not act; God 'relates' by uniting with nature. God does what God is, namely, love the world, as the poet Mary Oliver wrote, 'my work is loving the world'.[60] Love causes things to be what they are and to become more than what they are. God's acts by loving the world, and by loving the world, God emerges through love as God for the world.

The inextricable relationship of God and world is the full meaning of the divine Word incarnate. God is not a singular monad but plural— Trinity—and thus an open system of self-engagement. The self-engaged God is the Christ. Carl Jung shared a similar understanding of theogenesis with Teilhard. For Jung consciousness is the mirror that the universe has evolved to reflect upon itself and in which its very existence is revealed. He described God (and Christianity) as a patient in analysis for whom consciousness needs to be brought into its unconscious darkness in a self-transformative process, one of individuating and becoming whole. According to Peter Todd, 'it is precisely this expanded and higher consciousness which Jung believes God acquires through incarnation in humankind'.[61]

The evolution of God and the evolution of humanity cannot be separated. As we rise into higher consciousness, so too does God. He wrote: 'One should make it clear to oneself what it means when God becomes man. It means nothing less than a world-shaking transformation of God.'[62] God becomes human and the human becomes God through consciousness and love. Through this ongoing incarnation or Christogenesis, God is completed by humankind in directed evolution. Todd states: 'It is as an archetypal and cosmic reality rather than a purely theological concept.'[63] God incarnate is the fulfillment of natural evolution. 'This transformation in

---

59. Teilhard de Chardin, *Christianity and Evolutioni*, 178. Emphasis added.

60. Mary Oliver, 'The Messenger' in *Thirst* (Boston: Beacon Press, 2006), 1.

61. Peter Todd, 'Teilhard and Other Modern Thinkers on Evolution, Mind, and Matter' Part II, in *Science and Nonduality*, (November 18, 2014): 5. https://www.scienceandnonduality.com/article/teilhard-and-other-modern-thinkers-on-evolution-mind-and-matter-part-ii. This article is the online version of Peter Todd, 'Teilhard and Other Modern Thinkers on Evolution, Mind and Matter', in *Teilhard Studies*, 66 (2013): 1–18.

62. Todd, 'Teilhard and Other Modern Thinkers', 6.

63. Todd, 'Teilhard and Other Modern Thinkers', 8.

consciousness', Todd writes, 'is the divinization or resacralization of the world'.[64] As God rises up through higher levels of consciousness, the human evolves to a new level of completion and thus a new vision, a new knowing, and a new way of acting in the world.

Ecopoietic Theogenesis

Teilhard was keenly aware that we can say nothing about either matter or God apart from human consciousness and experience. God's being is God's relationship, a depth of divine relationship that impels material existence toward more complexified relationships of greater consciousness and attraction. Love defines this movement of matter toward spirit. God 'acts' by 'loving the world'. This empowering divine presence bestows freedom to nature and depends on the freedom of nature to act according to the highest good. 'A tree does nothing more than be a tree', Thomas Merton wrote, 'and in being a tree it gives glory to God'.[65] Nature is self-making and God-making: as God emerges through evolution, nature finds its own identity in relation to that which is it not, namely, God, and God finds divine identity precisely in and through that which God is not, namely, nature. Hence neither 'nature' nor 'God' can exist independently; each is dependent on the other for their own existence.

This relational interdependence defines the cosmotheandric whole. God is not outside the realm of complexifying relationships. Rather God is actively engaged in the world, 'Godding' in and through the world, precisely by becoming what God is not, namely, matter; and matter is actively engaged in becoming what it is not, namely God. The human person recapitulates this process of theogenesis in such a way that God's life affects our life and our life affects God's life. Moral living, therefore, is cooperating out of love. Our ethical life is a productive activity. 'Since God has been involved in evolution from the beginning, our love for God requires cooperating with God's activity in building up the world. There is no need for a separate sphere called "supernatural"'[66] The engagement of God in

---

64. Todd, 'Teilhard and Other Modern Thinkers', 8.
65. Thomas Merton, *New Seeds of Contemplation* (New York: Basic, 1961), 31.
66. Edward Vacek, SJ, 'An Evolving Christian Morality *Eppur si muove*', in *From Teilhard to Omega: Cocreating an Unifinised Universe*, edited by Ilia Delio (Maryknoll, NY: Orbis, 2014), 157.

the self-making of the world means it is religiously important that we cooperate in this project. 'Agnostics cooperate by working to promote the good and believers cooperate as an act of adoration.'[67] Sanctification, for Teilhard, means freely participating in this stream of life that is unyielding in its dynamic movement toward fullness. Fullness is a relational term, meaning to be incorporated into God's evolving world through a growth in consciousness and unity. For Teilhard, we will be saved by an option that has chosen the whole.

Teilhard's paradigm of theogenesis suggests divine dependency. God needs us to be God. Without human beings, God cannot realize God's vision of wholeness, unity and fecundity. Edward Vacek writes: 'God's activity is present whenever humans are enticed into committing themselves to improve the world . . . God not only needs human labor to build stable skyscrapers and dig deep oil wells . . . God uses and thereby depends on our thoughts and affections in discerning how to build the earth.'[68] Vacek continues: 'the will of God is not an antecedent plan to be discovered by us, but rather a plan to be co-created through the exercise of our own minds and hearts.'[69] Engagement with one another and with the earth means to love matter in all its brute reality, because engagement with matter is engagement with God. Teilhard's hymn on 'The Spiritual Power of Matter' captures this beautifully:

> Purity does not lie in separation from, but in a deeper penetration into the universe. It is to be found in the love of that unique, boundless Essence which penetrates the inmost depths of all things . . . bathe yourself in the ocean of matter; plunge into where it is deepest and most violent; struggle in its currents and drink of its waters. For it cradled you long ago in your preconscious existence; and it is that ocean that will raise you up to God.[70]

The heights of God are to be found in the depths of matter; and the key to matter is consciousness. Teilhard's religion of the earth, his

67. Vacek, 'An Evolving Christian Morality', 158.
68. Vacek, 'An Evolving Christian Morality', 159.
69. Vacek, 'An Evolving Christian Morality', 159.
70. Pierre Teilhard de Chardin, 'The Spiritual Power of Matter', in *Hymn of the Universe*, translated by Simon Bartholomew (New York: Harper 7 Row, 1961), 64–65.

'ecopoietic theogenesis', anticipates a collective unity of minds gathered into new unities of love. This is not a radical anthropocentrism; mind in this respect does not refer to the human mind but a much broader concept of mind as the field of awareness across all spectrums of life. That is, when we become conscious of belonging to the whole earth with its tremendous variety of life forms, when we act from a consciousness of divine presence empowering this whole earth and its rich variety of life, when we engage in this wholemaking process of evolution through living in the good, then we are part of cosmotheandric life oriented toward more life. Teilhard celebrates this life in his 'Mass on the World':

> Once upon a time [men] took into your temple the first fruits of their harvests, the flower of their flocks. But the offering you really want, the offering you mysteriously need every day to appease your hunger, to slake your thirst is nothing less than the growth of the world born ever onwards in the stream of universal becoming . . . Receive, O Lord this all-embracing host which your whole creation, moved by your magnetism, offers you at this dawn of a new day. This bread, our toil, is of itself, I known, but an immense fragmentation; this wine, our pain, is no more, I known, than draught that dissolves. Yet in the very depths of this formless mass you have implanted— and this I am sure of, for I sense it—a desire, irresistible, hallowing, which makes us cry out, believer and unbeliever alike: 'Lord, make us *one*'.[71]

God receives into God's self the good that occurs in creation; God expands through the choices for love. This is not the naturalism of the German idealists but a much more robust and participative enactment of ongoing creativity. Ecopoietic theogenesis is co-creative, cosmotheanrdic relational holism oriented toward the flourishing of life. The perfection of God *is* God's maximal involvement with all matter, from the smallest quark to the highest creature. If God could not be related to what goes on in creation, God would not be a God of love. God and matter belong together, all of matter: earth matter, universe matter, star matter. On the human level our lives and our work fill out God's relational self; however, we must make a conscious choice for love.

---

71. Teilhard de Chardin, 'Mass on the World', in *Hymn of the Universe*, 20.

Conclusion

Like a flower blooming in the garden, the evolutionary and ecological theology of Denis Edwards has been well fertilised by Teilhard de Chardin's cosmic vision. My aim here has been to overcome the Kantian split between matter and mind too often assumed in today's dialogue between theology and science; and I have sought to do so by retrieving the evolutionary epistemology and cosmology of Teilhard.

Teilhard's emphasis on cosmotheandric wholeness and the future has the salutary feature of making us responsible for the future. Our responsibility for evolution requires *more than* passing on a world no worse than the one we have inherited. Rather, a morality of movement requires a morality of involvement, one by which we improve the world.

Evolution has given us a better world and we are responsible for continuing that creative enhancement. This better world, however, will consist not in more things and more material resources, but rather in increased personal capacities, faith in God, faith in the world, faith in the future requiring a commitment to the earth and to one another through closer cooperation. Teilhard proposes an ethic based on evolving into the future through an increase of connected minds and connected hearts. His paradigm, therefore, impels us to replace the word 'naturalism' with 'evolution' because a consciousness of evolution alters the meaning of what we are doing. His cosmic synthesis refutes a supernatural religion and scientific reductionism that fails to explain the depth and movement of life. His approach shows that our ordinary ethical life has eternal meaning; that individual autonomy develops out of deep interconnectivity, that love leads not only to unity but to cooperative creativity, and that beyond self-fulfillment we are responsible for developing both the world and God's life onto the fullness of life.

Deep Incarnation and the Real Presence of Christ in the Lord's Supper

Jamie L Fowler

'When Christians gather for Eucharist they bring creation with them.'
– Denis Edwards[1]

Abstract: As a tribute to the late Denis Edwards, this project intends to shed light on the means by which Christ is physically present in the Lord's Supper. Such illumination appeals to deep incarnation (Niels Henrik Gregersen), the multidimensional unity of life (Paul Tillich), and the role of the Spirit as the mediator of Christ's presence in the elements of the sacrament. The deep incarnation of Christ into the multidimensional unity of life establishes a relationship between the divine and material reality that subsequently allows for the presence of the risen Body of Christ in the bread and wine. Finally, the manner and means of Christ's presence in the incarnation and the Sacrament of the Altar affirms Edwards' primary theological commitment to the self-giving nature of God.

Key Terms: Real presence of Christ, Lord's Supper, deep incarnation, multidimensional unity of life, spiritual presence

The field of *Theology and Science* has matured since its birth with Ian Barbour's introductory book in 1966, *Issues in Science and Religion.*[2] Denis Edwards has contributed much to that maturation process. Until his untimely death, Edwards was a renowned Australian theologian at the Australian Catholic University in Adelaide. Edwards' work focused on eco-theology, deep incarnation, and sacramentology. He was one of the original experts involved in the birth of Catholic

---

1. Denis Edwards, *The Natural World and God: Theological Explorations* (Adelaide, Australia: ATF Press, 2017) 135.
2. Ian G Barbour, *Issues in Science and Religion* (New York: Prentice Hall and Harper, 1966).

Earthcare Australia, a program that attends to ecological needs.[3] Serving God's church and creation was the center of Edwards' life and work. No matter the theological task, Edwards held fast to his belief in 'the self-giving nature of God'.[4]

In the spirit of Edwards' theological and faithful exploration, in this chapter I will attempt to advance the concept of deep incarnation by applying it to the sacrament of the Lord's Supper, especially as we find it in Roman Catholic and Lutheran traditions. One question both Roman Catholic and Lutheran theologians have sought to answer is this: how can we provide a coherent explanation of the *physical* presence of the divine within the elements of bread and wine?

Classically, Roman Catholics have appealed to transubstantiation. Lutherans have preferred a non-metaphysical affirmation of the real presence of Christ described by Martin Luther in his 'Confession Concerning Christ's Supper'[5] and various treatises on the Lord's Supper.[6] Luther states that the body and blood of Christ are present *in, with, and under* the bread and wine,[7] making no appeal to a transformed essence or substance. Luther's position intentionally falls short of explaining just *how* Christ is present because for Luther the employment of such philosophical categories is a human conception lacking revelatory basis.[8] In order to retain the belief in the real presence in today's scientific climate, Lutherans need

3. https://www.indcatholicnews.com/news/36728
4. http://www.adelaide.catholic.org.au/view-biography?guid=31530
5. Martin Luther, 'Confession Concerning Christ's Supper' (1528), *Martin Luther's Basic Theological Writings*, edited by Timothy F Lull and William R Russell, 2nd edition (Minneapolis: Augsburg Fortress Press, 2005), 259–276.
6. 'We may well allow it to be said, "he is in the bread, he is the bread, he is where the bread is", or whatever you wish. We do not wish to argue over words, just so the meaning is retained that it is not mere bread that we eat in Christ's Supper, but the body of Christ.' Martin Luther, 'That These Words of Christ, "This Is My Body", Still Stand Firm Against the Fanatics', (1527), *The Annotated Luther*, edited by Hans J Hillerbrand, Kirsi I Stjerna, and Timothy Wengert, 6 Volumes (Minneapolis: Fortress Press, 2015–2019) 3:163–274, here at 211.
7. *Formula of Concord Solid Declaration* VII.36–38 (*Triglot Concordia*, 983, 985); Theodore G Tapport *The Book of Concord: The Confessions of the Evangelical Lutheran Church* (Philadelphia: Fortress Press, 1959), 575–576.
8. Gordon A Jensen, 'Luther and the Lord's Supper', in *The Oxford Handbook of Martin Luther's Theology*, edited by Robert Kolb, Irene Dingle, and L'ubamir Batka (Oxford: Oxford University Press, 2014), 321–325.

a conceptualization of Christ's presence in the Lord's Supper that features the *biological* dimension of the physical presence.

In what follows, I will demonstrate that the Lutheran position regarding the real presence of Christ in the elements of the Lord's Supper finds valuable illuminative, if not explanatory, support from deep incarnation Christology. Indeed, Lutheran theology needs deep incarnation to develop a clear description of Christ's presence in the elements of the sacrament. I hope to show that in his presence, Christ is perpetually self-giving, really imparting grace to us in the Sacrament of the Altar. To that end, I hope to honor Edwards' belief in a self-giving and co-suffering God[9] and emphasise the importance of deep incarnation to Christian, especially Lutheran, theology.

I will begin with highlights of deep incarnation. Next, I will introduce the multi-dimensional ontology proffered by Paul Tillich's systematic theology. This ontological structure will provide the scaffolding for the existential relationships among creation, Christ, and the Holy Spirit. With this ontological structure in place, I will review the operation of the Lord's Supper from a Lutheran perspective. Finally, I will pull the pieces together into a conceptualization of the real presence of Christ in the Lord's Supper. I hope this concept of the real presence will affirm the importance and veracity of Edwards' theological commitment, the self-giving nature of God, in the Sacrament of the Altar.

Deep Incarnation

In 2000 deep incarnation was introduced by the Danish theologian, Niels Henrik Gregersen. He generated this concept in response to the question, 'How can we believe in the good, loving God of the Christian faith in the face of a creative process like evolution which carries an overwhelming cost, built-in suffering and death?' Looking for answers, Gregersen returned to the incarnation text John 1:14 'And the Word was made flesh and dwelt among us . . .'[10] Gregersen proposed that the 'flesh' taken on by the Word was not limited to the human body. Rather 'flesh' describes the connection between Jesus

---

9. Denis Edwards, *Deep Incarnation: The Cross as Sacrament of God's Redemptive Suffering with Creatures* (Maryknoll: Orbis Books, 2019) 124.

10. Jn 1:14 NRSV

Christ and other humans, the diverse community of life on earth, *and* the universe beyond.[11]

To answer his question, Gregersen posited that in the incarnation, the Word assumed the whole of material existence, including the entire cosmic history of said material. Christ assumed all sections of existence, such as electrons, cells, and self-consciousness. Gregersen named this concept 'Deep Incarnation', acknowledging that the incarnation extended beyond human life, deep into creation. Conversely, the depth of creation was drawn into the life of God, prompting Edwards to assert that the whole of creation is with Christ on the cross.

> In the twenty-first century, a theology of the cross as sacrament of God's redemptive suffering with creatures can enable us to say that the love poured out in the incarnation of the Word, which culminates in the cross of Jesus, can enable us to affirm the compassionate presence of God to all creatures of our evolutionary world.[12]

Christ who had assumed all flesh sacrificed himself to the cross. His sacrifice not only destroyed sin, suffering, and death for humanity. It also destroyed the suffering and death inherent to all life in the evolutionary process. In response, God gave the life of God's Son to end the problematic components of the evolutionary process. On this matter, Edwards along with Christopher Southgate share similar theological perspectives. Southgate states, 'The cross of Christ expresses God's loving solidarity with all creatures, particularly with the victims of evolution.'[13] Deep incarnation perceives that all of creation is united to Christ in his life and death on the cross. Deep incarnation Christology understands that Jesus Christ suffered to end all suffering, became the victim to end all victimization, and died to end all dying.

Deep incarnation Christology modernizes and biologizes Irenaeus' recapitulation Christology, according to which the incarnate word assumes all physical reality, including suffering and death. Christ has

---

11. Niels Henrik Gregersen, 'The Cross of Christ in an Evolutionary World', in *Dialog: A Journal of Theology* 40/3 (Fall 2001): 197–198.

12. Edwards, *Deep Incarnation*, 128.

13. Christopher Southgate, *The Groaning of Creation: God, Evolution, and the Problem of Evil* (Louisville: Westminster John Knox Press, 2008), 72.

therefore, in His work of recapitulation, summed up all things . . . in order that, as our species went down to death through a vanquished man, so we may ascend to life again through a victorious one; and as through a man death received the palm [of victory] against us, so again by a man we may receive the palm against death.[14]

Deep incarnation, similarly, recognises that power of death and suffering, the problematic components of evolution, ended when Christ—still united to creation—was raised to new, eternal life with the triune God.

If deep incarnation is carried through the Christological gamut, it leads to 'deep resurrection'.[15] Deep resurrection states that, because Christ assumed all material reality in the incarnation, he carries it to salvation through his resurrection. Consequently, all of creation is resurrected and made anew. God's astonishing response to Christ's death on the cross, to the death and suffering in creation, is to raise Christ—along with all material reality and cosmic history—to a new, eternal life filled with love, communion, and peace. Deep incarnation and deep resurrection maintain the self-giving nature of God revealed in the Christian faith in the face of evolutionary suffering.

The Multi-Dimensional Unity of Life

Deep Incarnation is an incredibly creative theological concept that meets the contemporary, scientific worldview head-on. In order to construct an illuminating concept of the real presence, a comprehensive ontological structure of reality that will allow for divine presence in material creation is necessary. The ontology must make sense both scientifically and theologically. On one hand, the structure of our ontological categories must be scientifically plausible. On the other hand, the scientifically structured picture of reality must be theologically accessible.

I suggest that we appeal to 'the multidimensional unity of life' in the ontology of Paul Tillich. This ontological structure incorporates an equanimous unity of multiple dimensions. Rather

---

14. Irenaeus, *Against Heresies,* 5:21:1; https://www.earlychurchtexts.com/public/irenaeus_on_recapitulation_in_christ.htm.

15. Elizabeth A Johnson, 'Jesus and the Cosmos: Sounding in Deep Ecology', in *Incarnation: On the Scope and Depth of Christology,* edited by Niels Gregersen (Minneapolis: Fortress Press, 2015), 142.

than combining previously separate elements such as we find in substance dualism, he orders a single created reality into multiple *dimensions*. Tillich states, 'One is justified in speaking of a dimension when the phenomenological description of a section of encountered reality shows unique categorical structures'.[16] What does this mean? First, Tillich relies on the philosophical presupposition that we come b knowledge through our perception of the world. Thus, any dimensional description is mediated through our experience.

Tillich tells us that we can identify a dimension when our experience yields a description that is consistently unique in category and structure to a section of reality. For instance, the consistent presence of carbon-based molecules and their unique chemical principles in our reality is identified by scientists as organic chemistry. The specific chemical patterns and rules, which accompany the carbon molecules, are the categorical structures of organic chemistry. Thus, the identification of organic chemistry as a dimension of existence is justified.

As the moniker states, the overarching relationship among dimensions is one of unity. Yet, three criteria nuance the unity.[17] The first criterion states that dimensions are authentic in themselves. Dimensions do contribute to the reality of other dimensions, like the inorganic dimension contributes to the organic. Even so, a single dimension retains its authentic boundaries and identity.[18]

The second criterion tells that dimensions, or parts of dimensions combine under certain conditions to create a new dimension.[19] Tillich states, 'the actualization of specific multidimensional structures gives birth to a new dimension'.[20] For example, when actualised structures from the inorganic (such as the presence of nitrogen, sulfur, and phosphate) and the organic (such as myelin sheaths and neurons) dimensions combine, the self-conscious dimension is born. Self-consciousness is an emergent property, an added dimension.

The final criterion asserts that a dimension cannot be reduced into its contributing components or be isolated from them. For instance, the self-conscious dimension cannot be reduced to the

---

16. Paul Tillich, *Systematic Theology*, 3 volumes (Chicago: University of Chicago Press, 1951–1963), 3:17.
17. Tillich, *Systematic Theology*, 3:22.
18. Tillich, *Systematic Theology*, 3:23.
19. Tillich, *Systematic Theology*, 3:22–23.
20. Tillich, *Systematic Theology*, 3:24.

organic and then to the inorganic without the loss of authentic existence.[21] Conversely, isolating the self-conscious dimension from its contributing dimensional structures would annihilate it.

In order to map out the relationships among dimensions, we might be tempted to propose a hierarchy, organizing dimensions into a tower of levels defined by increasing complexity. 'In this view reality is seen as a pyramid of levels following each other in vertical direction according to their power of being.'[22] However, a hierarchical structure of reality is a direct violation of Tillich's ontology. He adamantly insisted that leveling the dimensions would undermine the importance of each dimension to those that follow and the creative process of life. The actualised continuity of dimensions contributing to other dimensions in the creative process does not allow the formation of levels. In the multidimensional unity of life, Tillich orders a single reality into multiple dimensions, ranging from the physical to the spiritual.

One Reality, Multiple Dimensions

The possession of conceptual clarity regarding the structure and thesis of the multidimensional unity of life is essential to this project. I find that Fritjof Capra's worldview most helpful because it provides solidity to Tillich's abstract dimensions. Capra, a Vienna-born physicist and systems theorist, has explored the ways in which modern physics and other sciences are shifting our worldview, or paradigm, from a mechanistic one to a holistic and ecological one.[23] In his many works, he eschews mechanism and hierarchy. Instead, he unites the physical, chemical, biological, cognitive, social, and ecological dimensions of life into one unified vision.

---

21. Tillich belongs among today's emergence theorists, for whom the whole cannot be reduced to the parts or even the sum of the parts. The concept of holism recognizes '*a complex mutual conditioning between part and whole*. It recognizes different levels of complexity and recognizes as well that no one level can be thoroughly understood in isolation from its neighbors.' Nancey Murphy, *Anglo-American Postmodernity: Philosophical Perspectives on Science, Religion, and Ethics* (New York: Harper, Westview, 1997), 34, Murphy's italics.
22. Tillich, *Systematic Theology*, 3:13.
23. Fritjof Capra and Pier Luigi Luisi, *The Systems View of Life: A Unifying Vision* (Cambridge: Cambridge University Press, 2014), 8–15.

> [In other words,] the web of life consists of networks within
> networks. At each scale, the nodes of each network reveal
> themselves as smaller networks. We tend to arrange these
> systems, all nesting within larger systems, in a hierarchical
> scheme by placing the larger systems above the smaller ones
> in pyramid fashion. But this is a human projection. In nature
> there is no 'above' or 'below', and there are no hierarchies.
> There are only networks nesting within other networks.[24]

If we apply Capra's systemic thought to the multidimensional unity
of life, we encounter a web of dimensions equally and potentially
present to all actualized junctions or nodes. New systems, or realms,[25]
are created by the organisation and actualization among dimensional
components. '. . . all dimensions are always real, if not actually, at
least potentially.'[26] Meaning, the whole web of united dimensions is
potentially present at each node. Capra's conception of reality like
Tillich's does not allow for levels or hierarchies. Instead, they share a
similar vision that could be described as a continuous web of united
dimensions.

Here is the value of Tillich's multidimensional unity of life
for deep incarnation Christology: a single ontology incorporates
without tension the biological and spiritual dimensions without
relying on substance dualism. The incarnation spans all dimensions
from creation's physical basis through humanity, including other
creatures and the universe. The combination of the multidimensional
unity of life and deep incarnation seamlessly includes the inorganic
dimension along with all others in God's salvific acts. The inclusion
of the inorganic dimension is crucial to the current project. The very
elements of the Lord's Supper, which Lutherans believe bear the real
presence of Christ, belong to the inorganic dimension.

---

24. Fritjof Capra, *The Web of Life: A New Scientific Understanding of Living Systems*
(New York: First Anchor Books, 1996), 15–25.
25. Tillich defines realm as a section of reality in which a special dimension
determines the character of every individual belonging to the realm. In this
sense, one speaks of the vegetable realm or the animal realm. In all of them,
all dimensions are potentially present and some of them are actualised. Tillich,
Systematic Theology, 3:16.
26. Tillich, *Systematic Theology*, 3:16.

The Spiritual Dimension, The Spiritual Presence and Symbol

Tillich's multidimensional unity of life describes a single, but dimensionally differentiated reality, which holds the material and immaterial dimensions together. Tillich does not appeal to substance dualism. Whereas substance dualism tries frustratingly to connect the physical with the spiritual, the multi-dimensional ontology presupposes that the physical and spiritual are already dimensions of a single reality.[27]

The spiritual dimension is actualised in the human person. It is born of a specific constellation of conditions in the psychological dimension and united with the psychological, the organic, and the inorganic dimensions.[28] As far as we know, the spiritual dimension has only actualized in human beings, making it the home of the human spirit.

In the incarnation, the Word assumes the spiritual dimension of human existence. However, deep incarnation states that the Word assumes all flesh. So that when the Word enters the multidimensional unity of life via human persons, the Word receives all dimensions of existence, which have contributed to the actualization of the human person. Due to the unity of persons with other dimensions; or other creatures and environment; the Word is automatically deeply incarnate in all flesh, in all dimensions, when the Word becomes a human being.

The incarnation of the Word—and the Lord's Supper for that matter—are dependent upon the Holy Spirit. The Spirit, or as Tillich would say, the Spiritual Presence, relates to all dimensions as the creative power of existence. The Spiritual Presence is the unity of power and being, which structures an unambiguous life.[29] Spiritual Presence relates to the spiritual dimension of existence by entering the spiritual dimension and sending the spirit beyond itself.

---

27. Tillich, *Systematic Theology*, 3:17.
28. Tillich, *Systematic Theology*, 3:25.
29. Although the unambiguous life is related to complex polarities in Tillich's system, let's for the sake of brevity simply its meaning. The ambiguous life is a life lived in the tension of the polarities like holy and profane. In existence we are sinner and saint, very simply good and bad. Thus, an unambiguous life is a life of all things good, whole, and holy. The tension or ambiguities of existence is resolved.

> The spirit, a dimension of finite life, is driven into a successful self-transcendence; it is grasped by something ultimate and unconditional. It is still the human spirit; it remains what it is, but at the same time, it goes beyond itself under the impact of the divine Spirit.[30]

When the divine Spirit grasps human persons, it creates unambiguous life. In other words, when the Spiritual Presence grasps the person, it gives rise to faith. Tillich said, 'we experience a faith-generating connection with the Spiritual Presence'.[31] The Spiritual Presence envelopes the whole human person, including every dimension internal to the human person, in the act of faith.

However, it is not necessary for the Spiritual Presence to grasp the human person in order to relate to other dimensions. As the life-giving power to creation, the Spiritual Presence has direct access to each dimension of existence, including the physical. In the sacrament the Spirit directly establishes a unique and incredibly special relationship to the physical dimension, actualized in a particular object. 'Objects which are vehicles of the divine Spirit become sacramental materials and elements in a sacramental act.'[32]

Sacramental material, which are physical inorganic objects, are not signs pointing to a reality unrelated to itself. They cannot be transformed into a new substance. Rather, sacramental materials are symbols. According to Tillich, symbols participate in the power of reality to which they point.[33] For instance, the cross is the symbol of the forgiveness of our sins and, as such, participates in the death of the Christ that earned said forgiveness. Due to the participatory power of symbols, they function as a medium of the Spirit in the sacraments.

> A sacramental symbol opens up dimensions and elements of reality which would otherwise remain unapproachable but also unlocks dimensions and elements within us which correspond to the dimensions and elements of reality.[34]

---

30. Tillich, *Systematic Theology*, 3:112.
31. Paul Tillich, *The Dynamics of Faith* (New York: HarperCollins Publishers Inc, 2001) 49.
32. Tillich, *Systematic Theology*, 3:107.
33. Tillich, *The Dynamics of Faith*, 48.
34. Tillich, *The Dynamics of Faith*, 49.

Symbol is used by the Spirit to open new dimensions like faith and to mediate the presence of Christ.

The Spiritual Presence is at the heart of Christ's salvific acts. The Spiritual Presence of God makes Christ present in the sacramental elements, that is, through the symbol.[35] The Spirit also unites the Word with the multidimensional unity of life in the incarnation. To that end, the Spirit mediates Christ's righteousness to us by faith, granting us salvation.

Justification and the Real Presence

Having inherited the mass from the Roman Catholic tradition, Lutherans today locate Word and Sacrament together at the center of Christian worship and life. According to Luther, both Word and Sacrament are necessary for our salvation.[36] (Our discussion of the Word is limited since the focus of this work is the Sacrament of the Altar.) Lutheran doctrine employs numerous key terms to describe the operation of the sacraments. The most important categories for our current endeavor are: Promise, Fulfillment, External Word, Internal Word, Symbol, and Elements. 'The Promise is the proclamation of our salvation by the Word of God. Fulfillment is the reception of our coming salvation through sacrament.'[37] The External Word is the Word imbued with Christ's righteousness through the power of the Spirit; 'it is the risen Christ here and present among us'.[38] The Internal Word operates as a faith of the heart in the spiritual dimension, awakened by the Holy Spirit. Symbol, in this context, is the sacramental elements. Elements are the objects that carry Christ here and now, that is, the bread and wine.

To best understand the Lutheran conception of the Lord's Supper, a brief summary of Luther's doctrine of justification is helpful. Luther's anthropology states that human beings are bound to sin and cannot by our own means earn righteousness or salvation.[39] So God became

---

35. Tillich, *The Dynamics of Faith*, 52.
36. Regin Prenter, *Spiritus Creator* (Eugene: Wipf & Stock, 1953), 138.
37. Prenter, *Spiritus*, 107.
38. Prenter, *Spiritus*, 111.
39. Martin Luther, 'The Bondage of the Will' (1525), *Martin Luther's Basic Theological Writings*, edited by Timothy F Lull and William R Russell, 2nd edition (Minneapolis: Augsburg Fortress Press, 2005), 165–196.

incarnate in all flesh—in all dimensions—in Christ and died sinless on the cross, earning eternal righteousness, which is imparted to us in the act of faith by the Spirit. In his treastise on justification, *The Freedom of a Christian,* Luther writes,

> Here this rich and divine bridegroom Christ marries this poor, wicked harlot, redeems her from all her evil, and adorns her with all his goodness. Her sins cannot now destroy her, since they are laid upon Christ and swallowed up by him. And she has that righteousness in Christ . . .[40]

The result of Luther's happy exchange is the doctrine of justification by grace through faith. In other words, we are saved by faith in Christ alone.

This Christocentric approach, in which the gift of salvation is given freely by the bodily sacrifice of Christ, demands his real presence in the Sacrament of the Altar. Christ's organic, biological body died on the cross. Christ in his wholeness as an embodied human being, earned righteousness. Christ's body was redeemed and transfigured to a new life, which imparts justification to the faithful. Because Christ's salvific acts are bodily, the gift of that salvation to us in the Sacrament of the Altar must also be bodily. The fulfillment of the promise, the forgiveness of sins, in the sacrament can only be imparted by that which possesses it. Therefore, the resurrected body of Christ must be present in the bread and wine. Lutherans state, 'We maintain that the bread and wine in the Supper are the true body and blood of Christ and that they are not only offered to and received by upright Christians but also by evil ones'.[41]

The Reformation of the Real Presence

The Reformation generated multiple theological concepts and explanations for the presence of Christ in the Lord's Supper. The Lutheran position described above differed from the Reformed position, on the one side, and the Roman Catholic position, on the other. All three positions affirmed the presence of Christ in the Lord's

---

40. Martin Luther, 'The Freedom of a Christian' (1520), *Martin Luther's Basic Theological Writings,* edited by Timothy F Lull and William R Russell, 2nd edition (Minneapolis: Augsburg Fortress Press, 2005), 397.
41. Luther, 'The Smalcald Articles', *The Annotated Luther,* 2:457.

Supper. However, they each supplied a different answer to the same question: how is Christ present in the Sacrament?

Ulrich Zwingli's followers emphasised that today's Lord's Supper is a memorial of the ancient event. The Calvinists granted that the Holy Spirit makes Jesus Christ present in the sacrament; but it is not a physical presence in the bread and wine. Rather, it's a spiritual presence in the faith of the communicant. No biology. No physics. No body. Only Spirit.

The Roman Catholic position which preceded Luther affirmed the presence of the body and blood of Christ in the bread and wine. In addition to the evidentiary support of the real presence found in scripture,[42] the scholastic theologians developed a metaphysical explanation of the real presence.

> By the consecration of the bread and of the wine, a conversion is made of the whole substance of the bread into the substance of the body of Christ our Lord, and of the whole substance of the wine into the substance of His blood; which conversion is, by the holy Catholic Church, suitably and properly called Transubstantiation.[43]

To the communicant feeling and tasting, the accidents are that of bread and wine; yet the essence of both elements changes. The Fourth Lateran Council (1215) declared that Christ's body and blood are 'truly contained in the Sacrament of the Altar under the species of bread and wine, the bread being transubstantiated into the body, the wine into the blood by divine power'.

Like the Fourth Lateran Council, Luther was adamant about the real presence; but he rejected the transubstantiation metaphysics. 'Concerning transubstantiation', he wrote,

> we have absolutely no regard for the subtle sophistry whereby they teach that bread and wine surrender or lose their natural substance and that only the form and color of the bread remain and not the real bread. For it is in closest agreement with Scripture that the bread is and remains there, as St Paul himself indicates (1 Cor 10:16; 11:28).[44]

---

42. Matt 26:26–28; Mk 14:22–24; Lk 22:17–20; 1 Cor 11:23–25.
43. General Council of Trent, 13th Session, 'Decree Concerning the Most Holy Sacrament of the Eucharist', https://www.papalencyclicals.net/councils/trent.htm.
44. Luther, 'The Smalcald Articles', *The Annotated Luther*, 2:458.

In the same vein, Luther also wrote:

> The opinions of the Thomists, whether approved by pope or by council, remain only opinions, and would not become articles of faith even if an angel from heaven were to decree otherwise. For what is asserted without the Scriptures or proven by revelation may be held as an opinion, but need not be believed.[45]

'To Luther the doctrine of transubstantiation was more useless than false. To him it was not a heresy but a theologically and pastorally useless effort to explain Christ's sacraments by means of Aristotelian philosophy.'[46]

Luther rejected transubstantiation as a viable explanation for the real presence of Christ on two grounds, one pastoral and the other theological. His theological rejection was based on the absence of transubstantiation in Scripture.

> Luther and Lutherans to follow agree that Christ is present in the elements, but they are even more suspicious of the metaphysics of transubstantiation as lacking a clear basis in Scripture and so prefer to speak instead of Christ's presence 'in, with, and under' (rather than instead of) the bread and wine.[47]

Luther also rejected transubstantiation on pastoral grounds because it diverted the focus on the Lord's Supper from its true intention: the forgiveness of sins. 'Transubstantiation attempted to explain how and in what way the bread and wine become Christ's body and blood by using philosophical categories, in doing so it drew attention away from what is given in the meal: the forgiveness of sins.'[48]

Luther himself operated with a borderline physicalist pneumatology. 'All is spirit, spiritual, and of the Spirit, in reality and in name, that comes from the Holy Spirit, however corporeal, outward, or visible it

---

45. Martin Luther, 'The Babylonian Captivity of the Church' (1520), *The Annotated Luther*, 3:9–130, here at 31.
46. Jari Jokkonen, 'Eucharist', *Engaging Luther: A New Theological Assessment*, edited by Olli-Pekka Vainio (Eugene OR: Cascade Books, 2010), 108–137, here at 120.
47. Ian A McFarland, *From Nothing: A Theology of Creation* (Louisville KY: Westminster John Knox, 2014), 174–175.
48. Gordon A Jensen, 'Luther and the Lord's Supper', *The Oxford Handbook of Martin Luther's Theology*, 324.

may be.'[49] Or, to put it more modestly, God's Holy Spirit does not need to leap a metaphysical chasm between the physical and the spiritual. Because creation originates through the continually creative power of the Spirit, all of existence belongs already to the Spirit. The existential, especially its physical component, is united to the Spirit, hence the spiritual, from the moment of creation. Therefore, *dimensionality* better describes the single reality that both Spirit and biology co-inhabit.

Furthermore, Luther appealed to Chalcedonian Christology for his sacramentology. Luther noted, 'What is true in regard to Christ is also true in regard to the sacrament. In order for the divine nature to dwell in him bodily (Col 2:9), it is not necessary for the human nature to be transubstantiated . . . Both natures are simply there in their entirety.'[50] The Chalcedonian definition of Christ states, 'the divine and human natures are united in One Person',[51] the physical, biological, social, psychological, historical, and spiritual person of Jesus Christ. Luther applied this definition to the Lord's Supper, so that the divine nature, or the presence of Christ, is united to the physical material of the sacrament.

In an attempt to explicate the relationship of Christ to the elements, some Lutherans proposed the term *consubstantiation*.[52] According to which, the substance of the elements and the substance of the body and blood co-exist. Even still, most Lutherans were satisfied with a less metaphysical description, namely, the body and blood of Christ are simply present *in, with, and under* the bread and wine. The degree of explanation offered aside, the Lutheran position affirmed the co-presence of Christ in the bread and wine of the sacrament, rejecting any attempt to alter the elements.

The Real Presence, Deep Incarnation, and the Multidimensional Unity of Life

With or without scholastic metaphysics, our task here is to demonstrate that deep incarnation Christology and the multidimensional unity of

49. Martin Luther, 'That These Words of Christ, 'This Is My Body', Still Stand Firm Against the Fanatics' (1527), *The Annotated Luther,* translated by Amy Nelson Burnett, 6 volumes (Minneapolis: Fortress Press, 2015–2019), 163–274, here at 240.
50. Luther, 'The Babylonian Captivity of the Church' (1520), *The Annotated Luther,* 37.
51. Roger Haight, *Jesus Symbol of God* (Maryknoll, NY: Orbis Books, 1999), 285–288.
52. Erwin L Leuker, *Christian Cyclopedia* (St Louis: CPH, 1975), 89.

life illuminate the nature of Christ's biological and material presence in, with, and under the bread and wine in the Lord's Supper.

The work of the Spirit is crucial to this task. The Spirit transmits the presence of Christ's risen Body and Blood in the elements, bread and wine.[53] On the existential side of the Lord's Supper, the Spirit grasps the bread and wine in the inorganic dimension, 'making room' for the presence of Christ. (On this side, the Spirit also gives rise to faith.) On the ultimate or essential side, the Spirit mediates the presence of Christ to the elements. The bread and wine are, thereby, sacramental symbols, participating in the presence of Christ and the forgiveness of sins. The Spirit's work is at the heart of the Lord's Supper where the Spirit continually imparts righteousness, faith, and the forgiveness of sins through the perpetual giving of Christ in the sacrament.

Although the Spirit is the central actor in the Lord's Supper, nonetheless, Christ has a crucial task. Once made present by the Spirit, the risen body of Christ binds to the elements of the sacrament; this bond is established by way of Christ's original, created composition. As we have learned, the person Jesus Christ was structured according to the multidimensional unity of life, as well as the deep incarnation of the Word into every dimension of existence. When Christ died on the cross, the multidimensional unity of life died. Consequently, when Christ was resurrected, the multidimensional unity of life is transfigured into a new, whole, and unambiguous reality.

I propose that the resurrected multidimensional unity of Christ is an ultimate dimension, which contains all dimensions in simultaneous fulfillment and unity. It follows that Christ is present in the sacrament as the ultimate dimension. Christ seamlessly connects to the existential, inorganic dimension that the bread and wine inhabit. As the Spirit makes Christ present to the elements, the resurrected biological and physical dimensions connect to the existential inorganic dimension through their shared dimensions and mutual immanence. By the Spirit, the Ultimate Dimension envelopes the elements, surrounding the bread and wine with Christ's righteousness. The risen body of Christ also contains all material components of reality—credit to deep incarnation. In the Lord's Supper, the transfigured biological body of the risen Christ connects to the existential inorganic material, bread and wine. This bond saturates the bread and wine with righteousness.

---

53. Prenter, *Spiritus Creator,* 61.

Therefore, the biological body of the risen Christ is present in the Lord's Supper as it warps and wefts in, with, and under the bread and wine.

At last, illumination. Finally, we are prepared to receive the sacrament! Denis Edwards sets the table for the Lord's Supper.

> When Christians gather for Eucharist, they bring creation with them. The one loaf of bread and the one cup of wine, fruits of the Earth, work of human hands, given and received at a common table, are the signs in which Christ gives himself to us. Eating and drinking this bread and this cup together continually points to our inter-relationship with all the living creatures of Earth, and with the land, the atmosphere, the rivers and the seas that support life. At the heart of the Eucharist is the memorial of praise and thanksgiving. It is fundamental to an ecological theology to understand this as memorial of God's marvelous deeds that include creation as well as redemption and the promise of final transformation.[54]

As the sacrament is prepared, the Words of Institution are spoken. Our faith is awakened by the coupling of the Internal Word and the Holy Spirit. Our hearts believe God is with us. So, we eat the bread and drink the wine. The risen Christ is taken into our bodies. We receive Christ, his righteousness, and the forgiveness of our sins. Our humanity is changed as we are simultaneously enveloped and saturated by Christ, who draws us ever closer to God's Kingdom. The ultimate dimension, which is say the risen body of Christ or the righteousness of Christ, envelopes us from the inside out in the same way that it engaged the sacramental elements. The bread and wine, the body and blood, the resurrected Christ, become a part of us. We receive the real, risen body of Christ, the grace of Christ who forgives us our sin. Yet, here and now the sacrament grants us the endurance necessary to live a Christian life of faith unto death.

Conclusion

Together the multidimensional unity of life and deep incarnation Christology form a conceptualisation of the Lutheran doctrine of

---

54. Edwards, *Natural World and God,* 96.

the real presence that is both sensible to our scientific worldview and theologically accessible. It is scientifically sensible because the multidimensional unity of life describes reality as a gradient of emerging dimensions, consistent with emergentism and systems theory. It is theologically accessible because God's actions reach into everything in the deep incarnation. Christ is present as his transfigured body; Christ's presence in the sacrament must be physical and biological because Christ's salvific acts are bodily. The combination of deep incarnation Christology and the multidimensional unity of life offers a comprehensive description of the physical and biological presence of Christ in the Lord's Supper. They illuminate the means by which Christ is present in, with, and under the bread and wine.

Deep Incarnation and the multidimensional unity of life together shine a light on the self-giving nature of God, illuminating the degree of intimacy that Christ has with us in the Lord's Supper. The depth of the incarnation and the bonds between the existential and Ultimate dimensions reveal the love and care God has for creation. God gifts us with Christ's real presence, Christ himself, as well as his righteousness is born of the love God has for creation. Edwards would say, 'God is the fullness of love, always remains the fullness of love, but his love is of such a kind that it can involve giving of self to a world of creatures'.[55] The depth of the incarnation extends to all of creation, so that God can resurrect and transform it for new, eternal life with God. 'The divine nature is revealed in Christ as the self-giving, self-humbling, kenotic love.'[56]

In conclusion, the illumination of Christ's real presence in the bread and wine of the Sacrament of the Altar set forth herein has reached three goals. The first goal was to demonstrate the importance of deep incarnation Christology to Lutheran, indeed Christian, theology in today's scientifically minded climate. The second goal was to advance deep incarnation as a theological concept by applying it to the Lord's Supper. Finally, and perhaps most importantly, the third goal was to affirm the foundation of Denis Edwards's work, theology, and faith through the illumination of Christ's intimate presence and God's loving self-bestowal to us in the Lord's Supper.

---

55. Edwards, *Deep Incarnation*, 87.
56. Edwards, *Deep Incarnation*, 118.

The Eucharist and Ecology

Anthony J Kelly, CSsR

'Both the scientific worldview of our time and the ecological crisis we face require a renewed theology of the natural world . . . A central emphasis of my own work has been the attempt to locate a theology of the natural world right at the heart of Christian faith.'[1]
– Denis Edwards

Abstract: A more inclusive life as 'sublime communion' begins with a fresh way of imagining our world of nature and culture. We here focus on the Eucharist as a primary symbol within the life of Christian faith in its affirmation of the value of the natural world and the varied wonder of life on this planet: the Eucharist expresses the overture of faith working within the natural world and in a universe of grace to promise the healing, fulfilment and transformation of all creation. Our thinking on both ecology and the Eucharist has been mightily assisted by the writings of Denis Edwards who now awaits us in the Light.

Key Words: Nature, culture, death of the Lord, resurrection, evolution, ecological praxis.

Denis Edwards was a genial pioneer of ecologically attuned theology. His multi-facetted contribution continued through many years with its distinctive blend of patristic resources, up-to-date scientific references, collegial recognition of fellow theologians—and always within a profound trinitarian dynamic as in his recent *The Natural World and God: Theological Explorations*.[2]

---

1. Denis Edwards, *The Natural World and God: Theological Explorations* (Adelaide, SA: ATF Theology, 2017), 8–9.
2. *The Natural World and God: Theological Explorations*. Hereafter, TNWG +page number.

For many years I enjoyed collegial exchanges with Denis, especially on the topic of the Eucharist and its ecological relevance. Through him I came to appreciate the planetary significance of the Eucharist and its cosmic ramifications—as we celebrated Mass here on planet earth, warmed by the Sun in this corner of our galaxy, the Milky Way, in which 200 billion stars are said to shine (TNWG 172). Denis often reminded me of Maximus the Confessor with his emphasis on the multi-relational character of human existence. Maximus wrote that 'the human person . . . is the laboratory in which everything is concentrated and itself naturally mediates between the extremities of each division, having been drawn into everything in a good and fitting way through becoming . . .'[3] His respect for the *logos* of each created entity and for the role of humanity in building a cosmic peace are so marked that an ecologically-minded theology must find rich resources in his writings.

Given Edwards' special concentration on trinitarian and incarnational dimensions of creation, it was no surprise when he adopted St Athanasius as a special mentor in elaborating many aspects of the 'sublime communion' of all living things within the gracious dispensation of the Word of God and the Spirit Lord and 'giver of life'. His entire theology was informed by 'a mysticism of ecological praxis' (TNWG 182): A sense of the interconnectedness of all reality, and of the 'sublime communion of all life', promoted an awareness of relationships, either newly known or long ignored, as with the earth itself, with the biosphere of this planet, within the emergent process of the cosmos itself, and with the sacraments of Christian faith.

The thought and sensibilities of our wise and gracious colleague was earthed in Australia, especially through his appreciation of Brachina Gorge, Willunga Hills, and that red river gum that so focused his attention (TNWG 82). In his priestly and theological ministry, he was indeed a 'priest of all creation' (TNWG 149–151), in a spirituality that consecrates all life and takes with it the world of nature. (TNWG 155) A 'a theology that truly embraced the natural world' (TNWG viii) necessarily brings an ecological dimension to a theology of the Eucharist—my assigned topic in this commemorative collection.

---

3.   Andrew Louth, *Maximus The Confessor* (London: Routledge, 1996), 157.

Ecology of God's Self-Giving

As we now turn to ecological dimensions of the Eucharist, it is clear that the earthy elements of bread and wine that sustain human life and communication are given an essential place in the 'ecology' of God's self-giving in Christ. In this respect, the Eucharist brings together many gifts and many forms of giving—it is a holy communion within a universe of grace and giving. From nature's giving we have the grain and the grapes. From the giving expressed in human work and skill, we have the gifts of bread and wine. In recalling the generous giving of family and friends there is a long history of good meals and festive celebrations. From Jesus' self-giving at the Last Supper, the disciples were given his 'body and blood', the food and drink to nourish life in him. After his resurrection, his giving continues as he breathes into his disciples his Holy Spirit. And working in and through all these gifts and kinds of giving, there is the gift of the Father who so loved the world. So it is that when the Church celebrates the Eucharist, all these gifts come together to nourish our lives in this world in anticipation of the life of the world to come. In such a context, there are the kind of gifts and giving that Denis Edwards embodied for so many of us, as a priest, theologian, friend, colleague, and companion.

The oft-cited phrase found in Vatican II's *Constitution on the Liturgy* refers to the Eucharist as 'the summit and source' of the life of the Church.[4] Caught up in the updraught of his ascension, the Eucharist of the Church is both a gathering in and a going out, a communion and a mission, a thanksgiving and a hope, an enactment of Christ's presence, and a hope for his final return, as the life of faith opens out to the full measure of the mystery of Christ. By receiving the body and blood of the Lord, Christians lift up their hearts and 'seek the things that are above, where Christ is, seated as the right hand of God' (Col 3:1).

The Eucharistic Paradigm

The sacramental economy reaches its paradigmatic form in the Eucharist. The risen Lord takes representative fragments of creation, the elements of our earthly reality which nature and history have combined to produce, to transform them into something more, in

---

4. The Documents of Vatican II, *The Constitution on the Sacred Liturgy*, 10.

anticipation of a new totality: '*This* is my body; this is my blood . . .' Jesus' transforming identification with the matter of our world is continued through history as the Eucharist is celebrated: 'Do this in memory of me.' In effect, Christ invites his followers to connect with the created cosmos as he has done and continues to do. By receiving the eucharistic gift of his body and blood, we are in fact claiming this world as our own in the way that the Christ already possesses it.[5] By assuming our humanity, the divine Word makes his own the world and the universe to which that humanity is essentially related.

The Eucharist, then, is the master-symbol within the sacramental life of the Church. It is expressive of the whole mystery of Christ and of our participation in it—the essential effect of the paschal event enacted in the death, resurrection and ascension of Christ. The identity of Christ, the Word made flesh, overflows into the corporate identity of the Church as the Body of Christ, in the daily enactment of his words, 'Do this in remembrance of me' (Lk 22:19).

In the Eucharist, faith is confronted with the gift that comes with a giving and from a giver beyond any worldly horizon. Mundane horizons of the possible, the real and the knowable are interrupted by a vertical in-breaking of a sacramental event 'not of this world'. There are dimensions of height and depth and breadth, of the present and what is to come, inscribed into the eucharistic experience. A gift is given from beyond all human giving, from a giver who is not of this world. At the same time, it deeply affects our notions of the Creator of that world, and of God's self-giving in Christ. Further, it enters into every dimension of the world, and of our being in the world. As St Paul would put it, 'for those who are in Christ, there is a new creation' (2 Cor 5:17). Our understanding of the Eucharist and its relationship to life on Planet Earth is not a matter of thinking *about* some religious ritual or even sacramental event, but more a way of thinking from *within* it, by participating in the experience of life on this planet within the community of the faith in this time and space.

A New Consciousness

Thankfully, our day is marked with an increasing appreciation of the diversity of life and with a concern to protect the unique wonder of

---

5.   See Anthony J Kelly, *Eschatology and Hope* (Maryknoll, NY: Orbis, 2006), 187–192.

our biosphere. But something more than a purely scientific calculation is needed, namely, a more integrated sense of the whole. The cosmic scale of the Eucharist is powerfully evoked in the following paragraph from *Laudato si'*:

> The Lord, in the culmination of the mystery of the Incarnation, chose to reach our intimate depths through a fragment of matter. He comes not from above, but from within, he comes that we might find him in this world of ours. In the Eucharist, fullness is already achieved; it is the living centre of the universe, the overflowing core of love and of inexhaustible life. Joined to the incarnate Son, present in the Eucharist, the whole cosmos gives thanks to God. Indeed the Eucharist is itself an act of cosmic love: 'Yes, cosmic! Because even when it is celebrated on the humble altar of a country church, the Eucharist is always in some way celebrated on the altar of the world'[6] (TNWG 236).

In the depth and breadth of the Eucharist, the universe is revealed, not as an anonymous fact indifferent to life or death, but as opening into the heartland of God. It presupposes that everything has its part in God's creation and that everything has been owned by the divine Word in the incarnation and involved in the great transformation already begun in his resurrection. All are connected in a universe of gifts and giving, at the heart of which is the self-giving love of God. We are living and dying into an ever-larger selfhood: 'Unless a grain of wheat falls into the earth and dies, it is just a single grain; but if it dies, it bears much fruit' (Jn 12:24). The true self is realised in a network of relationships within a communion pervading the whole of the universe, and shaped by the trinitarian relationships that constitute the very being of God.

The Eucharist as thanksgiving inspires us to welcome the great, generative reality of the cosmos and the ecological reality of our planetary biosphere. To obey Jesus' command, 'Do this in memory of me', is to 're-member' all that has been dismembered in the sterile imagination of modern culture. The eucharistic does not bypass either the universe or our planetary home. Spiritual progress is not an escape from what we are, but a generous reclamation of the

---

6. Citing John Paul II, Encyclical Letter *Ecclesia de Eucharistia* (17 April, 2003), 8: *AAS* 95 (2003), 438.

world as destined for transformation that hope awaits. (TNWG 154, 170) We cannot set nature aside, for it is our own flesh and blood. Loving our neighbour means loving the whole cosmic and planetary neighbourhood of our existence. In the measure we share the charged reality of the Eucharist, the Christian imagination expands to its fullest dimensions. Paul's prayer begins to be answered:

> I pray that you may have the power to comprehend, with all the saints, what is the breadth and length and height and depth, and to know the love of Christ which surpasses knowledge, so that you may be filled with all the fullness of God (Eph 3:18-19).

The time and space of our earthly existence moves with the energies of true life. Here and now, we are destined, not only to be jubilant participants in the feast but also, through all the giving and service that love demands, to be with Christ as part of the meal. We contribute the energies of our lives to the great banquet of the new creation. With Jesus, we fall as grains of wheat into the holy ground to die, in order not to remain alone (Jn 12:24). As Denis Edwards sums up,

> Every Eucharist is a living memory of Christ that is also an anticipation of the transformation of all things in Christ . . . we celebrate the three-and-a-half billion-year history of life that finds its radical yes to God in the paschal event of Christ . . . All creatures are embraced and loved in this divine Communion . . . It is to remember every sparrow that falls to the ground and to know that it has its place in God. (TNWG 73)

The Cost of Evolution

Any celebration of the Eucharist necessarily begins with the resurrection of the Crucified (3). In this, it contains a dangerous and provocative memory, not repressing, but proclaiming, the death of the Lord until he comes (1 Cor 11:26)—Paul's wholesome reminder was designed to counter the convivial exuberance of Paul's Corinthians. The crucified One has entered into the violence, vulnerability, the suffering and dying present in nature and culture, just as his resurrection assures a victory over evil and death (TNWG 28–32). Ecological awareness, however, cannot but be confronted with the agony of the world and the cost of evolution, with its deaths, extinctions, violence, and dead ends: 'the whole of creation has been groaning in labor pains until now' (Rom 8:22). Though birth, not death, is the hope, Denis Edwards remarks that 'competition, pain, and death (are) intrinsic to evolutionary processes'.[7] In the agony and struggle inscribed in nature itself, and ever convulsing human history, Christian hope is wise to focus on 'the Lamb that was slaughtered before the foundation of the world' (see Rev 13:8, 5:6, 7–8, 11–12). It implies that self-sacrifice on the part of God is primordially constitutive of creation itself, and that an aboriginally self-sacrificial divine love is constitutive of divine providence.

Aspects of a prevenient, self-giving love come to expression when Paul affirms that Christ Jesus emptied himself because he was in 'the form of God', so as to take on the form of a slave (Phil 2:5–7).[8]

As Edwards remarked, 'Evolution is a costly process . . .' (TNWG 15; *cf* 74–97, 228); in view of the casualties, extinctions, and the bland metaphor of the food chain, only hope recognising the primordial self-giving of the Lamb slain before the foundation of the world can suggest a positive approach in the midst of universal death. Likewise, in later Pauline developments, the Letter to the Colossians describes the Christ as 'the image of the invisible God, the first born of all creation . . . He himself is before all things, and in him all things hold together' (Col 1:15, 17). Similarly, the Letter to the Ephesians proclaims: 'He chose us in him before the foundation of the world to be holy and blameless before him in love' (Eph 1:4). At the foundation of Johannine Christology is the intimate union between the *Logos* with God that pre-existed 'the beginning' (Jn 1:1–2). In his final prayer, the Johannine Jesus prays to his Father that he might return to the glory, which was his, in God's presence 'before the world existed' (Jn 17:5).

The New Testament addresses the mystery of pain, suffering, death, and human failure without hesitation, and, in the light of the death, burial, and resurrection of Jesus (*cf* 1 Cor 15:3–19), looks to the new creation. Nor does this hope forget that the risen and glorified body of Jesus still bears the wounds of the cross; and that the Eucharist both proclaims and invites communion with Christ in his death.

---

7. Denis Edwards, *Partaking of God: Trinity, Evolution and Ecology* (Collegeville, MN: Liturgical Press), 88, 130–146.

8. For informed and widely shared approach to the Christ Hymn in Phil 2:5–11, see Bonnie B Thurston, *Philippians and Philemon*, Sacra Pagina 10 (Collegeville, MN: Liturgical Press, 2005), 80–92.

The Christening of the Universe

The Eucharist emerges from the creative imagination of Jesus; and, in turn, shapes the imagination of the Church as it registers the impact of what has been and is being revealed. The reality of his presence transcends the categories and capacities of the world. At the same time, he draws those who receive him to the singular excess of divine self-giving and to the original and ultimate Giver, within a universe of grace.

In its ecological significance, the Eucharist is a 'Christening' of the universe. Catholic theology applies the hallowed term, 'transubstantiation', to the manner in which the bread and wine are changed into the Lord's body and blood. But a larger cosmic perspective is implied when the mystery of the Eucharist is set within a cosmic process of transformation.[9] The physical, the chemical, the biological structures underpinning earthly life have culminated, through a succession of transformations in human consciousness in our minds and hearts. Thus, the universe has become aware of itself as an expanse of wonder. Contemplating such a universe and existing as part of it, we live and breathe, aware that no one of us is the centre or origin of all this great happening. We are ecstatic beings, thankful for the sheer gift of our existence. We become a question: Are we to live on this earth through which we have been given so much, yet to have no responsibility to be part of the giving—as life-givers, love-givers, care-givers? What are we to do with ourselves as the stream of life lifts us up, carries on, and confronts us with the fact that we were not here, nor will we be here, forever? The span of human history (two hundred thousand years?) and the eight decades or so of any given life, are only the merest instant in the fourteen thousand million years that have gone into the making of our world and of this moment. And yet, as been so well said, 'We are nature's big chance to become spirited'.[10]

Eucharistic faith envisages human existence indwelling in an all-inclusive mystery. It invites believers to see their world charged with communication of all kinds—a great field of relationships, reaching

---

9. For a wide-ranging and, I think, seminal work, see Gustave Martelet, *The Risen Christ and the Eucharist World*, translated by René Hague (New York: Crossroad, 1976).

10. A happy phrase borrowed from David S Toolan, SJ, "Nature is a Heraclitean Fire'. Reflections on Cosmology in an Ecological Age', in *Studies in the Spirituality of the Jesuits*, 23/5 (November 1991): 36.

to everything and everyone. In this respect, the mystery of Christ is the all-unifying attractor, the direction inscribed into its origin, the goal drawing it onward, and holding it together. All reality, be it the physical world, all forms of life, the distinctive life of human consciousness, its cultural creations, and its transformation in the Spirit, is embodied in the *pleroma* of the Risen One.

As the Spirit animates transformed humanity, Christian faith blossoms into its sacramental imagination: symbols, gestures, words, relationships and biological processes of our world come to be appreciated in different sacramental contexts as 'visible signs of invisible grace' (Augustine). These reach their most intense and comprehensive form in the Eucharist. The risen Lord takes fragments of creation, the elements of our earthly reality which nature and history have combined to produce, to transform them into something more, yet in anticipation of a new totality: 'This is my body; this is my blood . . .' Jesus' self-embodying identification with the matter of our world is continued through history as the Eucharist is celebrated: 'Do this in memory of me.' By receiving the eucharistic gift of his body and blood, we are in fact claiming this world as our own in the way that Christ has done. In this way, we become immeasurably larger selves in a world of divine incarnation. Such an understanding neither implies nor commends some vague form of pantheism, but is the recognition of the reality of the Incarnation itself. In a Christian sense, it enables believers to contemplate the world as the 'body of God'.[11] By assuming our humanity, the divine Word necessarily makes his own the world and universe to which that humanity is essentially related.

The Eucharist, therefore, is a celebration of both the holiness and wholeness of creation. It is *holy* in that the earthy elements that sustain our lives and communication have such a central place in the eucharistic gift. Unless creation were radically from God, it could not figure so largely God's relationship to us. Moreover, the eucharistic imagination embraces the *wholeness* of creation. Matter, life and the human spirit are connected in the one God-created cosmos. The fruits of nature and the work of human creativity are integrated in a cosmic sense of how God communicates god's self to us in Christ.

---

11. Hans Urs von Balthasar, *The Glory of the Lord. A Theological Aesthetics. I: Seeing the Form*, translated by E Leiva-Merikakis, edited by J Fessio and J Riches (Edinburgh: T&T Clark, 1988), 679.

Nature and history commune and interpenetrate. In this regard, the produce of the earth is instanced in the wheat and grapes. The productions of human creativity are exemplified in that the grain and grapes are made into bread and wine. The expressiveness of human culture appears in the manner in which such food and drink are used in the convivial communication of our meals and festive celebrations.

More radically, the eucharistic meal embodies Christ's self-gift. In its turn, Christ's self-giving incarnates the love of the Father himself: 'For God so loved the world that he gave his only Son, so that everyone who believes in him may not perish but may have eternal life' (Jn 3:16).

An Ecological Vocation: Eucharistia

This all-embracing eucharistic imagination suggests an ecological vocation for human beings within creation. The highest moment of communion with God is at the same time the most intense moment of our communion with the earth. For 'the fruits of the earth and the works of human hands' are not magically vaporised by the action of the Spirit. They come into their own as bearers of the ultimate human mystery. Put most simply, in the idiom of John's Gospel, the bread and wine become '*true* food and *true* drink' (Jn 6:55). 'Transubstantiated' in this way, the sacramental reality anticipates the cosmic transformation that is afoot, not as something that leaves the created cosmos behind, but as promising its healing and transformation.

Through the eucharistic imagination, a distinctive ecological vision and commitment take shape. The literal meaning of *eucharistia* is 'thanksgiving'. In the comprehensive scope of such thanksgiving, we show gratitude for all the kinds of givings and gifts that nourish our existence. The 'one God and Father of all, who is above all and through all and in all' (Eph 4:6) acts by gathering up all things in Christ, the 'things of heaven and things of earth' (Eph 1:10). Whether our gaze is upward to God, or outward to the earth, we are confronted with the many dimensions of God's giving. We are indeed 'up to our necks in debt'.[12] Divine providence has guided the great cosmic processes over billions of years to create the conditions in which planet earth could be a biosphere, a place of life. The same providence has worked through the evolutionary dynamics that have made us what we are—

---

12. David S Toolan SJ, 'Nature is an Heraclitean Fire', 43.

'earthlings', human beings, co-existing with a million other forms of life in the delicate ecology of this planet. In this continuing chain of giving and receiving, we live not only *with* but *from* and *off* from one another. Capping the long history of gifts, the creative providence of God's has led to the Incarnation of the Word, 'for us and for our salvation'. How are we to act in this economy of giving and grace?

The eucharistic command of the Lord, 'Do this in memory of me', arises from the imagination of one who gave himself unreservedly and wholly for the sake of the many and the all. By entering into the spirit of Jesus' self-giving, we begin to have a heart for all God's creation. We cannot refuse to leave out of our concerns any aspect of the good creation that the Creator has loved into being. By entering into Christ's imagination and becoming members of his body, we are in fact putting our souls back into our bodies. For we become re-embodied in him who is related to everything and everyone. In and through him, we co-exist with all creation. We begin to live in a new time-frame determined by the patient, creative goodness of God who is working to draw all things to their fulfilment. We start to have time, beyond the pressures and compulsions of instant demand, to appreciate the wholeness of God's creation. We begin to own, as truly our own, what we had previously disowned or bypassed—above all, our living solidarity with the world of nature.

Eucharist: Ecological and Cosmic

The eucharistic imagination thus stimulates new ecological perspectives. Everything has its part in God's creation. Everything has been owned by the divine Word in the incarnation. Everything is involved in the great transformation already begun in his resurrection. We are bound together in a giving universe, at the heart of which is the self-giving love of God. We are living and dying into an ever-larger selfhood to be realised in a network of relationships pervading the whole of the universe. It even reaches into the trinitarian relationships that constitute the very being of God.

The Eucharist, then, inspires an embrace of the great, generative reality of the cosmos and the ecological reality of our planetary biosphere. We begin to belong to in a larger spiritual space. For all this has its place in the Father's 'house of many dwelling places' (*cf* Jn 14:2). To obey Jesus' command, 'Do this in memory of me', implies a re-membering of all that has been dismembered in the sterile imagination of our culture. Loving our neighbour means loving the whole cosmic and planetary neighbourhood in which we exist. Here and now, we are enabled not only to be jubilant participants in the feast, but also, through all the giving and service that life and love demand, we are destined to be part of the meal, by contributing the energies of our lives to the great banquet of the new creation: 'Unless a grain of wheat falls into the earth and dies, it just a single grain; but if it dies, it bears much fruit' (Jn 12:24). With Jesus, we fall as grains of wheat into the holy ground to die, in order not to remain alone (Jn 12:24). One writer has given striking expression to the planetary consequences of a eucharistic imagination in contact with the ecological concerns of our day:

> the Earth as the Eucharistic Planet, a Good Gift planet, which is structured in mutual feeding, as intimate self-sharing. It is a great Process, a circulation of living energies, in which the Real Presence of the Absolute is discerned.[13]

From one point of view, eucharistic imagination envisions the world 'otherwise' because it contemplates it in its most radical bearing. The sacrament of Christ's body and blood nourishes our minds and hearts into such a sense of wholeness, and cures the imagination from the illness of planetary and cosmic solipsism. Relational existence nourished by the eucharist promises a sense of reality at odds with any self-enclosed individualistic vision. Jesus prays, '. . . that they may all be one. As you, Father, are in me and I in you, may they also be in us . . . I in them and you in me, that they may be completely one' (John 17:21–22). Our unity in God derives from the way the Father and the Son are united in the one divine life: the divine persons are not independent entities somehow managing to come together. Divine life is an eternal flow of one into the other, in relationships of mutual self-giving—the *perichoresis* of trinitarian theology. This reciprocal indwelling that characterises all reality: 'Instead of taking as the norm of Reality those things which are *outside* one another, he [Jesus] takes as a standard and paradigm those who are *in* one another'.[14] This deeply Johannine statement challenges the community of faith to imagine

---

13. B Bruteau, 'Eucharistic Ecology and Ecological Spirituality', in *Cross Currents*, (Winter 1990): 501.

14. Bruteau, 'Eucharistic Ecology', 502.

its inter-relationships in terms of mutual indwelling modelled on the union existing between the Father and the Son. We *are*—by being with, from and for the other to be. And the life-giving nourishment we give is not less than the gift of ourselves. We are *in* one another for the life of each other. By being from the other, for the other, and so, *in* the other, our earthly-human lives participate in God's own trinitarian love-life, while at the same time being embodied in the earth itself.

The first movement of Christian existence is to give thanks (*eucharistia*) for the wonder of the love that has called us to be part of a commonwealth of life. In terms of a Heideggerian wordplay, this kind of *thanking* deeply conditions the *thinking* necessary to address the urgent ecological problems of our day.

As the source and goal of the whole life of the Church, the eucharist relates us to Christ, connects us with one another, and re-embodies us within the life of planet Earth. The sacrament is celebrated within a field of transcendent, communal, planetary and cosmic belonging. Our universe is being drawn into the trinitarian life, toward that ultimate point at which 'God will be all in all' (1 Cor 15:28).

Conclusion: Eucharistic Ecology

Some might feel that religious symbolism is one thing, while the conflicts and strategies of practical ecological concerns are quite another. I can only suggest that the movement toward a richer and more inclusive life begins with a new way of imagining the world we live in. Great symbols orientate us within the wholeness of things, and give both the passion and patience to grapple with it. Touched by the need of such passion and such patience, we have focused on the Eucharist as a primary symbol within the life of Christian faith as it confronts the problems of our time. In every dimension of Christian responsibility, the Eucharist expresses the overture of faith, working as it must within a universe of grace. Its imagination radically re-shapes our experience, to make the unseen and unspoken glow with significance, even if the struggle to have words for such matters remains, and so much remains to be done. But our thinking on ecology and the Eucharist has been mightily assisted by the writings of Denis Edwards who now awaits us in the Light.

Eucharist:
Longing for the Bread of Justice

Mary E McGann, RSCJ

'At the heart of the Eucharist is the memorial of praise and thanksgiving.
It is fundamental to an ecological theology to understand this as
memorial of God's marvelous deeds that include creation as well as
redemption and the promise of final transformation.'[1]
– Denis Edwards

Abstract: In a world where hunger abounds, Earth suffers exploitation and where social-economic inequality marks relationships throughout the global community, eucharistic celebration invites communities to turn toward the suffering Earth community and recognise it as an arena of divine grace. Communicants need too enter more deeply Christ's paschal co-suffering with Earth's suffering peoples and the groaning Earth itself and, empowered by the Holy Spirit, to embody a eucharistic mission of feeding, healing, and liberation, in keeping with God's desires for the planetary community.[2]

Key words: Global food crisis, justice, mystagogy of suffering creation, eucharistic remembrance, deep incarnation, eucharistic banquet, planetary mission.

World hunger is on the rise. After a decade of gradual decline, the number of people suffering from hunger today exceeds 820 million.

---

1. Denis Edwards, *The Natural World and God: Theological Explorations* (Adelaide, Australia: ATF Press, 2017), 96.
2. This article on Eucharist and the global food crisis reflects the approach of Denis Edwards regarding Eucharist celebrated at a time of global climate change. See Denis Edwards, 'Celebrating Eucharist in a Time of Global Climate Change', in *The Natural World and God: Theological Explorations* (Adelaide: ATF Press, 2017), 157–172. See also his 'Climate Change and the Theology of Karl Rahner: A Hermeneutical Dialogue', in the same source, 361–380.

Twenty percent of the population of Africa and twelve percent of Asians suffer from undernourishment. A recent UN report states that over two billion of the world's people do not have regular access to safe, nutritious and sufficient food.[3]

The situation is clearly a matter of injustice. More than enough food is produced today to feed everyone in the world, yet millions do not have enough to enable them to lead healthy and active lives.[4] Chronic undernutrition is not a consequence of overall scarcity of food, but of unequal access: to land, to technology, to education, and to employment. Conflict and climate disruption further exacerbate the situation. Climate change alone is predicted to decrease both the yield and the nutrition of food grown around the world.[5] A recent Oxfam report made this chilling prediction: 'Increased hunger is likely to be one of climate change's most savage impacts on humanity.'[6]

Where is the God of Justice, whose heart is moved by the longings of Earth's poorest for bread and for equity? And how do Christian communities encounter this God when they gather at their eucharistic tables? This chapter identifies some critical dimensions of the global food crisis. It then explores how engagement in eucharistic celebration can be transformative for communities over time, drawing them into greater solidarity with the longings of those who hunger for the justice of bread, and uniting them with the empowering work of the divine Spirit who transforms these longing into mission on behalf of God's nourishing intentions for the world.

Along with the hungry, Earth herself suffers. The late twentieth century's "green revolution" was sold to countries around the globe by US corporations as the answer to dwindling crops and hungry people.[7] For a brief time, its fertilizers, pesticides and fossil-fuel machinery

---

3. *The State of Food Security and Nutrition in the World, 2019.* Report issued by the FAO (UN), IFAD, UNICF, World Health Organization and the World Food Programme.
4. Erik Milstone and Tim Lang *The Atlas of Food: Who Eats What, Where and Why?* (Berkeley: University of California Press, 2013), 18.
5. Bill McKibben, *Falter* (New York: Henry Holt and Company, 2019), 36–39.
6. Oxfam, 'Extreme Weather, Extreme Prices: The costs of feeding a warming world', September, 2012. https://www-cdn.oxfam.org/s3fs-public/file_attachments/20120905-ib-extreme-weather-extreme-prices-en_3.pdf Accessed September 13, 2019.
7. For a much more complete look at the corporate food industry and its global impact, see my *The Meal that Reconnects: Eucharistic Eating and the Global Food Crisis* (Collegeville: Liturgical Press, 2020).

managed to push global crop yields upward.[8] But the cost to the Earth and its productivity has been severe—soils depleted by excessive use of fertilizer, waters polluted by pesticide runoff, biodiversity decreased, and Earth's atmosphere made toxic by herbicides and machinery emissions. Today, displaced peasant farmers around the globe swell the planet's vast slums, unable to feed their families, and themselves hungry.[9]

The stark contrast in available calories per person in various parts of the world tells its own story: more than 3,500 calories per day are available in much of North America and Europe; while populations in parts of sub-Saharan Africa have access to some 2,000 calories.[10] Food prices reveal a similar inequality: while in the US only fourteen percent of household spending is on food, Bangladeshis spend some fifty-five percent and Rwandans, seventy-four percent.[11] Unfortunately, these latter cases are more typical of food expenditures worldwide.

Crop yields and prices are especially vulnerable to climate disruption.[12] Even slow onset changes in temperature and precipitation will decrease global harvests, causing the price of staple foods such as maize to double in the next twenty years. But with the number of severe and extreme weather events on the rise, markets will be further destabilised, provoking price spikes that will spell disaster for people already living in poverty. Six months after the devastation inflicted by cyclone Idai—which killed a thousand people in Mozambique, Malawi and Zimbabwe—hunger continues to escalate. The number of people in need of food has risen by twenty-five percent since April of this year alone.[13] Hunger has become the silent killer of those who survived the cyclone.[14]

---

8. McKibben, *Falter,* 36.
9. McKibben, *Falter,* 36.
10. Milstone and Lang, *The Atlas,* 19. This is significantly more than the 2,500 calories recommended for daily consumption by many nutritionists.
11. Milstone and Lang, *The Atlas,* 18–19, 28.
12. This paragraph based on Oxfam, 'Extreme Weather'. Bill McKibben notes that two-degree C rise in the planet's temperature—which is the current *goal* of world climate response—would cut US corn yields by eighteen18 percent and sorgum yields by seventeen percent. See *Falter,* 36–37.
13. Oxfam, 'Six months after cyclone Idai: Farmers are fainting in fields because of hunger.' https://www.oxfam.org/en/pressroom/pressreleases/2019-09-13/6-months-after-cyclone-idai-farmers-are-fainting-fields-because. Accessed September 18 2019.
14. Oxfam, 'Hunger is spiraling, but has fallen off the political agenda.' https://www.oxfamamerica.org/press/hunger-spiraling-has-fallen-political-agenda-says-oxfam/ Accessed September 19 2019.

Mozambique is not alone. The FAO calls on governments around the world to respond quickly to the crisis, building new strategies that can tackle the key drivers of hunger—a mounting climate crisis, endless conflict, and a global food industry that is focused on increased profits alone and not on the urgent needs of hungry communities. Others note that rising amounts of food waste world-wide, gender inequality, the diversion of food crops such as corn and soy to biofuel production, and massive global flows of migrating peoples, further cripple the ability of Earth's poorest and most vulnerable to survive in the face of rising hunger.

Our global situation prompts a spiritual and moral crisis that cries out to Christian communities worldwide. Food is not only an human right, guaranteed by international law,[15] but integral part of the common good, an essential component of God's good and life-furthering creation that belongs to all.[16]

In *Laudato si'*, Pope Francis appeals to Christians and to all persons of faith to allow themselves to be drawn into the heartbreaking awareness of the sufferings of hungry sisters and brothers and of the devastation of Earth herself. He urges them to embrace not only a knowledge of the situation but to allow themselves to be touched affectively,[17] to feel with the sufferings, and to share the longings of those who experience hunger and malnutrition, joining them in their search for liberating justice. Commenting on food waste, Pope Francis highlights the reciprocal nature of our sharing the world's abundance:

'whenever food is thrown out it is as if it were stolen from the tables of the poor.'[18]

Eucharistic Sharing in Hunger and Fulfillment

How is the eucharistic table, at which Christians eat and drink deeply of God's nourishing wellsprings, related to these 'tables of the poor'?

---

15. Food was designated a human right in the UN's 1948 Universal Declaration of Human Rights, as part of the right to an adequate standard of living.
16. See Cynthia Moe-Lobeda, 'Climate Injustice: truth telling and hope', in *Anglican Review of Theology.* 99/3 531–540, on the meaning of *tov* as used in Genesis as 'life-furthering'.
17. *Laudato si'* No 89.
18. *Laudato si'* No 50.

How might the longings for the food of justice that reverberates around the globe become the longings of each eucharistic community as they gather for worship? Most specifically, how do these longings for nourishment and dignity, and for a regenerated Earth, touch the hearts of communities who dwell in affluence—those who live in comfortable settings and experience a quality of life far beyond that of the poor of the Earth?[19] These communities especially, notes *Laudato si'*, need for an experiential encounter that can bring deeper awareness of the human tragedy of poverty and hunger. Such lived encounter can lead to compassion and an imaginative response to how the world might be different.[20]

Eucharist can likewise invite change—a reorientation of communities, invited and facilitated by God's Spirit. Joined with the self-offering of Christ, eucharistic communities can become more deeply aligned with the kingdom of justice he came to proclaim. In what follows, I will first explore Karl Rahner's understandings of eucharistic celebration as a 'mystagogy' of God's great liturgy-of-love-poured-out in a suffering world, and inviting communities to become emissaries of that grace-filled love on behalf of hungry people and a struggling Earth. Second, I will explore how conversations about Christ's 'deep incarnation' bring new insight to theologies of Eucharistic remembrance of Christ's death and resurrection, and to a community's self-offering in communion with Christ. Finally, I propose that eucharistic celebration gathers communities around the table of God's justice and hospitality, there to be formed, nourished and sent as disciples in a suffering and hungry world.

Eucharist: Mystagogy of the Suffering Creation

In midst of a suffering world, eucharistic celebration calls communities to turn *toward* the world, in all its beauty and pain, and discover it again as an arena of God's grace.[21] From the beginning of time, the humble and merciful love of the triune God has coursed through

---

19. These questions raised by Pope Francis, *Laudato si',* Nos 49–50.
20. Pope Francis *Laudato si'* Nos 49–50.
21. This perspective, based in the work of Karl Rahner, is quite in contrast with perceptions of Eucharist, or any liturgy, as a turning *away* from the world toward a liturgical arena of grace, or at least as a moving into a more sacred realm of divine presence.

the evolving cosmos, sustaining the lives of each beloved creature. But despite its pervasiveness, the mystery of this divine gift is often hidden within the experience of everyday life: obscured by human violence and greed, lost from view by the taken-for-grantedness of inequality and injustice, and masked by a growing disruption of the biosphere. Eucharistic liturgy, proposes Karl Rahner, must become a '*mystagogy*'[22] of this great mystery of divine grace at the heart of a suffering world; a summons to eucharistic communities to awaken to the outpouring of God's mercy and justice in the world and in their daily lives, which, although obscured and often hidden, is seeking to find a public voice, a communal witness, and calling communities of faith to participate in the divine lovingkindness toward all God's creatures, especially those suffering, hungry, and most in need.[23]

Rahner speaks of God's great outpouring of love in human history as the 'Liturgy of the World': God's reconciling and liberating self-communication throughout history that evokes, invites, and welcomes the thankful surrender of human love. This is the foundational and primordial liturgy. Unfolding within a world where terror, misery and injustice abound, this liturgy of God's radical love, hidden by human failures, is never extinguished. Rather, it is constantly emerging within the lives of human communities, seeking their response of love and commitment, inviting them to deeper engagement in the work of God's kingdom in the midst of everyday life.

While this Liturgy of the World is radically caused and sustained by God, it is at the same time something that human communities accomplish through their active participation in the life of the world.[24] It is precisely here that eucharistic celebration becomes a mystagogy: an event that awakens communities to the divine milieu in which

---

22. The term mystagogy points to a process that helps people notice, understand, accept, and appropriate the experience of God that is present throughout the course of daily life. It is more than education about God; rather, it is direction or guidance toward the mystery of God. See Michael Skelley, *The Liturgy of the World: Karl Rahner's Theology of Worship* (Collegeville: Liturgical Press, 1991), 78–79.

23. See Karl Rahner, *Theological Investigations*, volume 6 (New York: Crossroad, 1983), 141–149. See also Skelley, *The Liturgy of the World*, 92–105, for a good summary of Rahner's understanding of the relationship between the 'liturgy of the church' and the 'Liturgy of the World'. I draw on Rahner and Skelley in what follows.

24. Skelly, *The Liturgy of the World*, 99

they live. As communities engage actively in the many modalities of embodied prayer—through word and song, deep reflection, thanksgiving, confession, attentive listening, exuberant praise, eating and drinking—their self-surrender to God's work of mercy and justice in the world can be repeatedly invited and reinforced, as they are drawn more deeply into the grace that fills the universe.[25]

It is important to note that moments of God's grace and invitation are not only perceived in experiences that are positive—events of beauty and joy, times of intimate love and mutual recognition, that speak of God's benevolence and care. God's grace and invitation may be masked in profoundly negative experiences: intractable, discouraging, even life-threatening. Oppression, violence, and injustice are encountered daily; human acts of terror and misery seem to dominate what is often experienced as the tragedy of daily life. Confronting issues of poverty and hunger, of global climate chaos and its impact on vulnerable peoples, can lead communities to a sense of failure, frustration, and powerlessness in the face of larger political forces.[26] Yet in Rahner's perspective, as communities resist cynicism and despair and continue to act in hope and trust, these situations can become places of God and God's liberating grace.[27] In Eucharistic celebration, a community's acts of forgiveness and healing, of recommitment in the face of failure, of acknowledging the intolerable injustice of hunger and assaults on the Earth, and of rekindling their desire to do all in their power to alleviate injustice— become acts of profound faith in the abiding presence of the God of mystery. What seemed like emptiness and darkness can be revealed as places where Love is with them, where they are held in divine Love.[28]

The biblical narratives read in eucharistic celebration reveal a God of steadfast love who is not distant but near to those in need—a God who chooses solidarity with the suffering, hearing the cries of the

---

25. Ibid., 95.
26. Edwards addresses negative experiences such as climate change in relation to Rahner's theology. See 'Climate Change and the Theology of Karl Rahner', in *The Natural World and God: Theological Explorations* (Adelaide: ATS Press, 2017), 369–370.
27. See Karl Rahner, 'Experience of the Holy Spirit', in *Theological Investigations*, volume 18 (New York: Crossroad, 1983), 189–210.
28. Edwards, 'Experience of Word and Spirit in the Natural World', in *The Natural World*, 198.

oppressed and burdened; a God who is remembered as 'merciful and gracious, slow to anger, and abounding in love and faithfulness . . . to the thousandth generation' (Ex 34:6–7a).[29] Moreover, the response of this God-of-tender-love to the cry of the oppressed is to engage the human community in the liberating process that God intends. Moses, addressed in the burning bush by a God who sees, hears, and knows the sufferings of the enslaved Hebrew people was sent to address Pharaoh on their behalf (Ex 3:1–12). The Hebrew prophets, called to speak the word of God to the people, summoned them to obedience and love, and in times of exile, spoke God's word of comfort and reassurance. Jesus' disciples are sent to announce good news and to engage in the healing and feeding ministries Jesus himself embodied. Rooted in these biblical narratives, liturgical preaching becomes a mystagogy, inviting communities to recognise the parables of grace and of disgrace unfolding in the world around them,[30] and awakening them to their own often challenging role in the work of God's liberating love and justice.

Moreover, the divine Spirit, emissary of godly love for suffering people and their planet, is actively present when Christians gather for Eucharist. In his letter to the Romans, St Paul describes the whole human-biotic creation as groaning, as it searches for liberation and redemption; laboring, struggling in an effort to give birth to a redemptive wholeness that has yet to be realized (Rom 8:19–27).[31] That same Spirit, Paul contends, cries out within the praying community, interceding from within their hearts 'with sighs too deep for words',—sighs that rouse the heart of God, who 'knows the mind of the Spirit because the Spirit intercedes for the saints according to the will of God' (Rom 8:26–27).

As communities attune their prayer to the Spirit's groans, interceding for a hurting Earth community, their commitment to

---

29. See Elizabeth Johnson, *Creation and the Cross: The Mercy of God for a Planet in Peril* (Maryknoll: Orbis Books, 2018), 60–63.

30. Image of 'parable of grace and disgrace' taken from Mary Catherine Hilkert, 'Natures Parables and the Preaching of the Gospel', in *The Wisdom of Creation*, edited by E Foley and R Schreiter (Collegeville: Liturgical Press, 2004).

31. See Brendan Byrne, 'An Ecological Reading of Rom. 8:19–22: Possibilities and Hesitations', in *Ecological Hermeneutics*, edited by David G Horrell, *et al* (London: T&T Clark, 2010), 83–93, for reflections on a contemporary ecological interpretation of Paul's imagery.

those who search for the bread of justice can increase, and their hope be strengthened. This divine Spirit, writes Pope Francis in *Laudato si'*, possesses 'an infinite creativity . . . which knows how to loosen the knots of human affairs, including the most complex and inscrutable . . . The Spirit of God has filled the universe with possibilities and therefore, from the very heart of things, something new can always emerge.'[32]

Eucharist: Entering Christ's Redemptive Co-Suffering with all Creation

At the heart of the 'Liturgy of the World', unfolding over time, is the revelation of God's redemptive love enfleshed in Jesus Christ. In his life, death, and glorious resurrection, Christ both revealed the depths of divine love and embodied the fullness of human self-surrender to the living God.[33] Eucharistic celebration invites communities to enter this mystery of Christ's life, given for the life of the world; to embrace his paschal self-offering as their own; and to be empowered by Christ's action to participate in Christ's saving work.[34] This entire process is a dynamic remembering—an *anamnesis* of Christ's saving work, that places his self-emptying love at the center of the community's faith and prayer.

Eucharistic *anamnesis* is made explicit in the great eucharistic prayers of thanksgiving.[35] Remembering Christ, who emptied himself on behalf of humankind, allowing himself to be broken so that his life-giving love might be poured out on behalf of all, the praying community 'offers [itself] in praise and thanksgiving, as a holy and living sacrifice, in union with Christs' redemptive sufferings on behalf of humankind.[36] Through the power of the Holy Spirit, the community's self-gift is made possible; its union with his death and resurrection, and its mission to be Christ's body in the world, are more deeply affected.

---

32. *Laudato si'*, No 80.
33. Denis Edwards, *Ecology at the Heart of Faith* (Maryknoll: Orbis Books, 2007), 63.
34. See John F Baldovin, *Bread of Life, Cup of Salvation* (Latham: Rowman and Littlefield, 2003), 162.
35. Baldovin, *Bread*, 162. This paragraph offers a cursory summary of that source.
36. From a US United Methodist Eucharistic Prayer, cited in Baldovin, *Bread*, 169.

Today, these understandings of liturgical *anamnesis* are enriched in at least five ways by new theological explorations of Jesus' 'deep incarnation' developed by Denis Edwards and other theologians.[37] First, the term deep incarnation stretches understandings of incarnation to include not only Jesus' birth, but the entire event of the Word of God becoming flesh—his life and ministry, his 'deep cross and resurrection', and his future coming in glory.[38] Thus Christ's paschal mystery is enfolded in a larger event of his enfleshment, and the dynamic relationships that flow from this mystery. Second, in this total act of 'taking flesh', Christ joined himself not only to human existence, but to the whole interconnected web of creaturely existence—the 'flesh' of earthly life—uniting himself with the entire human-biotic community of life. Third, in a similar way, deep incarnation stretches understandings of redemption in Christ, accomplished through his death and resurrection, beyond the human community to include the eschatological destiny of all created life. Hence, the entire ecological world of nature and its future destiny are dynamically related to Christ's salvific paschal mystery.[39] Fourth, the whole reach of Christ's incarnate existence is 'mediated by the Holy Spirit of God at every point',[40] thus emphasizing the critical role of the Spirit in uniting a community in Eucharist to Christ's redemptive self-gift. Finally, deep incarnation underscores in a poignant way the radical identification of Christ with the whole suffering community of life, culminating in his agonising death. Images of his compassionate accompaniment of suffering creatures add urgency to the eucharistic community's action with Christ on behalf of all who long for healing, for food, and for dignity.[41]

---

37. The term was first introduced by Niels Hennrik Gregersen, 'The Cross of Christ for an Evolutionary World', in *Dialog: A Journal of Theology*, 40 (2001): 205. See Denis Edwards, *Deep Incarnation: God's Redemptive Suffering With Creatures* (Maryknoll: Orbis Books, 2019), for an excellent summary of work by various theologians.
38. Edwards, *Deep Incarnation*, xvii. Incarnation is therefore inclusive of Jesus' paschal sacrifice but includes, as well, the greater arc of his entire life as one act, inclusive of his future coming in glory. The image 'deep cross and resurrection' is taken from Elizabeth Johnson, *Creation and the Cross*, 187.
39. *Creation and the Cross*, 187.
40. Edwards, *Deep Incarnation*, 32. See also 106–110.
41. Elizabeth Johnson speaks of her work in *Creation and the Cross* as a 'theology of accompaniment'. See 158–194.

While a full exploration of these understandings is not possible here, some additional comments will clarity how deep incarnation expands perceptions of eucharistic *anamnesis.* In assuming flesh, Jesus entered the very tissue of biological life, the interdependent web-of-life, revealing divine lovingkindness and mercy present in a radically new way at the heart of planetary life.[42] Christ sanctified not only individual lives, human and other-than-human, but the interconnections between them: the entire kinship structure of earthly existence with its potential for solidarity and for aggression. From within these relationships he reveals, in a new way, that God is not absent from situations of human distress or earthly disfigurement, but present with boundless love and mercy, seeking to heal what is torn apart and reconcile what has been estranged. In eucharistic remembrance, those who seek to join Christ in his self-offering are called to do likewise.

Having entered the whole of planetary life in his incarnation, Christ's anguished death becomes 'an icon of God's redemptive co-suffering with all of sentient life',[43] revealing the compassionate presence of divine love-made-flesh in the midst of even the most destructive of earthly situations. The cross signals that God is never absent from suffering or anguish, from destructive forces that diminish and extinguish human life and dignity, or that compromise or contaminate Earth's precious resources. Rather God is radially present in the midst of anguish, bearing every creature and all creation forward with an unimaginable promise, accompanying them with unspeakable tenderness and fidelity.[44]

The cross is the culmination of the compassionate love that flowed from the entire arc of Jesus' life. The cross places him on the side of the suffering and dispossessed,[45] in alliance with all who foster life rather than the powerful to seek to extinguish it. 'The cross is where

---

42. 'The Word assumes the creaturely humanity of Jesus with all its ecological and cosmic interconnections, and these interconnections are by divine intention co-constitutive of the Word incarnate.' Edwards, *Deep Incarnation,* 132. See also Johnson, *Creation and the Cross,* 183–187.

43. Gregersen, 'The Cross', 205. See also Johnson, *Creation and the Cross,* 187–194.

44. Johnson, *Creation and the Cross,* 189.

45. Gregersen underscores that Jesus 'takes the side of the victims of the horrors that human beings inflict upon one another'. As quoted in Edwards, *Deep Incarnation,* 24

believers in Christ find their God, vulnerable to the brutality and power of the privileged',[46] and challenging all those who would follow him as disciples to do likewise. As preached by Shawn Copeland, 'We can stand with our God only insofar as we stand beside and wait in active and compassionate solidarity with children, women, and men who suffer concretely, unbeautifully, and actually in our world which is God's world . . .'[47] Eucharistic memory invites communities to stand with Christ, with all creatures of flesh whom he has embraced, to enter his self-offering passion and death and in so doing, to identify with the longing of countless members of the Earth community for the bread of justice and dignity. Hearing the groaning Earth, the suffering of the poor ones whose lives are threatened by human selfishness and greed, communities are invited to embody the saving mystery of Jesus' cross in the present and into the future.

The cross is incomplete without the resurrection. Risen from the dead, 'Jesus has been reborn as a child of the Earth, radiantly transfigured',[48] while at the same time, carrying the memory of the suffering ones, who are imaged forever in the wounds of his risen body.[49] Thus, the resurrection of Christ holds out a dynamic vision of hope for a world in the throes of diminishment and struggle[50]—a promise that God's healing and reconciling love are already active in this world and summoning all who follow Christ to act in union with this redemptive flow of divine life.[51] Christ's resurrection is a promise that all creatures will one day be reconciled in him, born anew into an unimaginable relationship of redemptive fullness and peace, where every tear will be wiped away, and death will come no more (Rom 8:18–25; Rev 21:4). Joined with Christ's paschal solidarity, eucharistic communities are invited to live into this promise in union with all who suffer, to embody a future-present in acts of feeding, healing, protecting, and reconciling, in union with the self-surrender of the Risen Christ.

---

46. Johnson, *Creation and the Cross*, 179.
47. Words preached by Shawn Copeland, as quoted in Johnson, *Creation and the Cross*, 179.
48. Johnson, *Creation and the Cross*, 190
49. Edwards, *Ecology at the Heart*, 106.
50. Edwards, *Ecology at the Heart*, 106.
51. Edwards, *Deep Incarnation*, 133.

As communities unite themselves with Christ's paschal self-offering, the divine Spirit, giver of life and of love, moves within those gathered for eucharist—urging them along the way, uniting them as the body of Christ in the world, releasing new visions of human-biotic wholeness and flourishing, and moving them to new life-styles and life-ways in solidarity with those most afflicted.[52] At the heart of the eucharistic celebration, the life-giving and creative Spirit is invoked in the *epiclesis* of the eucharistic prayer of thanksgiving. Voiced in the name of the community, the *epiclesis* calls on this font of divine energy to transform this worshiping community to be the hands and heart of Christ in the world; to embody his self-sacrificing love on behalf of those most in need—the hungry, poor and excluded—and in situations where Earth's most precious resources have been destroyed. Through the Spirit's power, Christ is dynamically present with these communities, leading them more deeply into the mystery of his redemptive love alive and active in the world.

But for eucharistic communities to be truly awakened to the mystery of Christ's redemptive solidarity with all creation, and their place in bringing it to fruition, the entire eucharistic celebration—especially the preaching, intercessory prayers, song lyrics, and well-crafted eucharistic prayers of thanksgiving—must reverberate with this invitation and the reorientation it implies. Moreover, the voices of those who suffer here and now, their stories, their cries, need to be heard in the gathering, enabling the community to encounter Christ's body, in all its needs and longings, and opening the community's vision to the work of God's justice and discipleship.

Eucharist: Gathering at God's Table of Hospitality and Justice

Finally, eucharistic celebration invites communities to gather at the table of God's justice and hospitality to be formed, nourished, and sent as disciples in and for a suffering world. Eucharist finds its deep roots in the memory of Jesus' table fellowship recorded in all four gospels: in narratives of Jesus' sharing food, eating and drinking with friend and stranger alike, each event an acted parables by which Jesus taught

---

52. *Laudato si'*, which reminds its readers that the Holy Spirit can always effect something new, spells out in great detail the 'new life-styles and new life-ways'. See especially Nos 202–245.

his disciples about inclusion, ministry, redemptive hospitality, and covenantal love.[53] Biblical scholars point to the critical significance of Jesus' meals in relation to his incarnate mission. Commenting on meals in the Gospel of Mark, Ched Meyers contends that 'Jesus chooses this site as the symbolic center of [his new] community. In place of the temple is a simple meal which represents participation in Jesus' 'body'", and that underscores the centrality of human need to the radically new symbolic system Jesus was inaugurating.[54]

It is important to note that in the socio-political context of Jesus' meal fellowship, food was in crisis and hunger pervasive.[55] Roman emperors, intent on keeping the price of bread low in imperial cities and providing for their legionnaires, pressed small Palestinian farmers and landholders to surrender their surplus grain, often leaving them without adequate provisions for daily consumption. Many who were drawn to Jesus' ministry and preaching suffered from hunger and malnutrition. Within this context, Jesus' preaching about seeds and growth, harvests and banquets, as well as his dining with those considered unrighteous and 'outside the orbit of grace', took on a distinctly Messianic significance: a new society was in the making, forged around an egalitarian table where there was not only enough for all but food to spare (Jn 6:12–13). Jesus' table sharing was not almsgiving—power giving to need—since almsgiving reinforces social-economic divisions rather than making people equal. Instead of offering charity, Jesus' meals created a common table, a sharing of spiritual and material resources, where each person was both giver and receiver, host and guest, nourisher and one nourished.[56]

Narratives of Jesus table fellowship can awaken communities to the significance of their eucharistic action as a meal of justice and divine hospitality for all God's creatures. Situating the origins

---

53. Eugene Laverdiere traces these themes in the meal stories in Luke's Gospel. See *Dining in the Kingdom* (Chicago: Liturgy Training Publications, 1994), 1–32. See also Robert Karris, *Eating Your Way Through Luke's Gospel* (Collegeville: Liturgical Press, 2006).

54. Ched Meyers, *Binding the Strongman:(A Political Reading of Mark's Story of Jesus* (Maryknoll: Orbis Books, 2008), 443.

55. See Michael Northcott, 'Faithful Feasting', in *A Moral Climate* (Maryknoll: Orbis Books 2007), 248–250.

56. This section based on Nathan Mitchell, *Eucharistic as Sacrament of Initiation* (Chicago: Liturgy Training Publications, 1994), 87–89.

of eucharistic eating in those events where Jesus satisfied hunger, announced the arrival of God's reign, and provided healing and hope for the poor and needy underscores that the eucharistic table is never far from the tables of Earth's most destitute of peoples.[57] The earliest account of Christians in Jerusalem gathering for the 'breaking of the bread', reveals a community life of sharing that privileges the care of the needy (Acts 2:43–47). There is no true eucharistic table, contends David Power, without this kind of common table, where distinctions of wealth, gender, race or status, fall away; where communion is not only signified but embodied in acts of love, mercy, and compassion; and where Earth's fruits are recognised as belonging to all.[58]

The production of food placed on eucharistic tables today is complexly linked to massive social, economic, and political forces— forces that, in a globalized world, shape patterns of wealth and poverty that leave so many of Earth's neediest peoples longing for the bread of justice.[59] The 'gifts' of bread and wine, used for a community's celebration, are concretely related to these forces, shaped by systems of production that are complicit in denying many their most basic needs, and embroiled in patterns of food production that destroy Earth's life-systems.[60] Placing these gifts on the table brings to the heart of the celebration the lives of those who suffer most from forces of oppression and economic conflict embedded in the production of bread and wine. Eucharistic communities must 'discern the body', as Paul instructs early believers in Corinth—acknowledging the impact of their eucharistic eating on other communities and the Earth herself. Are the cries of the Earth and of the poor heard and felt? Are communities drawn into Christ's redemptive action on behalf of those who eat daily the bread of affliction?[61] And what liberating and creative forces come into play within the community when the Spirit of Christ is invoked over this eucharistic food and drink?

---

57. See Mitchell, *Eucharistic as Sacrament of Initiation*, 102–103.
58. David Power, 'Eucharistic Justice', in *Theological Studies*, 67 (2006): 861.
59. This paragraph based in part on Power, 'Eucharistic Justice', 865. See also Timothy Gorringe, *The Sign of Love: Reflections on the Eucharist* (London: SPCK, 1997), 33–45.
60. See McGann, *The Meal that Reconnects*, 189–197.
61. This question and the one that follows based on Power, 'Eucharistic Justice', 874.

Conclusion

Today, as communities gather for the eucharistic meal, there is a strong connection between the body of Christ, remembered and shared in the breaking of bread, and the body of Christ alive in the world, including his cosmic body, the whole of creation.[62] The same Spirit who anointed Jesus for his solidarity with the poor ones (Lk 4:19–19); who sent him to bring good news and to enact liberating justice on behalf of all God's beloved creatures—that same Spirit sends each community to embody Christ's healing and feeding. Jesus' command, 'Do this in memory of me' reverberates in the mission that flows from the eucharistic table. In acts of breaking bread and shared food, a community's deep communion in the mystery of the Risen Christ, alive in the entire 'flesh' of the planetary community, is celebrated as a 'sublime communion.'[63]

Remembering Christ's ministry to the poor and marginalized can inspire communities to embrace his liberating action, to be Christ's flesh in the world, present in solidarity with those who are invisible and voiceless, with all who hunger for the justice of bread, and with the suffering Earth. Eucharistic participation calls communities to a more human and generous lifestyle, inviting them to challenge the structures of the world that keep some people hungry, and to question the inordinate desires and policies of those who work to maintain those structures.[64] It forms communities for the reign of God yet to come in a world dying for justice, for bread, and for peace.[65]

---

62. See Edwards, *Deep Incarnation,* 22, citing Gregersen 'Jesus and the Cosmic Story', *Theology and Science,* 11, no 4 (2013): 370–393, here at 385. To notions of the body of Christ as the historical Christ, his post-resurrection body, the social body of the church, Gregersen adds the whole creation as cosmic Body of Christ.
63. 'Sublime communion' is used in *Laudato si'* to reference the deep, interspecies communion of the human-biotic community with the living God (no 89).
64. Monica Hellwig, *Eucharist and the Hungers of the World* (Kansas City: Sheed and Ward, 1992), 78–81.
65. See Don E Saliers, *Worship as Theology: Foretaste of Glory Divine* (Nashville: Abingdon, 1994), 185.

From Spirit to Life in a Scientific Age

Stoeger and Edwards on Divine Action: The Intelligible Action of the Incomprehensible Mystery

Lawrence Ng Yew Kim

'God acts through all . . . the laws of nature which all things obey—gravity, electromagnetism, chemical bonding, natural selection—to create and sustain all things in existence . . . But God also acts in a special way toward persons—in a personal way—through other persons, through special events and experiences, through communal life and revelation. These involve laws of an order and depth which are outside the present and perhaps even the future limits of the sciences.'[1]
– William Stoeger, SJ

Abstract: This essay explores not only how theologian Denis Edwards collaborated with the work of Jesuit Priest and astrophysicist William Stoeger on divine action, but also how their tradition and orientation as Roman Catholics shape their conception of divine action. It is within this context too that their work shines. While they speak of the incomprehensible mystery of the transcendent God, they also speak of the immanence of God within the processes of creation. Beyond sharing Stoeger's concern with conceiving divine action in a way that is intelligible with contemporary science, Edwards's thoughts on divine action are also related to his pastoral ministry.

Key Terms: divine action, incomprehensible mystery, secondary causes, transcendence, immanence, constitutive relationships, laws of nature, miracles, prayer, Catholic priest, Denis Edwards, William Stoeger, SJ.

Theologian Denis Edwards mentioned his collaboration with astrophysicist William R Stoeger, SJ for his work *How God Acts: Creation, Redemption, and Special Action*. However, the influence of

---

1. William Stoeger, SJ, 'Can God Really Act in Our World and in Our Lives?', in *God for the 21st Century*, edited by Russell Stannard (Philadelphia and London: Templeton Foundation Press, 2000), 166.

Stoeger's thoughts is evident in many of his other writings as well.[2] Stoeger's scholarship reveals a concern of making intelligible the universe we live in, between the truths given in revelation and the knowledge gained the discoveries of science. For Stoeger, science can inform and enrich our faith and theology. Edwards's writing appears to take cue from this as he locates his discussion between science and theology within the concrete realities of this world.

More specifically, Edwards drew on evolutionary perspectives to account for divine action within the realities of suffering and death. He drew from Stoeger's thoughts on the laws of nature to speak of special divine acts and miracles. What is common between both scholars, in no small part due to the same tradition they share as Roman Catholics, was the continual assertion that God is an incomprehensible mystery and that God's action is understandable only in relation to us. It is within this context that they speak of God working through secondary causes, possible due to God who is immanent within the processes of creation. God is immanent precisely because of God's transcendence. Edwards expounds the Thomistic framework of secondary causes and speaks of God working through the interplay of chance and lawfulness.

This chapter will show that Edwards' and Stoeger's treatment of divine action reflects not only their concern of making God intelligible within their world they live in as a person of faith but also true to their tradition and orientations as Roman Catholics. It is within this context too that their work shines. My own recommendation for future treatment of divine action is not far from the Thomistic framework espoused by Stoeger and Edwards. The only addition I would make is how the framework or the method we adopt in our project of relating between theology and science is differentiated and can shine through our own historically conditioned context as a person of faith rooted within our own tradition.

Background

In a discussion with a fellow graduate student about my project of applying the theological work done on the relationship between

---

2. Edwards also made a mention of his collaboration with Stoeger in his book, *How God Acts*. Denis Edwards, *How God Acts: Creation, Redemption, and Special Divine Action* (Minneapolis, MN: Fortress Press, 2010).

theology and science within the context of Asian Christianity, the first question he asked me was, "Who are you writing as?" I was not surprised by the question from a fellow Asian and that is not an easy question to answer for me. It deals with the question of identity, language, culture, ethnicity, and religion. There is also the issue of what has formed my core academic orientation. It is my conviction that our historical situatedness affects our orientations, and our orientations give shape to our theological expressions. Theologian Robert J Schreiter points out to us on the importance of context in theology. The classical definition of theology may be faith seeking understanding. The issue is not in the faith aspect of it but rather the historical context of the person by which faith comes through. Schreiter states, 'Local theologies make us keenly aware that 'understanding' itself is deeply colored by cultural context.'[3] This points to the question of whether there can be such a thing of 'theology' as just 'theology'? Schreiter tells us that theology is like the way any human knowledge is experienced, which 'although communicable across cultural boundaries, is nonetheless largely shaped by local circumstances.'[4]

I follow Schreiter here regarding local theology as I asses both Stoeger and Edwards. I begin with a brief biographical introduction of both Stoeger and Edwards before exploring their approaches to divine action. This essay will not only attempt to present how Edwards built his thoughts on Stoeger but also on how his catholic roots might have shaped the questions about divine action he is grappling with.

Stoeger and Edwards: Scholar, Catholic, and Priest

Astrophysicist and Jesuit Priest Fr William R Stoeger (1943–2014), and Lecturer and Diocesan Priest Msgr Denis Edwards (1943–2019) both discusses how we can speak of divine action today in the light of contemporary science. Stoeger is considered an influential proponent of theistic evolution.[5] Stoeger earned his doctorate in astrophysics from the University of Cambridge, where he studied under Astronomer

---

3. Robert J Schreiter, *Constructing Local Theologies* (London: SCM Press, 1985), 75.
4. Schreiter, *Constructing Local Theologies*, 75.
5. Robert Russell, 'William R Stoeger, SJ (1943–2014): Physicist, Cosmologist, Friend, and Leader in Theology and Science', in *Theology and Science* 12/4 (2014).

Royal Sir Martin Rees and had Stephen Hawking as a classmate.[6] He was a staff astrophysicist at the Vatican Observatory until his death in 2014. Stoeger specializes in theoretical cosmology and high-energy astrophysics, and he also made contributions in elucidating the interrelationships between science, philosophy, and theology.[7] Stoeger was part of the team that organized a major international conference on science and religion that was co-sponsored by the VO/ CTNS.[8] In his theological writings, Stoeger articulates a weakly critical-realist approach to God's action, which aims to be 'faithful to the sources of revelation and at the same time understandable in light of our scientific knowledge of creation'.[9]

It is evident from his writings, Edwards engages Stoeger's work with some seriousness, and there was even collaboration between both of them.[10] While Edwards may build his work of Stoeger's thoughts, there is also distinctness to his conception of divine action. Edwards engages the scriptures and viewed with some seriousness the thoughts of the Church Fathers, such as Athanasius and the works of German theologian Karl Rahner, which Stoeger did not.[11] Edwards states that his "methodological approach might be described as a hermeneutic of critical retrieval," and it is 'an attempt to reclaim trajectories from the history of theology that can assist in the envisioning of a renewed theology of the natural world'.[12]

---

6. Denis Edwards, 'Toward a Theology of Divine Action: William R. Stoeger, SJ., on the Laws of Nature', in *Theological Studies* 76/3 (September 1, 2015): 485.

7. Edwards, 'Toward a Theology of Divine Action', 485.

8. Pope John Paul II calls for the Vatican Observatory to organise a conference to further the theology-faith dialogue in commemoration of the 300th anniversary of Isaac Newton's Principia. As a result, a series of international research conferences on 'scientific perspectives on divine action' was held from 1990–2005. The series of conferences were co-sponsored and co-organized by the Vatican Observatory (VO) and Center for Theology and Natural Sciences (CTNS) and in total produced six volumes of work from 1993–2007. Edwards also participated and produced an article which was printed in the second volume.

9. William R Stoeger, 'God and Time: The Action and Life of the Triune God in the World', *Theology Today* 55/3 (October 1998): 365.

10. Edwards mentions their collaboration in the preface of his book. Edwards, *How God Acts*, xiv.

11. For example, Denis Edwards, *Christian Understanding of Creation: The Historical Trajectory* (Minneapolis, MN: Fortress Press, 2017); Denis Edwards, 'The Attractor and the Energy of Love: Trinity in Evolutionary and the Ecological Context', *The Ecumenical Review* 65/1 (March 2013): 130–145.

12. Edwards, *Christian Understanding of Creation*, viii.

Edwards offers a renewed theology of divine action, which in part, is built from the work of Stoeger. A renewed theology of divine action enables Edwards to situate his work within his concerns for ecology, suffering, prayer, and miracles.[13] This is where Edward's roots as a catholic become visible. Edwards's renewed theology of divine action did not stand apart but is related to life as a diocesan priest and also as one who was shaped by his diocesan seminary training within the Catholic tradition. His concern on issues of miracles and prayer, amidst his thoughts on suffering, reflects this.

Edwards's approach to divine action does not read like a typical academic endeavor. His theological writings in *How God Acts* also reads like spirituality and this aspect is visible in his other writings. For example, while speaking about God working through secondary causes, he also writes that 'the test of what leads to true happiness is to see all these things in relationship to the one thing that is our ultimate happiness—our life in God'.[14] Edwards expanded a chapter in his book on intercessory prayer for Christians who consider this matter to be essential.[15] In his chapter on 'Miracles and the Laws of Nature', Edwards speaks about how 'some of the pastoral practice of the church seems to be based on an assumption that, in miracles, God intervenes in a way that suspends or bypasses the laws of nature', and therefore, 'an alternative theology of miracles is needed . . .'[16] Edwards sees himself not only as a theologian but also as a 'presbyter of the Archdiocese of Adelaide . . .'[17] In a chapter that he contributed to the book *The Spirituality of the Diocesan Priest*, he said that he grew from the understanding of his priestly role, from that of *alter Christus* to a spirituality that is 'fundamentally relational and communal'.[18]

In another place, he writes on the connection between the Eucharist and ecology, asking, 'Are there authentic and intrinsic links between the Eucharist and the way we think, feel and act with regard

---

13. This is visible in his book of collected articles. Denis Edwards, *The Natural World and God: Theological Explorations* (Adelaide: ATF Press, 2017).

14. Edwards, *How God Acts*, 176.

15. Edwards, *How God Acts*, 167–179.

16. Edwards, *How God Acts*, 77.

17. Denis Edwards, 'Personal Symbol of Communion', in *The Spirituality of the Diocesan Priest*, edited by Donald B Cozzens (Collegeville, MN: The Liturgical Press, 1997), 73.

18. Edwards, 'Personal Symbol of Communion', 81.

to the natural world'?[19] This question makes sense if we consider that the Eucharist is central in the lives of practicing Catholics, and it will not make sense to see the act of worship as having no bearing in their daily lives.

The threads above sew together theology with ministry. At some level, Edwards recognises that the work of dialogue between theology and science can benefit Catholic theology. This explains further his decision to collaborate with Stoeger. Edwards tells us 'that Stoeger's argument constitutes an important breakthrough in the theology of divine action, one that, though largely unrecognized in the literature, is highly significant not only for the science–theology field but also for broader Catholic theology'.[20] He added that if Stoeger's 'insights, so deeply based in the sciences, were to find acceptance in the Catholic theology of creation, incarnation, providence, and miracles, for example, then new possibilities might well open up for dialogue with contemporary culture and for evangelization in today's world'.[21] Edwards states, 'Stoeger's argument constitutes an important legacy to twenty-first Century theology, one that calls for wide discussion and debate in Catholic theology'.[22] Edwards's view reflects that of Saint Pope John Paul II, who believes that both theology and the sciences can benefit from their interchange with each other. The late pope writes, 'Science can purify religion from error and superstition; religion can purify science from idolatry and false absolutes. Each can draw the other into a wider world, a world in which both can flourish'.[23]

Approaches to Divine Action

Thus far, this essay argues that Stoeger's and Edwards's Catholic orientations gave shape to their theological expressions. Peter MJ Hess

---

19. Denis Edwards, 'Eucharist and Ecology: Keeping Memorial of Creation', in *Worship*, 82/3 (2008): 194.
20. Edwards, 'Theology of Divine Action', 487.
21. Edwards, 'Theology of Divine Action', 487–489.
22. Edwards, 'Theology of Divine Action', 489.
23. Pope John Paul II, 'Message of His Holiness Pope John Paul II', in *Physics, Philosophy and Theology: A Common Quest for Understanding*, edited by Robert John Russell, William R Stoeger, SJ, and George V Coyne, SJ (Vatican City State: Vatican Observatory, 1988), M13.

and Paul L Allen write that after Vatican II, there has been a stream of Catholic thinkers who works with various academic disciplines but yet is rooted in tradition. One important point they make is that the 'Catholic strength in philosophy is one reason why Catholic contributions to science-theology dialogue have been indirect and yet comprehensively framed'.[24] This is visible in the approach of Stoeger and Edwards, who offers an indirect and yet comprehensive treatment of divine action. Besides pointing out the Catholic strength in philosophy, Hess and Allen offer three characteristics found in Catholic thinkers after Vatican II, which might help us understand Stoeger and Edwards better. They are: (1) the idea that faith is a strongly personal pursuit, (2) Catholic thinkers emphasize the unity of reality, and (3) Catholic scientists and philosophers of science continue to be strong advocates of a realist epistemology.[25] I now turn to their approaches to see how these characteristics play out in their consideration of divine action.

Both Stoeger and Edwards speak of divine action in two categories. They are: '(1) God's creative and sustaining action of all that is not God; and (2) God's special action with respect to creation, for example, God's revelation to God's people through prophets and through God's "mighty acts" in answer to the prayers and the cries of God's people'.[26] An important consideration of speaking about divine action today involves the question of whether God intervenes or bypasses the laws of nature as we understand them. Like most Catholic thinkers, Stoeger and Edwards develop their theologies of divine action 'in a more or less Thomistic vein'.[27]

Edwards explains his decision to speak of divine action through secondary causes 'because it represents a foundational metaphysical understanding of the God-world relationship, which is at the heart of

---

24. MJ Peter Hess and Paul L Allen, *Catholicism and Science* (Westport, CT: Greenwood Press, 2008), 120.

25. Hess and Allen, *Catholicism and Science*, 120–121. Hess and Allen speak of a realist epistemology as meaning that 'truth can be both discovered and verified, in science and theology, though in different ways. With some expectation, Catholic thinkers tend to hold out of the reliability of sense perception, the understanding of the intellect, and the reflective knowledge of judgement as key cognitional levels that are active in developing truthful knowledge.' Hess and Allen, *Catholicism and Science*, 121.

26. Stoeger, 'God and Time', 365.

27. Hess and Allen, *Catholicism and Science*, 121.

the Christian tradition and which [he finds] intellectually coherent and religiously meaningful'.[28] He writes, 'At its center is the idea that the Creator is present to all creatures, closer to them than they are to themselves, conferring existence and the capacity to act on every entity and every process'.[29] An important reason for Catholic thinkers who works with Thomistic philosophy, and this is visible in Stoeger's and Edwards's work, is that it 'upholds the absolute mystery and transcendence of the Creator, and resists any tendency to see God as one cause among others in the world'.[30] For Edwards, it is 'an approach that is less likely than some other options to exacerbate the theological problem of suffering'.[31] This thought exposes the unitive aspect of Edwards's thinking.

Edwards also addresses the common objection of the limitations of God acting through secondary causes argument as it does not clearly explain how God acts through them. He points to the apophatic aspect of our understanding of God. Edwards explains that it is 'important to say that from a theological perspective, we do not know how God's creative act works. What we know is the result of this act but not the act itself. There is a very good reason for an apophatic stance in relation to God's creative act'.[32] God's 'creative act is God', and 'whatever science studies, is not God', as 'we have no direct access to God's creative act, only to its effects, the universe of creatures we find around us, with the relationships between them and the laws that govern them'.[33] Expressing his own kind of negative theological disclaimer, Edwards writes that 'what we know about the nature of God comes from the Christ-event and, on this basis, we can say important things about divine action, but we can no more comprehend the nature of God's act any more than we can comprehend the divine essence'.[34]

This is not to say Edwards does not believe that science cannot give us insights into how God acts because his work engages the findings of contemporary science. Stoeger can provide us with

---

28. Edwards, *The Natural World and God*, 215.
29. Edwards, *The Natural World and God*, 215.
30. Edwards, *The Natural World and God*, 215.
31. Edwards, *The Natural World and God*, 215.
32. Edwards, *The Natural World and God*, 215.
33. Edwards, *The Natural World and God*, 215.
34. Edwards, *The Natural World and God*, 215.

insights into Edwards's thinking on this, and it is a point that speaks to the aspect of faith grounded by a certain realist epistemology. Stoeger tells us that despite upholding the 'radical mystery and transcendence of God, *we do* have manifestations—revelations, self-communications—of God in persons and in experiences addressed to us which we can appropriate.'[35] God is 'disclosed to us in creation', and the 'characteristics of creation manifested to us by natural sciences are in harmony with, and even indirectly support, many fundamental qualities of God's creative action.'[36]

Stoeger On Divine Action

Stoeger relates God's creative action to his conception of *creatio ex nihilo* and *creatio continua*. It is important to note that for Stoeger, he does not tie the Christian understanding of creation to the scientific theory of the Big Bang. Stoeger writes, though it is suggestive of such, there is no warrant at all for identifying the Big Bang with the moment of creation from nothing.[37] To do so is a very dangerous move, constituting a 'God of the gaps' explanation and perpetuating the illusion that cosmology can delineate or isolate the 'creation event'.[38]

For Stoeger, 'creation' or 'creation event' refers to '*creatio ex nihilo*', which at the same time also refers to 'the radical preservation in existence ("creation continua"), which is just as important as bringing something into being'.[39] Stoeger does not limit creation to just only a moment in time and points us to the direction of participation. This is because 'the creator is always sustaining, or conserving, all that is in its existence'.[40] For us, it might be helpful to conceive the relationship of creation as a participation in the being and activity of the creator, and in this regard, to conceive this creator as a verb, rather than as a noun (an entity).[41] Thus we might say that creation is the 'limited participation of whatever exists in the pure, self-subsisting

---

35. Stoeger, 'Conceiving Divine Action', 234.
36. Stoeger, 'Conceiving Divine Action', 234–235.
37. William R Stoeger, 'What Does Science Say About Creation?', *The Month* (August/ September 1988): 808.
38. Stoeger, 'What Does Science Say About Creation?', 808.
39. Stoeger, 'What Does Science Say About Creation?', 808.
40. Stoeger, 'God, Physics and the Big Bang', 181.
41. Stoeger, 'God, Physics and the Big Bang', 182.

being, activity, and creativity of the creator'.[42] Elizabeth Johnson who examines the notion of participation in her work, tells us that all creation participate and have the source of their being in God who is the 'loving Giver of life'.[43] In this sense, 'participation signifies this intimate and profound relationship'.[44]

The image of conceiving the creator as a verb and the language of participation raises two important points. First, it takes away the image of God as intervening in the processes of nature. Second, the language of *creation continua* tells us that God respects the processes of nature by enabling and empowering creation to be what it is.[45] Johnson describes it poetically when she writes, 'To be imaginative for a moment, it is as if at the Big Bang the Spirit gave the natural world a push saying, "Go, have an adventure, see what you can become. And I will be with you every step of the way."'[46]

In Stoeger's framework, God is distinct from secondary causes. *Creatio ex nihilo* is meant to drive home the point that God 'the Creator, is the primary, first, or ultimate 'cause' of everything, and as such is uncaused'.[47] God is then the source of everything and the ground by which all things exist. Since God is distinct, God is not a cause among other causes because 'God is the ultimate or foundational "cause," . . . of order as well as of existence . . .'[48] This point is important to note because for both Stoeger and Edwards, since God is distinct, God is not accessible to the methods of science because God is 'completely distinct from other, scientifically accessible causes'.[49] However, it would be incorrect to say that God has nothing to do with creation. Stoeger explains this through the concept of transcendence and immanence. It is because that 'God is transcendent (subject to no barriers or constraints), God is radically immanent (interior)

42. Stoeger, 'God, Physics and the Big Bang', 182.
43. Elizabeth A Johnson, *Ask the Beasts: Darwin and the God of Love* (London: Bloomsbury, 2014), 143–150.
44. Johnson, *Ask the Beasts*, 148.
45. Stoeger, 'God, Physics and the Big Bang', 182.
46. Johnson, *Ask the Beasts*, 156.
47. William R Stoeger, 'Conceiving Divine Action in a Dynamic Universe', in *Physics, Philosophy and Theology: A common Quest for understanding*, edited by Robert J Russell, William R Stoeger, SJ, and George V Coyne, SJ (Vatican City: Vatican Observatory, 2005), 229.
48. Stoeger, 'Conceiving Divine Action in a Dynamic Universe', 229.
49. Stoeger, 'Conceiving Divine Action in a Dynamic Universe', 229.

to all that is—but in a highly differentiated way, according to the character of each process, relationship or object'.[50] One can now begin to understand why Stoeger and Edwards framed their treatment of divine action indirectly. It is because while we can say something about God in relation to us, there is also the emphasis that God 'is unlike any other cause or act, transcending what we can describe or articulate'.[51] Stoeger writes, 'this negative theological disclaimer must always be applied to whatever we end up saying about God's action', though this should not be taken 'that absolutely nothing at all can be asserted about God'.[52]

Stoeger's thoughts on special divine action are built on this framework of God's creative action. Stoeger writes that special divine action is 'a particular manifestation or mode of that divine creative action, more broadly conceived'.[53] It refers to the particular action, such as through prophets or the person of Jesus. They are 'turning points within creation, or within history and are specially revelatory of God's immanent creative presence'.[54] The point here is that God's special divine action happens within what is already set in place by God's creative action. Stoeger writes that special divine acts are in 'deeper harmony with God's intended purposes and with the essential structures and relationships already established with creation itself'.[55]

Edwards's on a Renewed Theology of Divine Action

Edwards may follow Stoeger's line of thinking when speaking of divine action, but in contrast to Stoeger, he situates his conception of how God acts within his concerns on suffering. He addresses these concerns, 'not by attempting a theodicy, but by contributing to a renewed theology of divine action'.[56] It is not possible to see the broad picture Edwards paints in addressing his concerns since this essay focuses on how he builds his thoughts from the work of Stoeger. However, Edwards did not think it is possible to offer a full explanation

---

50. Stoeger, 'Conceiving Divine Action in a Dynamic Universe', 229.
51. Stoeger, 'Conceiving Divine Action in a Dynamic Universe', 229.
52. Stoeger, 'Conceiving Divine Action in a Dynamic Universe', 229–230.
53. Stoeger, 'Conceiving Divine Action in a Dynamic Universe', 244.
54. Stoeger, 'Conceiving Divine Action in a Dynamic Universe', 245.
55. Stoeger, 'Conceiving Divine Action', 245.
56. Edwards, *Natural World and God*, 225.

on suffering, whether in general or in the costs built into evolution but instead attempts to offer 'a view of God working creatively and redemptively in and through the natural world to bring it healing and wholeness'.[57] We can see Edwards's attempt to emphasize the unity of reality by offering a theology that sees 'God as working in and through the natural world rather than as arbitrarily intervening to send suffering to some and not to others'.[58] To answer the problem of suffering which offers no immediate solution, Edwards speaks of a need for a 'theology in the light of the cross, whereby God's action is understood as embracing the limits of created entities and processes, waiting upon creation in love, living with its processes, accompanying each creature, rejoicing in every emergence, suffering with every suffering creature, and promising to bring all to healing and fullness of life'.[59] Finally, 'God's action in creating an emergent universe would need to be understood in the light of the resurrection and its promise that all things will be transformed and redeemed in Christ'.[60]

The Christ-event is central and is the lens to how Edwards understands and views divine action. This is visible in much of his thoughts, as we have seen earlier. For Edwards, the life, words, and works of Jesus tell us a lot of who God is, even if it is in relation to us. As Edwards describes it, the 'best model we have of divine action is the Christ-event, culminating in the cross and resurrection of Jesus'.[61] In it, 'God was not passive in the rejection, humiliation, and crucifixion of Jesus'.[62] What the Christ-event tells us is that 'God was with Jesus in his suffering, holding him in love, and acting powerfully in the Spirit, transforming his failure and death into the source of healing and liberation for the world, and raising Jesus up as the beginning of life for the whole creation'.[63] The Christ-event affirms for Edwards that God's love is the kind 'that respects and works with the limits of

---

57. Edwards, *Natural World and God*, 225. Costs built into evolution follow the argument from the 'the evolutionary biology of the past two centuries that competition for resources, predation, death, pain, and extinction are built into the evolution of life', Edwards, *How God Acts*, 12.
58. Edwards, *How God Acts*, 12.
59. Edwards, *How God Acts*, 12, 225–226.
60. Edwards, *Natural World and God*, 226.
61. Edwards, *Natural World and God*, 226.
62. Edwards, *Natural World and God*, 226.
63. Edwards, *Natural World and God*, 226.

creaturely processes'.[64] The Christ-event then is foundational in the thought of Edwards because the Christ-event in Christian theology shows us that 'God can act only in accordance with the divine nature', and this 'nature is revealed in the Christ-event as radical self-giving love'.[65] Edwards also claims that the Christ-event tells us of 'a divine and transcendent love, a love that has an unimaginable capacity to respect the autonomy and independence of creatures, to work with them patiently, and to bring all things to their fulfillment.[66]

Constitutive Relationships

My essay has just presented an overview of both Stoeger's and Edwards's thoughts, the reasoning behind Edwards's collaboration with Stoeger, and how their orientations as Catholics frame their discussions of divine action. The elements of faith and the emphasis on the unity of reality is visible in their thoughts, including a certain realist epistemology. Now, this essay turns to Edwards's and Stoeger's thoughts on constitutive relationships, the laws of nature, miracles and prayer.

Related to Edwards's concern for suffering is his socioecological suffering. His thoughts on how God acts in creation calls for a response in concern for the earth. In his writings on ecological theology, he stresses the aspect of interconnectedness and relationship, and locates 'human beings within the community of creation'.[67] It may be for Edwards that it does not makes sense to speak of God as the source of creation if it does not lead towards a trajectory of a 'theology of the human-in-relation-to-other-creatures'.[68] It is also clear that Edwards's language of interconnectedness is related to Stoeger's conception of the universe as constituted by patterns of relationships. Constitutive relationships tell the that there is an interrelatedness in nature at all levels. It involves 'all those interactions that incorporate components into a more complex whole, and relate that complex whole into another level of unity'.[69] He added, 'They may be physical, biological,

---

64. Edwards, *Natural World and God*, 226.
65. Edwards, *Natural World and God*, 226.
66. Edwards, *Natural World and God*, 226.
67. Denis Edwards, *Ecology at the Heart of Faith: The Change of Heart that Leads to a New Way of Living on Earth* (Maryknoll, NY: Orbis Books, 2006), 119–123.
68. Edwards, *Ecology at the Heart of Faith*, 7.
69. Edwards, *Ecology at the Heart of Faith*, 6.

or social in character'.[70] For Edwards, constitutive relationships show that 'we are dependent upon and interrelated with the universe'.[71] In a statement that shows his emphasis on the unity of reality, Edwards writes, 'Closer to home, we become who we are in relationship to families, communities, and the land to which we belong, with its animals, birds, trees, flowers, insects, and bacteria'.[72]

On a theological level, Edwards argues that the constitutive relationships at all levels of nature are part of our story and God's, which is the story of God's creation. It shows a patient God 'working in and through the laws of nature', and one who 'not only enables but respects and waits upon the processes by which things evolve in more and more complex ways'.[73] It is God's creative act that 'enables the creaturely world to flourish in its own integrity and proper autonomy'.[74] It is the relationship of 'ongoing creation' in which the 'the indwelling Creator Spirit is present to each creature, enabling it to be and to become in a world of interconnected relationships'.[75] This perspective also enables Edwards to speak of God as the God of evolution and the God of mutual friendship.[76] All of 'created reality is to be understood as relational', where 'to be is to be in communion', and at the 'most fundamental level, being is communion'.[77] Edwards's view is related to Stoeger's view on the interrelatedness of the cosmos. On this, Stoeger writes, 'What in fact is being given at each moment in the evolutionary process of some system or manifold, whether it be of a star, a planet, a region on the planet, or a compartment within a larger system, is an ecology—a rich interrelated network of conditions, processes, and entities'.[78]

---

70. Edwards, *Ecology at the Heart of Faith*, 6.
71. Edwards, *Ecology at the Heart of Faith*, 6.
72. Edwards, *Ecology at the Heart of Faith*, 6.
73. Edwards, *Ecology at the Heart of Faith*, 6.
74. Edwards, *Natural World and God*, 209.
75. Edwards, *How God Acts*, 6.
76. Denis Edwards, *The God of Evolution* (New Jersey, NY: Paulist Press, 1999).
77. Edwards, *The God of Evolution*, 29.
78. William R Stoeger, 'The Immanent Directionality of the Evolutionary Process, and Its Relationship to Teleology', in *Evolutionary and Molecular Biology: Scientific Perspectives on Divine Action*, edited Robert J Russell, William R Stoeger, and Francisco José Ayala (Vatican City State: Vatican Observatory and CTNS, 1998), 184.

The Laws of Nature

Stoeger develops his thoughts on constitutive relationships together with his conception of the laws of nature. Thus, it makes sense now to explore Stoeger's thoughts on the laws of nature as Edwards locates this discussion within the issue of miracles and prayer. Stoeger delves into the question of whether the laws have a reality in itself or that it 'constitute physical reality?'[79] He answers that they do not because 'these laws and theories are actually 'models', or approximate descriptions, albeit very accurate and detailed ones'.[80] In this respect, the laws of nature are descriptive and not prescriptive, as they describe 'reality as it is for us and in relation to us'.[81] These are two crucial points about the laws of nature as Stoeger conceives it. He stresses that these laws 'do not prescribe how physical reality itself behaves—they rather describe some of its fundamental and unchanging regularities in its continual transformations'.[82] Stoeger explains, 'We use these models and laws to probe the phenomena and to understand and describe the physical realities manifested through them'.[83] It may be that 'God can be conceived of as acting through the laws, but the ones through which God is acting principally are not "our laws", but rather the underlying relationships and regularities in nature itself, of which "our laws" are but imperfect and idealized models'.[84] Stoeger's realist epistemology is visible here too when he states, 'the theories and models and the laws they encompass have a definite basis in reality as we observe and experiment with it'.[85]

There are two notable points about Stoeger's conception of the laws of nature. First, it underscores the transcendent aspect of how God acts. Second, we are limited in our ability to grasp God and that is especially true of what science can give us. The tools of science will not enable us to grasp the divine. Science can tell us a great deal about

---

79. William R Stoeger, 'Contemporary Physics and the Ontological Status of the Laws of Nature', in *Quantum Cosmology and the Laws of Nature: Scientific Perspectives on Divine Action*, edited by Robert J Russell, Nancey C Murphy, and CJ Isham (Vatican City State: Vatican Observatory, 1993), 211.
80. Stoeger, 'Contemporary Physics', 212.
81. Stoeger, 'Contemporary Physics', 223.
82. Stoeger, 'Contemporary Physics', 220.
83. Stoeger, 'Contemporary Physics', 220.
84. Stoeger, 'Contemporary Physics', 233–234.
85. Stoeger, 'Contemporary Physics', 234.

ourselves but there is a limit to what science can give us, and science cannot peer fully into the mystery of God as God. Stoeger tells us this much, and speaks of a 'cosmological limit', when he says,

> As we realize that we have arrived at the cosmological limit, and then continue to strive to move beyond it with our concerns and questions, we quickly begin to sense that there are aspects of reality which are fundamental, incredibly rich and profound that we shall never be able to comprehend adequately or master. And yet they exist, are very insistent and demand our attention. In a very real sense, *we cannot grasp them—they grasp us.* This is the dawning—and eventually consuming—awareness of Mystery, of the inexhaustible richness and depth, at the heart of the reality that embraces us.[86]

Miracles and Prayer

Stoeger's discussion on the laws of nature enables Edwards to address the issue of miracles more robustly. Edwards proposes that 'Stoeger's account of the laws of nature helps us understand miracles in a noninterventionist but genuinely theological way that builds on Aquinas'.[87] Any 'Christian theology of divine action needs to discuss miracles, above all because they are central to the ministry of Jesus'.[88] As we have seen earlier, the issue of miracles also stems from Edwards's concern that the way miracles are understood in the pastoral practice of the Church is not intelligible with the findings of contemporary science. Edwards may even be considering the implications of 'conflict' between faith and science, even if it is not in consideration at the pastoral level of ministry. The argument from the laws of nature enables Edwards to reconcile between the issue of miracles and divine action from a non-interventionistic perspective.

Following Stoeger's line of thought, Edwards argues that the laws of nature are descriptive based on scientific models, which are 'the

---

86. William R Stoeger, 'The Quest for Understanding and Meaning: From Process and Complexity to Meaning and the Transcendent', Presented at *Metanexus Institute Conference*, Phoenix, AZ, 2009. http://www.metanexus.net/essay/quest-understanding-and-meaning-process-and-complexity-meaning-and-transcendent-0. Emphasis is mine.
87. Edwards, 'Theology of Divine Action', 499.
88. Edwards, *How God Acts*, 77.

result of imaginative and conceptual abstraction guided by continued observation and experiment'.[89] Then, there is no 'justification for the idea that they correspond in a direct way to the entities, structures, and relationships of physical reality as it is in itself'.[90] Edwards also points out that the laws of nature do not comprehensively cover all aspects of life, such as one's religious experiences or a cherished value. He states, 'The existence of parts of reality that defy scientific analysis, such as personal relationships or deeply held values, is an indication not that these phenomena are illusory but that the laws of nature, meaning the natural sciences as we know them, do not model or describe central aspects of reality'.[91]

There are two parts to this argument which Edwards makes. First, if there are parts of reality that science cannot model—or have reached a 'cosmological limit' as Stoeger identifies it—then, it 'suggests that marvelous manifestation of the Spirit, such as an act of healing, may take us beyond the laws of nature understood in the first sense—as our limited models of reality'.[92] But, 'it may not be beyond the laws of nature understood in the second sense, as the relationships and processes that function in reality, which are more than we have fully understood or adequately modeled'.[93] In this respect, miracles still work within the structure of this world established by God's creative action. They are theologically 'secondary causes'.[94]

Before this essay considers Stoeger's thoughts on miracles, it might be helpful to consider Edwards's concerns on the prayers of intercession as they are interrelated. The interesting question posed by Edwards is that 'if God is not an interventionist God', then, 'is there any reason to ask God for things? What is the point of intercessory

---

89. Edwards, *How God Acts*, 86.
90. Edwards, *How God Acts*, 86.
91. Edwards, *How God Acts*, 86. The source of Edwards's thoughts is from Stoeger's article, 'The Mind-Brain Problem', 134–135. I opted to cite them to show the close connection of Edwards's thoughts to Stoeger's work. The argument on parts of reality not measurable by the sciences but is not any less real, resembles closely to Stoeger's argument of the 'deictic' aspect reality, such as meaning and spiritual experiences. William R Stoeger, 'What Contemporary Cosmology and Theology Have to Say to One Another', in *CTNS Bulletin*, 9/2 (March 1989): 8–9.
92. Edwards, *Natural World and God*, 264.
93. Edwards, *Natural World and God*, 264.
94. Edwards, *Natural World and God*, 264.

prayer?'[95] Related to his view on miracles, Edwards writes, 'I see no opposition between intercessory prayer and this idea of a God who acts consistently through creaturely causes, because I believe that God can and does respond to our prayers through such secondary causes and that in this prayer God invites our further participation in the praxis of the kingdom.'[96] The fact that Edwards devotes a chapter on this exposes the fact that his pastoral concerns motivate his questions.

Stoeger would agree with Edwards's point on speaking of God acting through secondary causes on the issue of miracles and prayers. He writes,

> Thus, an apparent divine intervention on our behalf—a miracle—in answer to our prayers, for instance, a healing of a disease of paralysis which cannot be explained by contemporary medical science, does not of itself manifest the direct action of God, *though it does manifest God's personal loving and life-giving action towards us.* We always experience it through some intermediary datum or agent—through some sacrament.[97]

Paul J Schutz, who explores Stoeger's work in his dissertation, explains the reasoning behind Stoeger's thoughts and how Stoeger respects the boundaries of each discipline. Schutz writes, 'Stoeger does not seek to explain by what means God effects miracles; rather, he seeks to acknowledge that purported miracles are known by their character, in and through their manifest coherence with who God is and what God intends on the basis of revelation.'[98] Stoeger's 'interpretation of miracles seeks to respect the epistemological boundaries that separate theology and science in such a way that gives each its due

---

95. Edwards, *How God Acts*, 167.
96. Edwards, *How God Acts*, 168.
97. William R Stoeger, 'Describing God's Action in the World in Light of Scientific Knowledge of Reality', in *Chaos and Complexity*, edited by Robert J Russell, Nancey C Murphy, and Arthur R Peacocke (Vatican City State: Vatican Observatory, 1995), 251.
98. Paul J Schutz, 'Ineffable Cosmos, Ineffable Love: Divine Action and the "Laws of Nature" in the Theology of William R Stoeger, SJ', (PhD dissertation, Fordham University, New York, 2017), 250, ETD Collection for Fordham University, AAI10621484, https://fordham.bepress.com/dissertations/AAI10621484/.

without subjecting one to the other.'[99] Thus, Schutz adds, 'because the Creator respects the integrity of creation, divine action is inherently constrained by the secondary causes in which it operates.'[100] Schutz also adds a point which this essay did not explore. It relates to Stoeger speaking of all things flourishing according to it its kind. Schutz states, 'In terms of Stoeger's overall system, then, God's action guides all things to flourish according to their own kind, as they exist and operate on the basis of their knowledge in the concrete experiential contexts they inhabit.'[101]

Conclusion: The Horizons from Where We Stand

Philosophy in its basic sense, is the art of inquiring and knowing. The Greek ancient phrase, 'Know thyself', tells us something that this art begins with us as knowers. William Stoeger, SJ, employs the tools of philosophy in his critical dialogue between theology and science. In his reflections about the art of knowing, Stoeger tells us that 'in coming to know ourselves as both knowers and agents we come to know our strengths and our limitations in understanding, relating to, and affecting the world around us . . .'[102] He writes, 'Concern with ultimate issues brings about a poignant consciousness of the limits.'[103] It is then, Stoeger tells us, that we 'strive and struggle to transcend those limits by scouring our radical experience as knowers to find a way of knowing something of what lies beyond them—of rendering the horizons revelatory!'[104]

The point Stoeger makes is one worth considering. It is not only in the fact of us as knowers, but there is something to be said about the awareness of who we are and our strivings to know something beyond the limits. It is during my time at the Graduate Theological Union, Berkeley that my strivings are enriched by my encounters with other like-minded fellow pilgrims who also seek to transcend and find their way to know something of what lies beyond the horizons. It is my conviction that I am richer for it because they come from a place

---

99. Schutz, 'Ineffable Cosmos, Ineffable Love'.
100. Schutz, 'Ineffable Cosmos, Ineffable Lov.
101. Schutz, 'Ineffable Cosmos, Ineffable Lov.
102. Stoeger, 'Contemporary Physics', 237.
103. Stoeger, 'Contemporary Physics', 237.
104. Stoeger, 'Contemporary Physics', 237–238.

where they are true to themselves and their traditions, whether as a Lutheran or as an Anglican. I see the beauty of them trying to express something of the divine in a way that is true to them. They taught me to think ecumenically and inter-religiously.

Along with Denis Edwards, I recommend that our treatments of divine action are at its best work when we are true to ourselves and our traditions while keeping our sights set on the transcendent. This is because consideration of divine action is not a competition though a healthy debate is necessary. It is one that should not claim or pretend to be an 'objective' or a 'pure' theology, devoid of any tradition, and that it can be universally applied across all traditions and cultures. Rather, let the universal comes from the personal. Asian theologian Peter C Phan tells us, 'All theologies, without exception, just as rationality itself, are therefore unavoidably context-dependent, and any theology's pretensions to universal applicability and permanent validity can be easily unmasked as symptoms of either intellectual naiveté or hegemonic ambition'.[105] My point on future treatments may be saying a lot or it may be saying nothing at all. If this essay points to anything at all, it is this. As a Roman Catholic, it seems fitting that I am both indirect and comprehensive.[106]

---

105. Peter C Phan, *Asian Christianity: History, Theology, Practice* (Maryknoll, NY: Orbis Books, 2018), 102.
106. I am thankful to Professor Ted Peters who invited me to participate in this project, and for his comments and suggestions. I also want to express my thanks to Paul Schutz who had made valuable suggestions and comments, which has been very helpful.

Contributions of Walter Kasper's Pneumatology to a Theology of Deep Incarnation

Julie Trinidad

'The person who grows in faith will be enabled to see the world a little more like the way that God sees it and to love it a little more like the way God loves it. God's attitude to the world is revealed in the Incarnation. Growth in faith means a taking on of the eyes of Christ and the heart of Christ.'
– Denis Edwards[1]

Abstract: Denis Edwards has incorporated much of Walter Kasper's pneumatology; but Edwards has proceeded further to apply this pneumatology to creation, incarnation, and ecology. A pneumatologically-conditioned trinitarian understanding of the nature of God as inter-relational, as Kasper has developed and Edwards has drawn upon and taken further, leads to the profound realization that the fundamental nature of all reality, not only that of humans, is relational, mutually responsible and oriented to love.

Key Terms: Pneumatology, ecology, kenosis, deep incarnation, Trinity, Spirit-Christology, Denis Edwards, Walter Kasper

These words cited above, written by Denis Edwards in 1979, provide a foretaste of his profound legacy which, forty years later, comes to fruition as a theology of deep incarnation.[2] Edwards' expansive, dynamic, bold and future oriented theology of the Holy Spirit is central

---

1. Denis Edwards, 'The Dynamism in Faith: The Interaction between the Experience of God and Explicit Faith. A Comparative Study of the Mystical Theology of John of the Cross and the Transcendental Theology of Karl Rahner' (unpublished Doctoral Thesis: Department of Theology, Catholic University of America, 1979), 513.
2. Denis Edwards, *Deep Incarnation: The Cross as Sacrament of God's Redemptive Suffering with Creatures* (Maryknoll, NY: Orbis, 2019).

to his ecological work. One of his interlocutors in the development of a contemporary theology of the Spirit is German theologian Walter Kasper.

Edwards' appreciation of Kasper's pneumatology is shared by Elizabeth Johnson whose study of Kasper's work concludes that 'theological consideration of the Holy Spirit runs like a golden thread through all of Cardinal Kasper's work.'[3] Kasper's pneumatology has been put to the service of deepening the identity and mission of lay and ordained ministries, to strengthening the theology and practice of ecumenical and interreligious dialogue and to other major theological questions and pastoral concerns.[4]

However, Johnson calls upon him to turn his attention to a different issue that she is confident would benefit from his attention: the current ecological crisis. Though Kasper has not directly taken up this challenge, his pneumatology has been drawn on and developed in the ecological theology of Denis Edwards. The foundations for a theology of deep incarnation lie in a renewed appreciation of the role of the Spirit in the dynamism of God, creation and history. For Kasper, the Holy Spirit is the power of God who is both the source and enabler of the emergence of the new from deep within the processes of life and death.

Edwards specifically notes that his own body of work has been influenced 'particularly [by] Walter Kasper.'[5] However he makes clear that he wants to go further than Kasper. Edwards is convinced that Kasper's *communio* theology and ecclesiology can be developed into a profound theology of communion of all creation.[6] *Communio* theology has its foundations in the trinitarian unity-in-diversity

3. Elizabeth A Johnson, 'Pneumatology and Beyond: "Wherever,"', in *The Theology of Cardinal Walter Kasper*, editerd by Kristen M Colberg and Robert A Krieg (Collegeville, MN: Liturgical Press 2014), 98.
4. This chapter draws from Julie Trinidad, 'Walter Kasper's Theology of the Spirit and Its Implications for the Reception of Lay Ecclesial Ministry in the Catholic Church', (unpublished Doctoral Thesis: Department of Theology, Australian Catholic University, 2017).
5. Denis Edwards, *Partaking of God: Trinity, Evolution and Ecology* (Collegeville, MN: Liturgical Press, 2014), 3.
6. Denis Edwards, *The Natural World and God: Theological Explorations* (Hindmarsh, SA: ATF Press, 2017), 446.

dynamism of God and the specific role of the Holy Spirit who personally communicates God's freely offered, self-giving love to each creature. Edwards explains his position: 'It is not that I now reject this theology—far from it. I embrace it and find it essential to a theology of the Trinity for today. But I think more is needed . . . I now think what is needed is a more dynamic account of the Trinity in action— particularly for a theology of the natural world that has emergent, evolutionary character.'[7] In his last book *Deep Incarnation* Edwards presses this point further:

> I am convinced that an evolutionary and ecological theology
> for our time must be a theology of the Spirit creatively at work
> in the emergence of the universe of creatures, as well as in all
> aspects of salvation in Christ. Deep incarnation needs to be a
> Trinitarian theology of Word and Spirit.[8]

Edwards affirms that Kasper's pneumatology is a valuable resource for the development of a theology that meaningfully engages the Christian tradition with contemporary understandings of the natural world:

> With Kasper I want to suggest that it is the life-giving
> Spirit who is the source of the new, the power that enables
> creatures to transcend themselves. It is the Life-giver who
> enables the movement of the unfolding of the early universe
> from the Big Bang, the beginning of nuclear processes in
> stars, the formation of our planetary system, the emergence
> of life on Earth, and the evolution of self-conscious human
> beings.[9]

In his study of the Trinity in relation to the natural world, Edwards draws on Kasper's understanding of the Spirit as God who enables the emergence of newness and life's hope-filled transformation:

---

7. Edwards, *Partaking*, 4.
8. Edwards, *Deep Incarnation,* 106.
9. Denis Edwards, 'For Your Immortal Spirit Is in All Things', in *Earth Revealing, Earth Healing: Ecology and Christian Theology*, edited by Denis Edwards (Collegeville, MN: Liturgical Press, 2001), 51–52.

> In a particular way [Kasper] understands the Spirit as source
> of the new in both the evolutionary unfolding of the universe
> of creatures and in human culture and life. In Kasper's
> thought, the Holy Spirit who enables creatures to participate
> in God's being thus also constantly enables them to become
> something new.[10]

Edwards' *Deep Incarnation* develops a contemporary theology of
Jesus Christ, drawing on the thought of Irenaeus of Lyons (second
century), Athanasius of Alexandria (fourth century) and Karl
Rahner (twentieth Century).[11] Each of these theologians contributes
key elements from the Christian tradition for such a theology: the
immediate presence of God to each creature; the goodness of all
creation; the intrinsic value of each creature and 'all flesh' in which
God dwells; creation being directed 'from eternity' toward the
incarnation; the self-humbling nature of God revealed by the Cross;
the interconnection between the Word and Spirit in a fully trinitarian
theology; the concern for theology to address the causes and impact
of suffering on both humans and non-humans; and the nature of
God's redemptive presence especially to suffering creatures. In this
chapter of tribute to Edward's theological legacy I propose that he
might well have included another chapter in his book that could
also make a contribution to the development of a theology of deep
incarnation: Walter Kasper's Pneumatology.[12] If he had included such
a chapter, I propose that there could be five themes that Edwards
may have explored based on themes he draws on in a number of

---

10. Edwards, *Partaking*, 80.
11. Edwards also outlines how the concept of deep incarnation has been taken up by
    selected contemporary theologians: Niels Gregersen, Elizabeth A Johnson, Celia
    Deane-Drummond, Christopher Southgate and Richard Bauckham.
12. The theological work of German born theologian Cardinal Walter Kasper spans
    almost sixty years. His career has included teaching, writing and exercising
    significant ecclesial leadership. More recently he has been described as Pope
    Francis' theologian. See for example: David Gibson, 'Cardinal Kasper Is the
    "Pope's Theologian"', *National Catholic Reporter* June 3 2014. https://www.
    ncronline.org/news/vatican/cardinal-kasper-popes-theologian.

his publications:[13] (1) In and through the Spirit, God dwells deeply, respectfully and lovingly within creaturely processes and experiences of life and death to bring about the new; (2) The Spirit brings about the Incarnation of the Logos of God; (3) The Spirit communicates the eternally 'self-giving' or kenotic nature of God; (4) The Spirit reveals God's power as transformative vulnerability; (5) The Spirit, whose healing and transformative power is known in the Cross and Resurrection of Jesus, draws all creatures into their unique, inter-connected and hope-filled fulfillment.

---

13. As examples, Edwards draws on Walter Kasper's work in the following eighteen publications: Denis Edwards, *Called to Be Church in Australia: An Approach to the Renewal of Local Churches* (Homebush, NSW St Paul, 1989); *Jesus the Wisdom of God* (Homebush, NSW: St Pauls, 1995); *The God of Evolution*, (Mahwah, New Jersey: Paulist Press, 1999); 'For Your Immortal Spirit Is in All Things', in *Earth Revealing, Earth Healing: Ecology and Christian Theology*, edited by Denis Edwards (Collegeville, MN: Liturgical Press, 2001), 45–66; *Breath of Life: A Theology of the Creator Spirit*, (Maryknoll, NY: Orbis, 2004); *Ecology at the Heart of Faith: The Change of Heart That Leads to a New Way of Living on Earth*, (Maryknoll, NY: Orbis, 2006); 'Celebrating Eucharist in a Time of Global Climate Change', *Pacifica*, 9 (February 2006); 'The Holy Spirit as the Gift: Pneumatology and Catholic Re-Reception of Petrine Ministry in the Theology of Walter Kasper', in *Receptive Ecumenism and the Call to Catholic Learning: Exploring a Way for Contemporary Ecumenism*, edited by Paul Murray, 1–15 (www.oxfordscholarship. co: Oxford Scholarship Online, 2009); *How God Acts: Creation, Redemption and Special Divine Action* (Hindmarsh, SA: ATF Press, 2010); 'Eucharistic Living: An Applied Theology of Priestly Life in the Church of Adelaide' (written for the Archdiocese but generally attributed to Denis) (Catholic Archdiocese of Adelaide, 2010); *Jesus and the Natural World: Exploring a Christian Approach to Ecology* (Mulgrave, Vic: Garratt, 2012); 'The Attractor and the Energy of Love: Trinity in Evolutionary and Ecological Context', *The Ecumenical Review*, 65/1 (2013): 129–44; 'Catholic Perspectives on Natural Theology', in *The Oxford Handbook of Natural Theology* edited by. John Hedley Brooke, Russell Re Manning and Fraser Watts (Oxford, UK: Oxford University, 2013), 182–196; *Partaking of God: Trinity, Evolution and Ecology* (Collegeville, MN: Liturgical Press, 2014); 'Creation Seen in the Light of Christ: A Theological Sketch', in *The Natural World and God: Theological Explorations*, (Hindmarsh, SA: ATF Press, 2017); *The Natural World and God: Theological Explorations* (Hindmarsh, SA: ATF Press, 2017);*Deep Incarnation: The Cross as Sacrament of God's Redemptive Suffering with Creatures* (Maryknoll, NY: Orbis, 2019); 'The Triune God and Climate Change', in *The T&T Handbook of Christian Theology and Climate Change*, edited by Ernst M Conradie and Hilda P Koster, (London: Bloomsbury, 2019).

The Indwelling Spirit Who Brings About the New

Kasper describes the Spirit as the power of God at the heart of created reality, sustaining, transforming and bringing all life to fulfillment.[14] The Spirit dwells deeply within creaturely existence. In this way, the Spirit inspires and empowers creatures to transcend themselves:

> [T]he Spirit is . . . the source of movement and life in the world. Wherever something new arises, whenever life is awakened and reality reaches ecstatically beyond itself, in all seeking and striving, in every ferment and birth and even more in the beauty of creation, something of the being of God's Spirit is manifested.[15]

The Spirit is the personal communication of the transcendent God who enables and empowers the fecundity, wonder and evolution of life. The Spirit's presence can be discerned by 'listening' and responding to reality with a compassionate heart:

> [T]hrough looking for and listening to traces, expectation and futilities of life, through 'attention to the signs of the times' which are to be found everywhere that life breaks forth and comes into being, everywhere that new life as it were seethes and bubbles, and even, in the form of hope, everywhere that life is violently devastated, throttled, gagged and slain. Wherever true life exists, there the Spirit of God is at work.[16]

Such discernment leads to human beings taking risks for what is right, following their consciences and selflessly taking up responsibilities out of love for God and others.[17] With the planet and its creatures in peril due to the impacts of environmental devastation, the Spirit is at work in those individuals and movements that take on ecological responsibilities and commitments to address and relieve the suffering of God's creation. Human wisdom and action that emerge in response to the realities of sin and suffering, whether in the spheres of nature, society, law, politics or elsewhere is, for Kasper, a gift of the Spirit

---

14. Walter Kasper, *The God of Jesus Christ*, new edition (London: T&T Clark International, 2012), 201.
15. Kasper, *God*, 228.
16. Kasper, *God*, 202
17. Kasper, *Jesus*, 255.

of God.[18] The Spirit is the force of love that attracts each creature to unity with God from within the contexts of their unique experiences and commitments.

Spirit-Christology

The Spirit continually beckons creation and history toward its final fulfillment, the Reign of God, which is, in person, Jesus the Christ. For Kasper, pneumatology and Christology can never be separated. Furthermore, ecclesiology is always a function of pneumatology, not the other way around. Kasper writes that Jesus is both the 'the goal and culmination' of the work and mission of the Spirit.[19] In the Spirit, God has expressed and communicated God's self in all aspects of the life and destiny of Jesus Christ.[20]

This self-communication includes every aspect of his bodily, creaturely life. In and through Jesus' history and destiny, the Spirit makes God's self-revelation as the *Logos* possible. Kasper's Spirit-Christology understands the Spirit as bringing about the Incarnation of the *Logos* of God. The unity of Jesus with the Logos of God is made possible through the Spirit-filled 'event' of the Incarnation. Through this event, which presupposes the trinitarian life of God, Jesus Christ externalises what is most hidden and interior in God: freely offered, other-centred, self-communicating love.[21]

In short, in the Spirit, Jesus communicates God's self as *Logos* in and through his own unique, creaturely history. Kasper's understanding of Christ's unity with God does not dissolve human-divine difference, but profoundly affirms it. Jesus' identity with the *Logos* is not reduced to the sameness of his 'substance' with the Father, but is expressed through the uniqueness of his dynamic relationship 'in the Spirit' lived out through personal and total commitment to God's 'mission' and in fidelity to his unique identity. In the Spirit, the communion of love between the Father and the Son, incarnated in Jesus Christ, opens to include all and bring all creatures to their eschatological fulfillment. Kasper shows that in Jesus, God assumed not only a human

---

18. Walter Kasper, *Jesus the Christ*, new edition (London: T&T Clark International, 2011), 243.
19. Kasper, *Jesus*, 243.
20. Kasper, *Jesus*, 157.
21. Kasper, *Jesus*, 237.

nature but also a history of relational commitments. In the Spirit, God's assumption of history also revealed its goal of transforming relationships and creating interconnections between all creatures.

Kasper does not understand Christology to be the culmination or universalisation of anthropology, but its unique and never-to-be-repeated particularisation.[22] He places value on the uniqueness of each person's relationship with God. He emphasises that the Logos of God and the humanity of Jesus Christ were fully united in the uniqueness and concreteness of Jesus' relational identity and life.

The Incarnation is not only an assertion of Jesus' divine and eternal identity as Logos. The Incarnation is also God entering and fulfilling history as Pneuma. The deep incarnation of God in creation, revealed in its fullness in the life and destiny Jesus Christ, is a theology of the Spirit. Jesus' life, passion, death and resurrection, not only confirm his divine identity as Logos but also enable a new understanding of God's presence as Spirit who is at the heart of the transformation of history:

> That does not imply an abandonment of faith in the Incarnation, but instead its transformation into a total interpretation of the history and activity of Jesus, so that it states that God assumed not only a human nature but a human history, and in that way introduced the fulfilment of history as a whole.[23]

Jesus Christ's historically mediated, humanly expressed freedom-in-love is united with and assumed by the Logos of God to become part of God's eternal relational life of love. It is worth noting Kasper's language for the Spirit's action in the Incarnation: the Spirit is the power within God which *impels* God, freely and out of love, to go beyond God's self to be united with what is other than God.[24] In that movement outwards, God draws or attracts creation into divine

---

22. See also Walter Kasper, 'Orientations in Current Christology', in *Theology Digest*, 31/2 (1984): 108. Here Kasper refers to Jesus' capacity, in his personal uniqueness, to open up new understandings about how God is present in and through what is unique and personal in our human histories. He writes: 'Christology reshuffles the alphabet of our humanity'.

23. Kasper, *Jesus*, 25.

24. Kasper, *Jesus*, 238. (Italics mine) Kasper uses the German verb *drängen* which can be translated as impel, urge, push, press, thrust, forge. These verbs express a powerful and dynamic, not static and lifeless, understanding of God as Spirit.

love while respecting creaturely freedom to respond. The event of the Incarnation, inspired and impelled by the Spirit, expresses the effusive overflow of divine love that seeks to bring all creation into a 'communion of essence' with the Father and Son's super-abundant, inclusive mutual love.

The Incarnation is an act of divine freedom-in-love, involving each of the divine persons who are experienced in history according to their creative, redeeming and sanctifying roles. Kasper considers the metaphysical starting point of scholasticism and the Latin tradition it came to represent, as privileging the unity or sameness of the divine essence, and thus each 'person' of the Trinity, more than the unique, yet inter-dependent trinitarian persons. This latter understanding is attributed more often to Eastern theology. Scholasticism came to privilege the action of the Logos, rather than the Spirit, in the union of the human and divine in Jesus. In continuity with the traditions of early patristic theology, Kasper seeks to redress this imbalance.

Patristic theology spoke of the 'unction' or anointing of Jesus Christ by the Spirit while scholastic theology spoke of the *gratia unionis* which involved bestowal of the gifts of the Spirit on Jesus at the Incarnation as a consequence of his *Logos* identity. In scholastic theology the grace of union was thus attributed to the *Logos* not the *Pneuma*. In this theology, the hypostatic union of the *Logos* with humanity is the cause of Jesus' life being gifted by the Spirit. However, Kasper contests this theology, arguing that it must be 'freed from its one-sidedness'.[25] Instead, he considers the Spirit as the pre-condition for the hypostatic union. In other words, if the *Logos* were the cause of the divinisation of Jesus' humanity through the Spirit, little room can be found for the inclusion of Jesus' relationships, responsibilities and consciousness of his personal mission in the inner life of the Trinity. A consequence of this scholastic theology is that God's incarnation in Jesus elevates his divinity and devalues his unique humanity in the work of God's salvation.

This one-sided Christology, Kasper argues, is inconsistent with the claim of Chalcedon that the fullness of Jesus' divinity and humanity *together* mediate God's salvation. The Spirit sanctifies the humanity of Jesus, thus enabling him to be God's self-communication, the Logos

---

25. Kasper, *Jesus*, 239. The original German word Kasper uses for 'freed' is *befreien* which can also be translated as 'loosened' or 'unknotted.'

of God.[26] Because Jesus is anointed by the Spirit, he is the Son of God, not vice versa. Kasper says explicitly that Jesus is 'the Son of God because he is a Spirit-creation'.[27] The action of the Spirit is the presupposition, not the consequence of the unity of the Logos with Jesus' humanity.

The pneumatological foundation for Kasper's Spirit-Christology is God's self-communication in the Spirit, as well as through the Son. The Spirit communicates God's desire for creaturely participation in God's trinitarian life:

> The Father communicates himself in love to the Son, in the Spirit this love is aware of its freedom; hence, in the Spirit, this love has the possibility of communicating itself outside the Trinity. In the Spirit, of course, an inverse movement also occurs. The creature filled with God's Spirit becomes in freedom an historical figure through which the Son gives himself to the Father.[28]

In and through the Spirit, the Word communicates the relationship of freedom-in-love between the Father and Son into history.[29] This love is oriented to include all creation in its embrace without detriment to the development of the unique identity of each creature.

Kasper's Spirit-Christology rebalances the Christian tradition's emphasis on the relationship of identity between Jesus and the *Logos* by focusing attention also on the distinctiveness of the personal relationship between the Father and Son mediated through the uniqueness of Jesus' life 'in the Spirit'. Kasper's theology of the Spirit holds together the dynamic nature of Jesus' unity with God as Logos as well as the relational distinctiveness of Jesus with his 'Father'. He points out that for the writer of John's Gospel, 'it is significant that [the evangelist] is concerned not so much with the unity between Jesus and the Logos, but more so with the unity between Jesus and the Father: 'I and the Father are one (10.30).''[30] Kasper understands the relation between Jesus and the Logos, the Word of God's self-

---

26. Kasper, *Jesus*, 239.
27. Kasper, *Jesus*, 239.
28. Kasper, *Jesus*, 240.
29. Kasper, *Jesus*, 240.
30. Kasper, *Jesus*, 221.

expression in human history, only in relation to the communion of unity-in-difference between Jesus and the Father.[31] He uses the term 'community of essence' to describe the active, personal and relational dynamic between the Father and Jesus.[32] In summary, according to Kasper, the reality of inter-relationship between the Father and the Son, incarnated in the Spirit-filled history of Jesus of Nazareth, is the foundation for knowing him as the *Logos* of God.[33]

The Kenotic, Self-giving Nature of God

For Kasper, the Son-Christology of the New Testament finds its full meaning as Spirit-Christology, which he later terms *kenosis*-Christology.[34] Kasper sees the Spirit as God's mysterious, free and personal self-communicating love and life that overflows into creation. In fact, for him the Spirit is 'the theological transcendental condition of the very possibility of a free self-communication in history'.[35] In other words, God is only able to communicate beyond God's self because God is self-communication 'within'.[36] Thus the word 'Spirit' is the language symbol that seeks to express the going forth or 'ecstasy' of God's self-giving intra-trinitarian love.

According to Kasper, understanding Jesus' 'oneness of being' with the Father, interpreted as Son-Christology and later as Logos Christology, needs further refinement. He recognises that these Christologies correctly emphasise the inner dynamics relationship and communication between Father and Son revealed through Jesus' life and ministry. However, he thinks that they seem inadequate to

---

31. Kasper, *Jesus*, 221.
32. Kasper, *Jesus*, 221.
33. See Kasper, 'Orientations', 111.
34. In the new introduction to *The God of Jesus Christ*, Kasper makes use of the term 'kenosis theology' to describe his pneumatologically-conditioned trinitarian theology. This is a significant development in the light of the terminology of 'Spirit-Christology' that he used in *Jesus the Christ*. The relation between Christology and the Trinity remained undeveloped in *Jesus the Christ*. However, in *The God of Jesus Christ* Kasper argues that 'kenosis theology' deepens understanding of God in line with the Augustinian analogy of the nature of self-giving inter-personal love. This understanding is dependent on the role of the Spirit in the trinitarian relations that give, receive and extend love.
35. Kasper, *Jesus*, 238.
36. Kasper, *God*, 227.

communicate the meaning of the experience of God's *kenosis* in Jesus' death and resurrection. They neglect a trinitarian theology of God's freedom and the self-emptying love experienced in the whole 'event' of the incarnation. He questions whether a classical Logos-Christology goes far enough in valuing the biblical testimony, especially found in John's Gospel, that God became a human person with all its frailty, suffering and commitments:

> The Incarnation thus already suggests a Christology of the cross and of kenosis, according to which in Jesus Christ God empties himself and, as it were, reveals himself in his opposite, so that God's revelation of himself is at the same time a revelation of his hiddenness. This element of self-emptying is neglected in the classical Logos-Christology. This fact constrains us not indeed to renounce the classical solution but rather to take it a step further and deeper in the idea of self-emptying.[37]

Kasper builds on the theology of Augustine and Aquinas who both understood God's Spirit as eternally 'giveable'.[38] The Spirit shows that God's love is not self-contained, but is a dynamic relationship of self-bestowing love.

Western theology typically begins with consideration of the one divine essence that all persons of the Trinity share and which the Spirit externalises in history. Eastern theology, on the other hand, begins with consideration of the Father as source of divinity, from whom both Son and Spirit proceed. This theology emphasises the unique saving role of each of the trinitarian persons. In the West, the Spirit came to be understood as the more inactive divine third person who brings to completion the mutual love between Father and Son, but often does not seem to have its own personal identity. The Spirit closes the circle of love, so to speak, with the result, Kasper writes, that trinitarian 'operation *ad extra* is in this view common to all three divine persons'.[39] In the East, on the other hand, theology generally emphasises the more active personhood of the Spirit who, Kasper explains, is understood as 'the excess, the overflow of the love

---

37. Kasper, *God,* 188.
38. Kasper, *God,* 226.
39. Kasper, *Jesus,* 245.

manifest in the Son . . . the revelation of the very being of the Son, just as the Son reveals the very being of the Father . . . the Spirit is, as it were, God's outermost and uttermost.'[40]

Kasper's trinitarian theology of God's *kenosis* in the Spirit does not begin with the 'being' of God but with the eternal 'sending' or 'giving' of God's self as freedom-in-love in the missions of the Son and the Spirit. These missions in time presuppose and maintain the divine mystery of the eternal processions or relations of the Son from the Father and the Spirit from the Father and the Son. Kasper draws on the theology of Albert the Great who understood the processions in God as 'an ecstatic going-beyond-oneself and self-transcending, a being-out-of-oneself such as is proper to love'.[41] Eastern classical theological language about God's eternal processions (or self-communication) expresses an understanding of distinct relations within God.[42] Kasper insists that these relations, in the end, express that 'the final word [about God] belongs not to the static substance, to divine self-containment, but to being-from-another and being-for-another'.[43] Distinction between 'persons' in God is based on relation, not substance. More precisely, the 'being-from-another' and 'being-for-another' relationality of the divine persons *is* God's substance.[44] For Kasper, God does not 'have' relations. God 'is' relations. Thus, Kasper can write: 'the ultimate reality is conceivable not in terms of a self-subsistent substance but of a person who is fulfilled only in a selfless, dynamic relationality of giving and receiving. It could also be said that the meaning of being, from the Christian point of view, is love.'[45]

The Vulnerability of God's Love

Something new in history and for history comes about in the experience of Jesus' cross and resurrection. Here God's nature as other-centred, vulnerable and self-limiting is fully revealed. The new understanding of God and reality as a whole that Jesus Christ

---

40. Kasper, *Jesus*, 246.
41. Kasper, *God*, 279.
42. Kasper, *God*, 279.
43. Kasper, *God*, 280.
44. Kasper, *God*, 280.
45. Walter Kasper, *Transcending All Understanding: The Meaning of Christian Faith Today* (San Fransisco: Ignatius Press, 1987), 98.

reveals and mediates is that of the power of divine vulnerability. For Kasper, in the light of Christ's resurrection, questions of God and suffering necessarily go together. In fact, he argues that 'the question of suffering alters the question of God'.[46] The theological ground of hope for those who suffer is that God identifies with their condition and redeems it:

> God's self-emptying, his weakness and his suffering are not the expression of a lack, as they are in finite beings; nor are they the expression of a fated necessity. If God suffers, then he suffers in a divine manner, that is, his suffering is an expression of his freedom; suffering does not befall God, rather he freely allows it to touch him. He does not suffer, as creatures do, from a lack of being; he suffers out of love and by reason of his love, which is the overflow of his being.[47]

In Jesus' life, but above all through the self-giving love of his death and the hope made possible by the resurrection, unexpected newness emerges in history. In Jesus, God as a creature freely suffers out of love. Such suffering does not diminish God. On the contrary, it affirms the nature of God's 'Godness'. Kasper explains this theology with the image of a lover:

> Th[is] lover must take himself back because his concern is not with himself but with the other. More than this, the lover allows the other to affect him; he becomes vulnerable precisely in this love. Thus love and suffering go together. The suffering of love is not, however, a passive being-affected, but an active allowing others to affect one. Because, then, God is love he can suffer and by that very fact reveal his divinity.[48]

Thus, suffering and love in God are not necessarily contradictions, though suffering is definitely not something God wants or wills for creatures. Kasper writes 'only an almighty love can give itself wholly to the other and be a helpless love'.[49] God's vulnerability is communicated as compassion and mercy that can and does transform suffering and death into new life and hope.

---

46. Kasper, *God*, 160.
47. Kasper, *God*, 195.
48. Kasper, *God*, 196.
49. Kasper, *God*, 194.

Salvation is Inter-relational and Opens up the Future

A recurring theme in Kasper's writing is that of hope. For him, hope for the future is what makes life meaningful, and even bearable.[50] Hope in the future, the power of freeing love and the question of salvation are linked. The Spirit is guarantor that hope can be placed in the power of love to bring all things to their completion. Such love is expressed when humans break out of selfishness, overcome divisions, offer and accept forgiveness and offer mercy without condition: 'Wherever there is love something of the world's final completion and transfiguration is anticipated even now.'[51] Since Jesus Christ, in the Spirit, incarnates the eschatological reality of the love of God, it is made clear that everything done in love and for love is never lost.[52] Kasper's theology of salvation is deeply inter-relational:

> While salvation and judgment always concern the individual, one whom no one else can represent, it is still an individual who by his very being can exist only in an I-you-we relationship. Because of this bond with all fellow-creatures, the individual can attain perfect fulfillment only when all the others have also attained to perfect fulfillment.[53]

In other words, resurrection hope is not limited to the individual person, turned in on him or herself, but opens out to include the whole of creation and history.[54] Kasper has a broad and inclusive theology of salvation. Individual salvation is not possible until the whole of the cosmos is included.[55] The creative and redemptive power of the Spirit

50. Walter Kasper, 'Individual Salvation and Eschatological Consummation', in *Faith and the Future: Studies in Christian Eschatology*, edited by John Galvin (New York: Paulist, 1994), 9.
51. German Bishops' Conference, *The Church's Confession of Faith: A Catholic Catechism for Adults*, Communio (San Francisco: St Ignatius Press, 1987), 186. In the introduction David L. Schindler, General Editor of *Communio Books*, writes: 'The book we have chosen to publish first [in English] is a catechism for adults, authored mainly by Walter Kasper under the aegis of the German Bishops' Conference.'
52. Walter Kasper, 'Hope in the Final Coming of Jesus Christ in Glory', in *Communio* 12 (Winter 1985): 383.
53. Kasper, 'Hope', 337.
54. Kasper, 'Hope', 378.
55. Kasper, 'Hope' 378.

draws all creation and history into a hope-filled, inclusive future. This power, that completes all things, 'gives us wings and encourages us to take responsibility for our own and our common historical future'.[56]

Conclusion

In the Introduction to *Deep Incarnation* Denis Edwards outlines two reasons for writing his book. First, he wants to ground contemporary Christian ecological theology in Christology. He poses the question: 'what relationship is there between the wider world, the world of galaxies, and the life, death and resurrection of Jesus Christ?'[57] The second reason is to provide a meaningful theological response to the reality of loss and suffering in creation and history. His question here is 'what relation is there between the suffering, predation, extinction, loss and death that are found in the natural world and the incarnation of God in Jesus Christ?'[58]

This chapter has outlined five themes from the pneumatology of Walter Kasper that I think contribute valuable theological resources for responding to these questions and thus to the development of a theology of deep incarnation. These five themes are: in the Spirit, God 'dwells' respectfully and lovingly within the processes of creation to make possible the emergence of the new; in the Spirit, God leads creation and history 'from eternity' toward the incarnation; in the Spirit, God's trinitarian 'identity' is fully revealed in the self-humbling and self-giving vulnerability of the Cross; in the Spirit, God identifies with, bears the costs of, and transforms the causes and impact of suffering on both humans and non-humans and; in the Spirit, God draws all creatures into their unique, hope-filled and co-responsible fulfillment.

I have shown that Edwards has not only drawn upon these themes but taken them further in the development of a theology of deep incarnation. While Kasper's pneumatological concerns focus on the meaning of Jesus' humanity for Christology, the focus of deep incarnation is the reality and interconnectedness of Jesus' creaturely

---

56. Walter Kasper, 'Religion und die Zukunft des Menschen', in *Internationale Katholische Zeitschrift Communio*, 36, no. Mai-Juni (2007): 312.

57. Edwards, *Deep Incarnation*, xv.

58. Edwards, *Deep Incarnation*, xvii.

life, including his biological identification with the emergent processes of creation. A theology of deep incarnation transforms Kasper's more anthropocentric incarnational theology into one that is more inclusive of the significance of Jesus Christ for all creatures. Kasper's work seeks to be in dialogue with the spiritual questions that arise from everyday human experience, especially the experience of suffering. He writes:

> Whereas modern theology's partner in dialogue used to be the unenlightened believer, the partner in dialogue of any contemporary theology is suffering man (sic) who has concrete experience of the persisting situation of disaster and is therefore conscious of the weakness and finiteness of human existence.[59]

However, a theology of deep incarnation broadens Kasper's engagement with the question of suffering to include the contemporary concerns of the planet and its creatures, especially the poor. Kasper's Spirit-Christology affirms the Spirit's nature as respectful and encouraging of the capacity of humans to contribute to their own self-emergence and to that of the whole creation. However, Edwards contributes to a more inclusive consideration of the precious uniqueness of all creaturely identities and histories when he emphasizes that the source of the movement toward God is mysteriously intrinsic not only to humans but to each and every creature:

> [T]he power of self-transcendence comes from *within* [the] creation itself, but it is a power that finally comes not from nature but from the ongoing creative activity of God. God upholds and empowers the process of evolution from within, as the power enabling creation itself to bring about something new.[60]

With Kasper, Edwards understands God's omnipotence as involving the capacity for loving self-restraint: 'God's power (is) constrained by God's love and respect for creatures'[61] God's love is expressed as the kind of vulnerable and inter-relational power that can and does bring

---

59. Kasper, *God,* 160.
60. Edwards, 'Your Immortal Spirit', 51.
61. Edwards, *Natural World and God,* 297.

about the new. Such power involves 'the infinite capacity for self-giving love, and for enabling the integrity of the other'.[62] Understanding divine power as vulnerability communicates a theology that affirms God's desire for and choice for active participation in creaturely life with all its associated costs.[63] God's humble power works in, with and through creaturely processes to bring about the new. Though such love and respect 'costs', it is never lost in eternity: '[t]he Gospel tradition of the glorious risen Christ still bearing the wounds of the cross suggests that the sufferings of creation are forever remembered and taken up in the healing, compassionate love of God'.[64]

A pneumatologically-conditioned trinitarian understanding of the nature of God as inter-relational, as Kasper has developed and Edwards has drawn upon and taken further, leads to the profound realisation that the fundamental nature of all reality, not only that of humans, is relational, mutually responsible and oriented to love.[65] Such understanding is foundational for a theology of deep incarnation. This theological legacy now awaits its future fulfillment through the new research and praxis it inspires.

---

62. Edwards, *Natural World and God*, 241.
63. Edwards, *God of Evolution*, 41.
64. Edwards, *Natural World and God*, 17.
65. Edwards, *God of Evolution*, 27.

The Spirit of Life in a Scientific Age: Towards A Sophianic Pneumatology in Dialogue with Denis Edwards

Celia Deane-Drummond

'The Spirit of God is the Life-Giver who enables and empowers the emergence of galaxies and stars, the Sun and its solar system, with Earth placed at the right distant from the Sun to enable life, the first forms of prokaryotic life, more complex life forms, the extraordinary flourishing of sea creatures, flowering trees and shrubs, the diversity of land animals, mammals and human beings with their extraordinarily complex brains.'[1]
– Denis Edwards.

Abstract: Finding ways to articulate theologically the work of the Spirit in creation is not just a theoretical challenge, but remains essential in order to spur new hope in an era of existential hopelessness and ecological anxiety. At the same time the cultural influence of scientific narratives and evolutionary origins of life is increasing. How can an articulation of the continuing work of God in the natural world understood in pneumatological categories still make sense? This chapter will explore the pioneering work of Denis Edwards in articulating a theology of the Spirit in the natural world and a metaphysic of primary and secondary causation in the light of newly emerging philosophies of nature. I will consider briefly if there are theological alternatives to Edwards' developed Rahnerian notion of self-transcendence.

Key words: Spirit, evolution, ecology, Denis Edwards, philosophies of nature, Karl Rahner, Michael Serres, Erazim Kahák, Sergius Bulgakov

In mounting global pressure from climate change, ecological devastation and massive biodiversity loss and species extinction, the possibility of ecological anxiety and despair is high on the agenda,

---

1. Denis Edwards, *The Natural World and God: Theological Explorations* (Adelaide, Australia: ATF Press, 2017), 18.

especially in Western societies.[2] One of the reasons for that despair is the sense of loss that arises not just from knowledge of climate change, but from ecological destruction and massive species extinction on a scale sometimes known as the sixth great extinction event[3].

EO Wilson, perhaps, among all biologists, is one who has consistently sought to press home the complexity, intricacy and wonder of the natural world around us. One of his key points is that right from the start of Neolithic civilisation, humanity assumed that the natural world would support human life indefinitely. 'Civilisation was purchased by the betrayal of nature.'[4] Above all, we have lost the ability to value the diversity of wild species-reliance on specialised monocultures make human societies highly vulnerable. The 'second betrayal' he identifies is in technocratic societies that rely on urbanised computer driven environments.[5] Knowing the immense ignorance that still confronts us, including the fact that uncounted millions of species exist and yet are still not yet identified,[6] he claims that 'scientific knowledge, humanised and well taught, is the key to achieving a lasting balance in our lives.'[7]

Or is it? Certainly, one can agree with Wilson that understanding and learning to observe the natural world away from our 'cocoons of urban and suburban material life' are important, but science alone will not necessarily change our deepest desires in the way promised from religious insight and experience. And change these desires we must if we are to face the immense challenge of climate change, biodiversity loss and threat of Earth System disfunction. Wilson recognises this in part, which is why, as other scientists have done, he creeps towards what can only be called a type of nature mysticism.[8]

2.   Panu Pihkala, 'Eco-anxiety, Tragedy and Hope: Psychological and Spiritual Dimensions of Climate Change', *Zygon*, 53/2 (2018): 545–569.

3.   Elizabeth Kolbert, *The Sixth Extinction: An Unnatural History* (London: Bloomsbury, 2014).

4.   EO Wilson, *Creation: An Appeal to Save Life on Earth* (London: WW Norton and Co, 2007), 11.

5.   Wilson, *Creation*, 12

6.   Wilson, *Creation*, 109.

7.   Wilson, *Creation*, 12

8.   Ursula Goodenough achieves something similar in her work, where she argues that contemplation of the natural world through its cosmic and ecological history leads inspires a sense of the sacred Ursula Goodenough, *The Sacred Depths of Nature* (New York: Oxford University Press, 1998).

Contemplation of the mystery of millions of years of evolution triggers 'a new theater of spiritual energy'.[9]

Sometimes given the label 'new materialism', this weaving in of spiritual language into the language of science is a relatively new development, and a sign that ecologically attuned scientists recognise that science reliant on materialistic philosophy and methodological reductionism as described in standard scientific articles and papers will not stir the human heart and imagination in the same way as talk of the spirit. It also appeals to the jaded sensibilities of many young people towards the established church.

I will argue in this chapter that there is a need not only to develop an adequate theology of the Spirit in creation, but also situate this alongside an awareness of current philosophical currents that are influencing popular science to speak either directly or indirectly in the language of the sacred in the natural world. As a first step in working out the former I will draw on the work of Denis Edwards, while in the second step I will highlight the work of two important contemporary philosophers of nature, Michael Serres and Erazim Kahák.

Breath of Life[10]

Denis Edwards' anticipated the need for a systematic theology of the work of the Spirit in creation in his pioneering work *Breath of Life: Theology of the Creator Spirit*. Ideas developed in this book reappear in his two most recent publications, *Deep Incarnation* and *The Natural World and God*, but also earlier works, *How God Acts*, and *Partaking of God*.[11] In *Breath of Life*, like many other scholars who are inspired by grand scientific cosmologies of nature, he adopts that cosmological narrative in working out what the work of the Spirit entails. For him 'God's Spirit has been breathing life into the processes of the evolving universe from the very first. The laws of nature and the initial conditions of the early universe exist because of the empowering

9. Wilson, *Creation*, 109.

10. Denis Edwards, *Breath of Life: A Theology of the Creator Spirit* (Maryknoll: Orbis, 2004).

11. Denis Edwards, *Deep Incarnation* (Maryknoll: Orbis, 2019); *The Natural World and God: Theological Explorations* (Adelaide, ATF Press, 2017); *Partaking of God: Trinity, Evolution and Ecology* (Collegeville: Liturgical Press, 2014); *How God Acts: Creation, Redemption and Special Divine Action* (Minneapolis: Fortress, 2010).

presence and action of the Creator Spirit'.[12] This 'story of the Spirit'[13] also includes all the processes of evolution, and the 'Breath of God' 'leads creation into an open future, who makes all things new'.[14]

The Spirit is active in 'creatively empowering a world in process', which, at the same time, 'has its own integrity and proper autonomy', so being 'a world of contingencies and chances, a world that evolved in its own way'.[15] Time and again he insists that the activity of the Spirit is not according to some pre-set design or plan (thus rejecting ideas of intelligent design), but is inclusive of scientific understandings of the evolution of life, including Darwin's understanding of evolution as well as Ilya Prigogine's concept of dissipative systems. The Spirit is one who 'embraces the chanciness of random mutations and the chaotic conditions of open systems'.[16] At the same time the work of the Spirit is 'boundless love at work in the process of the universe'.[17] The Spirit is, in this view, an enabler who still honours the proper autonomy of natural systems as described through scientific observations.

In order to support his position Edwards draws on Irenaeus' proposal of the Word and Spirit acting as the two hands of God in one act of creation, Athanasius envisaging that the Spirit is the immanent presence of God in creatures and creating through the Word but in the Spirit, and Basil, who understood the work of the Spirit through the communion of the Trinity, dwelling in the diverse creatures of the universe, and 'enabling them to exist from the divine Communion'.[18] Overall, because Edwards supports ideas such as the emergent Universe that were not accepted theories in the classic era, such theological ideas about the work of the Spirit in the ground of existence need supplementing with a greater stress on the idea of becoming. He draws heavily on Karl Rahner's theology in order to develop this aspect of his work. Accordingly, 'He calls this process whereby God empowers creation itself to produce something radically new "active self-transcendence."'[19]

---

12. Edwards, *Breath of Life*, 33.
13. Edwards, *Breath of Life*, 33.
14. Edwards, *Breath of Life*, 34.
15. Edwards, *Breath of Life*, 34.
16. Edwards, *Breath of Life*, 34.
17. Edwards, *Breath of Life*, 34.
18. Edwards, *Breath of Life*, 44.
19. Edwards, *Breath of Life*, 46.

How does Edwards navigate the difficult task of affirming scientific descriptions but also holding onto a strong theological narrative? He achieves this by both affirming explanations 'at the level of science', as well as 'at the deepest metaphysical and biological levels it is God who enables and empowers this becoming. God is the inner power of evolutionary emergence . . .'[20] This is not, Edwards insists, some sort of 'intervention' from the outside, rather 'God empowers the whole process of ongoing creation from within by constantly giving to creation itself the capacity to transcend itself and become more than it was'.[21] We might ask in what way might such activity take place. For Edwards, it is by developing Rahner's trinitarian thought further, thus; 'It is the Spirit who is the immanent divine principle that empowers the new, enabling creatures to transcend themselves'.[22]

How convincing is this approach? Certainly, from a theological perspective, it makes sense, and Edwards' extension of the work of the Spirit into the dynamic processes of the Universe enlivens and informs the task of theology, updating traditions that were originally premised on a static cosmology.[23] I am in broad agreement with the overall stance that Edwards takes, namely, that it would be inappropriate to try and work out in too much detail how God acts in the world, and the classic tradition of primary and secondary causation protects, to a large extent, having to make such explanations. A primary and secondary causation model secures the idea of God being present to creatures everywhere in the Universe, while also giving that Universe

20. Edwards, *Breath of Life*, 46
21. Edwards, *Breath of Life*, 46.
22. Edwards, *Breath of Life*, 46–47.
23. Edwards, *How God Acts*, 61. Edwards distinguishes his position on special divine action in non-interventionist terms from four other alternatives. These are first process theology, where divine action is understood as the inviting lure of God which does not pre-determine the outcome; second, the idea of God's action in indeterminacy of quantum events, following by Robert John Russell, Nancy Murphy, George Ellis and Thomas Tracy; third, John Polkinghorne's top down imparting of information working within the openness of nature in chaotic and complex systems, fourth, Arthur Peacocke's understanding of God acting on the whole system in a way analogous with whole/part causes in the natural world and finally his own adoption of the classic tradition of primary and secondary causation, promoted by the work of William Stoeger among othersEdwards does not mention Elizabeth Johnson, though her work also adopts primary and secondary causation model. See, for example, Elizabeth Johnson, *Ask the Beasts: Darwin and the God of Love* (London: Bloomsbury, 2014), 163–168.

its own autonomy integrity.[24] The main alternative, which Edwards rejects, is that of process thinking on the basis that it loses important theological concepts about divine transcendence. The challenge, then, is to hold together creaturely autonomy and divine transcendence, and resist understanding God as one more cause among others in the world. It also allows some diffidence about precisely how God acts in the world, so the search for an empirical basis for God's action is bound to fail.[25] Importantly, for Edwards, the way God acts in the world is that of divine self-bestowal, an act of love.[26]

The Spirit in Evolutionary Creation

The difference between my own position and that of Edwards has to do with where and in what sense it might be possible to describe the evolutionary process *also* as an act of the Spirit in creation, *and* being the result of primary and secondary causation. I think there are theoretical challenges here that need closer attention.

The first challenge is scientific, and the second one relates to the application of Thomistic ideas in contemporary scientific contexts. On the scientific front, if, as Edwards claims, the processes and systems are to have their own integrity as discovered by science, the natural process of evolution by natural selection is in a fundamental way non-teleological. The most that can be said of natural selection, according to some theories, is that it fosters convergence along lines of constraint.[27] Even the rather more imaginative niche construction theories which have some resonance with theological ideas, support the notion of agency, but resist notions of teleologically directed outcomes.[28]

---

24. Edwards, *How God Acts*, 62.
25. Edwards, *How God Acts*, 63.
26. Edwards, *How God Acts*, 64.
27. As in the work of Simon Conway Morris, for example. See Simon Conway Morris, *Life's Solution: Inevitable Humans in a Lonely Universe* (Cambridge: Cambridge University Press, 2003) and *The Deep Structure of Biology: Is Convergence Sufficiently Ubiquitous to Give a Directional Signal?*, edited by Simon Conway Morris (West Conshohocken: Templeton Foundation Press, 2008).
28. For a more developed discussion of alternative contemporary theories of evolution see Celia Deane-Drummond, *Christ and Evolution: Wonder and Wisdom* (Minneapolis: Fortress, 2009), 1–30 and Celia Deane-Drummond, *Wisdom of the Liminal: Evolution and Other Animals in Human Becoming* (Grand Rapids: Eerdmans, 2014), 194–209; 219–222.

Although Edwards correctly rejects any idea of a fixed 'design', his repeated insistence on the idea of the Spirit 'empowering' the whole process through what sounds like a form of accompaniment of the Sprit in nature, harks back to ancient evolutionary theories that supported the idea of a positive life force influencing the evolutionary process, rather than the weaker, and more negative theory of evolution by natural selection. It is therefore not consistent with Darwinian understanding of biological evolution in the way that Edwards intends. This is articulated in more depth through Rahner's developed theory of self-transcendence.

What is particularly interesting is that contemporary philosophers have begun to discuss the possibility of the transcendent in the natural world, as in the work of Thomas Nagel, for example, in *Mind and Cosmos*.[29] However, such theories, which I will explore more fully below, tend to lean more towards what I would call a Whiteheadian process approach, which, of course, Edwards resists. The fundamental problem is whether it still makes sense to hold to primary causation in terms which allow for God's action of the Spirit in the created world and yet still allow those sciences to have integrity as science of nature. A yawning gap opens up between creation and nature.

The second challenge relates to a metaphysical framework of primary and secondary causation. When Thomas Aquinas talked about the *Division and Methods of the Sciences*, for example, what he had in mind was, in a fundamental sense, ontologies and philosophies of nature, rather than observational and empirical sciences which are characteristic of post-Enlightenment cultures.[30] The contemporary view of universal, reasoned knowledge arising out of the empirical sciences is very different from Thomistic understanding of science as 'knowledge of things through their causes' bringing to light properties of things through 'intelligible relations to their causes'.[31] It aims, therefore, at the 'very being and structure of things' and is not content simply with 'empiriological knowledge gained through controlled observation and measurement of the physical world'.[32]

---

29. Thomas Nagel, *Mind and Cosmos: Why the Materialist NeoDarwinian Conception of Nature is Almost Certainly False* (New York: Oxford University Press, 2012).

30. Armand Maurer, 'Introduction', Thomas Aquinas, *The Division and Methods of the Sciences*, translated by Armand Maurer, 4th edition [1956] (Toronto: Pontifical Institute of Medieval Studies, 1986), vii–xiv.

31. Maurer, 'Introduction', ix.

32. Maurer, 'Introduction', x.

While Thomas was aware of the emerging observational studies in biology, its range was limited, and therefore they only play a minor role in his understanding of the sciences.[33] What this implies, therefore, is the need for more work on a philosophy of nature if Thomistic thought is going to have relevance to contemporary observational sciences. In the middle-ages there was considerable optimism about the ability to understand the ontological structure of things and their intelligible natures. The physics of the Middle Ages was discarded by Newton and others, along with its approach to philosophy. Hence, the methods of controlled observation replaced that of ontological analysis, though such scientific positivism eventually gave way to other philosophical traditions such as phenomenology. Is it possible, therefore, to combine ontological approaches such as that of primary and secondary causation with affirmation and insistence on the integrity of the natural sciences?

Transcendence in Contemporary Science and Philosophies of Nature

In the light of the above, I have become convinced that theologians need to pay much more attention to current philosophical currents that may either help or hinder theological articulation of the work of the Spirit in creation, especially in so far as they adopt grand narratives of origin using metaphors arising from scientific analysis. I have arrived at this conclusion not least through reading Lisa Sideris' important contribution to this discussion, *Consecrating Science*.[34] In this work Sideris exposes the philosophical flaws relevant to environmental ethics that are latent in new cosmologies that bring together science and spirituality, arguing that in many cases they amount to disguised forms of anthropocentrism and an uncritical absorption of scientific narratives. It is the collapse of scientific *into* sacred narrative that she objects to most strongly. Among those narratives that she names as objects of particular critique are influential ideas such as the 'Epic of Evolution, the Universe Story, the New Story, the Great Story or Big History'.[35]

---

33. Maurer, 'Introduction', xi.
34. Lisa H Sideris, *Consecrating Science: Wonder, Knowledge and the Natural World* (Oakland: University of California Press, 2017).
35. Sideris, *Consecrating Science*, 1. Of course, evidence for such negative impacts are theoretical rather than necessarily found in practice. However, I think responsible forms of theology need to be aware of background assumptions and potentially negative environmental impacts.

The wonder that emerges in such movements is, she suggests, rather than counter cultural, as they claim, instead complicit with those cultural forces that have led to the domination of the planet in the first place and the environmental crisis. She argues that impoverished forms of wonder, especially those that celebrate technological advances as part of human history are particularly troubling in so far as they contribute to a form of 'creeping scientism'.[36] Her more constructive solution, to engage in more nuanced forms of wonder that are more richly in tune with ecological sensibilities open up the possibility of an alternative, but, in so far as she avoids explicit constructive forms of theology, leaves a great deal of room for development.

In order to begin to build the basis for an alternative approach, greater philosophical clarity with respect to a philosophy of nature is an important first step in laying the basic framework for robust theological discussions. While, with Aquinas, I would resist *reducing* theology to philosophical analysis, it is important to take current philosophical currents seriously, especially those that open up rather than close down theological articulations of our place in the natural world and the role of the Spirit in creation.

Michael Serres

Michael Serres and Erazim Kohák are two philosophers whose work I have found helpful in this respect. I will discuss just those aspects of their work that intersects with the twin ideas of immanent spiritual presence/transcendence that an understanding of the work of the Spirit in creation presents.

Michael Serres contribution, *The Incandescent*, begins, like Edwards, with a reflection on the incredible cosmic narrative described by scientists that has also been our history, but he aims to critically engage with it, rather than just absorb its assumptions.

Unlike EO Wilson, who traces the dawn of agriculture as a crucial negative moment in human history, Serres points to the impact of modernity on more traditional ways of being and becoming human that went with the flow of the natural world, whereas in the modern context 'the Neolithic has been brought to an end'.[37] Going back in

---

36. Sideris, *Consecrating Science*, 3.
37. Michael Serres, *The Incandescent,* translated by Randolph Burks [2003] (London: Bloomsbury, 2018), 223.

time and imagining ourselves as composed within that vast time of the universe and other creatures along the way to becoming human, he describes that process as a 'contingent masterpiece' that required 'billions of years of attempts, errors and deaths'.[38] It is considering this as part of our history, part of a grand narrative, that is part of a mushrooming bifurcating process that leaves Serres spellbound, so 'unpredictable when it advances, it becomes deterministic when one turns around'.[39] The disappearance of Nature as an entity after the Renaissance signified the use of the term Nature just as 'a set of properties of a being or thing'.[40] What is forgotten, he suggests, is *natura* in the feminine, from the Latin verbal root *nascor* which means, 'what is in the very act of or about to be born, the very process of birth, of emergence of newness'.[41]

Such reflection over billions of years places our limited historical acts in a different light. The violence and sacrifice displayed through the media amounts to what Serres provocatively describes as a return to a new polytheistic tradition, so, he asks, 'Are we aware that we live in a polytheistic era and that a sacred terror similar to that of archaic religions is invading our collectives, admittedly advanced as far as science, technology and reason go but thus returning to backwards times?'[42]

This grand narrative has the power and attraction of a form of enchantment, and while it speaks of 'unpredictable circumstances' and 'unforeseen consequences when the direction of time is followed', it 'seems coherent and directed towards some end or other when reread from downstream to upstream'.[43] The evolution of living things offers a seductive grand narrative that, like Sideris, has religious overtones, so 'thread by thread, piece by piece, act by scene, the sciences keep the world and its inhabitants on tenterhooks through their suspense'.[44] This memory of the past in the evolution of life is what Serres called the genotypic memory in common with every living thing.[45]

---

38. Serres, *The Incandescent*, 9.
39. Serres, *The Incandescent*, 13.
40. Serres, *The Incandescent*, 14
41. Serres, *The Incandescent*, 15.
42. Serres, *The Incandescent*, 16.
43. Serres, *The Incandescent*, 19.
44. Serres, *The Incandescent*, 20.
45. Serres, *The Incandescent*, 24

At the same time, unlike Sideris, he also suggests that we forget this memory of origins at our peril, so a philosophy of nature helps restore that memory to its proper place. He is therefore both critical of but appreciative of the possibilities latent in that memory.[46] In the advancement of evolution, Serres sees differentiation, in progressing it produces a multitude of diversity. Yet in regressing, in de-differentiation and forgetfulness, the human became 'totipotent, global and infinite', a 'counter-species'.[47] The differentiation now is through cultural change 'an ultrafine temporal film over the enormous thickness of the duration of bodies, objects of the sciences of living things . . .'[48] Within that framing of indefiniteness, in what Serres calls 'white concepts', a natural birth takes place, so 'the human is born so transparent, so incandescent that freedom enters into the white class. Not only does freedom concern us, it identifies us.'[49]

The significant contribution that Serres makes to the discussion on the work of the Spirit in creation seems to me is that he is acutely aware of the lure of the grand narrative of the sciences that conjure up archaic memories of the sacred, but also of the importance of situating ourselves critically within the memory of the grand narrative of cosmic history, but without losing a strong sense of human distinctiveness and how this has arisen. This need not lead to an unbridled anthropocentrism in the way that Sideris fears, but a modesty before the vast history of the universe. Humanity has both co-evolved with but is in distinction from the world around us. At the same time, Serres is aware of metaphysical implications. If sciences are going to contribute to contemporary theological discussion, becoming aware of the metaphysical implications of the life sciences that either go beyond their stated outcomes or become more explicit in forms of scientism is of critical importance.

Erazim Kohák

Erazim Kohák's book, *The Embers and the Stars*,[50] is another deeply reflective philosophy of nature, pointing to what we normally

---

46. Serres, *The Incandescent*, 33.
47. Serres, *The Incandescent*, 41.
48. Serres, *The Incandescent*, 43
49. Serres, *The Incandescent*, 62.
50. Erazim Kohák, *The Embers and the Stars: A Philosophical Inquiry into the Moral Sense of Nature* (Chicago: University of Chicago Press, 1984).

overlook in common everyday experiences of the ecological world within which humanity is embedded, but have commonly been overlooked. Instead of contemplating the nature of the cosmos, Kohák takes us to the depths of a forest and invites us to meditate with him on this experience. Like Serres, he finds the technological world in which we now live one of alienation, rather than comfort, though he does not read religious symbolism into it, and recognises that some technologies have the potential to be humanity's servant. And, like Serres, he understands the natural world to be ambiguous and, to an extent, representative of cruelty, rather than an ideal to be sought.

While averring nature romanticism, he insists on letting the natural world speak and absorbing that experience as a basis for his philosophising. For Kohák, humans are fundamentally 'at home in the cosmos', not thrown as in an alien context.[51] For him the dividing line is between the natural world and artefacts, rather than humans and nature, thus coalescing, to a degree, the moral and natural order.[52] The unity of being in the cosmos and the natural world that not only authors such as Aristotle and Aquinas promoted, but also found in the Platonic traditions, complexifies any stereotypes of dualistic thinking in the latter. Rather, the opposition is that 'between the rational order of the cosmos and the contingent, customary ordering of the human world'.[53] As Kohák acknowledges, 'the Christian cosmos is a creation, an ordered meaningful work of God's hands, and the human is set into it as its steward and its integral part'.[54] Christian thinking therefore embraced the idea of humanity as a 'homeward bound wayfarer', rather than 'homeless stranger'.[55]

Our lack of experience of the natural world has, he suggests, deadened our sensibilities and even our moral sense, and to recover that, we need to recover 'the moral sense of nature'.[56] Here he draws on the work of Czech biologist turned philosopher Emanuel Rádl, who understood the natural world as a 'living *physis*, whose multiform strivings are guided by a hidden yet powerful purpose, each creature

51. Kohák, *The Embers*, 8.
52. Kohák, *The Embers*, 9.
53. Kohák, *The Embers*, 10.
54. Kohák, *The Embers*, 10.
55. Kohák, *The Embers*, 11.
56. Kohák, *The Embers*, 13.

charged with its task'.[57] The human moral law is therefore one that is in tune with rather than against the cosmic order. And, in a critical move, like Serres who is exercised by the temporality that he sees in the natural world, Rádl points to the importance of 'the distinctive dimension of eternity which humans add to the temporality of the animate'.[58] What does eternity mean? Not so much infinite extension of time, but an awareness of 'the absolute reality of being'.[59] This comes back, therefore, to the ontological dimension that I raised in Aquinas' discussion of the various sciences. In this it goes further than the positive aspect of temporality found in the process philosophy of growth. Kohák rejects, however, Rádl's resort to tradition alone as being sufficient for the task, given its ambiguous moral history.

The insight that Kohák wishes to promote, instead, is that arising as embedded in the experience of the natural world, 'the moral sense that emerges when the fading daylight no longer blinds us to the deep bond among beings but darkness has not yet obliterated their distinctness. It is at dusk that humans can perceive the moral sense of life and the rightness of seasons'.[60] In reclaiming 'the gift of solitude' Kohák touches on a form of nature mysticism, that is then further elaborated through what he terms 'the gift of pain', which while it is 'an intrinsic part pf the rhyme and intimate part of life',[61] is one whose surplus is still necessarily resisted.[62] The power of nature is one that for him, has learnt the task of absorbing pain, rather than avoiding it. So, 'the forest is different, it lives, it absorbs the grief'.[63]

Towards a Sophiology of the Spirit in Creation

Like Kohák, Edwards' understanding of the natural world is also rooted in his existential experience of it. I have some sympathy for such an approach, as it grounds theological reflection in our own practice of love for and wonder in the face of the natural world, in all its power to attract and at times repel. While Serres and Kohák

---

57. Kohák, *The Embers*, 14.
58. Kohák, *The Embers*, 18.
59. Kohák, *The Embers*, 18.
60. Kohák, *The Embers*, 33.
61. Kohák, *The Embers*, 41.
62. Kohák, *The Embers*, 42.
63. Kohák, *The Embers*, 45.

made important philosophical contributions, their work falls short of a developed theology of the Spirit in creation. In his work on the Trinity as the attractor and energy of love in an ecological perspective, Edwards begins to work out in more detail what it means to speak of the work of the Spirit in creation, understood within a framework of the Trinity.[64]

Although, as I argued above, Edwards generally avoids discussing details of how God acts in the world, or a 'God of the gaps', he is prepared to suggest that the power of self-transcendence (drawn from Rahner) is particularly evident in critical transition points, including the transition from life to non-life and from life to the human.[65] Edwards maintains the integrity of the sciences by suggesting, following John Haught, that the Holy Spirit works at a different 'level' from scientific understanding of evolutionary processes.[66] What he does not discuss, as I indicated earlier, is conflicts in understanding that arise if both are taken equally seriously, or the philosophical and religious implications of scientific grand narratives. An area that I would like to develop towards the end of this essay is hinted at in Edwards when he suggests that 'All things are created through the wisdom of God and in the life-giving Spirit . . .'[67]

Sergius Bulgakov developed an elaborate understanding of the Trinity and the work of the Spirit in creation through his sophianic pneumatology.[68] Although a full discussion of his pneumatology and its relevance for ecological understanding in the light of current trends in science would require much further elaboration,[69] a brief summary is as follows. Bulgakov develops the importance of what he calls

---

64. This is discussed in Edwards, *Partaking of God*, 74–87 and Edwards, *The Natural World and God*, 67–109. Ecological aspects of the work of the Spirit are also developed in *The Natural World and God*, 100–133. While Edwards argued for the ecological relevance of a theology of both the Spirit and the Word, I am focusing on his understanding of the Spirit in this chapter.

65. Edwards, *Partaking of God*, 76.

66. Edwards, *Partaking of God*, 77.

67. Edwards, *The Natural World and God*, 117.

68. Sergius Bulgakov, *The Comforter*, translated by Boris Jakim (Grand Rapids: Eerdmans, 2004).

69. I have begun to work out this task in Celia Deane-Drummond, 'The Spirit of Wisdom: Sergius Bulgakov's Sophianic Trinitarian Ontology in Dialogue with Contemporary Biology', paper delivered at a conference entitled, *New Trinitarian Ontologies*, Cambridge University, 13–15th September, 2019.

trinitarity, which counters any mathematical logic in being one and three simultaneously. He also elevates the role of the Holy Spirit in a significant way, enlarging the idea of the self-revealing spirituality of the Spirit in the Third Hypostasis. The tri-hypostatic, self-revelation of Divine Love is the self-revelation of Ousia-Sophia. In the context of trends towards holism in contemporary biology, that are increasingly influenced by ecological science, his position remains coherent. However, just as Bulgakov was unafraid to name the distinctive contribution of theology in contradistinction from scientific narratives, any attempt to merge ecological thinking arising from the biological sciences and trinitarian theology is, I suggest, misguided. Bulgakov's distinctive trinitarian ontology offers a substantial alternative to deconstructive postmodern philosophies that tend to erode both theological and modern scientific frames of reference. In this respect it is a more robust alternative to Michael Serres' philosophical stance, who leans too far towards postmodern deconstruction, even while showing up in a clear way the limitations of alternatives.

Tentative conclusions

I began this chapter with a brief overview of Denis Edwards' pioneering understanding of the work of the Spirit in creation, probing specifically how he understood the action of God as Spirit in creation and its compatibility with evolutionary and ecological frameworks in the light of alternatives. While generally sympathetic to the use of the metaphysical principle of primary and secondary causation, I suggested that rather greater awareness of the medieval understanding of the sciences as natural philosophy is important if that metaphysic is to be adopted in a philosophically consistent way in a contemporary context. I also probed recent philosophies of nature, and the extent to which they compete with or complement Christian theological positions on the work of the Spirit in creation and their coherence for environmental ethics.

My conclusion overall is that a claim for science and theology working at different 'levels' is true in as much as the action of God is not of the same order of being as the operational world of things, but inconsistencies in conclusions need to be named rather than avoided. Theologians need not shy away from acknowledging divergence from scientific analysis. Gestures towards theological positions through secular discussions of the sacred and natural transcendence may be welcomed in so far as they leave room for a theological voice to be taken seriously, but treated cautiously if they are not going to replace rather than complement theological insights. Edwards' work on the role of the Spirit in creation as Rahnerian self-transcendence can fire up greater attention to the work of the Spirit in our own lives, transforming sensibilities towards rather than away from greater ecological responsibility.

I have suggested that Sergius Bulgakov's sophiology is also a valuable resource in constructing a theological ontology in so far as it elevates rather than minimises the role of the Spirit in both the life of the Trinity and in the created world. As such, learning to contemplate and dwell in participation with that Spirit will relieve our ecological anxiety and allow us to act in ways that respond to that Spirit dwelling in creation.

Acknowledgements

I am grateful to Ted Peters for the invitation to contribute this chapter, and of course, to Denis Edwards, who, though no longer with us in person, will continue to inspire future generations.

In Dialogue:
Athanasius, Rahner and Edwards on the Trinity

Joseph A Bracken, SJ

'Deep incarnation needs to be a trinitarian theology of Word and Spirit.'[1]
– Denis Edwards

Abstract: Denis Edwards employs the notion of deep incarnation as originally formulated by Neils Henrik Gregersen to link the Neo-Platonic understanding of the God-world relationship in the theology of Athanasius in the fourth century with the Neo-Thomistic understanding of the God-world relationship in the theology of Karl Rahner. The author argues that, despite certain linguistic similarities, the two world views are very different. One stresses the transcendence of God to the world; the other, the immanence of God in human self-awareness. Instead, one should work out an evolutionary metaphysics of becoming which places emphasis on change and evolution rather than on permanence and a fixed mode of operation.

Key Words: Neo-Platonism, Neo-Thomism, evolution, systems-oriented thinking, God-World relationship.

Shortly before his untimely death, the well-known Australian theologian Denis Edwards submitted to Orbis Books in the United States a manuscript entitled *Deep Incarnation: The Cross as Sacrament of God's Redemptive Suffering with Creatures*. It has since been published, read, and appreciated by many.

In this final testament, Edwards reviewed the understanding of the Christian God-world relationship first in contemporary systematic theology, then in the theology of Irenaeus and Athanasius in the Patristic period of the Church's history and the work of the

---

1. Denis Edwards, *Deep Incarnation: God's Redemptive Suffering with Creatures* (Maryknoll NY: Orbis, 2019), 106.

German theologian Karl Rahner in the mid-twentieth century. Afterwards, Edwards set forth his own understanding of the God-world relationship in terms of what Niels Henrik Gregersen has called 'deep incarnation', that is the proposal that the Divine Word has become incarnate not only in the person of Jesus of Nazareth but also in creation as a whole in virtue of becoming incarnate in Jesus.[2]

Edwards believes that there are clear inklings of the notion of deep incarnation in the writings of Irenaeus and Athanasius. For that purpose, he cites numerous passages out of their published works. Likewise, relying upon Rahner's insights into an evolutionary understanding of Christian eschatology, he sets forth the latter's thesis that in Jesus' descent into hell after his death on the cross and in his resurrection on Easter Sunday the triune God incorporated into the divine life the totality of the world of creation.[3] Then in the final chapter of the book Edwards elaborates on his own proposal that the cross of Christ is the sacrament of God's redemptive suffering with creatures and that Christ's resurrection is a promise of healing and fulfilment that embraces all creatures.[4]

A Critique of Edwards' Approach to Systematic Theology

As with his other writings in systematic theology, this latest book by Edwards is carefully crafted. He cites a wide variety of other theologians, past and present, in support of his chosen topic each time. Likewise, he tries to situate his specifically theological reflections in the context of an evolutionary world view as currently explained in contemporary natural science.[5] Finally, he employs an orthodox trinitarian understanding of the God-world relationship in line with

---

2. Niels Henrik Gregersen, 'Cur Deus Caro: Jesus and the Cosmic Story', in *Theology and Science*, 11 (2013): 370–93; also *Incarnation: On the Scope and Depth of Christology* (Minneapolis, MN; Fortress Press, 2015).
3. Denis Edwards, *Deep Incarnation: The Cross as Sacrament of God's Redemptive Suffering with Creatures* (Maryknoll, NY: Orbis Books, 2019), 96–99.
4. Edwards, *Deep Incarnation*, 120–128.
5. See, for example, *The God of Evolution: A Trinitarian Theology* (Mahwah, NJ: Paulist Press, 1999); *Breath of Life: A Theology of the Creator Spirit* (Maryknoll, NY: Orbis Books, 2004); *How God Acts: Creation, Redemption, and Special Divine Action* (Minneapolis, MN: Fortress Press, 2010); and *Partaking of God: Trinity Evolution and Ecology* (Collegeville, MN: Liturgical Press, 2014).

Church teaching. As a result, I find myself agreeing with his overall theological arguments without any difficulty.[6]

Even so, I am uneasy with the philosophical rigor of his thought. For example, if one sides with natural scientists in the claim that the route of cosmic evolution is not predetermined but based on a process of trial and error, how is this to be reconciled with the distinction between the primary causality of God and the secondary causality of creatures from moment to moment? Either the omniscience/omnipotence of God in classical metaphysics is compromised or the freedom of choice for creatures, above all, human beings, is called into question. If one further claims that God's self-bestowal from moment to moment 'enables and empowers creaturely self-transcendence',[7] then how is that claim to be reconciled with the difference between efficient and formal causality in God's activity vis-à-vis creatures? For God to empower an entity to achieve self-transcendence in a free choice, God must give that entity (for example, a human being) a new substantial form. But if God does that through divine efficient causality, is the creature free to accept or reject God's offer? If not, either God is not omnipotent or the creature is not genuinely free to make its own decision.

My intention here is not to reproach Edwards for inconsistency in thinking through the metaphysical implications of his basic understanding of the God-world relationship, but only to make clear how difficult it is reconcile with one another the categories and basically *apriori* approach to reality of the classical metaphysics of Being with the empirically oriented hypothesis/verification approach to reality in natural science. As a result, a philosopher/theologian such as Edwards may be strongly tempted to resort to metaphors drawn from Sacred Scripture or common-sense experience rather than to systematically ordered concepts to describe the God-world relationship. For example, is the term 'deep incarnation' more a metaphor with multiple possible interpretations vis-à-the work of previous theologians (ancient and modern) than a precisely defined concept within a fully developed philosophical cosmology? I return to that question at the end of this article.

---

6. See, for example, Joseph A Bracken, *The World in the Trinity: Open-Ended Systems in Science and Religion* (Minneapolis, MN: Fortress Press, 2014), 96–98.
7. Edwards, *How God Acts*, 43.

Comparing the Differing World Views of Athanasius and Rahner

In this second part of the article, however, I compare with one another the understanding of the God-world relationship in the theology of Athanasius and Karl Rahner. For they seem to reflect two different world views. That is Athanasius focused on God's transcendence to creation even in the work of bringing about its transformation and ultimate deification; Rahner focused instead on the self-transcendence of human beings in responding to the felt presence of God in their ongoing awareness of the world around them. Athanasius, accordingly, was operating out of a Neo-Platonic metaphysical frame of reference even in his description of God's loving 'condescension' to the world of creation.[8] Rahner was instead thinking more empirically or phenomenologically in his analysis of human striving for self-transcendence in virtue of God's felt presence to oneself. Furthermore, separating Athanasius and Rahner were many centuries of philosophical/theological reflection and major advances in the scientific understanding of physical reality.

At the beginning of the seventeenth century, for example, Francis Bacon proposed that induction, careful study of empirical data, should take precedence over deduction, rational argument from antecedents to consequences, in scientific research.[9] The easiest way to analyze the plethora of empirical data, however, is through mathematics: that is, the measurement of what is quantitatively measurable in the data while ignoring other qualitative features and then the formulation of universal laws of nature in terms of mathematical equations.[10] Copernicus, Galileo, Brahe and Kepler used this mathematical approach to reality in their research into astronomy with considerable success so that the ancient geocentric understanding of the cosmos was gradually replaced in scientific circles by a heliocentric understanding of the solar system. Shortly thereafter René Descartes grounded his philosophical world view not in God as Creator of heaven and earth, but in his own individual human experience: 'I think; therefore I am.'[11] Thereby Descartes

---

8.   Edwards, *Deep Incarnation*, 75.
9.   WT Jones, *A History of Western Philosophy*, 4 volumes, 2nd edition (New York: Harcourt, Brace & World, 1969), II, 77–87.
10. Jones, *A History of Western Philosophy*, 88–91.
11. René Descartes, *Meditations on First Philosophy*, II, in *The Philososphical Works of Descartes*, 2 volumes, translated by Elizabeth S Haldane and GRT Ross (Cambridge, UK: Cambridge University Press, 1978), I, 150.

shifted his starting-point for philosophical reflection from ontology, the study of Being in all its forms, to Human Being with a focus on individual subjective experience.

When it became apparent that this purely subjective approach to reality undercut the objectivity of the known laws of nature, Immanuel Kant in the late eighteenth century proposed a new 'Copernican Revolution': namely, that the laws of nature are to be derived not from direct observation of empirical data in the world outside the self but from introspection into the workings of the mind within the self.[12] Given his assumption that the human mind worked the same way in all human beings, Kant believed that he had thereby rescued the objectivity of the laws of nature.

In due time, of course, scientific research into the language and thought-patterns of human beings in different cultures and in different parts of the world made clear that clear proof of the objectivity of the laws of nature was still lacking in Kant's Copernican Revolution. The scientific community, however, was already working with a new understanding of what is meant by scientific method. That is, they had adopted, at least in practice, a hypothesis-verification approach to the study of empirical data with the prior understanding that any given hypothesis can and should be tested for its verifiability by other scientists in the same field of research.

Many, if not most, Christian systematic theologians at that time, however, did not endorse this hypothesis-verification approach to truth and objectivity in the presentation of their views. For, in their minds the truth-claims of any scheme in systematic theology must instead be in accord with the manifest truth of divine revelation in Sacred Scripture and/or the unchanging teaching of the Church over the centuries. At the same time, the influence of Kant's *Critique of Pure Reason* with its focus on individual subjectivity as the starting-point for philosophical reflection on physical reality was evident in the work of some French-speaking Roman Catholic philosopher/ theologians at the end of the nineteenth century who in turn significantly influenced the intellectual formation of Karl Rahner some years later.

---

12. Immanuel Kant, 'Preface to Second Edition' in *Kant's Critique of Pure Reason*, translated by Norman Kemp Smith (New York: St Martin's Press, 1956), B xvi.

From Pierre Rousselot, for example, Rahner gained the insight that, if God is Pure Spirit or pure intelligibility, then God is co-known in every act of human knowing. Hence, faith is not primarily based on objective acceptance of Church doctrine as a set of propositions but on a felt presence of God to a human being in the subjective act of cognition.[13] From Joseph Maréchal in his book *Le Point de Depart de la Metaphysique*, Volume 5, Rahner gained approximately the same insight: that the dynamism of the human mind is toward full intelligibility, namely, God as the perfect union of mind and matter.[14]

Still another influence on Rahner came, of course, from his doctoral studies at Freiburg in Breisgau where he attended classes taught by Martin Heidegger who had published *Being and Time* some years earlier. *Being and Time* was a phenomenological study of *Dasein* (Human Being) as Being-in-the-World.[15] Rahner's dissertation *Geist in Welt (Spirit in the World)* by its very title indicated that he too was interested in a more empirically oriented approach to traditional scholastic philosophy and theology. Perhaps for that reason Rahner's dissertation was rejected by his dissertation director at Freiburg, Martin Honecker. For, whereas in scholastic thought Being is identified with God as the supreme Being, Being for Heidegger is rather the power-to-be manifest to human beings in and through experience of the world around them. By grounding his own philosophical starting-point in human subjectivity rather than in God as the First Principle of Being, Rahner was betraying the scholastic tradition.

In fairness to Honecker, Rahner was in fact moving from the context of a strictly defined metaphysics of Being to that of a more fluid and empirically hypothetical metaphysics of Becoming. For example, in *Foundations of Christian Faith* published toward the end of his life in 1984,[16] Rahner discusses in success four interrelated topics: The Interlocking of Philosophy and Theology, Man as Person and Subject, Man as Transcendent Being, and Man as Responsible and

---

13. Pierre Rousselot, *The Intellectualism of St Thomas*, translated by James Mahoney (New York: Sheed and Ward, 1935).

14. Joseph Maréchal, *Le Point de Depart de la Metaphysique* (Paris: Desclée de Brouwer, 1964).

15. Martin Heidegger, *Being and Time*, translated by John Macquarrie (New York: Harper & Row, 1962), 107.

16. Karl Rahner, *Foundations of Christian Faith: An Introduction to the Idea of Christianity*, translated by William V Dych (New York: Crossroads, 1978).

Free. With reference to the first topic, Rahner asserts the necessity of a close link between the empirically based findings of philosophical anthropology and the faith-claims of systematic theology. In dealing with the second topic he claims that we experience ourselves 'precisely as subject and person insofar as' we become conscious of ourselves 'as the product of what is radically foreign to' us. 'Being a person, then, means the self-possession of a subject as such in a conscious and free relationship to the totality of itself.'[17]

Vis-à-vis the topic of Man as Transcendent Being, Rahner notes: the human person 'is and remains a transcendent being, that is, he [or she] is that existent to whom the silent and uncontrollable infinity of reality is always present as mystery. This makes [persons] totally open to this mystery and precisely in this way he [or she] becomes conscious of himself [or herself] as person and as subject.'[18] The infinity of reality that is present to human beings as mystery is in the first place God and in the second place the world as the virtually infinite reality of creation.[19] Finally, in discussing Man as Responsible and Free, Rahner asserts: 'By the fact that' we humans in our transcendence exist 'as open and indetermined, we are 'at the same time responsible for' ourselves. Each of us is left to ourself and placed in our own hands not only in our knowledge, but also in our own '*actions*'.[20]

Unquestionably, Rahner's focus on human subjectivity and the possibility of an interpersonal relationship with God as a felt presence in one's experience of self, others and the world of creation has much greater appeal to contemporary Christians than the classical Aristotelian-Thomistic understanding of the God-world relationship in terms of abstract cause-effect relations. But there is a danger in thus moving from ontology, the study of Being in all its finite ramifications, to psychology or philosophical anthropology, the study of Human Being on a much more empirical basis. One danger, of course, is anthropocentrism, seeing the natural world as ordered to the satisfaction of human goals and values rather than as an objective reality in its own right that is often resistant to the satisfaction of one's current needs and desires.

---

17. Rahner, *Foundations of Christian Faith*, 29–30.
18. Rahner, *Foundations of Christian Faith*, 35.
19. Rahner, *Foundations of Christian Faith*, 81–89.
20. Rahner, *Foundations of Christian Faith*, 35.

Furthermore, any such personalised world view can be challenged by others as self-deception or at least open to other interpretations. For example, to claim with Rahner, as noted above, that 'the silent and uncontrollable infinity of reality' is the tri-personal God of Christian revelation is strictly speaking a faith-claim, not an immediate inference from the empirical fact of 'being in the world'. For the world can be legitimately interpreted as a steady-state universe or a cyclical recurrence of a cosmic process, in both cases without beginning or end.[21] Or Jean Paul Sartre was possibly right in claiming that humanity 'is a useless passion', condemned to a futile grasp at a reality or an ideal beyond its comprehension.[22]

Thomas Aquinas in his *Summa theologiae* added rational plausibility to his faith-claim that God exists by employing the categories of Aristotelian causality (material, formal, efficient and final) to the analysis of empirical data from common sense experience.[23] But Rahner had no pre-given philosophical categories in which to set forth his new process-oriented understanding of human subjectivity and an interpersonal relation with God. Instead, he had to claim that the Aristotelian-Thomistic metaphysics of Being could be adjusted to an evolutionary understanding of the God-world relationship. For example, in *Foundations of Christian Faith,* Rahner says that humanity 'is the event of an absolute and forgiving *self*-communication of God'.[24] Rahner then adds: 'This self-communication means precisely that objectivity of gift and communication which is the climax of subjectivity on the side of the one communicating and the one receiving.'[25]

The above statement fits well within a metaphysics of inter-subjectivity such as that proposed by Martin Buber in his book *I-Thou:* 'I require a You to become; becoming I, I say you.'[26] But it is

---

21. Nancey Murphy and George FR Ellis, *On the Moral Nature of the Universe: Theology, Cosmology and Ethics* (Minneapolis, MN: Fortress Press, 1996), 45–47.

22. See, for example, Jean Paul Sartre's comments on *mauvaise foi* in *Being and Nothingness: An Essay on Phenomenological Ontology,* translated by Hazel Barnes (New York: Washington Square Press, 1992), 86–119.

23. Sancti Thomae Aquinatis, *Summa Theologiae* (Madrid: Biblioteca de Autores Cristianos, 1951), I, Q 2, art 3.

24. Rahner, *Foundations of Christian Faith,* 117.

25. Rahner, *Foundations of Christian Faith,* 118.

26. Martin Buber, *I and Thou,* translated by Walter Kaufmann (New York: Scribner's, 1970), 62.

not compatible with the causal relation between God and creatures in the *Summa theologiae* of Aquinas. Aquinas states very clearly that God is Pure Actuality, therefore perfect in every respect.[27] Hence, God is not internally affected by God's relation to creatures. God is merciful to creatures in virtue of God's infinite goodness, but not out of compassion or sympathy for a creature in its pain or suffering.[28] Finally, a fully reciprocal relation between God and creatures is impossible within a traditional Thomistic frame of reference in which God exercises primary causality for what happens and the creature only exercises secondary or instrumental causality in making it happen.[29]

A Systems-Oriented Trinitarian Theology

In the third and last part of this essay, I offer a sketch of a Trinitarian world view which is grounded in a systems-oriented approach to reality that has been used in the natural sciences, above all, the life-sciences, to explain the mechanics of evolution, that is, the emergence of higher-order systems out of antecedent lower-order systems that in and of themselves offer little or no explanation for the unexpected appearance of a higher level of structure and internal organization within physical reality. Admittedly, systems theory as employed in the natural sciences is not immediately applicable to a Christian trinitarian understanding of the God-world relationship. But, as Granville Henry points out in his book *Christianity and the Images of Science,* Christians have always tended to incorporate the best natural science of the day into their own understanding of the God-world relationship once the legitimate boundaries of both approaches to reality have been properly assessed.[30] Christian philosophers and theologians, accordingly, should be willing to experiment with models or paradigms from the sciences for use in their own discipline.

---

27. Aquinas, *Summa Theologiae,* I, Q 4, art 1.
28. Aquinas, *Summa Theologiae,* Q 21, art 3.
29. Aquinas, *Summa Theologiae,* Q 22, art 3.
30. Granville C Henry, *Christianity and the Images of Science* (Macon, GA: Smyth & Helwys, 1998), 4: 'I intend to show that images and philosophical perspectives derivative from science have conditioned most Christian's understanding about God, religious history, the divinity of Christ, miracles, the nature of the future, and our souls, as well as other biblical and theological topics.'

One key value of a systems-oriented approach to Christian systematic theology, of course, is the fact that it places fresh emphasis on the social implications of the gospel message. The mission of Jesus was not simply to 'save souls' from eternal damnation but also to reform the social order of his day.[31] No doubt, there are many reasons for an otherwise conscientious Christian to fail to see the intrinsic connection between concern for one's personal salvation and work for the reform of the social order in contemporary society. But one reason might be the enduring influence of the philosophy of Aristotle with its claim that 'substance', an individual entity existing in its own right, is the First Category of Being.[32] Common-sense experience likewise seems to suggest that only individual entities ultimately exist. Accordingly, communities and other socially organised institutions are all too often judged as transient realities that endure or fall apart, dependent upon the will of their individual members from one generation to another. Thus, for many theologians the focus in church teaching should be on fostering the spiritual well-being of the individual Christian rather than on studying the significant role that communities and other economic and political institutions play in the decisions made by that individual on a day-to-day basis.

Yet Charles Sanders Peirce makes clear the socially organised character of life with his primordial categories of Firstness, Secondness and Thirdness.[33] An individual entity is an instance of Firstness. But that entity is always dealing with other individual entities and the external environment in terms of Secondness, namely, that which stands over against Firstness as something to be dealt with. As a result, the individual entity (Firstness) sets forth its relation to others (Secondness) in terms of Thirdness, an external sign or symbol of that relationship. For example, a citizen of the United States gives witness to his citizenship and affiliation with other Americans in

---

31. *Cf* Joseph A Bracken, 'Personal Resurrection into the Mystical Body of Christ', in *The Way* (July 2016): 75–87. I use a systems-oriented approach to the notion of body to explore the connection between the desire for personal salvation and one's efforts at reform of the social order in contemporary society.

32. *Aristotle's Metaphysics,* translated by Hippocrates G Apostle (Grinnell, IA, 1979): Book Z 1028a.

33. *Collected Papers of Charles Sanders Peirce,* Volume 6, edited by Charles Hartshorne and Paul Weiss (Cambridge, MA: Harvard University Press, 1935), 32. NB: Reference is to paragraph number, not page number.

saluting the American flag or joining in celebration of the Fourth of July and other national holidays.

Hence, *pace* Aristotle and his notion of substance as the First Category of Being, no individual entity exists in and for itself alone. It comes into existence within a pre-given social environment, contributes to that system by its own individual existence and activity, and is ultimately absorbed back into the energy-field proper to the system when it ceases to exist. Admittedly, systems cannot exist without individual entities as its parts or members, but in the final analysis individual entities come and go but systems remain even with gradual changes in their structure and mode of operation over time.[34]

If then systems of various kinds rather than individual entities are the real 'building-blocks' of physical reality, it makes sense to experiment with the notion of system as the model or paradigm for a process-oriented metaphysics within which to set forth a new evolutionary understanding of the God-world relationship. Here a Christian may immediately object that the God of biblical revelation is clearly not an impersonal system but a transcendent individual entity. But one should realise that the triune God of Christian belief can, in fact, be quite readily explained as a system, that is, a community or a corporate unity of dynamically interrelated parts or members. There are, of course, many kinds of systems. Some systems constitute the existence and activity of individual entities (for example, a human being or some other higher-order animal as a functioning mind-body system). But other systems govern the existence and activity of corporate realities (for example, communities or physical environments). Both types of systems fulfil the generic definition of a system as an ongoing unity of dynamically interrelated parts or members.

Furthermore, if in line with classical metaphysics one still thinks of the triune God as a transcendent individual entity, then logical inconsistencies within classical metaphysics immediately arise: for example, Aquinas's understanding of the divine persons as 'subsistent relations' in his *Summa theologiae*.[35] Since relations in Aristotle's metaphysics are treated as contingent qualifications of an already existing substance or individual entity, then, if the divine persons are

---

34. Alfred North Whitehead, *Adventures of Ideas* (New York: Free Press Paperback, 1967), 204. Whitehead uses the term 'society' rather than 'system'. But reference is to the same reality of an ongoing social reality.
35. Aquinas, *Summa Theologiae*, I, Q 29, art 4.

considered to be relational entities, they do not endanger the unitary reality of God as One.[36] But if each of the divine persons are likewise 'subsistent relations', then each of them is identical with the full reality of God (the divine essence),[37] But then, how can three entities that exist in their own right still be only one individual entity? Thinking of the triune God as a community or corporately organized system, however, seems to make more sense since it corresponds more closely to common sense experience. Quite possibly Aquinas himself may have been aware of the logic of that argument but felt obliged to treat Questions 27–43 of Part One of the *Summa* as an exception to his customary use of Aristotelian categories to explain the God-world relationship everywhere else in the *Summa*. Yet, while this line of thought might have been too big an 'imaginative leap' for Aquinas to make in his day, is it still too big a leap for contemporary Christian philosophers and theologians, given widespread acceptance of the dynamically interrelated character of physical reality?[38]

Moreover, if one accepts the notion of the Trinity as a divine life-system, then one has a logical precedent for thinking of all the finite things of this world as likewise systems or components of systems. In other words, the classic understanding of the image of God (*imago Dei)* in systematic theology should no longer be restricted to individual human beings in the exercise of their mental powers but should be extended to all living entities and their components insofar as they are linked together to constitute specifically social realities (for example, human communities, animal herds, flocks of birds, schools of fish, overall physical environments, etc). Thus understood, only the cosmic process as a whole can adequately represent the corporate image of God as Trinity.

In addition, within this systems-oriented understanding of the God-world relationship, the world of creation not only imitates the divine being from afar through the principle of the analogy of being as in classical Aristotelian-Thomistic metaphysics,[39] but actively participates in the divine life as a set of hierarchically ordered subsystems that still retain their own finite mode of operation.

36. Aquinas, *Summa Theologiae*, I, Q 30, art 1.
37. Aquinas, *Summa Theologiae*, I, Q 29, art 4.
38. The phrase 'imaginative leap' is borrowed from Whitehead, *Process and Reality,* 4. *Cf* also Joseph A Bracken, 'Subsistent Relation: Mediating Concept for a New Synthesis?', in *Journal of Religion,* 64 (April, 1984): 188–204.
39. Aquinas, *Summa Theologiae*, I, Q 13, art 6.

Mini-systems such as atoms, for example, do not cease to function as atoms when they become co-constituents of a molecule; similarly, molecules do not lose their specific identity when they are parts or members of cells as still more complex systems. Hence, the notion of panentheism in which creatures can exist within the divine being without ceasing to be themselves as finite realities in their own right seems to make quite good sense within a field-or systems-oriented approach to reality.

A systems-oriented interpretation of the Christian doctrine of the Incarnation illustrates my point here. In the conciliar decree of the Council of Chalcedon, one reads that Jesus as the Incarnate Word exists in 'two natures unconfused, unchangeable, undivided and inseparable'.[40] If the two natures be understood as dynamically interrelated life-systems, then the life-system proper to the humanity of Jesus exists in subordination to the life-system proper to the divinity of Jesus but retains its own finite mode of operation. That is, the human life-system of Jesus necessarily places restraints on the way that the divine life-system within Jesus could work. Jesus felt fatigue and hunger along with periodic feelings of joy or sadness, even anger, in dealing with other people. The divine life-system normally works in and through the human life-system with all its creaturely limitations. But sometimes the divinity or divine life-system in Jesus notably enhances the natural capabilities of Jesus's humanity or human life-system (for example, in the working of miracles and in the exercise of unexpected wisdom and resourcefulness both in preaching and in dealing with other people).

In similar fashion, one can employ this systems-oriented approach to the Christian doctrine of creation so as to provide a solid conceptual basis for the notion of deep incarnation as set forth by Niels Henrik Gregersen and endorsed by Edwards (*cf* above). My argument here is as follows. First of all, in line with one's understanding of the mode of operation of other systems in physical reality, one presupposes that the divine life-system or the communitarian life of the three divine persons is itself grounded in an all-encompassing energy-field. That is, by their ongoing dynamic interrelation the divine persons both draw from and contribute to an underlying energy-field as the vital source of their life together.

---

40. *Cf The Teaching of the Catholic Church*, edited by Josef Neuner, Heinrich Roos and Karl Rahner, translated by Geoffrey Stevens (Staten Island, NY: Society of Saint Paul, 1967), 154, No 302.

Second, if, as most theoretical physicists believe, the cosmic process (or at least the current 'epoch' of the cosmic process) began with a 'Big Bang' within a pre-existent energy-field, then it conceivably began within God, that is, within the unbounded energy-field proper to the three divine persons in their ongoing dynamic interrelationship. Accordingly, the world has never existed apart from God. It has always existed within and drawn its capacity for growth and development from the divine energy-field even though the world as a cosmic process still functions according to its own organisational principles.

Third, the cosmic process as a result puts constraints on the way that the divine persons can interact with their creatures. That is, if the divine persons wish to share the divine life with their creatures, they have to conform to the laws governing the growth in size and complexity of the cosmic process.

Accordingly, the self-manifestation or 'incarnation' of the divine persons within the world of creation logically had to begin with the Big Bang. That is, the first manifestation of the divine life in this world was an enormous burst of energy from the divine energy-field. Over billions of years that same spontaneous burst of energy condensed and took shape in terms of galaxies of stars and planetary systems. This growth in size and complexity at the pre-animate level of existence and activity thus represented a more advanced 'incarnation' of the divine life in the world of creation. Finally, after a long period of growth and complexity in the various kinds of plant and animal species that eventually appeared on this earth, the triune God became much more intimately incarnate in Jesus of Nazareth as a divine-human individual person.

The Christian doctrine of the Incarnation, however, is best understood as an ongoing process rather than as a singular event for one individual entity within the cosmic process. Hence, while in Jesus the self-manifestation of the divine life in this world reached a definite climax, the end-goal of this incarnational process has yet to be achieved and will only take place at the end of the world when the cosmic Christ (as prophesised in Ephesians and Colossians) will be fully acknowledged as the summation of all things in heaven and on earth.

As I see it, only in this way does the term 'deep incarnation' move beyond the realm of symbol or metaphor and into a systematically organised world view that is basically compatible with the traditional understanding of the Christian God-world relationship. This systems-oriented understanding of the Christian God-world relationship is, nevertheless, tentative and inevitably perspectival. For, it is clearly contingent upon the possibility that a metaphysical scheme better than the current systems-oriented explanation of the God-world relationship will become available for use in Christian systematic theology. But for the moment, a systems-oriented approach to the God-world relationship seems to represent a more timely and logically consistent explanation of Christian doctrinal belief than that provided by Aristotelian-Thomistic metaphysics even in the hands of a creative thinker like Denis Edwards.

Following the Deeply Incarnate Christ: Discipleship in the Midst of Environmental Crisis

Joseph E Lenow

'Both the scientific worldview of our time and the ecological crisis we face require a renewed theology of the natural world . . . A central emphasis of my own work has been the attempt to locate a theology of the natural world right at the heart of Christian faith.'[1]
– Denis Edwards

Abstract: This essay assesses the significance and offers three proposals for extending the theology of deep incarnation, a major theme in Denis Edwards's later writings. Deep incarnation maintains the virtues while avoiding the failures of each of the three dominant approaches to environmental theology: (1) ecojustice, (2) stewardship, and (3) ecological spirituality. Finally, I propose three trajectories for deep incarnation's future development: movement toward a 'Christic ecology' that recognises the interconnection of natural and biological process; the localisation of analysis of Christ's presence in the natural world, in service of eco-liberation; and the development of new liturgical and devotional practices rooted in deep incarnation.

Keywords: deep incarnation; christology; environmental theology; climate change; bioregionalism

Theology often arrives too late. Christian supersessionism and an attendant anti-Judaism propagated themselves almost entirely unchecked across two millennia before coming under serious scrutiny in the wake of the Shoah. Settler colonialism and the transatlantic slave trade were enthusiastically supported by the dominant theological tradition for hundreds of years, in spite of what now seem to us their evident moral horrors. Judged against the timescale of church history,

---

1. Denis Edwards, *The Natural World and God: Theological Explorations* (Adelaide, Australia: ATF Press, 2017), 8–9.

we have only just begun the work of disentangling our theology and ecclesial life from the evils of patriarchy and racism; and the world of academic theology has only just begun to acknowledge the damage that has been wrought by homophobia and transphobia. Whether we describe this state of affairs in a spiritual register as a consequence of the ignorance of the Good produced in us by sin, or more concretely as a result of the Church's accommodation to the worldly institutions which offer it wealth and power, theology is often inexcusably tardy. Theology is only able to identify sin after the damage has already been done.

It remains to be seen whether theology is too late to prevent the ecological catastrophe unfolding around us. If we are not it will be because of thinkers such as Denis Edwards, one of his generation's most perceptive and influential thinkers on the relation between God and the natural world. Edwards compellingly set forth a theological vision in which being joined to Christ's death and resurrection and being knit into the Body of Christ necessarily affects how we relate to the non-human creation. Ingredient to our redemption from sin and reconciliation to God is a changed relationship to the world that God has made.

In the last fifteen years of his life, Edwards increasingly articulated this conviction through a theology of deep incarnation and the emphasis that he placed on this concept in his later works would alone be enough to commend it to us as a resource for rethinking our place within the natural world.[2] As developed by Edwards and other leading thinkers at the intersection of systematic and environmental theology, deep incarnation holds the potential to be one of the most important christological movements of the twenty-first century, providing a key link between the Christian intellectual tradition and

---

2. Edwards' first discussion of deep incarnation may be found at Denis Edwards, *Ecology at the Heart of Faith: The Change of Heart that Leads to a New Way of Living on Earth* (Maryknoll, NY: Orbis Books, 2006), 52–60; see also his *Partaking of God: Trinity, Evolution, and Ecology* (Collegeville, MN: Liturgical Press, 2014), 54–67, and most fully, Denis Edwards, *Deep Incarnation: God's Redemptive Suffering with Creatures* (Maryknoll, NY: Orbis Books, 2019). Gregersen first coined the term in his article 'The Cross of Christ in an Evolutionary World', in *Dialog: A Journal of Theology,* 40/3 (2001): 192–207.

the desperately needed transformation of the way we relate to the natural world.[3]

In this essay, I will offer first an account of *why* deep incarnation is such a promising christological option in the present moment of environmental crisis by placing it in conversation with the three major approaches to environmental theology outlined by Willis Jenkins following the sociologist Laurel Kearns: (1) ecojustice; (2) Christian stewardship; and (3) ecological spirituality.[4] Second, I will offer some indication of how deep incarnation might develop so as to realise this promise moving forward. I admit at the outset that this is merely one window into a conversation threading through many and diverse theological projects.[5] Rather than offering a programmatic statement attempting to capture the whole of this movement, this essay should be read as offering one entry within the emergent discourse of what deep incarnation is and might be—justified by the fact that the intellectual project of deep incarnation itself reflects its scholarly emphases on interrelation, mutual implication, and evolutionary development.

The Promise of Deep Incarnation

At the heart of the theology deep incarnation is a simple claim: the incarnate God is present to and present within all that is, the full scope and depth of creation in all its materiality and processual character.[6]

---

3. The best entry point to discussions of deep incarnation is the collection *Incarnation: On the Scope and Depth of Christology*, edited by Niels Henrik Gregersen (Minneapolis: Fortress Press, 2015), hereafter cited as *Incarnation*. See also Celia Deane-Drummond, *Christ and Evolution: Wonder and Wisdom* (Minneapolis: Fortress Press, 2009); Christopher Southgate, *The Groaning of Creation: God, Evolution, and the Problem of Evil* (Louisville: Westminster John Knox Press, 2008); Elizabeth A Johnson, *Creation and the Cross: The Mercy of God for a Planet in Peril* (Maryknoll, NY: Orbis Books, 2018).

4. Willis Jenkins, *Ecologies of Grace: Environmental Ethics and Christian Theology* (Oxford: Oxford University Press, 2008), 18, citing Laurel Kearns, 'Saving the Creation: Religious Environmentalism', Dissertation (Emory University: 1994).

5. See Gregersen's own evaluation at 'Deep Incarnation: Opportunities and Challenges', in *Incarnation*, 361–379.

6. *Cf* Gregersen's comment at *Incarnation*, 374: 'What is central to deep incarnation, as far as I'm concerned, is an understanding of the material ('natural') basis for all God's works, including in eschatological fulfillment.'

Nestled within this central affirmation are a number of subsidiary claims. Before the birth of Christ, the Word is present within creation as *Sophia*, the Wisdom of God, setting and sustaining all creatures in their proper relations to one another.[7] In the incarnation, this *Sophia* comes to be present in creation in a new way, not only in, with, and under the proper life of the world, but *as* one part of it: Jesus of Nazareth, the human who is God. By living not only as the divine power within all creatures, but as a fellow-inhabitant of the material cosmos, the incarnate Christ opens a new possibility of relation to God for all that God has made—leptons, white dwarf stars, basalt formations, live oak, ospreys. The Wisdom of God comes to share in the vulnerability and mortality of creation, both as one whose body is shaped by an evolutionary process dependent upon millennia of creaturely suffering and death, and as one whose body is itself subjected to torture and execution. It is through becoming implicated in these biological and social histories that God joins God's own life to the groaning of the human and nonhuman world on the Cross. Perhaps most importantly, it is as the one who has taken on the dissolution and death of the cosmos rises triumphantly on Easter morning that a new possibility is opened for all creation, a deep resurrection offering the hope that each creature might be transfigured and united to God in its very particularity.[8]

This capacious incarnational sensibility is not, of course, unprecedented within the history of Christology, yet the concreteness with which it engages the material processes of the natural world— evolution preeminently, but physical, microphysical, and biological processes more generally—leave it especially well-positioned for

---

7. Elizabeth Johnson and Celia Deane-Drummond have each foregrounded the importance of wisdom theology, the former especially its ability to broaden the theology of deep incarnation beyond exclusively masculine namings of God; see Johnson, *Creation and the Cross*, 175–187, and Celia Deane-Drummond, 'Deep incarnation between Balthasar and Bulgakov: The form of beauty and the wisdom of God', in *Envisioning the Cosmic Body of Christ: Embodiment, Plurality, and Incarnation*, edited by Aurica Jax and Saskia Wendel (London: Routledge, 2019), 101–113.

8. On deep resurrection, see also Elizabeth Johnson, 'Jesus and the Cosmos: Soundings in Deep Christology', in *Incarnation*, 133–156.

development in concert with ecological theology.[9] Deep incarnation's distinctive contribution can best be appreciated through contrast with the three approaches Jenkins and Kearns identify as dominant within contemporary environmental theology: ecojustice, Christian stewardship, and ecological spirituality.

Ecojustice grounds Christian environmental practice in each creature's intrinsic value, given through the creature's independent relation to God and God's purpose for it within creation. Human exploitation of the environment fails to give it what it is properly owed as the creation of God, and therefore should be resisted as injustice. While some ecojustice theologies may be faulted for describing this independent value of nature apart from the histories of Israel, Jesus, and the Church,[10] at its best this approach takes the life of Christ and the whole arc of salvation history to be an indispensable guide to the shape of Christian ecological responsibility. Where this strategy can falter, in Jenkins's estimation, is in portraying the experience of the natural world and working for justice within it as disconnected from the upbuilding of Christian virtue and growth in the love of God. As Jenkins writes, 'for ecojustice to mold normative practice by the character of creation, it must show how the sanctifying practices that generate description of creation's integrity are themselves ecologically shaped'.[11]

---

9. In addition to tracing the Scriptural sources of deep incarnation (see here especially Niels Henrik Gregersen, 'Cur deus caro: Jesus and the Cosmos Story', in *Theology and Science*, 11/4 (2013): 370–393), proponents of deep incarnation have offered substantive engagements with Irenaeus, Tertullian, Athanasius, the Cappadocian Fathers, Bonaventure, Hans Urs von Balthasar, Sergius Bulgakov, and Karl Rahner. See Gregersen, 'The Cross of Christ'; and *idem*, 'The Idea of Deep Incarnation: Biblical and Patristic Resources', in *To Discern Creation in a Scattering World*, edited by Frederiek Depoortere and Jacques Haers (Leuven: Peeters Publishers, 2013), 319–341; 'The Emotional Christ: Bonaventure and Deep Incarnation', in *Dialog*, 55/3 (2016): 247–261; Deane-Drummond, 'Deep incarnation between Balthasar and Bulgakov'; see *idem*, *Christ and Evolution*, 128–155; and 'Deep Incarnation and Eco-Justice as Theodrama: A Dialogue between Hans Urs von Balthasar and Martha Nussbaum', in *Ecological Awareness: Exploring Religion, Ethics and Aesthetics*, edited by Sigurd Bergmann and Heather Eaton (Berlin: LIT Verlag, 2011), 193–206.
10. This is the critique that stewardship approaches often level at ecojustice theologies; see Jenkins, *Ecologies of Grace*, 80–84.
11. Jenkins, *Ecologies of Grace*, 74.

Happily, deep incarnation provides precisely such a connection between the work of justice in nature and growth in the love of God. Deep incarnation begins from the recognition that *Sophia*— the Wisdom of God—is doubly present within the materiality of the created world: present as the divine pattern producing both harmonious order and generative disorder within creation, but present too as Jesus Christ, a part of this physical creation. The *Sophia* encountered in the steel-grey sea of a November morning or the gentle stream flowing from a high mountain lake is the very same Wisdom who was baptised at the hand of John. It is the connection between these natural processes and the particularity of one human life forged in the flesh of Christ that opens the sort of exchange Jenkins imagines between experience of the natural world and sanctificatory Christian practice.

Deep incarnation reminds us that because of the Word has become implicated in material creation, Christian devotion must attend to the stones or trees out of which our churches are built, the land on which they stand, the baptismal waters that are subject to pollution by our economic orders, the grain and grapes grown according to our modern agricultural processes, the wax altar candles produced by the labors of bees threatened by the use of pesticides in those very same fields. The intrinsic value of the natural world thus derives not only from its dependence on the Word as creatures, but on the new relations between God and the world given through the incarnation. The creatureliness of Christ, joined to the Church's profession that this creature is also the Word in whom all things hang together, allows Christians to see the natural world as itself a medium of revelation through which Christians are called to holiness and the work of environmental justice.

Where ecojustice begins with the natural value of creation in its relation to God, Jenkins's second approach of Christian stewardship emphasises the operation of God's covenantal grace. The natural world is brought into the sphere of the covenant by the divine command: in making covenant with Israel, and above all in the life of Christ, God has decreed that human faithfulness requires certain patterns of relationship to both the human and non-human world. Human sin leads to damage of the good world that God has made and violence against one's neighbor, while faithfulness leads to the restoration of the land and sustainable patterns of living. Yet in its wariness of rooting environmental practice in any notion of natural value outside God's decree, Christian stewardship underdetermines precisely how we should *understand* God's covenantal grace. Does Christian discipleship require human protection of natural systems of predation, or does it require the taming of nature so that it comes to resemble a peaceable kingdom? As Jenkins asks, 'wolves pacified in zoos or wolves chasing rabbits?'[12]

Here again, deep incarnation preserves the best of this approach, while answering its potential weaknesses. Christian stewardship hinges on an understanding of discipleship as answering a vocation to faithful action in the world. By articulating how the cross of Christ is a sign of divine identification with the suffering of the non-human world, deep incarnation makes clear that participation in God's redemptive work entails a transformed relationship to the whole of creation. If Christ bears on the cross the pain and disintegration of evolutionary history, and if his victory over death means also a resurrection for each creature in its particularity, then the call to discipleship must be a call to the healing of our relationships with the natural world. Yet deep incarnation also resists the tendency of this second approach to slide into an anthropocentrism that sees humans as the ones who are called to *produce* the restoration of creation—through, for example, climate engineering, or the domestication and pacification of natural predators. Deep incarnation makes clear that on the cross, *God* takes accountability for the sufferings of evolutionary processes, because it is *God* who has willed to use predation and death as the mechanism through which biological complexity and diverse ecosystems and are created. Death may be recognised as both the last enemy of a cosmos bound for glory, and as a tool which God has employed to produce created diversity.[13] In view of this twofold recognition, deep incarnation has the conceptual resources to advocate for a land ethic that seeks environmental stability including processes like predation, rather than the artificial prevention of death in the natural world. Deep incarnation thus refuses to set the actual order and integrity of ecosystems aside in favor of a supposed anthropogenic beatitude.

---

12. Jenkins, *Ecologies of Grace*, 89.
13. Gregersen, 'Cross of Christ', 200.

Drawing especially upon the resources of Eastern Orthodox thought, Jenkins's third approach, ecological spirituality, understands Christianity's relation to the natural world through the doctrine of *theosis*, creation's progressive union with God. As *theosis* is characteristically understood as an ascetical process of spiritual growth, this third approach rests upon an ecological transformation of human subjectivity. Increased intimacy with the divine mystery allows us to see the face of God reflected ever more clearly in the non-human creation, and to love it with a love conformed to God's own. Yet ecological spiritualities often fall prey to two opposed temptations. On the one hand, they can portray the incarnation as the necessary endpoint of the evolutionary history of the cosmos, thus undercutting both the gratuity of the Incarnation and the integrity of the non-teleological mechanism of natural selection. On the other, they risk relativising the importance of christology by concentrating upon God's presence within all creation rather than the unique mode of God's presence to creation in the incarnation.[14]

As developed in the work of thinkers like Edwards, Celia Deane-Drummond, and Elizabeth Johnson, deep incarnation undoubtedly bears a close resemblance to theologies of ecological spirituality. This is most pronounced in Johnson's recent *Creation and the Cross*, the final chapter of which offers a series of spiritual exercises designed to produce precisely the sort of transformation of ecological subjectivity that Jenkins describes.[15] Edwards and Deane-Drummond both argue that deep incarnation offers the christological grounding tacitly presumed by Pope Francis's theology of 'ecological conversion' but left undeveloped in *Laudato si'*.[16] At the same time, deep incarnation

---

14. For examples of the first temptation, see Pierre Teilhard de Chardin, *The Phenomenon of Man*, translated by Bernard Wall (New York: Harper and Row, 1959) (Johnson deploys Teilhard as a spur to theologies of deep incarnation at *Incarnation*, 155–156). For the second, see Matthew Fox, *The Coming of the Cosmic Christ: The Healing of Mother Earth and the Birth of a Global Renaissance* (San Francisco: Harper and Row, 1988); Catherine Keller, *Intercarnations: Exercises in Theological Possibility* (New York: Fordham University Press, 2017).

15. Johnson, *Creation and the Cross*, 195–226.

16. Edwards, *Deep Incarnation*, 129, and more extensively, '"Sublime Communion": The Theology of the Natural World in *Laudato si'*', in Denis Edwards, *The Natural World and God: Theological Explorations* (Adelaide: ATF Press, 2017), 99–117; Celia Deane-Drummond, *A Primer in Ecotheology: Theology for a Fragile Earth* (Eugene, OR: Cascade Books, 2017), 73. See also Pope Francis, *Laudato si', On care for Our Common Home* (Libraria Editrice Vaticana, 2015), paragraphs 216–221.

manages to avoid the excesses of ecological spirituality, neither portraying the Word's assumption of flesh as a possibility emergent from creation's own evolutionary trajectory, nor as a general symbol of cosmic divinisation.[17] Deep incarnation is, first and foremost, a christological approach rather than a practical strategy of moral reasoning; it is thus principally concerned with incarnation as the gracious action of God, coming by divine power to accompany and dwell within creation in a new way. Though deep incarnation may *found* an ecological spirituality, it begins farther upstream theoretically, attending not only to human subjectivity and its experience of nature, but to concerns more commonly relegated to the subdiscipline of 'theology and science': quantum and particle physics, spacetime, geologic history, and snapshots of evolutionary history that have long since passed. These may have little to contribute to contemporary spiritual experiences of God in nature, but deep incarnation proposes them as objects of christological contemplation together with attention to the ecosystems in which we live.

Having situated deep incarnation within the landscape of contemporary ecological theology, we may render more precisely where the central promise of deep incarnation really lies. Deep incarnation offers a christologically rich foundation for theological engagements with the natural world, a christocentric framework for drawing together and considering in ordered fashion an expansive range of ecological and scientific concerns. It grounds the proper integrity and intrinsic value of the natural world not only in the fact of creation, but in the Word's will to become a co-participant with non-human creatures in natural and physical processes. In so doing, it allows us to name the violation of the natural world as sin and injustice, confronted and overcome on the Cross. It shows us how Christ's redemptive sacrifice issues a vocation calling all Christians to restored relationship with the natural world, and to responsibility for its care. It invites a praxis in which the natural world becomes a site of spiritual transformation, drawing us through the created materiality of Christ and the cosmos into union with God. By way of comparison with each of these traditions of ecological theology, it becomes clear that deep incarnation preserves their characteristic virtues while avoiding their characteristic failures. More than this, it

---

17. Gregersen rejects a ubiquitous incarnation at *Incarnation*, 364.

provides a christological substructure within which these approaches can be coordinated together, uniting considerations of creation's inherent value, God's redemptive work, and the implication of human subjectivity in the natural world. As a source of ecological thought and practice, deep incarnation reflects the work Christ accomplishes in history: theoretical elements that have seemed irrecoverably separate are reconciled to one another in the very fleshly body of Christ.

Deep Incarnation and Discipleship

We come to the critical question, then: what does it mean to follow the deeply incarnate Christ? Deep incarnation has so far been (rightly) preoccupied with advocating for an expansion in the scope and depth of our Christologies. A conceptual shift of this magnitude must, however, inevitably occasion changes in our understanding of discipleship. Deep incarnation requires a transformation in our understanding of how life in Christ relates us to the natural world, and in light of this transformation, I wish to propose three trajectories along which the theology of deep incarnation may—and I argue, should—develop in the future.

A first trajectory sees in deep incarnation an invitation to develop a 'Christic ecology'—sustained attention to the natural systems in which Jesus was implicated, and their effect upon his life and ministry. A full appreciation of the depth of incarnation invites contemplation of how Jesus' life was shaped by the ecological particularities of the Lake Region of Lower Galilee: the geographic and hydrological features of the region that shaped the dynamics of its urbanisation; the local flora and fauna that allowed Jesus and his followers to live as fishermen, shepherds, and carpenters; the epidemiological features of this lowland region that produced the need for his healing ministry.[18] Jesus was dependent upon his environment in a way that modern Western Christians generally try not to be. Considering these very local features of Christ's life encourages a bioregionalist sensibility, calling us to a very particular form of *imitatio Christi* responsive to the ecological particularities of our own environments and to a

---

18. Rene Alexander Baergen, 'Re-Placing the Galilean Jesus: Local Geography, Mark, Miracle, and the Quest for Jesus of Capernaum', unpublished doctoral dissertation (Toronto School of Theology, 2013).

reconciled attentiveness to the places we inhabit.[19] Disciples of Christ are called to a fuller engagement with each of the three patterns of human relation to the natural world that Holmes Rolston III has argued provide for 'a comprehensive experience of human identity': wilderness, rural settings, and urban settings.[20] Within Christ's own ministry, these settings figure prominently as the environmental contexts for solitary prayer, communal work including teaching and healing, and for Christ's redemptive self-offering. An ethic founded on a Christic ecology will not only incorporate all three settings as sites of spiritual growth and faithful discipleship, but will pursue a way of living in which the relations between these spaces are determined not exclusively by human ingenuity and desire, but in responsive relation to the natural features of local landscapes. Following Norman Wirzba, we can see deep incarnation as filling out the content of Genesis 1's command to exercise 'dominion' over nature. Deep incarnation teaches us that Christ is the Lord who has become servant to the natural world no less truly than to the human world—entering within, becoming responsive to, even becoming determined by natural process and history. Christian 'dominion' must necessarily resemble the true *dominus*, leading to an account of discipleship in which we become servants of the ecosystems we inhabit just as truly as we are called to serve our neighbors.[21]

This notion of Christic ecology also refines the theology of deep incarnation itself. M Shawn Copeland has written compellingly of human flesh as 'marked' by the social realities like race, gender, sexuality, abledness or disability, and histories of colonisation.[22] Deep incarnation pushes us to see our bodies as similarly marked by natural and biological process. More than this, deep incarnation pushes us to see that these ecological processes are *themselves* socially marked, marking our bodies in turn. As William Cronon has controversially

---

19. On Christianity and bioregionalism, see *Watershed Discipleship: Reinhabiting Bioregional Faith and Practice*, edited by Ched Myers (Eugene, OR: Cascade Books, 2016), especially Jonathan McRay's and David Pritchett's essays.

20. Holmes Rolston III, *A New Environmental Ethics: The Next Millennium for Life on Earth* (London: Routledge, 2012), 50.

21. Norman Wirzba, *The Paradise of God: Renewing Religion in an Ecological Age* (Oxford: Oxford University Press, 2003), 128–148.

22. M Shawn Copeland, *Enfleshing Freedom: Body, Race, and Being* (New York: Fordham University Press, 2010), 56–57.

observed, 'There is nothing natural about the concept of wilderness. It is entirely a creation of the culture that holds it dear, a product of the very history it seeks to deny.'[23] The land and the creatures that inhabit it bear the traces and wounds of our social histories, and our bodies— including Christ's—are reflexively shaped by the environments we have made. Christ takes up bread and wine in the Upper Room because the climate of Roman Palestine enabled wheat and grapes to thrive; the evolutionary histories of the varietals put to this sacramental work are shaped by the social realities of domestication and husbandry. A Christic ecology, both in its attention to Christ's flesh and in the broader context of Christian discipleship, will thus necessarily attend to natural and social process as an integrated whole, ever attentive to the ways that social and spiritual concerns are determined by and feed back into ecological concerns.

A second trajectory particularises the claims of deep incarnation by training our eyes not on *Christ's* environmental context, but on contemporary social and environmental sites where Christ's extended body resides. Jakub Urbaniak has unfavorably contrasted deep incarnation with the work of South African liberation theologian Tinyiko Maluleke, noting that while deep incarnation directs its gaze to the Word's presence within the whole of space and time, Maluleke resolutely concentrates on Christ's empowering presence in the midst of concrete social evils.[24] Yet as Urbaniak acknowledges, deep incarnation also highlights the entanglement of social oppression and environmental harm in a way that might enrich theologies of liberation, sharpening their descriptions of how the natural world figures into the domination of the marginalised by the powerful.[25] Urbaniak is thus mistaken to believe deep incarnation teaches 'that through Jesus's cross everything, without any differentiation, has been universally reconciled with God';[26] Gregersen and Edwards have been

23. William Cronon, 'The Trouble with Wilderness; or, Getting Back to the Wrong Nature', in *Uncommon Ground: Rethinking the Human Place in Nature*, edited by William Cronon (New York: WW Norton, 1996), 79. More extensively, see J Baird Callicott, 'The Wilderness Idea Revisited: The Sustainable Development Alternative', in *The Environment Professional*, 13 (1991): 235–247.

24. Jakub Urbaniak, 'Extending and Locating Jesus's Body: Toward a Christology of Radical Embodiment', in *Theological Studies*, 80/4 (2019): 774–797; here at 790.

25. Urbaniak, 'Extending and Locating Jesus's Body', 792.

26. Urbaniak, 'Extending and Locating Jesus's Body', 794.

clear that Christ's presence in the violence of a forced labor camp or a superfund site is quite different from Christ's presence among oppressed peoples, and deep incarnation takes as a basic axiom that 'God . . . takes side with the victims of evolution and social injustice.'[27] Johnson's 'theology of accompaniment' provides an especially vivid depiction of deep incarnation as one moment in a longer history, in which God's character is displayed above all through bringing Israel out of slavery in Egypt.

Nevertheless, Urbaniak would be quite right in saying that these insights have not yet born fruit in local contexts, being rigorously employed to describe Christ's presence in particular contexts of social and environmental oppression. This sort of specificity is encouraged by deep incarnation's claims about the Word's presence within the very concrete realities of natural and social process; it is past time for deep incarnation to begin realising these possibilities. Elizabeth Johnson's development of deep incarnation provides a particularly useful guide here, as her recognition of the mutual conditioning of social and ecological orders enables her to illuminate the connections between settler colonialism, patriarchy, racism, heterosexism, and environmental degradation.[28] Johnson provides a model for how deep incarnation may productively draw upon, for instance, the ecojustice theology of Larry Rasmussen, or the ecologically-attuned liberation theologies of Willie Jennings, Melanie Harris, or Daniel Castillo.[29] Deep incarnation must be able to speak not only about Christ's cosmic presence, but about Christ's presence in the ecological particularities of Hetch Hetchy or Warren County, North Carolina. Such engagements will enrich deep incarnation's ability to speak about Christ's identification with the victims of social and environmental harm. They will also demonstrate deep incarnation's

---

27. Niels Henrik Gregersen, 'Deep Incarnation: From deep history to post-axial religion', in *HTS Teologiese Studies/Theological Studies*, 72/4 (2016), http://dx.doi.org/10.4102/hts.v72i4.3428, 2.

28. See, for instance, Johnson's integration of these concerns in *Creation and the Cross*, 31–63.

29. *Cf* Larry L Rasmussen, *Earth Community, Earth Ethics* (Maryknoll, NY: Orbis Books, 1996); Willie James Jennings, *Acts: A Theological Commentary on the Bible* (Louisville: Westminster John Knox Press, 2017); Melanie L Harris, *Ecowomanism: African-American Women and Earth-Honoring Faiths* (Maryknoll, NY: Orbis Books, 2017); Daniel P Castillo, *An Ecological Theology of Liberation: Salvation and Political Theology* (Maryknoll, NY: Orbis Books, 2019).

utility as a resource for theologies which describe Christ's extended body as one marked by and redemptively present within the nexus of our political and biological ecologies. We might say: deep incarnation must learn to think globally and analyze locally.

A third trajectory asks how deep incarnation might generate novel practices of worship and piety contributing to ecological conversion. Put simply: how do Christians encounter the deeply incarnate Christ? How do they respond to him in love and praise? Describing deep incarnation as having 'provided a foundation' to her thinking,[30] Lisa Dahill argues, 'Living in a time of urgent ecological crisis, Christians need outdoor ritual experiences of their faith: of what is wild, of the living Earth, stranger faces of the divine: taking eco-alienated people out of the building and into the streets, the river, the forest.'[31] To this end, Dahill's work underscores how liturgy can both occlude and illuminate Christ's presence in the fabric of the material world. Recognising that eucharistic liturgies cultivate in us a sense of ourselves as consumers of the natural world, she wonders how the sacrament may help us confront death by helping us see ourselves as bodies that are presently edible by creatures like bears and crocodiles, and bound eventually to be metabolised by the natural world. In this recognition of our present vulnerability to predation, we might come newly to see the ecological peril to which we lie open.[32] Similarly, Dahill invites Christian baptismal practice to move back into local running waters, so as to tie our understanding of God's renovating presence to care for our natural waterways, ensuring that they are clean and accessible enough to signify the purification of the baptism.[33] In each case, novel liturgical practice—whether new forms of prayer, or changing the space within which sacramental worship is conducted—breaks down the separation between the human and natural world, preparing us to recognise the human Christ redemptively present to and within our environment, a concern that also figures prominently in Denis

---

30. Lisa Dahill, 'Eating and Being Eaten: Interspecies Vulnerability as Eucharist', in *Religions,* 11/204 (2020): 1–11; 9n.29.

31. Dahill, 'Eating and Being Eaten', 1.

32. Dahill, 'Eating and Being Eaten', 4–6.

33. Lisa E Dahill, 'Into Local Waters: Rewilding the Study of Christian Spirituality', in *Spiritus: A Journal of Christian Spirituality,* 16/2 (2016): 141–165; here at 152.

Edwards's work.[34] Yet if deep incarnation is to motivate new practices of prayer and worship, these new liturgical forms must (as Dahill recognises) attend to the specifics of the natural and social systems in which Christ is encountered. They must be generated from the particular histories of land use and population displacement, the particular environmental landmarks and ecological relationships, the particular sites of natural beauty and of nature's degradation, through which the deeply incarnate Christ makes himself available to his extended body. Christ invites us to follow after his own incarnational movement, leading us to follow him to the very ends of the Earth, and to worship him wherever we find him: in the deserts, in the forests, in the streams.

Conclusion

With an abundance of sources throughout the Christian theological tradition, an ecumenically broad range of voices driving its development, and a compelling message of Christ's presence to and in the midst of both human and non-human suffering, deep incarnation is poised to be a significant voice within contemporary theological responses to both the ecological crisis and environmental injustice. The central commitments of this approach allow for significant diversity, inviting further development through engagement with theological anthropology, ecological liberation theologies, and scholarship on environmental spiritualities. The damage to the natural world occurring all around us leaves no doubt: following Christ, today, demands radical alteration in our relation to the environment, before it is too late to avoid irreparable harm to the ecosystems we inhabit. Attention to the scope and depth of the Word's incarnation provides us a framework for describing this path of environmental discipleship. Centering on Christ's flesh, marked by biological process and social formation in inextricable relationship to one another, equips us to imagine how we might conceive of humanity's relation to the natural world anew, how we might work in particular contexts of social oppression and environmental harm, how our prayer and

---

34. See Edwards' essays 'Eucharist and Ecology: Keeping Memorial of Creation' and 'Celebrating Eucharist in a Time of Global Climate Change', in *The Natural World and God*, 137–172.

worship might reflect more fully the blessing that God communicates to all creation by dwelling within it. Christ is the *Sophia* of God active in both the harmonious order and generative disorder of the natural world; Christ is the human who lives from the land as a wandering rabbi and unites his life to the suffering of the world on local timbers. If we are called in this moment of environmental crisis to a new appreciation of the depth of incarnation, we are called also to a new understanding of the ecological and social depth of discipleship.[35]

---

35. Thanks to Christina McRorie and JW Pritchett for comments on this chapter.

From Deep Crucifixion to Deep Resurrection
Biblical Perspectives

Deep Incarnation, the Suffering of Creatures and the Letter to the Colossians

Vicky Balabanski

'. . . redemption in Christ involves, *both* forgiveness and life for human beings, and God's loving accompaniment and redemptive embrace of suffering creatures. For both of these meanings, there is a sacramental relationship between the cross of Jesus as the explicit expression, and the reality, which is saving grace for human beings through relationship with Christ on the one hand, and the Word's compassionate and loving presence in the Spirit to all suffering creatures on the other.'[1]
– Denis Edwards

Abstract: In *Deep Incarnation*, Denis Edwards argues that 'redemption in Christ involves *both* forgiveness and life for human beings, and God's loving accompaniment and redemptive embrace of suffering creatures'. He sees the cross as 'a sacrament of God's redemptive suffering with the whole creation'. This essay explores these insights from a biblical perspective, specifically in relation to Colossians. In the context of theological discourse about the suffering of creatures, the essay examines Colossians 1:14–20, including the Christ Hymn, with its emphasis on the reconciliation of *all things*. This chapter affirms that in Colossians 1:20, the cross is indeed an effective symbol or sacrament, revealing God's self-giving nature and redemptive purposes for the whole creation.

Key Terms: redemption, the cross, suffering creatures, all things, Christ Hymn.

The Australian summer of 2019/2020 has brought home the suffering of creatures in a way never before seen on this continent. As the fires raged across huge swathes of Queensland, New South Wales and Victoria, as well as South Australia and Western Australia, burning

---

1. Denis Edwards, *Deep Incarnation: God's Redemptive Suffering with Creatures* (Maryknoll: Orbis Press, 2019), 121.

rainforests, choking capital cities in smoke and threatening the national capital, the word 'unprecedented' was heard on a daily basis. The range of the fires, the temperatures of the fires, the way they created their own climate events—all these things were unprecedented. More than 16 million hectares of bushland burned, much of it national park, state forest and world heritage areas.[2] Countless unique ecosystems were damaged, indeed destroyed. It is estimated that a billion animals died in the space of these few weeks.[3] The suffering of wild creatures—first through the drought conditions in many parts of the country, then through the intense devastation of the fires and ultimately through the resulting loss of habitats—exceeds our human ability to comprehend.

Denis Edwards' book *Deep Incarnation: God's Redemptive Suffering with Creatures* brings theological questions about the suffering of creatures into the foreground.[4] In this his final work, Denis draws richly on the work of Irenaeus, Athanasius, and Rahner, as well as other contemporary theologians,[5] to articulate a theology that develops and underpins the prophetic teaching of Pope Francis' encyclical *Laudato si'*. As a leading trinitarian theologian who has over a lifetime brought ecological insights to the study of the Triune God, Denis considers with great clarity and compassion the significance of Christ's incarnation for all creatures. Denis himself did not live to see this summer, but his work is profoundly apposite as we begin to experience the real consequences of the climate crisis.[6]

In *Deep Incarnation*, Denis builds the case that 'redemption in Christ involves *both* forgiveness and life for human beings, and God's loving accompaniment and redemptive embrace of suffering creatures.'[7] Central to both aspects of this case is his understanding

---

2. Karen McGhee, 'Unbearable Loss', in *Australian Geographic*, 155 (March-April 2020): 56.

3. The New York Times cited the estimates of Professor Christopher Dickman of the University of Sydney https://www.nytimes.com/2020/01/11/world/australia/fires-animals.html

4. Edwards, *Deep Incarnation: God's Redemptive Suffering with Creatures*.

5. In particular, Niels Gregersen, Richard Bauckham, Celia Deane-Drummond, and Elizabeth Johnson.

6. I take the unusual step of using Denis' Christian name in this chapter, rather than the more usual practice of referring to a scholar by his or her surname. In doing so, I am writing of Denis Edwards using the cadence that is consonant with my respect for him as a valued colleague and friend, and as a man of deep Christian faith.

7. Edwards, *Deep Incarnation*, 121.

of the cross as 'a sacrament of God's redemptive suffering with the whole creation'.[8] This essay will explore these insights from a biblical perspective, specifically in relation to one key text to which Denis often refers: the Letter to the Colossians. After some introductory remarks setting the context of theological discourse about the suffering of creatures, we will begin with Colossians 1:14, which speaks explicitly of redemption, the forgiveness of sins, and makes clear that this aspect of redemption pertains to humanity. Second, we will examine these claims regarding the cross as a sacrament of God's redemptive suffering with the whole creation Deep Crucifixion in relation to the Colossians Hymn, Colosssians 1:15–20, which sets out the cosmic scope of Christ's role in and for creation, and culminates with the words 'making peace through the blood of his cross'. This chapter concludes—as indeed *Deep Incarnation* also does—by bringing these reflections into dialogue with Pope Francis' *Laudato si'*.

The Suffering of Creatures and the Scope of Theology

The suffering of creatures has not generally been deemed to be a core topic of theological discourse and reflection. Within Christian theology, the traditional concerns of human sin and redemption have an implicit anthropocentrism that leave little room for giving attention to the suffering of creatures more generally. This relative silence is being perceived by some contemporary scholars not simply as neglect, but as actively detrimental, as Hannah M Strømmen states:

> Judaism and Christianity have in fact frequently been deemed dominant and problematic traditions in animal studies. Andrew Linzey has for several decades engaged with the problems of Judaism and Christianity for propagating 'a range of ideas about animals which are hugely detrimental to their status and welfare'.[9]

---

8. Edwards, *Deep Incarnation*, 121–122.
9. Hannah M Strømmen, 'Encounters with Animals in Literature and Theology', in *Literature & Theology*, Vol/4, (December 2017): 383–390, here at 385. Citing Andrew Linzey and Dorothy Yamamoto, 'Is Christianity Irredeemably Speciesist?', in *Animals on the Agenda, Questionsabout Animals for Theology and Ethics*, edited by Andrew Linzey and Dorothy Yamamoto (London: SCM Press, 1998), xi, xi–xx.

This problem has begun to be redressed in recent years, particularly in the work of David L Clough.[10]

The trinitarian approach of Denis Edwards makes a significant contribution to reframing theological discourse away from anthropocentrism and towards a theology that reflects deeply on the suffering of creatures *as creatures*. Rather than approaching the theological dimensions of the suffering of creatures via questions of 'speciesism' or the rights of animals, Denis brings his expertise in Trinitarian theology to bear, interrogating our understanding of the incarnation and opening up the scope of the Word becoming flesh to embrace evolutionary processes and all creatures. Citing Rahner, Denis understands this to mean the Word became *matter*.[11] By affirming that the incarnation embraces not only human flesh, but matter in all its diversity, the scope of the incarnation can be more clearly seen it all its breadth and inclusivity. When the incarnation of the Word is seen in this way, the divide between human beings and other species is no longer a primary theological category. Instead, the emphasis lies on the extraordinary wonder of God's self-communication in grace, inviting all things into a process of self-transcendence.[12] This self-communication of God is efficacious not only for humanity, but for all creatures, commensurate with their specificity.[13] In keeping with his trinitarian approach, Denis expounds God's self-communication in several ways: in creation unfolding 'within' God,[14] in the personal presence of God interior to each creature through the Spirit,[15] through the incarnation of the Word and through the co-suffering of God through the cross.[16] In order to grasp God's self-communication in grace, we may view these various aspects of grace as separate categories; however Denis insists, together with Karl Rahner, that the

---

10. David Clough, *On Animals: Systematic Theology*, volume I (London: Bloomsbury T&T Clark, 2013) and *On Animals: Theological Ethics*, volume II (London: Bloomsbury T&T Clark, 2018).

11. Denis Edwards, *Jesus and the Cosmos* (New Jersey: Paulist Press, 1991), 83.

12. Edwards, *Jesus and the Cosmos*, 83–93.

13. Denis Edwards, *Breath of Life: A Theology of the Creator Spirit* (New York: Orbis, 2004), 119–120.

14. Denis Edwards, *The God of Evolution. A Trinitarian Theology* (New Jersey, Paulist Press, 1999), 28–34.

15. Edwards, *Breath of Life. A Theology of the Creator Spirit,* 119.

16. Edwards, *Deep Incarnation*, chapter 5.

self-expression of God in creation and the self-giving of God through the incarnation are integral to one another:

> We are entirely justified in understanding creation and incarnation not as two disparate and juxtaposed acts of God 'outwards' which have their origins in two separate initiatives from God. Rather in the world as it actually is we can understand creation and incarnation as two moments and two phases of the *one* process of God's self-giving and self-expression, although it is an intrinsically differentiated process.[17]

The word that Denis favours to describe the gracious salvific self-communication of the Trinity is redemption. The original semantic field of redemption is the metaphor of a slave redeemed from bondage, which at first glance would seem to be a specifically human metaphor.[18] This might even suggest that the sin of each individual human person was the only reference point: each individual redeemed from the bondage of sin. However, as stated at the outset of this chapter, Denis defines redemption in Christ as involving '*both* forgiveness and life for human beings, and God's loving accompaniment and redemptive embrace of suffering creatures'.[19] Redemptive embrace and redemptive suffering are integral to his theology of divine self-communication, and thus the cross is seen as 'a sacrament of God's *redemptive* suffering with the whole creation'. We now turn to the redemption named in Colossians 1:14.

Redemption in Colossains 1:14

As part of one long sentence, running from Colossians 1:9 through to 1:20, in vv 13–14 we have a brief epitome of the Gospel which

---

17. Edwards, *Jesus and the Cosmos*, 88, citing Karl Rahner, *Foundations of Christian Faith* (New York: Seabury Press, 1978), 197.
18. Friberg gives the literal meaning as 'an action a buying back of a slave or captive through payment of a ransom; hence setting free, release'. Figuratively it is used in Rom 3:24 and 8:23 of rescue from sin and the release of the body from earthly limitations and mortality liberation, deliverance. In 1 Cor 1:30, Christ is the one who sets free from sin as redeemer or deliverer. Timothy Friberg, Barbara Friberg and Neva F Miller, *Analytical Lexicon of the Greek New Testament*, Baker's Greek New Testament Library 4 (Grand Rapids, MI: Baker, 2000), 70.
19. Edwards, *Deep Incarnation*, 121.

the believers had embraced and into which they had been baptised. This is the Good News of salvation with an emphasis on what it has achieved for the believer:

> [13] He [God] has rescued us from the power of darkness and transferred us into the kingdom of his beloved Son, [14] in whom we have redemption, the forgiveness of sins.

In vv 13–14 we have four soteriological affirmations with diverse associations: firstly rescue—with its associations of danger; secondly transfer into the sovereignty of God's beloved Son—with associations of citizenship and safety; thirdly redemption—with its associations of being freed from slavery; and fourthly forgiveness, with its associations of redressing broken relationship. Rescue, transfer to safety, redemption and forgiveness offer a rich, interconnected articulation of the salvation that believers have accessed and in which they now live. To this list we should add two other key terms, namely reconciliation and peace-making, which are used in Colossians 1:20, and which will be discussed further below. No single metaphor or phrase can encompass everything that can be said about salvation. All of the analogical language that Paul and his associates use articulates an aspect of the saving movement of God, whose loving and saving presence reaches across those realities that prevent communion with God—both the external realities represented by the power of darkness, and also the internal reality of sin. Any one of these terms can function as a metonym for this saving movement of God. For Denis, redemption is the preferred figure of speech or metonym that conveys the reality that God's self-communication is restorative and restitutionary.[20]

In vv 13–14, the focus is on the redemption of the believers. This is in keeping with the emphasis in vv 9–12, which are also specifically focussed on the human person. Timothy and Paul[21] pray that the believers may be filled with knowledge, spiritual wisdom and

---

20. Redemption is a central concept in Ps 111:9, which alludes to the Exodus, when God redeemed the people from slavery in Egypt.

21. On the issue of authorship of this letter, see Vicky Balabanski, *Colossians: An Earth Bible Commentary. An Eco-Stoic Reading*, (London: Bloomsbury T&T Clark, 2020), 7–9, 97, 156, where I propose a position of 'co-authorship' or 'partial pseudepigraphy'. I see the primary author as Timothy, but with Paul still alive and visible in the opening and closing greetings.

understanding, living worthy lives and bearing fruit, being strong, prepared to endure, so that they may ultimately give thanks to the Father, who has incorporated them into the inheritance of the saints (Col 1:9–12). In order to do these things, and be free to do so, they must have been released and restored. Redemption, defined as the forgiveness of sins, is the necessary context of all the human-focussed aspirations or prayer-wishes of vv 9–12. The natural world is not in need of the forgiveness of sins. However, the whole of creation is in need of rescue and redemption from the consequences of human sin, both individual and corporate, defined as:

> . . . human distortion and abuse of the natural world, the human propensity to idolatry and the inability of humans to see the glory of God in creation and to reflect it truly in ourselves. Creation's subjection to futility and its slavery to perishability (Rom 8:20–21) are the result of this complex network of dysfunction—the anthropogenic forfeiting of right relationship between God, humanity and all things.[22]

The reality of sin, affecting as it does both humanity and nature, requires nothing less than divine redemption through the death and resurrection of the One through whom all things came into being.

The Cosmic Scope of Christ as First-born of all Creation and First-born from the Dead: Colossians 1:15–20

The one long sentence running from Colossians 1:9 right through to Colossians. 1:20 has, as we have seen, articulated the hopes for the believers (vv 9–12) and the breadth of their redemption (vv 13–14). In our English editions, such as the New Revised Standard Version, there is an editorial break at v 15, with the title 'The Supremacy of Christ' indicating the substantial shift of perspective in verses 15–20. Grammatically, however, vv 15–20 are still part of the same sentence, and so need to be read in close association with what has gone before.[23]

---

22. Balabanski, *Colossians: An Earth Bible Commentary*, 102.
23. For a discussion of the grammar of this section and a case for substantial break before v 23, see Vicky Balabanski, 'Colossians 1:23. A Case for Translating ἐπιμένετε (continue) as Imperative, not Indicative', in *Tyndale Bulletin*, 70/1 (2019): 85–94.

Many scholars, myself included, hold that there is an early 'Christ Hymn' embedded into vv 15–20. By embedding this hymn here, the authors are offering an extended meditation on the beloved Son named in v 13, the one in whom we have redemption, v 14. Grammatically, v 15 begins with the relative pronoun 'who' (*hos*), and flows on from the preceding verses without a break, opening up the vista of redemption to embrace all creation. All creation is named in v 15, and then from v 16, the creation of 'all things', *ta panta,* is emphasized.[24] This seamless connection between human redemption and the reconciliation of all things that the hymn sets out is important. It shows that the connection between the two is not superficial nor in any sense hierarchical—humans first, and other parts of creation as somehow lesser or an afterthought. Instead, through the incorporation of the Christ Hymn, the vista of salvation broadens, and we glimpse the true expanse of Christ's person and work. Christ, as the *eikon* or visible embodiment[25] of the invisible God, is proclaimed as the source and salvation of 'all things', *ta panta.*

The Christ Hymn is structured in two stanzas or movements, with Christ as firstborn of all creation (v 15), and the second with Christ as firstborn from the dead (v 18). Creation and new creation—understood as the reconciliation of all things—are depicted here as part of the same gracious self-bestowal of the invisible God. In the first stanza, Christ is the one in whom, through whom and for whom all things were created, the one who precedes all things ('He himself is before all things', v 17) and in whom all things cohere ('in him all things hold together', v 17). In the second, Christ's pre-eminence is revealed (v 18); in him all the fullness of God is pleased to live continually (v 19), and through him all things are reconciled to God (v 20). These eschatological realities are grounded in the peace-making achieved through the blood of his cross (v 20). Using the

---

24. The phrase 'all things' is used twice in v 16, twice in v 17, everything in v 18. Verse 20 concludes with the reconciliation of 'all things'.

25. On the translation of *eikon* as visible embodiment, see Balabanski: *Colossians: An Earth Bible Commentary,* 73. 'This term can refer to the image, representation or likeness of something (*cf* Mt 22:20), but this sense is too weak. I have translated the Greek word as 'visible embodiment'. Christ is no mere likeness, in the sense of a portrait or artistic representation; Christ is proclaimed in this hymn as God's active agent in creation . . . for those influenced by Stoic ideas, only embodied reality can be causative and can *effect* things. If Christ is the visible, tangible embodiment of God who is not seen, Christ is both the revealer and the agent of the unseen God.'

language of plerophory[26] to articulate things beyond articulation, the hymn shows Christ as the source, sustainer and saviour of all things, visible, invisible, heavenly and earthly.

It is striking that the 'blood of his cross', Colossians 1:20, is named as the means of peace-making and reconciliation for *all things*. Christians often celebrate the way in which Christ's blood shed upon the cross is the means of their salvation.[27] However, how often is it understood that Jesus' blood shed upon the cross reconciles *all things*? Before we explore the meaning of the cross reconciling all things, it is necessary to give attention to one other aspect of the Christ Hymn, namely the description of Christ as 'Firstborn of all creation'. The ecological significance of this phrase had already been emphasized by Pope John Paul II:

> The Incarnation of God the Son signifies the taking up into unity with God not only of human nature, but in this human nature, in a sense, of everything that is "flesh": the whole of humanity, the entire visible and material world. The Incarnation, then, also has a cosmic significance, a cosmic dimension. The 'first-born of all creation', becoming incarnate in the individual humanity of Christ, unites himself in some way with the entire reality of the human, which is also 'flesh' and in this reality with all 'flesh', with the whole of creation.[28]

As we have seen in Colossians 1:16, Christ is the One *in* whom, *through* whom and *for* whom all things have been created. Using the imagery of Christ as the Wisdom of God,[29] and the grammar of

---

26. A verbal depiction of abundant fullness, using synonyms, parallels and repetitions of 'all'. Balabanski, Colossians: An Earth Bible Commentary, 61.

27. For example, see the hymn by Charles Wesley 'O for a Thousand Tongues to sing' (1739), which celebrates redemption of the prisoner by Jesus' blood:
He breaks the power of cancelled sin,
He sets the prisoner free;
His blood can make the foulest clean;
His blood availed for me.

28. *Dominum et Vivificantem: On the Holy Spirit in the Life of the Church and the World*, paragraph 50: http://w2.vatican.va/content/john-paul-ii/en/encyclicals/documents/hf_jp-ii_enc_18051986_dominum-et-vivificantem.html%245K. Cited by Denis Edwards, *Deep Incarnation*, 109–110.

29. See Denis Edwards, *Jesus the Wisdom of God: An Ecological Theology* (Homebush: St Paul's, 1995), 33–37.

prepositional metaphysics,[30] the hymn positions Christ very close to the divine presence. However, as 'firstborn of all creation', Christ is also in some sense *birthed by creation*. 'Firstborn' is the language of incarnation—Jesus is indeed the firstborn son of Mary (Lk 2:7). 'Firstborn' is also reminiscent of the Passover, when all the firstborn in Egypt, whether humans or animals, were killed in the foundational struggle for liberating the people of Israel, God's 'firstborn son' (Ex 4:22–23). But the 'firstborn of all creation' is incarnation of an even grander scale—a birthing springing from all creation itself. Creation birthing the One through whom all things came into being presents us with a paradox. This view of creation as flowing both *from* and *towards* Christ articulates something profoundly mysterious.

In *Deep Incarnation*, Denis picks up something of this two-way flow of Christ and creation when he refers to the Word assuming the creaturely humanity of Jesus with all its ecological and cosmic interconnections, and that these interconnections are by the divine intention *co-constitutive of the Word made flesh*.[31] Denis explains this with reference to Rahner's extension of the saying by Gregory Nazianzus: 'What has not been assumed has not been healed':

> . . . what has been assumed in the flesh taken by the Word, is the whole of creaturely reality. Nothing remains outside this whole. Nothing remains outside the transfiguration and the deification, which beginning in Christ, draws all that exists into the life of God.[32]

Denis goes on to expand the concept of deep incarnation as a hypostatic union with the matter of the universe itself, with all its potentiality:

> By the divine intention, the flesh assumed in the incarnation is that of Jesus of Nazareth in all its internal relationality with other human beings, with the community of life on

---

30. Gregory E Stirling, 'Prepositional Metaphysics in Jewish Wisdom Speculation and Early Christian Liturgical Texts', in *Wisdom and Logos: Studies in Jewish Thought in Honor of David Winston*, The Studia Philonica Annual 28: Studies in Hellenistic Judaism 9, BJS 312, edited by David T Runia and Gregory E Sterling (Atlanta GA: Scholars Press, 1997), 219–238

31. Edwards, *Deep Incarnation*, 113 (emphasis mine).

32. Edwards, *Deep Incarnation*, 112.

our planet, and with the universe itself in all its dynamic processes. The flesh of Jesus is made from atoms born in the processes of nucleosynthesis in stars, and shaped by 3.7 billion years of evolution on Earth. Social, ecological, and cosmic relationships are not add-ons to the Word made flesh. They are constitutive of the Word made flesh. And if one takes up the position of Irenaeus, Athanasius, Rahner and Gregersen, then one would have to say that the creation of our cosmic, evolutionary and ecological world was always directed to the Word made flesh. In this sense the Word made flesh can also be said to be constitutive of our interconnected and evolutionary world.[33]

This expansive vision is richly resonant with the Colossians Hymn, and with the phrase 'Firstborn of all creation' in particular. All the processes of the universe, even death, are constitutive of the One whom we call the Firstborn of all creation; at the same time, the Firstborn of all creation (who is also 'Firstborn from the dead') is also constitutive of the universe. In this way, we see in relation to creation/all things, a movement both from and towards Christ. Both are, to use Denis' words, by divine intention 'co-constitutive of the Word made flesh'.[34]

In a similar way, the title of Christ as 'Firstborn from the dead' brings several disparate things into focus. The incarnation—understood as deep incarnationis again in view through the title Firstborn. By connecting the incarnation with both the death and resurrection ('re-birthing') of Christ, we see that the One who truly died and was truly raised from death is connected with all the processes of the universe. The very thing that characterizes creation—mortality, the finite creaturely reality that culminates in death, is assumed by Christ, 'Firstborn from the dead'. Christ assumes mortality and so redeems mortality.

The Cross and the Suffering of Creatures

In the final chapter of *Deep Incarnation*, Denis reviews the issue of God suffering with creatures, and the challenge that this appears to give to the transcendence of God and divine impassibility. He posits

---

33. Edwards, *Deep Incarnation*, 113.
34. Edwards, *Deep Incarnation*, 113.

that 'a God who can freely and lovingly enter into the pain of creation and feel with suffering creatures is actually more truly and fully transcendent than the concept of a God who is unable to do this.'[35] He goes on to state that divine transcendence is in fact re-envisioned in the light of the incarnation and the cross of Jesus; it is *enlarged* when viewed as 'the transcendence of divine love . . . the transcendent divine capacity to be with creatures of flesh.'[36] The key biblical text that Denis draws on, together with Athanasius, is the Philippians Hymn (Phil 2:6–11). This early Christ Hymn is indeed the clearest articulation of the kenotic self-humbling of the Word in the incarnation and the cross, which reveals the divine nature.

When we compare the Colossians Hymn with the Philippians Hymn, there are of course significant differences. The Philippians Hymn has the U-shaped structure of descent and ascent, kenosis and exaltation, with the cross named at the centre as the axis and turning point. The Colossians Hymn also evokes a two-fold movement— Firstborn of all creation, Firstborn from the dead. It does also invite the gaze to move from heaven to earth in v 16 and from earth to heaven in v 20, which, in the Greek, is the final phrase of the hymn. But the vision of the Colossians Hymn is not a U-shaped descent to the cross, and subsequent exaltation. Rather, it proclaims the panorama of all things in, through and for Christ, evoking the power of Christ as the source of things visible and invisible, surpassing thrones, dominions, rulers and powers, taking precedence over and yet sustaining all things. If there is a pivotal point in the Colossians Hymn, it is Christ as the Head of the Body, the Church (v 18). The self-emptying of Christ is visible when naming him 'Firstborn from the dead' in the second stanza of the hymn and adding 'so that he might come to have first place in everything' (v. 18). Having renounced first place, he is raised—or birthed—to his rightful place, namely primacy. All the fullness was pleased to dwell in him (v 19), which invites the worshipper to see this not only at Christ's exaltation, but throughout the hymn. Grammatically, the subject of v 19—all the fullness— continues to be the subject of v 20, so that we could translate these verses as:

For in him all the [divine] fullness was pleased to dwell.

---

35. Edwards, *Deep Incarnation*, 113–114.
36. Edwards, *Deep Incarnation*, 114.

And through him [all the divine fullness was pleased] to reconcile
all things to him,
Having made peace through the blood of his cross through him
Whether things on the earth or things in the heavens.

The cross is prominent at the conclusion of the hymn; this does
not, however, mean a downplaying of its significance. In Greco-
Roman thought, the final place was the one of greatest prominence
and honour. The cross plays as substantial a role in the Colossians
Hymn as in the Philippians Hymn—not as the pivot or axis but as the
climax of the story of reconciliation and redemption.

So what does the Colossians Hymn have to contribute to
theological thinking about the suffering of creatures? We have seen
that there are no grounds for 'speciesism' in the hymn—*all things*
are both created and reconciled in Christ, who makes peace through
the blood of his cross. It is this final affirmation, Colossians 1:20,
which claims the reconciling, peace-making act of God in the cross
of Christ that is key to this discussion. The surprise of this last phrase
is the introduction into a transcendent vision of heavenly (as well as
earthly) things a temporal, finite, particular moment in the history
of the world: the cross of Christ, and further, the identification of the
bodily self-giving—the shedding of blood—in this cosmic vision. Yet
as Denis argues, 'the saving effects of the cross are already quietly at
work throughout the world and throughout history, in the Spirit . . .
The effects of the cross are not confined to the period after the cross,
but are already present and at work, even if obscurely, throughout all
of history in the Spirit of Jesus Christ.'[37] The transcendent God is free
to make a temporal, historical event efficacious for all time and space.

The blood of Jesus on the cross is irrefutably an act of suffering.
Through this shedding of blood, 'God was pleased to reconcile to
[Godself] all things' (Col 1:20). The suffering of Christ on the cross
is God's reconciling, peace-making participation with all things that
suffer. All the divine fullness—God's being—is involved with deep
incarnation, understood as both the dwelling with us and the act of
reconciling all things. This does indeed expand our conception of the
transcendence of God. The Colossians Hymn enlarges the panorama
of self-giving love to show that all things are embraced in the divine
movement of love; no creature, no one and no thing is excluded from
this vision.

---

37. Edwards *Deep Incarnation*, 120.

The redemptive co-suffering of God with creatures that Denis reveals with great care and compassion is expounded in Irenaeus' vision of the cross,

> . . . where he sees the cross as inscribed across the whole creation, reaching across the sky and into the depths of the earth . . . The cross makes fully visible the cruciform activity of the Word of God, who acts invisibly in the height and in the depth, in the length and in the breadth of all creaturely reality.[38]

Irenaeus' vision is one that grasps and expands the vision of the Colossians Hymn, where through the cross, God reconciles and makes peace with all things. Denis concludes that this vision has implications for the suffering of creatures, as 'the biblical promise is for the final liberation and fulfilment in Christ of "the creation itself" (Rom 8:19), and for the recapitulation (Eph 1:10) and reconciliation (Col 1:20) of "all things" in him, and this includes, in some unforeseeable way, of other species and individual creatures'.[39]

The Colossians Hymn, embedded as it is in the context of Timothy and Paul's prayer that the believers may be filled with all spiritual wisdom and understanding (Col 1:9) and may grow in the knowledge of God (Col 1:10), alludes to the big picture of God's purposes for *all things*: rescue, citizenship—or just living space and habitat, redemption and reconciliation with God. It offers confirmation of Denis' claim that 'redemption in Christ involves *both* forgiveness and life for human beings, and God's loving accompaniment and redemptive embrace of suffering creatures'.[40] The cross in this hymn is indeed an effective symbol[41] or sacrament, revealing God's self-giving nature and redemptive purposes for the whole creation.

Pope Francis' Encyclical *Laudato si' . . . On Care for Our Common Home* connects the hymn with the eschatological vision of healing and wholeness. Drawing explicitly on Colossians 1:16, and then

---

38. Irenaeus, *Demonstration*, in St Irenaeus of Lyons. *On the Apostolic Preaching*, translated by John Behr (Crestwood, NY: St Vladimir's Seminary Press, 1997), 34, cited by Edwards, *Deep Incarnation*, 122.

39. Edwards, *Deep Incarnation*, 127.

40. Edwards, *Deep Incarnation* 121

41. Edwards, *Deep Incarnation*, 118.

Colossians 1:19–20, he links the destiny of all creation with the 'mystery of Christ':

> 'From the beginning of the world, but particularly through the incarnation, the mystery of Christ is at work in a hidden manner in the natural world as a whole, without thereby impinging on its autonomy. The New Testament does not only tell us of the earthly Jesus and his tangible and loving relationship with the world. It also shows him risen and glorious, present throughout creation by his universal Lordship: 'For in him all the fullness of God was pleased to dwell, and through him to reconcile to himself all things, whether on earth or in heaven, making peace by the blood of his cross' (Col 1:19–20). This leads us to direct our gaze to the end of time, when the Son will deliver all things to the Father, so that 'God may be everything to every one' (1 Cor 15:28).[42]

This section of the encyclical links the pre-incarnate mystery of Christ, the incarnate Jesus and the eschatological future of creation. It calls for a profound shift in our perception of the creatures of the world—they are valued and loved by God. It also calls for a shift in eschatology; Christ is also directing all things—all creatures— towards 'fullness'.

At this time of grief at the loss and suffering of creatures, the vision of the Colossians Hymn reminds us that divine grace and mercy are at work even in the dark and unknown places of history. All things hold together in Christ and all things are reconciled in him. The concept of mystery is prominent in Colossians,[43] but the mystery is not something that remains unknowable. Rather, it is specifically linked with the redemptive revelation of God through the gospel of Christ.

The life and work of Denis Edwards was—and is—a beacon of the reconciling work of Christ among us—a valued teacher and scholar who articulated the mystery of Christ clearly (Col 4:3–4).

---

42. Francis' *Laudato si' . . . On Care for Our Common Home*, 99–100.
43. Col 1:25, 26, 2:2 and 4:3. Note that Paul concludes with the imperative laid upon him to articulate the mystery clearly.

Earth Connectedness and Transfiguration: Luke's Story of Jesus' Death and Resurrection

Michael Trainor

Abstract: Denis Edwards was inspired by the theology of Karl Rahner. He affirmed Rahner's conviction that through Jesus' death and resurrection, Earth was transformed. Through these events God's heart became centered in Earth, transfiguring it from a place of impermanence and death. This chapter traces the Gospel underpinnings which Rahner explicates in his meditation on Jesus' death and resurrection. Luke's story of Jesus' death and especially the resurrection, drawing on Mark's earlier narrative, reveals environmental or Earth-related insights that capture the essence of Rahner's conviction. For the contemporary interpreter concerned about today's ecological challenges Luke essentially reveals how Earth is transformed by Jesus' suffering, death and resurrection and discloses the heart of God's presence.

Key Terms: Karl Rahner, Luke, Mark, Gospel, suffering, Jesus' death and resurrection, resurrection, narrative, Earth, ecology, eco-theology, Earth Bible, Earth, God's presence, intertextual dialogue, hermeneutic, Ecological biblical interpretation, Transfiguration, Incarnation ('Deep'), Psalms, Gethsemane, ecstasy, discipleship, women, burial shroud, Plutarch, Ovid, Joseph of Arimathea, Pilate, Kingdom, Easter.

Denis Edwards, friend, companion and mentor, was committed to eco-theology. The testimonies from colleagues and friends in this present work attest to this. He was inspired, among others, by the theology of Karl Rahner whom he studied intensely. Rahner's thought shaped his initial doctoral work and formed his eco-theological insights throughout his life, and especially in his final works.

In 1950, Rahner offered a meditation on the Earth-connectedness of Jesus' death and resurrection. Denis integrated Rahner's meditation in his own ecological reflections.[1] For Rahner, Jesus' resurrection was

---

1. Denis Edwards, *Christian Understandings of Creation: The Historical Trajectory* (Minneapolis MN: Fortress Press, 2017).

not an escape from the world or a flight beyond the present, into an eternity and heavenly glory removed from present human experience or life. His resurrection was not a disconnect from Earth after enduring the suffering of the cross. Rather, Rahner believed that Jesus entered more intimately into Earth's being through his death and resurrection. Rahner believed that death brought Jesus into Earth's depths, to its 'deepest regions'. In this journey, Jesus also brought God's very *being*, God's heart, into Earth's centre. Rahner writes,

> In his death, the Lord descended into the lowest and deepest regions of what is visible. It is no longer a place of impermanence and death, because there he now is. By his death, he has become the heart of this earthly world, God's heart in the centre of the world, where the world even before its own unfolding in space and time taps into God's power and might.[2]

God's heart lies at the centre of the Earth through Jesus' death.[3] His resurrection is not an abandonment of Earth and its creatures, 'but profoundly connected to all that is bodily' and all that is Earth-related. Deep Crucifixion yields to deep resurrection

Denis quotes Rahner:

> [Jesus] is risen in his body. That means: He has begun to transfigure this world unto himself; he has accepted this world forever; he has been born anew as a *child of this earth*, but of an earth that is transfigured, freed, unlimited, an earth that in him will last forever and is delivered from death and impermanence for good.[4]

---

2. Karl Rahner, 'A Faith that Loves the Earth', in *The Mystical Way in Everyday Life: Sermons, Essays and Prayers: Karl Rahner, SJ*, edited by Annemarie S Kidder (Maryknoll, NY: Orbis Books, 2010), 55, as quoted by Edwards, *Christian Understandings*, 222.

3. Edwards, *Christian Understandings*, 222. I capitalise 'Earth' to accentuate it as the common home of all living creatures and ecosystems. It as a bearer of vital interconnectivity and a total or global living organism bonded by organic and inorganic matter.

4. Rahner, 'A Faith', 55, as quoted in Edwards, *Christian Understandings of Creation*, 223. Emphasis added.

In this Chapter I trace the ecological underpinnings which Rahner elucidates in his meditation on Jesus death and resurrection. I show how Luke's story of Jesus' death and resurrection reshapes Mark. For the contemporary interpreter, Luke's 'reshaping' seems to explicate environmental or Earth-related features implicit in Mark. These have ecological implications for contemporary disciples concerned about climate change and the environmental disasters that confront us.[5]

It is important to note that the evangelists were not ecologists concerned with the same issues that preoccupy us today. However, it is possible through *intertextual* engagement, to allow our contemporary ecological concerns to act as a 'text' in engaging an ancient and revered document like the Gospel of Luke.[6] In this intertextual dialogue, one 'text' speaks to another as Earth's voice emerges from the Gospel story in an *ecological hermeneutic*.[7] The adoption of this ecologically-focused intertextual hermeneutic in Luke highlights resonances, of Jesus' communion with Earth in his death and resurrection, uniquely symbolised in the Gospel narrative. This leads to the conviction, not entirely radical, that Rahner explicated a theology intuited in the Gospels. As we shall see in drawing on Rahner's frame of reference, Luke can be interpreted as presenting Jesus as a 'child of this earth', and the Earth as transfigured through his resurrection, 'delivered from death and impermanence'. Towards the end of this Chapter I

---

5. For a snapshot of some of these ecological challenges see National Geographic's summary of the 2018 IPCC, 'Climate change impacts worse than expected, global report warns,' https://www.nationalgeographic.com/environment/2018/10/ipcc-report-climate-change-impacts-forests-emissions/; accessed 12 September, 2019.

6. Intertextuality in its classic sense is the absorption into one text of an earlier text and an understanding of the later text is assisted through an appreciation of the earlier one. See for example the work of Gail R O'Day, 'Jeremiah 9:22–23 and 1 Corinthians 1:26–31: A study of Intertextuality', in *Journal of Biblical Literature,* 109 (1990): 259–267, who describes intertextuality as 'a literary and hermeneutical category . . . [which] . . . refers to the ways a new text is created from the metaphors, images, and symbolic world of an earlier text or tradition.' (259) I take 'text' more broadly to indicate anything (personal history, social context) that helps the emergence of the '*textere*' (Lat, 'weaving') of existential meaning for a community. From this perspective, the environment and concern for Earth can be a 'text' for such an engagement.

7. While space prevents a thorough discussion on the legitimacy of this approach, see the explanation by Norman C Habel, 'Introducing Ecological Hermeneutics', in Norman C Habel and Peter Trudinger, *Exploring Ecological Hermeneutics*, (Atlanta: Society of Biblical Literature, 2008), 3.

briefly return to the affirmation of Rahner's insights in Denis' final works, *Christian Understandings of Creation* and *Deep Incarnation*.[8]

Mark's Story

The *Gospel according to Mark* is the story of God's beloved one who meets opposition, misunderstanding and ultimate rejection.[9] The climax of this comes on the cross. Jesus hangs naked before those who mock him urging him to self-salvation, a seductive temptation that he resists. But in the moment of his death screams, in the opening lines of Psalm 22, Mark's Jesus cries out to his God who seems to have abandoned him.[10] The auditor of the Gospel who would be familiar with the Psalm knows that the sentiment of its opening lines is not the last word. The Psalm moves to conclude with confident assurance that God's face is not hidden from the one who cries out in suffering (Ps 22:24).[11] This memory of the full Psalm offers another perspective, an interpretative key—albeit subtle or imperceptible—to the Gospel's auditor that what appears to dominate, namely the sense of divine abandonment and the experience of ultimate misunderstanding and loneliness, is not the final witness or meaning to the death of one whose life is lived faithfully in communion with God.

The apparent elements of Mark's scene of Jesus' death continue into the final Gospel story, the resurrection (Mk 16:1–8). There is continuity between the two scenes. However, an invitation awaits.

In the early morning, as light begins to dawn, the women come to the tomb with an intent to anoint the body of Jesus. The auditor

---

8. Denis Edwards, *Deep Incarnation: God's Redemptive Suffering with Creatures* (Maryknoll, NY: Orbis Books, 2019).

9. For a helpful overview of these themes of opposition, misunderstanding and rejection see Francis Moloney, *The Gospel of Mark: A Commentary* (Grand Rapids, MI: Baker Academic, 2012), 2–11. Also, Mark Goodacre, 'Scripturalization in Mark's Crucifixion Narrative', in *The Trial and Death of Jesus: Essays on the Passion Narrative in Mark,* edited by Geert van Oyen and Tom Shepherd (Leuven: Peeters, 2006), 46–47.

10. HN Roskam, 'Jesus' Death in Mark's Gospel', in *The Purpose of the Gospel of Mark in Its Historical and Social Context, Novum Testamentum Supplements Online* (Brill Online) volume 114, 189–207.

11. Mary Healy, *The Gospel of Mark* (Grand Rapids, MI: Baker Academic, 2008), 320–321.

already knows that he has already been anointed by the unnamed woman at the beginning of Mark's passion story (Mk 14:3–9). The action of this woman, anticipating his burial, looks forward to the final action of women at the Passion narrative's concluding story. Here the women approach the tomb as they start to query about removing the stone that would have blocked their access to the inner recesses of the tomb and Jesus' body. To their amazement the women see that the stone 'which was very huge had already been rolled back' (Mk 16:3)[12]. Mark's description of the size of the stone and the action that has already occurred to remove the stone from the tomb's entrance indicate that God is present. Something more, the divine presence, is active in a scene that seems quintessentially mortal.

The women enter the tomb to find a young man 'dressed in white clothing seated on the right' (Mk 16:5). Is this Jesus now resurrected and enthroned in heavenly glory 'on the right hand of the Father'?[13] Or an angelic agent of God's presence? Or the young man from an earlier scene (Mk 14:51–52) who fled Gethsemane as Jesus was arrested, now rehabilitated? Whatever Mark's intent by the figure, the words of the young man offer the evangelist's theology of the resurrection. The centrepiece of the angelic declaration reminds the women (and Mark's auditors) that Jesus, has been raised. He is not here. See (Gk *íde*) the place where they laid him.' (Mk 14:7)

Then comes the commission to announce the Easter message to Jesus' disciples as they return to Galilee, the place where they were first called by Jesus at the beginning of the Gospel (Mk 1:16–20). In Mark's concluding verse, the women flee from the tomb with fear and 'ecstasy' and say nothing to anyone 'for they were afraid' (Mk 14:8). What this concluding verse means is unclear, perhaps deliberately so. Like the whole of Mark's Gospel and Jesus' teaching, it is parable-like, a theme introduced in Mark 4.

In Mark 4, as Jesus presents the meta-parable of the sowed seed and other parables to his disciples, Mark concludes,

---

12. Here and elsewhere, unless otherwise indicated, the translation of the NT Greek text is by the author.

13. The place of the 'right hand' as a metaphor for agency and authority runs throughout the Bible. As the position which the Risen Jesus assumes in his relationship to God see, for example, Mt 22:44; Mk 12:36; 16:19; Lk 22:69; Acts 2:33; 5:31; 7:55, 56; Rom 8:34; Eph 1:20; Col 3:1; Heb 1:3; 8:1; 12:2; 3:22.

> With many such parables he spoke the word to them, as they were able to hear it; he did not speak to them without a parable, but privately to his own disciples he explained everything.' (Mk 4:33–34)

The Gospel's concluding verse echoes Mark's reflection on Jesus' parable-teaching:

> And going forth, they fled from the tomb for terror and amazement (Gk. *ekstasis*) seized them and they said nothing to anyone for they were afraid (Mk 16:8).

To the disciple it sums up the meaning of the Gospel—the women come to 'ecstasy' (*ekstasis*) at their recognition of the full implications of Jesus' resurrection. They are unable to explain this for 'fear' that it would be misunderstood, as Jesus himself was misunderstood. The only appropriate response is silence, that allows disciples to encounter the presence of the Risen One within their own life experience and on their own terms. For those 'outside' the discipleship circle, the ending will always remain enigmatic, parabolic perhaps, even, ironic.[14]

But what is that experience to which the tomb's young man points and brings the women to deep ecstasy and holy silence?

It is here that we enter the profundity of Mark's narrative of the dead and risen Jesus. It is also here that an aporia appears that allows the contemporary auditor, concerned about Earth and environmental degradation, to see the truth of Rahner's insights about death and resurrection.

The women are invited to 'See (Gk *íde*) the place where they laid him . . .' (Mk 16:6b). The invitation 'to see'(*íde*) is more than a casual look at an empty burial chamber. It is a deliberate direction from the young man to the women to observe and take note.[15] There is almost a tone of contemplation. What the women are to 'see' is more than the empty space. They observe the absence of what *was* present and contemplate what *is* present. These confirm Jesus' physical absence

---

14. On the irony of Mark's ending, see Norman R.Petersen, 'When is the End not the End? Literary Reflections on the Ending of Mark's Narrative', in *Union Seminary Review*, 34 (1980): 151–166.

15. WF Arndt and FW Gingrich, *Greek-English Lexicon of the New Testament and Other Early Christian Literature* (Chicago: The University of Chicago Press, 1979), 369.

and the meaning of the young man's declaration: Jesus has been raised. Their observation of Jesus' absence and the contemplation of what is present opens them to the deeper mystery of the resurrection. Their observation of the physical, Earth-related realia that surrounds them in the tomb prepares them for the encounter of the presence of the divine in the Risen Jesus, yet to be revealed in Galilee. What they are invited to 'see', to contemplate, is the absence of Jesus' body and the surrounds of the rock-hewn receptacle for a corpse. There is no corpse only Earth's presence. It is this presence which the women are invited to look at. For the contemporary auditor reflecting on Mark's story and searching for ecological meaning for a planet that is environmentally damaged, Earth becomes the conveyance of Jesus' resurrected presence. Though Jesus is physically absent in the space in which the women gather, the tomb shaped from Earth becomes the reminder of Jesus' resurrection. The link which the young man, the divine announcer, makes for the women, between the physical setting and Jesus' resurrection is clear. To return to Rahner's metaphor, Jesus, as Earth's Child, has begun to 'transform' Earth.

It might seem to today's Gospel auditor that this link between Earth and Mark's resurrection proclamation is rather tenuous or too implicit. The link becomes most explicit in the passion and resurrection stories in Luke and Matthew. Both evangelists draw on Mark's narrative but offer their unique insights that convey a clearer message which has ecological resonances testifying to Rahner's meditation. Our focus will be on Luke.

Luke's Story of Jesus' Death (Lk 23:26–49)

While Mark's passion story is more graphic, barren and tragic, Luke's offers a different tone and perspective. Jesus comes to his death accompanied by his disciples, women who have followed him from Galilee (Lk 8:1–3). As he journeys to the place of execution, he meets Jerusalem's women who lament for what will happen to him (Lk 23:27–31). He is crucified but, unlike in Mark, does not hang as a naked figure surrounded by taunts, but as one prepared to offer himself into the hands of his God while forgiving his executors (Lk 23:46). He does not utter a cry of dereliction but a word of communion.

Luke's Jesus is a dignified figure, still wearing the regal 'elegant/ luminous garment' (Gk *esthéta lampraán*) in which Rome's imperial agent, Herod, dressed him in an earlier trial scene (Lk 23:11). A closer look at the way Luke portrays the context of Jesus' crucifixion in comparison to Luke's source, Mark, on which the evangelist draws, attests to this.

Mk 15:22–24	Lk 23:33–34
And they brought him to the place of Golgotha which means place of a skull, and they offered him wine mixed with myrrh, he did not take it.	And when they came to the place which is called 'Skull' there they crucified him, and the criminals, one on his right and one on his left.
And they crucified him and, dividing his clothes, they cast lots for them to decide what each should take.	And Jesus said, 'Father forgive them for they do not know what they are doing'. They cast lots to divide his garments.

In Mark, Jesus is crucified. His garments are divided amongst his executors as they cast lots for this victim's clothing. The participial phrase, 'dividing his clothes' (Mk 15:24), indicates that they already have his clothing before them and Jesus is naked. The presumption is that it is easier to remove a victim's garments prior to crucifixion rather than after death. In Luke, Jesus' executioners cast lost *in order* to divide his clothing. Luke indicates that this will happen after his death. The garment Jesus wears is the Herodian 'elegant/luminous robe' (Lk 23:11) placed on him in the earlier trial scene. This is never removed prior to his crucifixion. There is no flogging from Pilate, as in Mark (Mk 15:15), nor any abuse and maltreatment from the regal guard who, in Mark 15:16–20, enact a mock royal investiture as they strip him, place purple around him and crown him with thorns.

For Luke, Jesus' dignity is unsullied. He retains Herod's garment, is condemned to execution by Pilate and then moves to the site of his death without maltreatment from Pilate's soldiers. Though Pilate announces that he will have Jesus flogged (Lk 23:22), this never happens. For Luke, the true representative of royal or noble presence, symbolised by Herod's 'elegant/luminous robe' goes to the cross as God's authentic regal representative, unlike Caesar's Jerusalem representatives, Pilate and Herod.

For the Gospel auditor the garment that accompanies Luke's Jesus to his death echoes the garment, the 'bands of cloth', that surround him at his birth and explicitly referred to in Jesus' birth story—a point to which we shall return shortly. And the royal garment that now dresses him in death will not be the last memory of clothing before the Gospel concludes. As we shall see, one final and important mention awaits.

But why this interest in Jesus' clothing?

Clothing in the ancient world was fashioned from the products of Earth: flax (from which linen was made), wool, silk, shell, cashmere, goat hair and cotton were all available to be fashioned into dress material.[16] Clothing gave identity to its wearer, warmth, status and dignity, and, in the case of Jesus' birth, security. Luke's mention of Jesus' clothing offers something further. They are reminders that Jesus is linked to Earth. This is borne out in Luke's combination of Jesus' cloth wrappings in birth and his placement in a stone-fashioned manger.[17] These gifts of Earth become the 'sign' (Gk *semeion*) to which Luke points the auditor more than once (Lk 2:7, 12, 16). The angel announces to the shepherds:

> This will be a sign (*semeion*) for you: you will find a child
> wrapped in bands of cloth and lying in a manger (Lk 2:12).

---

16. On the composition of the material of ancient fabrics, see Glennda Susan Marsh-Letts, 'Ancient Egyptian Linen: The Role of Natron and other Salts in the Preservation and Conservation of Archaeological Textiles—A Pilot Study', *BA (Hon) Thesis* (Sydney: University of Western Sydney, 2002); Eve Cockburn and Mary W Ballard, 'Cotton in Ancient Egypt: A Unique Find', *Proceedings of the First World Congress on Mummy Studies, Puerto de la Cruz, Tenerife, Canary Islands, February 3–6, 1992* (Santa Cruz, Tenerife: Archeological Museum of Tenerife, 1996), 625–631; Sheila Landi and Rosalind M. Hall, 'The discovery and conservation of an ancient Egyptian linen tunic', in *Studies in Conservation*, 24 (1979): 141–152.

17. The nostalgia and presumption that Jesus' birth manger was fashioned from wood comes to us from the many paintings of Jesus' birth by artists over the centuries. Archaeology presents us with a different story. The only archaeological evidence of mangers from the period under consideration is stone. On the manger, Martin Hengel, 'fa,tnh', *Theological Dictionary of the New Testament*, volume 9, edited by Gerhard Kittel and Gerhard Friedrich (Grand Rapids, MI: Eerdmans, 1964), 49–55. On its stone structure, see LG Herr, 'Stall', *The International Standard Bible Encyclopedia*, volume 4, edited by Geoffrey W Bromiley (Grand Rapids, MI: Eerdmans, 1995), 609–610.

The 'sign' is explicitly Earth-related. The child is a creature of Earth, indicated by the bands of cloth and the manger, gifts of Earth. If Jesus' Earth-connection is present in the early chapters of Luke's Gospel it is confirmed later towards the end of the Gospel, in his death and resurrection. Besides the 'elegant/luminous garment' as Jesus' death robe, it either remains or is added to as his shroud.

After his death, Joseph from Arimathea goes to Pilate and requests the body of Jesus (Lk 23:52). We notice that he,

> wrapped it in a linen cloth (Gk *sindón*) and laid it in a rock-hewn tomb where no one had ever been laid (Lk 23:53).

As in birth, Jesus is surrounded by cloth and placed in a stone receptacle, a 'rock-hewn' tomb. Earth gifts identify him. These become the final 'signs', echoing what the angels point out to the shepherds at Jesus' birth story. Cloth and stone prepare the auditor for the meaning of Jesus' resurrection. No longer a manger, but now a tomb. The 'bands of cloth' that earlier wrapped Jesus' infant body is now a shroud.

Significant is Luke's explicit description of this cloth that wraps his body. Only in the Gospel's final chapters (here, in Lk 23:53, and in the next chapter, the resurrection story in Lk 24:12) do we learn the *exact* nature of the material which surrounds Jesus. The evangelist calls it a *sindón*—'linen'. Linen substitutes the nativity 'bands of cloth' and, later, the 'luminous/elegant' robe placed on Jesus by Herod.

In the ancient and Jewish world, linen symbolized immortality.[18] Plutarch (46–120 CE), for example, tells his readers that 'flax springs from Earth which is immortal; it yields edible seeds, and supplies a plain and cleanly clothing'.[19] For this reason, says Plutarch, it was important that the priests wore linen, not wool. Wool was the 'the hair of domestic animals'. It was perishable and mortal.[20] The Roman poet, Ovid (43BCE–17/18CE), had earlier commented that anything made of animal skins reminded worshippers of death. It was to be excluded from a temple worship and those who conducted temple worship.[21] On the other hand, linen with its immortal and eternal association was considered the most appropriate clothing for priests and royals.

---

18. Johannes Quasten, 'A Pythagorean Idea in Jerome', in *American Journal of Philology*, 63 (1942): 207–215.

19. Plutarch, *De Iside et Osiride* 4.

20. Ovid, 1. 629.

21. Ovid, 1. 629.

Luke's Resurrection Story (Lk 24:1–12)

Luke's explicit identification of the linen garment that now surrounds Jesus' body reinforces both his eternal status and Earth-connectedness. Earth's gifts of stone and linen are the Gospel's final 'signs' that bring auditors to know Jesus' status as God's beloved one. Earth has become the revealer of the sacred and eternal.[22] This becomes clearer in Luke's story of the resurrection (Lk 24:1–12) as stone and linen again feature. This is anticipated in the note that Luke provides as Joseph of Arimathea approaches Pilate for Jesus' body.

> He took [Jesus' body] down, wrapped it in a linen shroud and laid him in a rock-hewn tomb where no one had ever been laid (Lk 23:53).

It is into a new, rock-carved tomb that Joseph places the linen-wrapped body of Jesus. The Earth-related images with its reminders of Luke's story of Jesus's birth are explicit. They feature as the women come to the tomb early morning with prepared spices intending to complete his burial anointment.

> On the first day of the week, at deep dawn, they came to the tomb bringing the spices they had prepared (Lk 24:1).

The women have already noted the place of Jesus' burial and 'how his body was laid' (Lk 23:55). This is an important detail. It is not only a matter of ensuring the women's witness to the *place* of what will become the site of Jesus' resurrection. They observe the *manner* of his burial, what surrounds him (the linen shroud) and Joseph's action. He places Jesus in the rock-hewn tomb. They note two Earth-related elements, linen and rock, which will become significant as the story unfolds. Luke notes that the women then prepare 'spices and ointments' (Lk 23:56b). This is a third element of Earth that is integral to the scene: aromatic spices and oils (Lk 23:56).

In Luke's opening verses of the resurrection narrative 'deep dawn' breaks revealing Earth's light and a new moment reminiscent of the dawning of Creation in Genesis 1. The women come to the tomb

---

22. On the ecological importance of stone, see Anne Elvey, *The Matter of the Text: Material Engagements between Luke and the Five Senses* (Sheffield: Sheffield Phoenix Press, 2011), 138–140.

with their spices and anointments. Whatever the women's intention for them, whether to anoint Jesus' body or perfume the tomb, the presence of the spices means that at another level of meaning, Earth, represented through the spices and aromatic oils, will also be a participant in what unfolds.[23]

Luke's women approach the tomb. There is no discussion, as in Mark's Gospel, about who will remove the stone for them from the tomb's entrance. Mark focuses on the stone's size ('it was very huge!' Mk 16:3) and the amazement of the women that the 'stone had already been rolled back' (Mk 16:4). Luke's women easily access the tomb because they find the stone covering the tomb 'rolled away' (Lk 24:2). Luke's verbal active form regarding Earth's stone ('rolled away') replaces Mark's passive verb ('had already been rolled back'). Luke's stone is an agent in allowing the women to enter the tomb. Along with the aromatic spices the women carry, it is a further participant in what unfolds and the revelation of God's definitive action in Jesus.

They enter the tomb and discover that Jesus' body is absent. As in Mark's equivalent scene, all they see is Earth's surround that allows them to know Jesus' corporeal absence and the potentiality of what is about to be revealed. What is implicit in Mark now becomes explicit in Luke. The women's perplexity over the absence of Jesus' body is clarified by the two heavenly clothed figures in the tomb before whom and in fear they bow their faces to Earth (Lk 24:5). It is a gesture of humility and honour frequent in the First Testament.[24] This leads to Luke's Easter proclamation.

'He is not here but has been raised' (Lk 24:6).[25]

---

23. On the function of aromatic spices and oils, see, μύρον in Gerhard Kittel and Gerhard Friedrich (editors), *Theological Dictionary of the New Testament*, Volume 4 (Grand Rapids, MI: Eerdmans, 1964–1976), 800–801; Also, Anne Elvey, *The Matter of the Text: Material Engagements between Luke and the Five Senses* (Sheffield: Sheffield Phoenix Press, 2011), 113.

24. For example, Gen 42:6; 43:26–28; 49:8; Ex 11:8; 18:7; Ruth 2:10; 1 Sam 2:36; 24:8; 25:23; Ps 72:9.

25. There is some doubt about the originality of this verse. For the textual evidence in favour of the Lukan authenticity for 24:6 supported by the third century CE Bodmer Papyrus, see the discussion in Joseph Fitzmyer, *The Gospel According to Luke X–XXIV* (Garden City, NY: Doubleday & Company, Inc, 1981), 1545. See also, I. Howard Marshall, *The Gospel of Luke: A Commentary on the Greek Text* (Grand Rapids, MI: Eerdmans, 1978), 885–886.

The two heavenly figures announce definitively that Jesus 'has been raised'. They remind the women to look for the risen Jesus 'among the living' (Lk 24:5). This has profound ecological implications for the Lukan audience. Jesus, as Earth' child, through his resurrection infuses all of creation with life. This means that Luke's Jesus is identified and bonded to Earth and God's presence (the 'kingdom') revealed through Jesus now pervades Earth. Earth's surround becomes the environmental context in which the women encounter the meaning of Jesus' resurrected life. It is now the place of divine encounter. The Earth-tomb is the environment that transforms and gives meaning to the words of the heavenly messengers. It becomes the place of transfiguration. This is because, in Rahner's words, Jesus 'has begun to transfigure this world unto himself.'[26] The tomb of Luke's Gospel is like a womb that gestates to bring forth life and permeates Earth at the initiative of God's action in Jesus.[27] What occurs next after the women's announcement confirms Earth's agency.

Peter's 'Amazement' (Lk 24:12)

The women go from the tomb and announce the Easter proclamation to the apostolic gathering of Jesus' disciples, the 'eleven and the rest' (Lk 24:9–10). Their words are disbelieved (Lk 24:11). Then,

> Peter got up and ran to the tomb; stooping and looking in,
> he saw the linen cloths by themselves; then he went home,
> amazed (Gk *thaumazo*) at what had happened (Lk 24:12).

What Peter perceives brings him to a sense of 'amazement' (*thaumazo*). In the classical Greek world *thaumazo* is often associated with an encounter with the deity.[28] Peter's thaumatological experience is not a simple act of curiosity or confusion over the tomb's emptiness, but a faith-filled response (*thaumazo*) that results from his sensory perception of everything. Two elements are explicit: the rock-hewn

---

26. Rahner, 'A Faith', 55.
27. On this gestational paradigm present in Luke's Gospel, see Anne Elvey, *An Ecological Feminist Reading of the Gospel of Luke: A Gestational Paradigm* (Lewiston, NY: The Edwin Mellen Press, 2005), 49–51.
28. See θαυμάζω in *Exegetical Dictionary of the New Testament*, volume 2 edited by Horst Balz and Gerhard Schneider (Grand Rapids, MI: Eerdmans, 1991), 134–135.

tomb, before which Peter has to stoop in order to look into it, and the 'linen cloths by themselves'.

But Peter encounters a third Earth-connected element implicit in the scene. This is the aromatic oils which the women had brought with them with the intention of anointing Jesus' body. There is no mention of these being carried away as the women go to announce the meaning of the tomb's emptiness to the apostles. Presumably, the spices with their accompanying fragrances remain in the tomb. They add to the Earth-related elements that Peter encounters. It is not the physical presence of the two angelic announcers or even the resurrected Jesus that brings Peter ultimately to Easter faith, but Earth's presence. The power of Jesus' deep resurrection permeates Earth, to use Rahner's expression, 'transfiguring it' to become the means of communicating God's action through Earth's resurrected child. Peter's engagement with Earth's gifts is equivalent to an encounter with the Risen Jesus.

This profound eco-theological conviction is confirmed a few verses later, after the two disciples return from Emmaus to Jerusalem to share with their apostolic colleagues their experience of the Risen Jesus in the 'breaking of bread'. They are told:

The Lord has risen indeed, and he has appeared to Simon! (Lk 24:34).

If we take the logic of Luke's narrative order and the last mention of Peter prior to this declaration, it is Peter's encounter at the tomb. There is no appearance of angelic announcers to clarify the meaning of the tomb's emptiness or even the appearance of the risen Jesus himself. The only encounter prior to this conviction of the appearance of the Risen Jesus to Peter is what has happened in the tomb. Its Earth-related elements—the rock of the tomb itself, the linen and the bouquet of the aromatic spices—confirm Jesus' resurrection. These are bearers of the truth of Jesus' resurrection. Through his resurrection, as Rahner puts it, 'God's heart' has entered Earth's being. This leads Peter to *amazement* and confirms the truth of the women's witness. In this sense, then, through Earth's elements, it can be truthfully affirmed that 'the Lord has risen indeed, and has appeared to Simon'.

Conclusion

Luke's story of Jesus' resurrection affirms that Earth is not a passive subject of human dominance. Rather, it becomes an agent of divine mediation. From Rahner's later theological perspective, Jesus is connected with Earth so intimately in death and his resurrection, that Earth bears the imprint of the Sacred. For Luke, this intimacy begins at Jesus' birth. He is from birth, Earth's child. Rahner's thought about creation and the meaning of bodily resurrection as refracted through Denis' own work is remarkably Lukan. Rahner considers Jesus as a 'child of this earth' being born 'anew'. Denis sees Rahner's interpretation as confirming that Jesus is at the heart of the yearning of all creation to participate with him in the transfiguration of his body. Denis concludes, 'Earth is our mother, and we are children of Earth, and we are called to love her'.[29]

From Rahner's perspective, then, Jesus is Earth's child and those attuned to him are Earth's children. These two images overlay the particular ecological approach in listening to the narrative dynamic in Luke's two volumes, the Gospel and the Acts of the Apostles. Luke-Acts is the story of *Earth's Child* and *Earth's Children*. The theological implications of this are deepened through Rahner's theology of the Incarnation and Denis' furthering of Rahner's thought in his final work, *Deep Incarnation*. The enfleshment of God's Word in Jesus means that a radical communion of God with Earth occurs. This 'deep incarnation' means that God's Word enfleshed in Jesus finds its expression in all ecological relationships. His presence is 'grounded' in these relationships, sacramentalised in the cross and revealed in the resurrection.[30] The cross discloses God's compassionate presence to all creatures.[31] Jesus' resurrection is the act of God's transforming the universe, 'the beginning of its glorification and fulfillment', an act of liberation and fulfillment of all biological life, and the ultimate moment of human communion with all creation.[32] Luke's Gospel stories of Jesus' death and resurrection, in which Earth plays a part to reveal God's revelatory intent through his death and resurrection, can underpin these fresh eco-theological insights from Karl Rahner and Denis Edwards.

---

29. Edwards, *Christian Understandings*, 223.
30. Edwards, *Deep Incarnation*, 117–119.
31. Edwards, *Deep Incarnation*, 123.
32. Edwards, *Deep Incarnation*, 137.

Chapter Quotations

'The resurrection of the crucified reveals the power of this divine love to heal, liberate, and bring creation to transfigured new life.'[1]
– Denis Edwards

'Deep incarnation needs to be a trinitarian theology of Word and Spirit.'[2]
– Denis Edwards
Bracken

'The transcendent God has the capacity to enter into the limits and suffering of creaturely existence.'[3]
– Denis Edwards

'The cross of Jesus can be understood as the sacrament of God's redemptive suffering with creatures.'[4]
– Denis Edwards

'At the centre of this theology is the Christian claim that the resurrection of Jesus Christ is the promise and the beginning of the final healing and divinisation of the whole of creation.'[5]
– Denis Edwards
Nesteruk

1. Denis Edwards, *The Natural World and God: Theological Explorations* (Adelaide, Australia: ATF Press, 2017), 18.
2. Denis Edwards, *Deep Incarnation: God's Redemptive Suffering with Creatures* (Maryknoll NY: Orbis, 2019), 106.
3. Edwards, *Deep Incarnation*, 117.
4. Edwards, *Deep Incarnation*, 117.
5. Edwards, *The Natural World and God*, 150.

'I have thought it important to keep creation and incarnation together as aspects of God's loving self-giving to creatures, and to see redemption, or salvation in Christ, as embracing not just human beings but the whole of creation. So the kind of ecological theology that I have worked on in these essays is one that seeks to embrace the natural world within a fully Trinitarian theology of creation and incarnation.'[6]
– Denis Edwards
Worthing

'Miracles are marvels of God's gracious self-communication that occur in different ways.'[7]
– Denis Edwards

'The Spirit of God is the Life-Giver who enables and empowers the emergence of galaxies and stars, the Sun and its solar system, with Earth placed at the right distant from the Sun to enable life, the first forms of prokaryotic life, more complex life forms, the extraordinary flourishing of sea creatures, flowering trees and shrubs, the diversity of land animals, mammals and human beings with their extraordinarily complex brains.'[8]
– Denis Edwards.
Celia-Dean Drummond

'God is interiorly present to the whole creation and to every part it, nearer to it than it is to itself, as the very ground and source of its existence, enabling and empowering it at every moment. Divine transcendence does not make God distant. It enables God to be more interior to things than any creature could ever be.'[9]
– Denis Edwards

---

6. Edwards, *The Natural World and God*, 9.
7. Edwards, *The Natural World and God*, 160.
8. Edwards, *The Natural World and God*, 18.
9. Edwards, *The Natural World and God*, 128.

'It is a Trinitarian act of self-bestowal: God gives God's self in the Word and the Spirit, in diverse ways, in creation, grace, incarnation, and final fulfillment.'[10]
– Denis Edwards

'At the heart of the Eucharist is the memorial of praise and thanksgiving. It is fundamental to an ecological theology to understand this as memorial of God's marvelous deeds that include creation as well as redemption and the promise of final transformation.'[11]
– Denis Edwards
McGann

'In Christian theology, a sacrament is a visible sign and agent of divine self-bestowal.'[12]
– Denis Edwards
Jamie Fowler

'The big bang and the expansion of our universe from a small dense hot state 13.7 billion years ago, and the evolution of life since its beginning on Earth 3.7 billion years ago—this whole story exists within the vision of the divine purpose.'[13]
– Denis Edwards

'There is a deep continuity between creation and new creation. This continuity is grounded ultimately in God's fidelity to what God has created.'[14]
– Denis Edwards

'The power of the cross is a power-in-love.'[15]
– Denis Edwards

10. Edwards, *How God Acts: Creation, Redemption, and Special Divine Action* (Minneapolis: Fortress Press, 2010). 39.
11. Edwards, *The Natural World and God,* 96.
12. Edwards, *The Natural World and God,* 135.
13. Edwards, *The Natural World and God,* 15.
14. Edwards, *How God Acts,* 158.
15. Edwards, *The Natural World and God,* 32.

'Every sparrow, every frog, the members of every threatened species—each is 'the object of the Father's tenderness', and each is enfolded with God's affection.'[16]
– Denis Edwards
Southgate

'God is present, in the Spirit, to each creature here and now, loving it into existence and promising its future. Creation is always an act of love. This means that in some way salvation begins in and with creation.'[17]
– Denis Edwards

'A fully Christian approach to the natural world cannot be limited to the theology of creation in isolation, but must also involve salvation in Christ. The theological meaning of mountains, seas, animals, plants, and the climate of our planet, the Milky Way Galaxy, and the observable universe will involve the whole story of God's self-bestowal to creatures in creation, incarnation, and final transfiguration.'[18]
– Denis Edwards

'I opt for the approach to divine action in which God is thought of as acting through secondary causes because it represents a foundational metaphysical understanding of the God-world relationship, which is at the heart of the Christian tradition and which I find intellectually coherent and religiously meaningful.'[19]
– Denis Edwards

'In response to the costs built into evolution, I think that a theology of divine action has to be able to offer a view of God working creatively and redemptively in and through the natural world to bring it to healing and wholeness.'[20]
– Denis Edwards

---

16. Edwards, *The Natural World and God*, 69.
17. Edwards, *The Natural World and God*, 59.
18. Edwards, *Deep Incarnation*, xvi.
19. Edwards, *The Natural World and God*, 131.
20. Edwards, *The Natural World and God*, 136–137.

'Both the scientific worldview of our time and the ecological crisis
we face require a renewed theology of the natural world.'[21]
– Denis Edwards

'The incarnation of the Word is, then, the incarnation of the
Attractor of evolutionary emergence.'[22]
– Denis Edwards

'The God of love dynamically empowers the emergent universe
through the presence of the indwelling Word and Spirit. Earth and
its creatures, its insects, birds and animals, its forests and seas, its
habitats and bioregions, all exist because the God of love is closer to
them than they are to themselves. The Trinity of love enables their
existence, their interaction and their becoming in the community of
creation.'[23]
– Denis Edwards

'I think that Gregersen is right to insist that in the evolution of
the universe and in the emergence of life on Earth, divine action
involves the historical, the unpredictable and the specific. I will
propose that divine action with regard to creation and grace is
intrinsically particular.'[24]
– Denis Edwards

---

21. Edwards, *The Natural World and God*, 8–9.
22. Edwards, *The Natural World and God*, 28.
23. Edwards, *The Natural World and God*, 271.
24. Edwards, *The Natural World and God*, 127.

Bibliography of Works

Denis Edwards

Compiled by Cris Henriksson, Gerard Kelly and Peter Malone MSC

Every attempt has been made to produce a comprehensive list of publications, but it may be incomplete.

Books in English (alphabetical)

Breath of Life: A Theology of the Creator Spirit, Orbis Books, New York, 2004.

Called to be Church in Australia: An Approach to the Renewal of Local Churches, St Paul Publications, Homebush, 1987.

Christian Understandings of Creation: The Historical Trajectory, Fortress Press, Minneapolis, 2017.

Deep Incarnation: God's Redemptive Suffering with Creatures, Orbis Books, New York, 2019.

Ecology at the Heart of Faith: The Change of Heart that leads to a new Way of living on Earth, Orbis Books, New York, 2006.

How God Acts: Creation, Redemption and Special Divine Action, Fortress Press, 2010, also published by ATF Press.

Human Experience of God, Paulist Press, New York, 1983.

Jesus and the Cosmos, Paulist Press, New York, 1991, St Paul Publications, Homebush, 1991, Limited edition, Wipf and Stock, Eugene, 2004.

Jesus and the Natural World: Exploring a Christian Approach to Ecology, Garratt Publishing, Mulgrave, 2012.

Jesus the Wisdom of God: An Ecological Theology, Orbis Books, New York, 1995.

Partaking of God: Trinity, Evolution and Ecology, Liturgial Press, Collegeville, 2014.

The God of Evolution: A Trinitarian Theology, Paulist Press, New York, 1999.

The Natural World and God: Theological Explorations, ATF Theology, 2017.

What Are They Saying About Salvation?, Paulist Press, New York, 1986.

Made from Stardust: Exploring the Place of Human Beings within Creation, Collins Dove, North Blackburn, 1992. Irish edition *Creation, Humanity, Community: Building a New Theology*, Gill and Macmillan Ltd, 1992.

Journal articles and chapters in books (in alphabetical order by title)

'Action for Justice and Peace, Contemporary Theology.' *Compass*, 19/2 (1985): 23–29.

'An Ecological Theology of the Holy Spirit.' Proceedings of the Annual Convention (Catholic Theological Society of America) 57 (2002): 204–205.

'An Ecological Theology of the Trinity.' *CTNS Bulletin* 13/3 (Sum 1993): 10–16.

'Apostolic Spirituality in the Light of the Parables of the Kingdom.' *Compass*, 14/4 (1980): 12–18.

'Apprentices in Faith to the Aboriginal View of the Land.' *Compass*, 20/1 (1986): 23–29.

'Athanasius' Letters to Serapion: Resource for a Twenty-First Century Theology of God the Trinity.' *Phronema*, 29/2 (2014): 41–64.

'Athanasius: "The Word of God in Creation and Salvation"', in *Creation and Salvation, Volume 1: A Mosaic of Essays on Selected Classic Christian Theologians* (Berlin: LIT Verlag, 2011), 37–52.

'Biodiversity & Ecology: An Interdisciplinary Challenge.' *Interface: A Forum for Theology in the World*, 7/1, 2004.

'Celebrating Eucharist in a Time of Global Climate Change.' *Pacifica,* 19/1 (February 2006): 1–15.

'Christopher Southgate's Compound Theodicy: Parallel Searchings.' *Zygon,* 53/3 (September 2018): 680–690.

'Climate Change and the Theology of Karl Rahner: A Hermeneutical Dialogue.' In *Confronting the Climate Crisis: Catholic Theological Perspectives,* edited by James Schaefer (Milwaukee, WI: Marquette University Press, 2011), 233–251.

'Creation Seen in the Light of Christ: A Theological Sketch', in *Creation is Groaning: Biblical and Theological Perspectives* (Collegeville: Liturgical Press, 2013).

'Dispossession.' *Compass,* 10/4 (1976): 6–13.

'Doctrinal Agreement and the Path to Unity.' *Lutheran Theological Journal,* 26/1 (May 1992): 51–62.

'Earth as God's Creation: The Theology of the Natural World In Pope Francis' *Laudato si*.' *Phronema,* 31/2 (2016): 1–16.

'Ecclesial Decision-Making: Exploring an insight from Karl Rahner', *A Forum for Theology in the World,* 5/2 (2018): 27–35.

'Ecological Commitment and the Following of Jesus.' *SEDOS Bulletin,* 41/7–8 (July 2009): 159–168.

'Ecological Theology: Trinitarian Perspectives.' Proceedings of the Catholic Theological Society of America 72 (2017): 14–28.

'Ecology and the Holy Spirit: The "Already" and the "Not Yet" of the Spirit in Creation.' *Pacifica,* 13/2 (June 2000): 142–159, also published in *Starting with the Spirit,* edited by Stephen Pickard and Gordon Preece (ATF Press, Adelaide: 2001), 238–260.

'Experience of Word and Spirit in the Natural World', in *The Nature of Things: Rediscovering the Spiritual in God's Creation* (Eugene: Pickwick, 2016), 13–26.

'Exploring How God Acts.' In *God, Grace & Creation,* edited by Philip J Rossi (Maryknoll, NY: Orbis, 2010), 124–146.

'Eucharist and Ecology.' *SEDOS Bulletin,* 41/7–8 (July 2009): 169–180.

'Eucharist and Ecology: Keeping Memorial of Creation.' *Worship,* 82/3 (May 2008): 194–213.

'Every Sparrow That Falls to the Ground: The Cost of Evolution and the Christ-Event.' *Ecotheology,* 11/1 (March 2006): 103–123.

'Everything is Interconnected: The Trinity and the Natural World in *Laudato si*.' *Australasian Catholic Record*, 94/1 (2017): 81–92.

'Evolution and the God of Mutual Friendship.' *Pacifica*. 10/2 (June 1997): 187–200.

'Evolution, Emergence and the Creator Spirit: A Conversation with Stuart Kauffman.' *Colloquium*, 42/2 (November 2010): 208–230.

'Experience of God and Explicit Faith: A Comparison of John of the Cross and Karl Rahner.' *The Thomist*, 46 (January 1982): 33–74.

'Final Fulfilment: The Deification of Creation.' *SEDOS Bulletin*, 41/7–8 (July 2009): 181–195.

'"For Your Immortal Spirit Is in All Things": The Role of the Spirit in Creation.' In *Earth Revealing–Earth Healing: Ecology and Christian Theology*, (Collegeville: Liturgical Press, 2001), 45–66.

'Humans and Other Creatures: Creation, Original Grace, and Original Sin.' In *Just Sustainability: Technology, Ecology, and Resource Extraction* (New York: Orbis, 2015), 159–170.

'Humans, Chimps, and Bonobos: Towards and Inclusive View of the Human as Bearing the Image of God', in *Turning to the Heavens and the Earth: Theological Reflections on a Cosmological Conversion: Essays in Honour of Elizabeth A Johnson*, edited by Julia Brumbaugh and Natalia Imperatori-Lee (Collegeville MN: Liturgical Press, 2016), 7–25.

'Incarnation and the Natural World: Explorations in the Tradition of Athanasius', in *Incarnation: On the Scope and Depth of Christology* (Minneapolis: Fortress, 2015), 157–176.

'Karl Rahner (1904–1984)—The Divine Self-Bestowal.' In *Creation and Salvation, Volume 2: A Companion on Recent Theological Movements* (Berlin: LIT Verlag, 2012), 61–65.

'Miracles and Laws of Nature.' *Compass* 41/2 (2007): 8–16.

'Original Sin and Saving Grace in Evolutionary Context.' In *Evolutionary and Molecular Biology: Scientific Perspectives on Divine Action*, (Vatican City: Libreria Editrice Vaticana, 1998), 377–392.

'Personal Symbol of Communion', in *The Spirituality of the Diocesan Priest* (Collegeville: The Liturgical Press, 1997),

'Planetary Spirituality: Exploring a Christian Ecological Approaches.' *Compass* 44/4 (2010): 16–23.

'Receptive Ecumenism and the Charism of a Partner Church: The Example of Justification.' *The Australasian Catholic Record*, 86/4 4 (October 2009): 457–467.

'Receptive Ecumenism and the Charism of a Partner Church: The Example of Justification.' *Lutheran Theological Journal* 43/3 (December 2009): 167–177.

'Reflections on Multicultural Australia in the Light of the Gospel Story of Jesus as one Who Shatters Barriers.' *Compass*, 23/4 (1988): 1–8.

'Resurrection and the Costs of Evolution: A Dialogue with Rahner on Noninterventionist Theology.' *Theological Studies*, 67/4 (December 2006): 816–833.

'Resurrection and the Costs of Evolution: A Dialogue with Rahner on Noninterventionist Theology.' In *From Resurrection to Return: Perspectives from Theology and Science on Christian Eschatology* (Adelaide: ATF Press, 2007), 112–133.

'Resurrection of the Body and Transformation of the Universe in the Theology of Karl Rahner.' *Philosophy & Theology*, 18/2 (2006): 357–383.

'Saving Grace and the Action of the Spirit Outside the Church.' In *Sin and Salvation* (Adelaide: ATF Press, 2003), 205–221.

'Sketching an Ecological Theology of the Holy Spirit and the Word of God.' *Concilium*, 4 (2001): 13–22.

'Sublime Communion and the Costs of Evolution.' *Irish Theological Quarterly*, 84/1 (February 2019): 22–38.

'"Sublime Communion": The Theology of the Natural World in *Laudato si*.' *Theological Studies*, 77/2 (June 2016): 377–391.

'Synodality and Primacy: Reflections from the Australian Lutheran/ Roman Catholic Dialogue.' *Pacifica*, 28/2 (2015): 137–148.

'Teilhard's Vision as Agenda for Rahner's Christology.' *Pacifica*, 23/2 (June 2010): 223–245.

'Teilhard's Vision as Agenda for Rahner's Christology.' In *From Teilhard to Omega: Co-Creating an Unfinished Universe* (New York: Orbis, 2014), 53–66, and in *Pacifica* 23/2 (2010): 233–235.

'The Attractor and the Energy of Love: Trinity in Evolutionary and Ecological Context.' *The Ecumenical Review*, 65/1 (March 2013): 129–144.

'The Church as a Community of Disciples.' *Compass,* 17/4 (1983): 5–10.

'The Church as Sacrament of Relationships.' *Pacifica,* 8/2 (June 1995): 185–200.

'The Church of Salvation.' *Compass,* 20/3 (1986): 1–4.

'The Cosmic Theology of Karl Rahner.' *Compass,* 25/1 (1990): 37–47.

'The Discovery of Chaos and the Retrieval of the Trinity.' In *Chaos and Complexity: Scientific Perspectives on Divine Action* ((Notre Dame IN: University of Notre Dame Press, 1997), 157–175.

'The Discovery of Chaos and the Retrieval of the Trinity.' *CTNS Bulletin,* 15/3 (Sum 1995): 13–24.

'The Diversity of Life and the Trinity.' *Lutheran Theological Journal,* 46/2 (August 2012): 92–96.

'The Ecological Significance of God-Language.' *Theological Studies,* 60/4 (December 1999): 708–722.

'The Holy Spirit as the Gift: Pneumatology, Receptivity, and Catholic Re-Reception of Petrine Ministry in the Theology of Walter Kasper.' In *Receptive Ecumenism and the Call to Catholic Learning: Exploring a Way for Contemporary Ecumenism* (Oxford: Oxford University Press, 2008), 197–210.

'The Integrity of Creation: Catholic Social Teaching for an Ecological Age.' *Pacifica,* 5/2 (June 1992): 182–203.

'The Ordination of Women and Anglican-Roman Catholic Dialogue.' *Pacifica,* 1/2 (June 1988): 125–140.

'The Redemption of Animals in an Incarnational Theology.' In *Creaturely Theology: On God, Humans and Other Animals* (London: SCM Press, 2009), 81–99.

'The Relationship between the Risen Christ and the Material Universe.' In *Constructive Christian Theology in the Worldwide Church* (Grand Rapids, MI: Eerdmans, 1997), 369–381.

'The Relationship between the Risen Christ and the Material Universe.' *Pacifica,* 4/1 (February 1991): 1–14.

'Theological Foundations for Ecological Praxis.' *Ecotheology,* 5 (July 1998): 126–141.

'The Triune God and Climate Change', in *T&T Clark Handbook on Christian Theology and Climate Change* (London: T&T Clark, 2019).

'Toward a Theology of Divine Action: William R Stoeger, SJ, on the Laws of Nature.' *Theological Studies,* 76/3 (September 2015): 485–502.

'Where on Earth is God? Exploring an Ecological Theology of the Trinity in the Tradition of Athanasius.' In *Christian Faith and the Earth: Current Paths and Emerging Horizons in Ecotheology,* edited by Ernst M Conradie, Sigurd Gergmann, Celia Deane-Drummond and Denis Edwards (London: Bloomsbury, 2014), 11–30.

'Why Is God Doing This?: Suffering, the Universe, and Christian Eschatology.' In *Physics and Cosmology: Scientific Perspectives on the Problem of Natural Evil* (Notre Dame IN: University of Notre Dame Press, 2007), 247–266.

Books in translation

Aliento de Vida: Una teologia del Espiritu creador, (Spanish) Editorial Verbo Divino, 2008, original *Breath of Life: A Theology of the Creator Spirit* 1st published by Orbis Books.

Bóg Ewolucji: Teologia Trynitarna, (Polish), Copernicus Center Press, Krakow, 2016, original *The God of Evolution: A Trinitarian Theology.* 1st published by Paulist Press.

El Dios de la evolución: Una Teologia Trinitaria, (Spanish), Sal Terrae, Cantabria, original *The God of Evolution: A Trinitarian Theology—* 1st published by Paulist Press.

Jak Dziala Bog?, (Polish), Wydawnictwo WAM, Krakow, original *How God Acts?* 1st Published by Fortress Press 2010.

L'ecologia al centro della fede: Il cambiamento del cuore che conduce a un nuovo modo di vivere sulla Terra, (Italian), Edizioni Messaggero, Padova.

Sopro de Vida: Uma teologia do Espirito Criador, (Brazilian Portuguese), 2007, Ediciones Loyola, Sao Paulo, original *Breath of Life: A Theology of the Creator Spirit.* 1st published by Orbis Books.

Biblical References

Author and Subject Index

CPSIA information can be obtained
at www.ICGtesting.com
Printed in the USA
VHW031631020821
3141BV00002B/96

9 781925 612059